W9-CER-435

DISCARD

UNIVERSITY OF CONNECTICUT — GROTON, CONN. — SOUTHEASTERN BRANCH LIBRARY

JUL 13 1970

A Middle East Reader

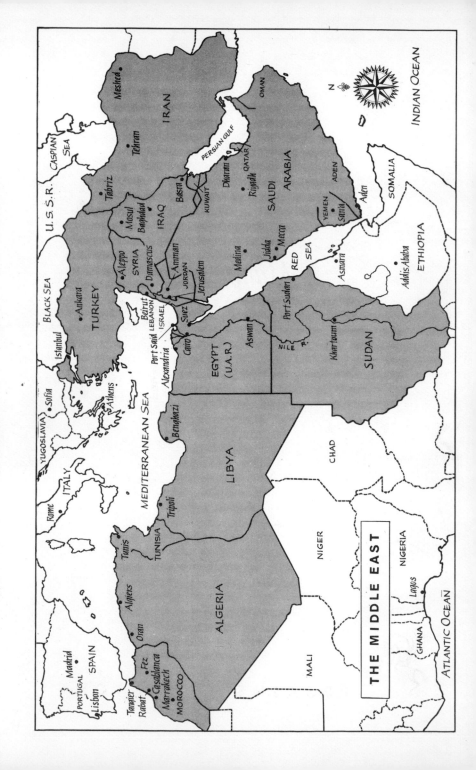

THE MIDDLE EAST

A

Middle East

READER

EDITED BY IRENE L. GENDZIER

PEGASUS · NEW YORK

FOR MY PARENTS

Copyright © 1969 by Western Publishing Company, Inc. All rights reserved.
This book, or parts thereof, may not be reproduced in any form
without permission of the publisher. Printed in the United States of America.

Library of Congress Catalog Card Number: 70–91615

Editor's Note

With a few exceptions, foreign names and places have been rendered in a simply transliterated style in order to avoid confusion and to facilitate reading.

Table of Contents

Contents

Introduction

THE PURPOSE of this book is to introduce readers to certain aspects of recent Middle Eastern history. While it is hoped that it will provide something of a guide into the labyrinthian world east of the Mediterranean, it is not intended as a comprehensive survey. The most modest objective is to clarify a number of the topics which are critical to an understanding of the contemporary situation of the region. Organized into four sections, the essays deal first with the nature and practice of radical change, with particular emphasis on the United Arab Republic, Syria, Iraq, and Israel (Parts 1 and 2); then with certain often unemphasized aspects of Israel's foreign policy and the problematic question of Arab unity (Part 3); and finally with the tangled web of the Arab-Israeli question (Part 4). In a more general sense, however, a single theme unites these separate subjects: that of change, total societal change as it has been conceived and implemented in the contemporary Middle East.

"Change" is referred to more frequently under the all-inclusive term, "modernization," but I have retained the simpler word in order to avoid the specialized vocabulary that belongs more properly to the political scientist, and to emphasize that it is not modernity, as such, with its neutral political connotations, that is the object of so much effort, but a very special kind of change, dominated by a specific if still ill-defined set of ideals. The radical change that preoccupies so much of the Middle East today, whether as a goal or an accomplished fact, is a reaction to an extended period of disruption, disintegration, and disenchantment. It stems from the conviction that the present state of Middle

Eastern society is corrupt and untenable, and that it should be replaced by conditions which will make it possible for a new type of man to emerge. Those who are preoccupied with radical change think in terms of total change, not piecemeal reform. They have a conception of political commitment that is at the least, inflated, and at its worst, dangerous—because it expects resurrection as well as social change from the passion with which politics is approached. Some would say that such utopian thinking is outmoded, a virtual guarantee of failure, and that it would be preferable to replace it with the solid, sober, realistic thinking which is characteristic of more cautious politicians elsewhere. Is this a realistic choice? Are the exponents of radical change, who are on occasion also the exponents of radicalism, men noted for their high style but poor politics? And what of their objectives in terms of the masses and of the democracy they still regard as their goal? What has change wrought, and why, indeed, has it become so urgent to the Middle East today?

In the following essays these and other questions are raised more or less directly, as each author and his subject indicates. But in all cases, whether the issue is the impact of the creation of the State of Israel or the problems of Arab unity, the dissatisfactions with the past and the visions of the future remain constant.

Given more space it would have been desirable to begin a consideration of the contemporary Middle East with the period of World War I and the consequences of the demise of the Ottoman Empire. Arab nationalism, in its early form, was already in existence, and locked in combat with Ottoman as well as European *realpolitik*. Zionism was a subject for discussion in the Arab press, while in Palestine Jewish settlers confronted the realities of Arab life, both geographically and politically. With World War I and the disruption of the empire, a new phase in the historical development of the region was reached. Partition and the occupation of the Arab states by the mandatory powers, as well as the more direct occupation of other areas, generated anti-foreign sentiments of impressive proportions. France and Great Britain, sometimes in cooperation and sometimes in mutual opposition, ruled over Syria, Lebanon, Palestine, Transjordan, Egypt, and Iraq. It was hardly surprising that independence from foreign rule became a practical and immediate objective, or that reunification of the Arab world loomed so insistently in the nationalists' vocabulary. Political cynics may contend that foreign empires have ruled over a multitude of people since time immemorial. The novelty then becomes the success with which the Western powers managed to "civilize" their subjects and the seriousness with which these subjects absorbed the alien ideas of self-determination, natural rights, and other such dangerous thoughts. But they had indeed absorbed them, adapted them; and when they wished to implement them, nationalism had come of age. Seen in this context, the colonization of Palestine by devoted Zionists was bound to be regarded as but another instance of the danger and the challenge represented by a western people in the Middle East. With the passage of time and the worsening of relations between Palestinian Jews and Arabs, and with the defeat of the first Arab-Israeli War of 1948, Israel became the symbol and the reality of the West, a symbol of the wounds as well as the desires of a generation. Between 1948 and 1968—the period covered in this book—wars punctuated the uneasy truce that marked relations between Israel and the Arab states. But as important as the absence of peace was the momentum for change that swelled the ranks of the young, humiliated by defeat and long disaffected by the course of events within their own countries.

Eric Rouleau has written of the June war of 1967 that "all the present Arab governments now risk disappearing from the political scene as did the elites who ruled the Arab world on the eve of the first Palestinian conflict in 1948." That conflict was indeed followed by a series of political tremors that marked the start of a new phase in the Arab world. But the most striking characteristic was not the disappearance of familiar political elites but the appearance of a new political mood, a new temperament, a new, more profound reaction to and evaluation of the nature of the past defeats, of which 1948 was but the most dramatic and most recent example. The time had come once again—as it had for the generations of the 1870's and 1880's before the occupation of Egypt in 1882—to ask the question: Why has the East declined while the West has progressed?

In the earlier period, those who asked this question answered it with a variety of analyses that added up to a general diagnosis of the ills of their society. Islam had been threatened, it was not as strong as it ought to be. It had been a source of unity and strength, but the West had diabolically sapped it of its power and the people had complied in their own defeat. The relationship between the potential power of a nation—a concept unfamiliar to this region on any level—and the ideology that holds it together—also a foreign notion—was nevertheless tentatively considered. But events seemed to interrupt the deliberations of those most prepared and concerned to extricate their land from imminent disaster. The occupation of Egypt in 1882, followed by World War I and the collapse of an Empire, created new conditions for which the questions and answers of an earlier age were no longer satisfactory. Without their having come to terms with the secular nature of European nationalism, the political independence they assumed as synonymous with becoming a separate nation nevertheless became the goal of a people living under foreign occupation. And woven into this dream of restored freedom was the vision of an Arab-Muslim world also restored. (The Arab and the Islamic quotient varied, depending on the exponent and the time and the place at which he spoke.) Nationalism and Arab unity became the slogans of those reformers bent on undoing the work of partition and occupation carried out by the West. By 1948, the nations had become political realities and unity was no longer impossible. But by then too, the difference between political independence and national viability had become clearer.

Nationalism was no longer seen as an end in itself. The dynamics of social life, the need to invigorate the economy, to educate the populace, to create a nation where a state existed—all these considerations came to supersede the political quest now satisfied. It has become a commonplace that the difficulties facing underdeveloped nations are greater after independence than before. The brotherhood of political conspirators is replaced by politicians who rediscover their private interests and their animosities. The old balance returns and the cause of independence and national survival is, once again, put aside. This description applies, in many instances, to the Middle East; and more particularly to the Arab states. In the case of Israel, the motivation to create a new image, to bring about a renaissance in which the ghetto stereotype and the emasculated self-hating Jew would be replaced by another breed of men, preceded the creation of the state itself. Not that the Arab world also did not have to await partition and the reluctant departure of its occupying mandatory powers. The recognition of the existence of legally separate entities served to confirm what had existed earlier under another name. But there had not yet been a pervasive popular movement to transform the Arab world; there had not yet been a renaissance built on the rejection of existing conditions and the desire to create a more humane society. That came about after World War II, specifically, after 1948. Then the intellectual expression of a brooding social and political discontent rose to the surface.

Chronologically, the essays in this book deal with the ideas and events that followed this period, the final years of "ancien régime" governments. They reflect largely the thinking of the left, which does not represent the entire ideological spectrum of the Arab East or of Israel. It does demonstrate clearly, however, the ambitions and the difficulties of a particular group of people and a particular outlook, one that has become important in the contemporary politics of the region. As for the balance in time as well as ideas between Israel, Zionism and socialism, and the exclusive nationalism and socialism that are emerging in the Arab world, this obviously remains a difficult subject to explore. Some attempt to do so appears in a number of the essays that follow. More often, however, I have tried to indicate the possibilities inherent in this kind of comparative study by the juxtaposition of certain essays.

Part 1, as its title indicates, is a series of reflections on the nature of radical change in the Arab East and in Israel. It seems appropriate to introduce this section, and indeed the entire collection, with an essay that is learned but also reflects the self-consciousness of a western liberal confronting "Arab radical notions of democracy." While Malcolm Kerr dissects and analyses the roots of Arab thought on this subject from the outside, Hisham Sharabi writes as an analytic participant, engaged less in the need to rationalize developments than to describe their inevitable course. Clovis Maqsud, a convinced socialist, concentrates on the role of the military in the evolution of national liberation movements, describing and warning against dangers which since the time of his writing (1959) have recurred with alarming frequency. In the fourth essay, Nachman Syrkin turns away from Arab developments to examine the complicated evolution of socialist Zionism before its transplant to Palestine. His article is included here as a tribute to the importance of socialist Zionism in the ideological development of the Zionist movement. But it is also included to offer a comparison, which is pursued in Part 2, between certain conceptions and goals of change in the Arab and Jewish milieus.

Kerr's article is an elaborate investigation into the significance

of the radical conception of democracy in the contemporary
thought of certain Arab socialists. But while he concentrates on
specific individuals and parties, it is clear that the mood he describes is common to an entire generation. It involves a bitter
criticism of parliamentary democracy and an implicit eulogizing
of what J. L. Talmon has referred to as "totalitarian democracy."
It includes a rejection of pluralism and a lessening of respect
for those institutions that guarantee the decentralization of power.
The historian who is curious about the causes of this disenchantment will be sympathetically led by Kerr to consider the experience of Syria and Lebanon, as well as other Arab states, during
the interwar period. He will find that from these experiences a
profound rebellion against the excesses of individualism, and an
identification of the worst features of individualism with capitalist
bourgeois society resulted. And from this certain conclusions, not
entirely foreign to the Islamic history of the area, are drawn.
The structure and economic roots of capitalist society come
under attack. "Unity of purpose and action at all political and
social levels" replaces the vices of individualism with the virtues
of collective action. The objective of such change is nothing less
than the restructuring of society, with the aim of incorporating
the masses into the life of the nation. It is an attempt to redefine
the nation, eliminating the political and socioeconomic aristocracy
of the past. Democracy and justice must be total. In a socialist
society, individualism is permanently suppressed in order to allow
the masses, who have been disenfranchised, to regain their just
place.

To say that liberal virtues and political propositions are no
longer put at a premium is a very considerable understatement.
This obviously worries Kerr, as it would most western liberals
whose confidence is not restored by socialist slogans. Kerr expresses his concern in the remark which he reserves for the end
of his essay. There, he warns readers that unless ideas are provided that will shape and determine the course of events, the
events will, in their grotesque fashion, determine their own irregular course. The only comment one can make to this is
surprise that the two are not seen as intimately related; especially since the brunt of the difficult story outlined by Kerr is
that the events of the recent past have conspired to push certain
ideas to the surface, which in turn are responsive to the current
needs and wishes of society. The ideas to which western liberals
are sympathetic are now deemed inadequate and inappropriate.

But the mere offer of new ideas—some of which are not germane
to the problems of Arab society—cannot solve the problems so
vehemently exposed by Kerr.

As a man who has been moved and molded by the events he
describes, Hisham Sharabi sees the transformation of ideology in
the Arab world as nothing less than a total rebellion, on every
level, against Europe and the system of political and social
values it stands for. In some respects he appears to share the
approach to politics that characterized the Arab radicals discussed by Kerr. Sharabi points out that for the younger generation (and generational differences are prominent in his presentation) the search for identity and reconstruction of the nation
are conceived through political action. "To be committed now
meant to be politically committed." Yet this is to ask that politics
be permanently transformed into ideology, a role that the mere
machinations of political life can hardly be expected to sustain.

On another level, it is also apparent that what Sharabi calls
"political action," even if broadly interpreted, hardly matches
the usual sense of the term. Hence, when he seeks to clarify
what is meant by the total repudiation of Europe, an action
which he sees as characteristic of the mentality of the young
revolutionary elite, he says: ". . . it is not enough to keep the
West politically at bay; the West must again be reduced to an
alien entity, to be made wholly other." But extrication and being
made "wholly other" belong more accurately to the category of
cultural catharsis than political action. Sharabi's final reference
to Frantz Fanon suggests a sympathetic reading of the works of
the prophet of apocalyptic history.

In his discussion of the transformation of ideology, Sharabi
develops a generational chronology which is instructive in following the pattern of intellectual development he outlines.
According to this scheme, the pre-World War I generation witnessed the initial political and economic pressure applied by
Europe to the Middle East. It saw this transformed into outright
occupation and expansion, but it was left to the interwar generation to experience the full brunt of life under European, that is
to say, French or British occupation. The postwar generation,
on the other hand, had the dubious pleasure of watching the
disintegration of Europe during World War II, and of seeing it
reluctantly remove itself from the Middle Eastern scene. The
final phase of Europe's demise is seen in the emergence of "revolutionism," which is both the ultimate heritage and the fatal

weapon used against the West to "extricate" it from the Middle East. The generational differences are reminiscent of a comment made by Margaret Mead to the effect that "events which have been sequential in the lives of his [man's] forebears become contemporaneous in his own life, and his responses will differ accordingly." ° In the case of the Middle East, one might well formulate Sharabi's argument in another way and say that while the pre-World War I generation watched the coming of the West with a mixture of apprehension, curiosity, and ignorance as to what the outcome would be, succeeding generations perceived the changes brought by the West contemporaneously, and were thus freer to understand them and to react to them in a more direct and vigorous way. Reversing the process of integration and adaptation that normally distinguishes second-generation immigrants' children from their parents, the interwar and postwar generations in the Arab world rejected the temptations of coexistence and assimilation which the European powers in the Middle East had offered. Alienated by the contradictions which underlay such theories, they chose to restore and redefine their identity as nonwestern peoples by searching for their own authentic intellectual, as well as political and economic, modes of operation. Whether or not such authenticity, which avoids chauvinism, is possible today is a question worth considering.

"Identity" and "activism" which have become terms of worldwide significance, are very much a part of the political vocabulary of the Arab East. With apparent consensus the younger revolutionaries, in particular, endorse the position that what makes them so different from their predecessors is that they are not bound by the dogmas of ideology, though they share a generally well-defined ideological position, and that they conceive the quest for a national identity through activism as a collective—not an elitist—movement. This outlook is reflected in the third essay of Part 1, that by Clovis Maqsud, entitled, "Democracy and Military Regimes." According to Maqsud, "Democracy implies a form of organization and a definition of the relations between the individual and society through which the people have an active participation in all fields of life." The emphasis is on consent and participation. Participation implies that the masses must be brought into public life; consent reminds

° Mead, Margaret, "Culture Change and Character Structure," in *Identity and Anxiety*, M. R. Stein, A. J. Vidich, and D. M. White, eds. (New York, 1960), p. 93.

us that the best form of participation is that which is total. The legality of authority is determined by the unanimity of the people's approval. It is the will of the majority that represents the nation, and this majority, therefore, represents the only legitimate source of government authority. Maqsud is not unaware of the dangers inherent in such a position, although his caution is directed more toward the danger of military "protection" than the possibility of mass tyranny.

Reviewing those instances in which the military were called in to protect revolution-in-the-making, Maqsud makes it clear that even when military revolts take place to save the popular cause, unless they abandon their military vocation, such coups are apt to deny the popular movements they allegedly arose to protect. The subject continues to be relevant to the Middle East, where the connection between military rule and popular revolution is a common theme running through the recent histories of "progressive" as well as "reactionary" nations of the region. It is implicit in the more general form of the role of the military in developing nations in all the articles included in Part 2, as well as elsewhere throughout the book.

Kerr, Sharabi, and Maqsud agree that the vanguard among the Middle Eastern revolutionary intelligentsia today is made up of Arab socialists. The subject of socialism in the Arab world is discussed below (xix–xxiii), but is mentioned here to draw a parallel with the very different world to which Nachman Syrkin introduces us. What is most striking about Syrkin's essay here is how distant the world of the Russian Pale is from the Arab East. The splinter groups that were a feature of the Russian political landscape appear far removed from the political associations common to the Middle East. But these differences do not obliterate certain essential similarities. When he writes of the Heirut Party, the first socialist-Zionist organization, Syrkin notes that it "set itself the goal of becoming a socialist-Zionist organization which would arouse the Jewish masses to struggle for a Jewish homeland and a new society." The concepts of the masses, of struggle, and of creating a new society, are precisely the same as we find in the writings of the observers of Arab society. Syrkin was impressed by the predicament of the Jewish proletariat in contrast to the privileged Jewish bourgeoisie. The latter could be seduced into feeling assimilated, and its economic situation soothed what social difficulties it experienced. But the masses suffered from the dual deprivation of political and social exploita-

tion, as well as from the economic exploitation which their own
fellow bourgeois Jews inflicted on them. Their enthusiasm for
Zionism lay in their need to escape the problems of homelessness; hence their socialist inclination, their wish to create a new
society in which they would be free of exploitative conditions.
If there is talk of redemption here, it is not simply in religious
or spiritual terms. Redemption can take place only in Palestine,
but it will come about through the "religions" of labor and socialism, which will combine to create a new man and a new
society. The conflict between Jewish settlement, socialist or no,
and Arab settlement in Palestine was to place virtually insurmountable obstacles in the way of both communities. On an
ideological level, it began to raise the question of the nature and
sincerity of the respective socialisms of Arabs and Jews, arguments that seemed irrelevant in the days of Syrkin, when the
Arab East was still regarded as feudal territory, but which would
become significant to members of a later generation.

Part 2 opens with a number of acerbic quotes taken from the
novel *Hunters in a Narrow Street* by Jabra I. Jabra. Jabra's bitter
wisdom seems most appropriate to the events which are described
with less wit and less fantasy in the following selections. In many
respects the essays of Part 2 illustrate themes which have already
appeared in Part 1. The conception of total change, the meaning
of the left in the Arab world and Israel, generational attitudes
toward the question of nationalism, and the controversial role of
the military as the arm or the emasculator of popular revolutions, have all been emphasized as central to the contemporary
thought of the Middle East.

Don Peretz and Anouar Abdel-Malek both describe the course
of the Egyptian revolution, at an interval of eight years. Both
men agree on the impact, within the region, of Nasser's success.
Peretz is impressed by the profound changes brought about by
the land reform program, although he recognizes that the difference between the redistribution of land and increased productivity
could endanger the goal of the redistribution itself. He emphasizes the national as opposed to the socialist slogans current in
1959, the Egyptian as opposed to the pan-Arab sentiments popular at the time, and the relative absence of ideological indoctrination in a movement that considers itself socialist. In conformity with a mood described earlier, Peretz found that there
was little patience with the niceties of parliamentary government
at this point, that democracy was regarded as a luxury, and that

the public virtues were order, unity, and work. That military rule—reflected in the predominance of officers in the countryside and the political administration, as well as in their more traditional settings—was untroubled by the paradox of "controlled democracy" seemed an ominous sign. But this was still a period of transition. Total social engineering was not practiced, nor even considered desirable; if anything, a truly socialist economy with its combination of experimentation and planning was still new.

After the June 1967 war, Abdel-Malek reviewed Egypt's situation with the bitterness mingled with hope that comes from combined devotion and disappointment. The central problem which continued to perplex Nasser and Egyptians was how to transform a national revolution into a social revolution. While Peretz reflected in a general manner on the paradox of the military position, Abdel-Malek saw the problem of the military in more precise terms as the need "to synthesize Islamic fundamentalism in its radical variant, that is, hostile to the ideology of the Muslim Brothers, with the principles of freedom and social justice which derived from the revolutionary tradition of the industrial era." The ideology which embodied this thought was later called "Arab socialism," and eventually, "scientific socialism." But labels did not transform the social or political realities. Like Peretz, Abdel-Malek recognized that a genuine and profound transformation of the economic and social structure of the country had taken place. This had involved the active participation of the officer corps, and it had resulted in the development of "an empirical and dirigiste ideology." But the avowed objective of building a socialist state and carrying out a social revolution was not possible without the participation of the masses, and it was this omission which rendered the entire accomplishment less than successful. The masses, in whose name the revolution had taken place, were conspicuously absent. It is Abdel-Malek's ability to explain why, under existing circumstances, they should have been missing which makes his analysis of Egypt in 1967 (and the analysis can be extended to the present) so important.

Abdel-Malek's critique applies to Egypt as a whole, but it is clear from this essay, as from his other works on Egypt, that he places great emphasis on and faith in the Egyptian left, in its contributions both before and, under great difficulties, after the revolution. While this undoubtedly reflects a personal viewpoint, it also raises the more general question as to what is the role and nature of the left in the Arab world. In the two essays on

Syria by Walter Laqueur and Eric Rouleau, some attempt is made
to answer this with reference to the most ideological of Middle
Eastern political parties, the Ba'th. Writing in 1957, Walter
Laqueur describes the emergence of the left in the Arab world
with the familiar skepticism which Europeans reserve for this
subject. But the tone in no sense invalidates the question which
Laqueur and others have raised: What does the left mean in the
Middle Eastern context? Laqueur answers it by saying that in
the Arab countries the left "opposes the social and political
set-up at home, favors domestic reforms, combats the 'feudal'
forces. But it certainly does not conform to the established western left-wing pattern of radical democracy, humanism, internationalism, and so on." And later, speaking of the radicalism of
the Syrian Ba'th, he says: "This radicalism is admittedly of a
vague character, and their pro-Nasser, pro-Soviet orientation
has less to do with Marxism-Leninism (or any other ideology)
than with a general feeling that these are dynamic, purposeful
movements which somehow 'get things done.' "

It has been customary to expose this very difference from
European leftism—the absence of a familiar ideology in full dress
and the presence of a general activism and spirit of negation—
as final proof of the immaturity of Arab leftism and socialism.
It is quite clear that there are several kinds of Arab socialists
and that ideological rigor, in the traditional sense, is to be found
among some Ba'thists as among some Communists, in and out of
jails. Laqueur's analysis of the move toward the left—which took
place at the time of the Baghdad Pact controversy (1954–1955)—
and his description of the bizarre allies who collaborated in the
creation of the Syrian Ba'th Party justifies skepticism, if one
insists on political consistency and clarity. Rouleau is not much
more generous in his exposé of what the Syrian enigma is all
about. But the accusation that the Arab left is not left because
it is mainly a form of activated negativism, not expressed in
European terms, is relevant. Certainly it is more palatable than
the view that socialism is merely the current intellectual content of a society in transition, the implication here being that
once this uneasy period has been transcended, more acceptable
ideas—less superficially fashionable and more native to the area
in their origin—will make their appearance.

The expansion of socialism into a worldwide movement, and
particularly its adoption by the Third World, has obviously affected its interpretation. It may be argued that to stretch a

definition of the left to include the original European roots of the term and its nonwestern variants is not possible without rendering the word "socialism" meaningless. Compromises and adaptations have been made, mainly for political reasons. Thus the Soviet Union, after 1956, found it possible to include the Egyptian revolution and its leaders in the lower echelons of the formally recognized socialist hierarchy, although even the most willing Soviet theorists appeared embarrassed at the prospect of having to approve the mixture of Arabism, Islam, and socialism which constitutes Arab socialism. This merely emphasizes the fact, however, that the Arab left is a world in itself, sharing certain conceptions—presumably the essential ones—with the rest of the socialist world.

The concept of the left in the Arab world is precisely the negation of existing social and political conditions. It does mean the struggle with feudalism and it does emphasize domestic reform. This is regarded as purposeful, and relies on activism for its implementation. And it does place such matters above the questions of Marxism-Leninism. Does this mean that it is not "left"? Or can we say, following the lead of the Polish philosopher Leszek Kolakowski, that the concept of the left "is a movement of negation toward the existing world"? Such negation is defined by its direction and by the utopia which animates that direction. Thus, it is paradoxically positive, within specified limits. But here difficulties arise. Given the success of socialism in the world and the establishment of allegedly socialist parties and governments, these have often come to stray from the fold with the same impunity as politicians of other persuasions. There is left and left. Kolakowski's criticism was directed at the Polish Communist Party, and particularly at the left within the party that emerged after it split. In his definition of the objectives of the left Party, he offers a description which I find relevant to the wishes of the most committed Arab leftists, Ba'thists or not, in and out of socialist parties:

> The Party Left was made up of those who fought to abolish all forms of privilege in social life, to recognize the principle of equality in dealings among nations, and to oppose local and foreign nationalism, reserving the right to call it by its real name of nationalism. The left stands for the abolition, without chicanery, of all kinds of anti-Semitism [in Poland], for freedom of speech and discussion, for victory

over dogma and over dull, doctrinaire or else magical thinking in political life, for legality in public relations, for the
maximum increase in the role of the working class within
the system of government, for the liquidation of the law-
lessness of the police.°

Does this describe the goals of Arab leftists within existing
parties; more specifically, does it describe the Baʿth? Eric Rouleau's
perceptive analysis of the roots of the Baʿth and its development
since the coup of February, 1966 offers the best answer to this
complicated question. The socialism of Michel Aflaq and Salah
al-Din al-Bitar, two of the more famous founders of the party in
Syria, was a mixture of nationalism, Arabism, and reformism.
It was not until 1948 that the party radicalized, and within a
few years after that differences among party members began to
crystallize around the question of more or less socialism, of the
scientific variety. In 1963, at the Sixth Party Congress, the exponents of Marxist socialism, imbued with the ideas of class
struggle and international solidarity, took the lead in what rapidly
became an internal struggle of important dimensions. Writing in
1967, Rouleau was impressed by the "authenticity" of the party's
radicalism and by the extent of the agrarian reform that had been
carried out. But the masses were neither in, nor supportive of,
the party; and internal differences, whose origins it is sometimes
difficult to discern, threatened what had already been accomplished. In spite of the increasing political sophistication of the
Baʿth regimes, secularism and internationalism remain at least
two of the topics that continue to be highly controversial in the
party and the nation. The leftism of the Baʿth has been secular
in theory, if inconsistently so. Under the leadership of Aflaq,
the mission of the Arab nation was conceived in quasi-religious
terms and Islam was recognized as the indivisible root of the
Arab genius. According to some commentators, Arab socialism
has merely transplanted or rechanneled the religious devotion
of its adherents from more traditional to more contemporary,
political concerns. But the fear of offending the masses by openly
criticizing religion is a problem that will one day have to be
faced in Syria, as in other Arab states. It is not merely that

°Kolakowski, Leszek, *Toward A Marxist Humanism* (New York, 1969), p. 78.
Translated from the Polish by Jane Zielonko Peel. Copyright © 1968 by Leszek
Kolakowski. Published by Grove Press, Inc.

socialism is secular; it is rather that the ability to contemplate the past—religious and sacrilegious—with dispassionate criticism is a prerequisite for the enlightenment which must precede any attempt at modernization. There can be no taboos, no prohibiting criticism of the army, religion, or the state, if the society is to progress, modernize, and otherwise survive. Obviously, these sentiments are shared by a large number of intellectuals, who understand the difficulties as well as the urgency of coping with them.

The question of nationalism, in the sense in which Kolakowski refers to it, is another matter. Here again, one has to recall that the impetus for social transformation, and the attraction of socialism, developed in the Arab world as a fulfillment of nationalism. The Egyptian revolution was motivated by nationalist considerations. The Ba'thists were nationalists before they were socialists. In the discussions of Arab unity, held in Cairo in 1963, two years after the dissolution of the Syrian-Egyptian unity (1958–61) in the form of the United Arab Republic, Nasser and the Ba'thists found it preferable to refer to nationalism as "regionalism." The choice of term is significant in that it reflects a certain discomfort with the persistence of nationalist sentiments considered inappropriate to a socialist society. On the other hand, regionalism cannot disguise or eliminate nationalist feelings—whether their appearance is appropriate or not.

It was not always necessary to qualify or apologize for the persistence of nationalism. Such persistence was one of the characteristics, in fact, that marked the interwar period, as we saw earlier. In the two selections which deal with Iraq, a contrast is offered between the views of the interwar generation, represented by Dr. M. Fadhel Jamali, former minister under Nuri al-Said and King Feisal II, and Khaldun al-Husri, historian, analyst, and socialist, committed to the new wave of revolutionary politics. Nationalism, the nature of the nation, and the price of change, are discussed by both men in their essays. Jamali defends Nuri's views on nationalism, emphasizing that his brand was not exclusive, as Arab nationalism has ironically become since independence. But this nationalism, which was a "matter of language, culture and history," was also an elitist concept. The nation was that part of the population fit to rule. It was not the Third Estate, proportionally larger than its counterpart in

eighteenth-century France. In this context, the revelation that
Nuri rather admired Western democracy is understandable, but
it reflects contempt. Western democracy, it turns out, was ad-
mirable but hardly fit for people who were "ultra-individualists
and very eruptive." That describes the Iraqis, whose individualism
made "cooperative political work very difficult." If the nation
is a naughty child, it cannot be allowed to rule or to play seriously
with politics. It needs control, education, and discipline. Is it
surprising that the events which have taken place since July,
1958 are not cause for celebration among those who favor the
"nation-as-child" approach? It would be worse than foolish or
flippant to deny that the Iraqi revolutions have not brought impressive signs of progress. At this stage, it seems nothing short
of a miracle that they have not brought total disintegration. But
does the failure of revolution retroactively pardon the sins of
the past?

Nuri was a revolutionary in his day. But when political liberation was accomplished, he failed to respond to the need to transform the national revolution into a social one. It is perhaps
unnecessary to suggest that revolution was a contrived foreign
import, and Khaldun al-Husri, who takes on Jamali with energetic anger, is insistent on stressing the national character of the
1958 revolution. Speaking for the angry young men who hope
to usher in the new nations of their dreams, al-Husri contests
the view that Nuri was genuinely interested in material reform
or that Iraq was a parliamentary democracy. Instead, he points
to the small clique that ran the country, the obstacles in the way
of a genuine parliamentary government, and (as a final insult)
to the fact that the police budget exceeded that for education.
It is little consolation that the police budget in a socialist state
also tends to run high, although the names of the enemies have
changed. Jamali's statement that Iraqis today are "yearning for
security, stability and prosperity" wins little sympathy from al-
Husri, who points out that few Iraqis enjoyed those conditions
before 1958.

Al-Husri's reference to education in relation to the police budget is well worth probing. It is not common for revolutionaries
to have much patience with the slow evolutionary process automatically assumed by education, but without education, the goals
of the most ardent national reformers are threatened with failure.
It is one of the many paradoxes of underdeveloped countries that
they are often unconscious of and unresponsive to the very sense

of solidarity and mutual responsibility that are indispensable to their development. Iraq is a perfect example of the extraordinary problems of shaping a nation out of a state.

The last two essays in Part 2 deal with Israel and with some of the problems it faces in its changing history. National solidarity again preoccupies David Ben Gurion in his analysis of the Histadrut. And the obsolescence of Zionism, which was both a cause and a result of this sentiment of solidarity, is scrutinized by Dan Avni-Segre.

It was stressed earlier that the process of development in Israel and the Arab world occurred not only at different rates but in different directions. Zionism, and particularly socialist-Zionism, preceded the establishment of a political state in Israel. The fabric of a nation that was not yet a state but was very conscious of its past as well as its future, was undoubtedly one of the sources of strength that enabled Israelis to withstand the pressures of war. If Zionism, with its exceptional endorsement of what Dan Avni-Segre calls the " 'collective aristocracy' of the land and the 'cooperative aristocracy' of labor," is becoming less viable as a result of the combined impact of industrialization and its relation to the changing nature of the population, then Israel may be said to be entering a new phase of development in which its own nationalism will undergo profound change.

Ben Gurion's essay on the "Histadrut and the State," written in 1955, reflects the position of the Zionist aristocracy, with its conceptions and concerns for the state. It is indispensable reading for an understanding of the role which the Histadrut, "the heart of the liberation movement," has played in the creation of the nation. Describing Israel as situated halfway between capitalism and socialism, Ben Gurion defines the role of the labor movement as the primary instrument in carrying out "achievement of our aims of national and socialist liberation." Reviewing its activities during the mandate period, he expresses concern at the reduction in the intensity of the pioneering spirit and at the increase in partisan, personal, professional, and economic interests. In debating how to imbue new immigrants with the requisite sense of belonging, Ben Gurion outlines a program which, with appropriate changes, is not very different from that applied in neighboring countries. They too share a comparable wish to raise the mass of the population to a new level of living, materially and spiritually. Resources, material and human, make the essential difference, but the objectives remain comparable if not always compatible. The state, according to Ben Gurion, must provide for education, technology, and the cultural-spiritual needs of the people. It must foster a "spiritual and social communion with the laboring class." But what distinguishes the recent members of that class from those of the pioneering days is that the pioneers arose from conviction as well as need, whereas the present generation is motivated primarily by need. And it comes from feudal societies which "know little of national and social liberation movements and still less of modern Hebrew or any other culture that were the molds which fashioned the immigrants to Israel before the Second World War." The danger is that the new immigrants will not share belief in the values of labor and colonization.

Avni-Segre begins his analysis of Israel with the assumption that the days of the Zionist plantocracy and the accompanying social and economic structure have passed, and that they have been replaced with the emergence of an unsentimental, industrially oriented technocratic elite. The complicated repercussions of this process, which have come to the surface in dramatic fashion after the June war—in part as a result of it—have affected diverse strata of Israeli society, and have filtered through various crises from the matter of German compensations to the Lavon Affair. But what is crucial is the gap separating the generation of Ben Gurion and Lavon, the Affair notwithstanding, and the men represented by Shimon Peres, creator of the Israeli Defense Establishment. For Peres, the emphasis is on productivity and not on ideology, on promotion based on merit and not in recognition of services to the cause. Industrialization, which has already transformed the social structure of the country and which now promises to transform its political and perhaps its international situation, is the key here. The war of 1967 reinforced the position of industry; it also provided "a new framework of unity centered on a community of interests, and on a more Jewish than Zionist national symbolism." The impact of the war in allowing the self-assertion of the new elite, and the presence of the Palestinians in "an already realized territorial unity of economic exchange," suggests yet another series of possibilities, this time concerning Israel's relations with the Arabs, which Avni-Segre alludes to with regrettable discretion. But the inescapable conclusion of all of this is that the long-range effect of this phase of development represents a critical transformation of the state—

and, potentially, a change in its dealings with the Arab world.

The balance between internal developments and foreign policy is one of the underlying themes in Part 3 of this book. Two general areas are explored: one, the controversial matter of Israel's position vis-a-vis the Middle Eastern states, and two, the question of Arab unity, its genesis as a movement and its possible implementation as a political reality. All of the essential ingredients brought together here have already been hinted at or discussed earlier. In the case of Arab unity, the primary instinct is the desire to restore unity to a fragmented and therefore weakened region. But it is also a response to a specific situation, namely, the existence of Israel and the realization that no single Arab state is strong enough to deal with Israel alone. However, Arab socialists also envisage the possibilities of regionalism as a means of bringing together Arab states that vary greatly in their natural resources and hence their wealth. What will this mean for the entire Middle East, Israel included? One of the objectives of Part 3 is not to stress the hostility that persists between Israel and the Arab world (which is sufficiently well documented) but rather to point out how much the existence of each is central to the policy making of the other. Arab unity, with its enormous if as yet unrealized possibilities for the Arab world as a whole, was given great momentum by the fear which Israel inspired. But Arab unity cannot be viewed merely as a vast defensive mechanism. As for Israeli attitudes to the Arab world, a series of complicated reactions (which are often unjustly simplified) are again at work here. Is Israel's western orientation, an axiom in the language of Third World progressives, inevitable? Has it always been so? What options existed earlier and why were they rejected? There are no simple answers to the problems raised here, but it is hoped that these essays will at least air questions which may one day be looked into and answered with greater promise.

In Parts 1 and 2 radical change was discussed primarily with reference to the left. In Parts 3 and 4 the issues are not presented in sectarian terms, although the dissenting views presented are often those of the left, and especially of the Mapam group in Israel. Arab unity has become the ambition of Arab politicians, whether of the left, center, or right, although they may differ on the nature of the governing apparatus that would administer such unity. In the case of the Arab-Israeli controversy, however, while the Arab left was not in the past consistently hostile to

rapprochement, it has become so—particularly since 1956. And
in Israel, after 1967, it is no longer possible to assume automatically that optimism is a prerogative of the left, although
those articulate advocates of reconciliation with Palestinian Arabs
are, in fact, often to be found among the left-wing socialists.

The virtue of Nissim Rejwan's article, which opens Part 3, is
that it immediately points up the connection between the dominant conception of Israeli nationalism, the relations between
western and nonwestern citizens of Israel, and the total effect
of this on Israel's attitude toward the Arab world. There are,
in addition, a number of salutary surprises. Thus the remark that
"the Zionists managed to create Arabism and Arab nationalism
in their own exclusivist image" is startling to those who assume
that Arab nationalism, in its recent form, and Zionism, are not
movements that had an influence on one another. But Rejwan
is persistent in exploring the European roots of Zionist nationalism,
and in questioning the relevance of such roots to the nonwestern
subjects of Israel. And he is equally persistent in exploring the
almost unconscious tendency on the part of some Zionists, including Ben Gurion, to conceive of Arabism as the Arab version
of Zionism, with unexpectedly negative results. Both Zionism
and militant Arab nationalism assumed a conception of the state
that had been foreign to the Middle East, that is to say to Middle
Eastern Jews, Muslims, and Christians. Its emphasis on homogeneity is of concern to people, in Israel and in the Arab world,
who regard exclusive nationalism as a dangerous condition.

Moving for a moment to the essay by Cecil Hourani, which
deals with the Arab League and the moderate nationalism it
encourages, we find an attitude similar to that expressed by
Rejwan. Hourani is equally concerned with the xenophobic
nationalism which he sees, and he reminds us that "Arab society
was not based on the Greco-Roman political tradition, and has
never had a concept of a strong sovereign state. . . . Arab society
has never been exclusively racial, but has consisted of racially
and religiously heterogeneous groups bound together by a common Arabic culture and world of thought." Hourani is interested
in presenting a reasoned case for the need for Arab unity, in
moderate style, through the means offered by the Arab League.
It is relevant in considering both Hourani and Rejwan to think
back to the attitude toward the state discussed by Kerr, Sharabi,
and Ben Gurion. Does this allow for the kind of heterogeneity

which Rejwan and Hourani endorse? Socialists, particularly in the Arab world, who are concerned with the imperative socio-economic needs of their society think invariably in terms of a strong central state, without which little seems possible. Can such states, even under socialist regimes, remain heterogeneous in composition, or must they become (as is indeed happening) homogeneous, exclusive states in which national and religious identity are the criteria for admission and participation? In Israel, the Zionism which Ben Gurion describes as the heritage of the pioneering days differs from that which Avni-Segre sees as the wave of the future. But how much do both tolerate differences—which again would render a homogeneous population unlikely? This question is crucial to Israel, which was born as a Jewish state.

In the three essays dealing with Israel's foreign policy, echoes of the problems exposed by Rejwan are constantly heard. Israel's foreign policy, since independence, has been affected by its rejection by the Arab world. But it is useful to avoid clichés of unchanging hostility or permanent alliances, and to consider the impact of reciprocal influence. To some observers, particularly those of the New Left, Zionism appears to dictate an inevitable conflict with the Arab world. But in practice—and the emphasis is on the practice, not the theory—there have been times when collaboration almost seemed possible. Certainly Israel's relations with the nonwestern world were not permanently blocked from birth. Simha Flapan points to three problems which have affected Israel's foreign policy although they cannot be considered the sole causes for Arab hostility. But the question that constantly emerges in Flapan's study, and indirectly in those of Shlomi and Nahumi, is whether or not different action on Israel's part might have provoked substantial changes on the Arab side. Thus Flapan is critical of Israel because it did not take sufficient account of the intensification of great power rivalry in the Middle East, of the rise of Arab nationalism, and of the retreat of colonialism. He recognizes the price paid for Israel's association with Great Britain and particularly with France, the two countries against which the Arab states directed their own struggle for independence. The tragedy is that this was not inevitable. "There exists no real contradiction between Arab aspirations for liberation, independence, and unity, on the one hand, and the existence of an independent, sovereign Israel integrated into the Middle East Area, on the other."

David Shlomi sees Israel's vocation as involving "cooperation with the Arab peoples awakening to a new spirit of activity after the destruction of the Ottoman Empire." But he puts the blame on the Arab states and the nations of the Third World for their inability or unwillingness to recognize the difference between "Jewish immigration to Israel and English colonization in Rhodesia or Kenya, or French settlement in Tunis and Algeria." This mistrust is not easily explained or allayed, but Flapan, without answering Shlomi directly, does provide at least a recognition of the reasons for it and for the ensuing "error" in Arab assumptions.

If there was a greater possibility of collaboration between Israel and the Arab states, it was in the period before the Bandung Conference of 1955, when Israel's relations with the nonwestern world were more fluid. The essay by Mordehai Nahumi is devoted to this proposition, taking as its illustration the example of Israeli-Chinese relations. Before the Bandung Conference, at which Chou En-lai launched his friendship with Nasser, friendly commercial relations had existed between China and Israel. This inspired Chou to discuss "steps [that] would be taken to exchange diplomatic representatives with . . . Israel." Even at Bandung, Chou did not attack Israel, which testifies to his enduring interest. But the pressures applied to Israel by the United States discouraged the further attempts that might have been made in this direction. Could it have been otherwise? Might China have become less pro-Arab, and Israel less pro-western? The answers that Nahumi offer are hardly optimistic, but he is careful to review some of the attitudes which accounted for Israel's earlier decisions, and the effect which these in turn have had on its later choices and policies.

By 1955–56 there had come a parting of the ways, at least in retrospect. Israel's collaboration with Great Britain and France in the Sinai-Suez campaign was a point of no return. Israelis and Arabs who had spoken publicly or privately in favor of an end to hostility were profoundly distressed, and coexistence once again dissolved into a distant dream. That Israel should have cooperated so closely with the former enemies of the Arab world, who were so obviously bent on defeating Nasser and what he represented, encouraged an attitude of self-defense and anti-western neutralism that found expression in the enormous popularity of the move for Arab unity. "Israel will insure Arab unity. If this does not happen, there will be no more Arabs," says Edmond Rabbath, prominent constitutional lawyer and articulate spokesman for the unity movement. ". . . . The Arabic speaking peoples today recognize a common denominator by which they, more or less confusedly, expect to resolve the economic and social conflicts still separating them." Rabbath, writing in 1956, is well aware of the factors making for confusion, and of the differences among Arab states which it was no longer then possible to overlook, but he writes with obvious concern for the long-range safety of the Arab world and for its defense, which he understands to embrace technological as well as military security.

At the end of his essay, Rabbath refers to the work done by the Congress of Arab Graduates, which had tried to "provide the solution by planning for a federal Arab state." In Selection 7 of Part 3, the results of this work are published in full. The Draft Constitution for the Arab Union is interesting for several reasons, among them the fact that its existence does away with the frequent allegation of total unpreparedness often leveled at partisans of unity. Rabbath, and a number of other Middle Eastern constitutional experts, had collaborated in the writing of the document, which was subsequently presented to Egyptian experts, having received the support of both President Nasser and King Hussein. The basic rules of the projected Arab Union assured the human rights and freedoms guaranteed to all citizens in the Universal Declaration of Human Rights, "regardless of race or creed" (Art. 6). It further guaranteed to "all religions and sects in the member states their respective traditions and their particular systems . . . insofar as they do not conflict with the national unity and the welfare of the Federal State" (Art. 7). The federal state itself would ensure the "organization, autonomy, constitution and frontiers of each member state" (Art. 5). It would control the foreign affairs, national defense, economic and educational matters falling under its jurisdiction (Art. 12), which included an interest in "oil and questions appertaining thereto" (Art. 13, Section 12). Legislative authority was vested in the Congress, which included a House of Representatives and a Senate (Chapter 3). And most interesting, in the light of the rather different experience which the years of unity (1958–61) produced, the executive authority was to be exercised through a conciliar system. Five members of equal rank and authority were to constitute the Council of the Union; they, in turn, would elect a President, who would rule for one year, and a Vice-President, to replace the President if necessary (Art. 36).

In practice, when the Baʻth precipitated the unity move with Egypt, the hope of influencing Nasser in more liberal and socialist directions proved useless. Instead of transforming him into a partisan of its brand of democratic centralism, the Baʻth was reduced to an inferior status and forced to dissolve itself. The essay by Patrick Seale, one of the more astute observers of the Syrian scene, on the break-up of the United Arab Republic discusses the forces which made unity near impossible, and the benefits which President Nasser's rule gave to Syria. He is unsparing in his evaluation of those factors in Nasser's entourage which made his rule in Syria highly unpopular, and he is equally sober in his estimate of the prospects of success, given Syria's hectic political past. It is more surprising to read that "few theorists of Arab nationalism have bothered to give the aspiration for unity a constitutional definition." But perhaps this reflects the failure—forced or not—of those men who had indeed given their dreams precise definition, but who were not present to implement them. Certainly in the light of the efforts of the Congress of Arab Graduates it does not seem just to conclude that Nasser's appeal was so powerful that it led his supporters to "overlook the importance of robust institutions and constitutional safeguards." Perhaps the proposed safeguards were *too* robust and did not fit in with the compromises which President Nasser was willing to make, given his own reluctance to accept unity in 1958. Pious wishes aside, after the June war of 1967 Arab unity no longer has the same fervor. It may revive in time and be stronger as a result of past experiences. But the present dissension within the Arab world—and particularly the severe disaffection with Arab governments and the charge of false promises of unity leveled by the Palestinians against other Arab states—seems to have considerably cooled the enthusiasm for unity.

Part 4 of this reader is, in some respects, the hardest to introduce. It is familiar to most people, since it is a part of the nature of the Arab-Israeli conflict that it touches on the most diverse interests and peoples. It represents a subject which—at its simplest—remains controversial and painful to those with memories of the recent European past, as well as to those Middle Easterners who first became familiar with the Jewish question in 1948. In a sense, this disparity in the memories of those who share an interest, even a stake, in Israel and the Palestine problem is at the heart of the issue. There is no way to make sense out of the profound grief and the persistent passion which animates partisans of both sides unless one accepts and understands the historic roots from which their respective positions emerge. And to understand why Zionism was a necessity to Jews, and why Palestinians left their homes or why they could not find a way of dealing with Jews in Palestine to their mutual satisfaction before 1948, is to confront the full and diverse history of Palestinian Arabs and European Jews. In the essays which I have included in Part 4, an attempt is made to show the genesis of the Arab-Israeli question as well as to listen to some men whose attitudes suggest a glimmer of hope. The emphasis, however, is certainly not on bringing together the most militant exponents of both sides. On the contrary, the reader may feel that he has been deprived of the literature he has come to accept on this subject. To such an objection, my only reply is that serious readers will detect enough anger and hate, implicit or explicit, in the material that follows to remind them of the "normal" dimensions of the conflict. If the same reader unexpectedly finds a new way of looking at the question, or voices of sanity and hope where he had come to anticipate only more despair, then I, for one, will feel that this presentation has more than justified itself.

The decision to begin the section with the essay by Chaim Weizmann has already been explained by the references to the European aspect of the problem which was to find its solution in Palestine. Written in 1942, Weizmann's article was an elaborate answer to the initial question it posed, on behalf of European Jewry. "The experience of the past twenty years, and the vexed problem of 'minorities' which has caused so much trouble in Europe, hardly give much ground for hope of a satisfactory solution on the spot . . . The hunted and disinherited will once more be faced with the eternal question: 'Whither?'" Meticulously reviewing the possibilities offered by allegedly interested European powers, Weizmann leads his readers to Palestine, pointing out as he does so that this most obvious choice seems to have been willfully overlooked by Great Britain. Weizmann's article is not based on an appeal to sentiment, and he presents a sober evaluation of the prospects and interests of those governments most concerned with the Palestine-Jewish problem. But he makes no compromise with the essential feature which dominates his thinking: that Palestine exists as the only place to which European Jews faced with extinction can and ought now to be able to go. But by 1942, Jewish settlement in Palestine had become extensive, and Weizmann was able to write in terms of concrete possibilities, for Jews and Arabs, based on the experiences of the past decades.

Judah L. Magnes, writing in 1947 when the horrors of the situation Weizmann had begun to describe had come to pass, responded to the same concern with a different voice. Magnes was not less realistic than Weizmann, nor was he less Zionist. But he answered the question: How shall Jews survive in Palestine? in a different fashion. What he feared was that a Jewish state could only be established and maintained, against Arab opposition, by force. Instead of supporting such a policy, he recommended the creation of a bi-national state. "We want a bi-national State, because we think the Jewish genius for government can be given full play through the bi-national State. How do we expect to get it? Through argument, persuasion, and finally through life itself." Magnes maintained that he had had conversations with "important representatives of the Arab world" who favored his plans. But the representatives were too few, too vulnerable. Perhaps their story has yet to be written with more optimistic results. Twenty years after Magnes's talk appeared in print, Moshe Dayan, as Defense Minister of the State of Israel, reflected on another figure (and undoubtedly on his own past) when he reviewed the phases through which Arthur Ruppin, Zionist, economist, and humanist, had passed in his attempt to come to an understanding of the Arab problem and the Jewish question in Palestine. Dayan's historical essay, which is written with persuasion and passion, with the authenticity of a man telling of his own experience in a manner not usually expected of military men, ends with the pessimistic conclusion:

> The Arabs do not agree to our venture. If we want to continue our work in Eretz Israel against their desires, there is no alternative but that lives should be lost. It is our destiny to be in a state of continual warfare with the Arabs. This situation may well be undesirable, but such is the reality.

Not the least frustrating aspect of the problem is that the nature of reality often appears to shift with the side one is on. In 1948, immediately after the State of Israel had come into existence, the Arab Higher Committee presented its tabulation of realities to the United Nations. What for Israel had been the consummation of decades of effort and vision was for the authors of the Arab Higher Committee report an act of treason. They recommended that the Palestine case be referred to the International Court of Justice, and that that body consider the status of Palestine after the end of the mandate. Two other questions were to be offered for discussion: "Whether the minority of the Palestine Jewish citizens, who are no more than 18 per cent of the citizens of Palestine, can proclaim a state in an Arab country. Whether the entry of Arab armies in Palestine, on the invitation of the overwhelming majority of the citizens of that country, is a violation of the [U.N.] Charter."

Although many Arabs endorsed the position of the Higher Committee, those who felt its arguments to be inadequate increased with time. With the establishment of Israel as a sovereign state new forces came into play, but it was still necessary to understand how Israeli success had been possible and why Arab defeat had been possible. As in other instances, military capability was hardly the whole answer. The need to come to grips with the causes of defeat led to analyses which, in turn, led far away from the incontrovertible proof of the battlefield. The "challenge and disaster" of Palestine referred to the challenge which the Arab states had missed to modernize their societies and, hence, to deal with a western people in their terms.

Musa Alami's "The Lesson of Palestine" was directed to this same question. But the lesson was a long and difficult one to learn, and two more wars, culminating in the June war of 1967, suggest that the impact of the analyses of this genre had not taken root. In "The Moment of Truth," Cecil Hourani returned to the same question, amplifying it as he saw fit, until it was nothing less than an indictment of self-deluding tyranny and indifference.

> This essay is addressed to the educated classes in the Arab countries: to those who still participate actively in the political, social, and intellectual life of their countries, and to those who have been excluded forcibly by their own free will. To all I trust it will have a message of hope. Destructive as much of my argument is, my aim is positive and constructive. On the understanding of our errors in the past may be built the new society of the future.

The catalogue of errors included tactical mistakes committed by

Palestinian Arabs in their dealings with the Jews and the British under the mandate. They included the rejection of compromise where the alternative spelled failure and even disaster. They involved the need to review and reassess the conduct of inter-Arab as well as international relations, and they involved the need to confront the real meaning of "progressive" and "reactionary" so that these two words should not become merely the labels for yet another myth.

Hourani's analysis followed on the last—that is to say, the most recent—of the Arab-Israeli confrontations, that of June 1967. It is placed in this text immediately after an account of the war written by Charles W. Yost, the present United States Ambassador to the United Nations, although it was actually written before his assumption of office. Yost's article is included because it places the events of June in perspective and because it takes into account the major power's interests and activities. But the war appears to have affected the ability or the willingness of the interested parties, primarily Israelis and Palestinians, to take the advice of the major powers. This realization that, when all is said and done, the question remains one to be adjudicated by Jews and Arabs, and more particularly by Israelis and Palestinians, is one of the striking results of the 1967 war. It has made the period since 1967 markedly different from that which accompanied earlier phases of the Arab-Israeli conflict, and it promises to affect the solution of that conflict in the future. Still, as of the time of writing (July 1969), this development has remained unrecognized on official levels; that is to say, the conflict remains one—in official parlance—between Israel and the "Arabs." The Palestinians have not yet been accepted as one of the parties to the conflict. Unofficially, although in an underground style that is relatively open and even publicized, Israelis and Palestinians do confront each other, and not only as occupiers and occupied. The selection entitled, "Arab-Israel Parley," is an example of such a confrontation. On the 28th of August 1968, a meeting between five distinguished Palestinians and five Israelis, with an Israeli moderator, took place in Jerusalem under the auspices of *Israel Magazine*. The participants represented divergent political attitudes, but both groups, Israelis and Palestinians, were devoted to their respective nations as well as to the need to find some more viable means of coexistence. The series of talks ranged from the objectives of Arabs vis-à-vis Israel, Arab views of Israeli ambitions, and the situation that would have occurred given an Arab victory, to the practical matter of achieving peace, and the urgent matter of dealing with Palestinian resistance, terrorism, and big power intervention. With the knowledge that their conversations would be reproduced and their views thus publicized, the assembled group of men nevertheless spoke with candor, expressing the frustrations, mistrust, and the deep passions which are common to the subject. Only one of the parleys is reprinted here, the third in the series, which deals with the question of how a political settlement is to be reached. It seeks to answer the following questions:

> How do we proceed toward a political settlement? In stages, beginning with a peace pact between Israel and the Palestinians alone, or between Israel and the Palestinians plus Jordan? Do you consider such a piecemeal arrangement desirable, practicable? Or are you of the opinion that peace is to be had only through an all-embracing settlement right off between the whole Arab world and Israel?

Amnon Cohen, the first of the Israeli speakers to tackle these problems, offered the suggestion that "we have to examine . . . the possibility of peace between Israel and the Palestinian Arabs, to serve as the basis of a wider peace that will emerge some time in the future." But the desire to localize the conflict, generally shared by all participants, was not in itself a final answer. What practical steps were necessary to achieve this end? What form of government would best serve Palestinian interests, and who would be responsible for introducing it? What would be the relationship between such a projected Palestinian entity— more or less "independent," given the individual views of the speakers—and the state of Israel?

The spirit animating these talks unfortunately already seems to belong to another age. In spite of profound discord, the Palestinian and Israeli delegates spoke together on the assumption that neither betrayed his people by doing so and that, through discussion, some clarification and hence some amelioration of the existing situation might result. One could be optimistic about the possibility of achieving clarity, if not a solution pleasing to all. But above and beyond all other considerations was the conviction that survival, in a meaningful sense, was the issue. This sentiment is reflected by an Arab-Israeli novelist and journalist in the last essay of this book. A man who belongs to two

worlds, Atallah Mansour represents a group of men who may
yet be the "bridge" between Israelis and Arabs. His essay reflects the possibilities of understanding as well as the persistence
of pride in one's country. Although the formulation of his conclusions may leave political pragmatists unsatisfied, as it must
inevitably dissatisfy those who prefer exclusive visions of their
own, Mansour's essay serves to remind us that the Arab-Israel
problem is, above all, a human one. Its various implications may
affect national and international relations, but the tragedy inherent in it is that which can be heard in a single voice, the voice
of a Christian, a Muslim, or a Jew.

It is a pleasure to thank Barbara Henson of the Center for
Middle Eastern Studies, Harvard University, for her consistently
cheerful help in typing parts of this manuscript. John Mong, of
Pegasus, deserves a citation for his patience, encouragement, and
interest, none of which is taken for granted. Finally, a word of
gratitude to those friends whose personal involvement in the
matters considered here first awakened my own interest. I hope
that they will not only be reminded of those past conversations
which we believed to be so vital, but that they will continue
to uphold the right to raise unpopular questions, and that they
will continue to have the courage to believe in the value of the
critical spirit.

Irene L. Gendzier
Cambridge, Massachusetts
July 1969

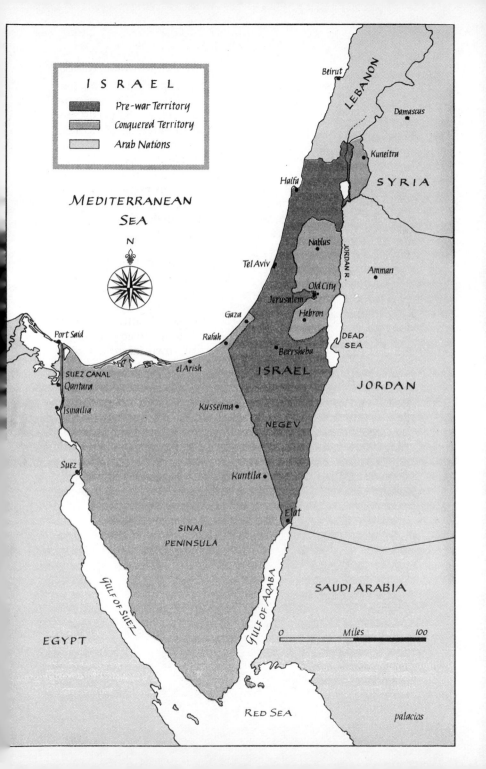

A Picture-Writer once coined a phrase, "The Unchanging East," and Time has turned round and taken revenge upon him. The East is to-day the place of change— of changes so great and swift that in comparison with it our Europe is standing still.

T.E. Lawrence, "The Changing East," *Oriental Assembly*, ed. A. W. Lawrence London, 1939.

PART I

Reflections on Radical Change
In the Arab East and Israel

Ling to A.D.

Cher Monsieur,

Europe calls forth few beautiful ghosts, and I have come to her with hostile curiosity. The illusions which she has created in us Chinese are too indefinite for us to find instruction or pleasure in modifying them: the influence of books and of our own anguish has made us investigate the thought of Europe rather than her forms. Her present attracts us more than the broken frame of her past, from which we seek only enlightenment as to the source of her strength. . . .

An unceasing creation, renewed by action in a world destined to act—that is what then seemed to me the soul of Europe, where all was subordinate to man's will.

André Malraux, *The Temptation of the West*. Trans. R. Hollander, New York, 1961.

1. Arab Radical Notions of Democracy

BY MALCOLM KERR

SINCE THE PALESTINE war, and more particularly since the Egyptian Revolution, it has been increasingly remarked that Arab nationalist political and social ideas were entering a new radical phase and that the age of liberalism was at an end. The stream of Western social and political values that had begun to trickle into the East at the time of Napoleon and had reached flood tide by the 1920's seems by now to have been somehow diverted, or dried up. The ideas themselves—notions of constitutionalism, individual civil rights, the electoral competition of political parties, and so forth—are as familiar as ever to educated Arabs; but they no longer strike an enthusiastic response. Often Arabs are now heard to say that these ideas are irrelevant to their needs; that they are of superficial value unless preceded by a social and economic revolution; that democracy is a fraud without social justice; that the West no longer has a monopoly of ideas, any more than a monopoly of arms for sale; that they, the Arabs, will shop in the open marketplace of the world at large for political, social and economic ideas, buying only what suits their taste wherever they find it; and finally that they have no need or wish to import artificial ideologies, but will develop their own indigenous product out of their own experience.

The simplest explanation given for this new radicalism is that the brief experience of several Arab states since 1920 with Western-style constitutional systems was an unhappy one, and therefore the experiment was abandoned on pragmatic grounds. A

Excerpt from "Arab Radical Notions of Democracy," St. Antony's Papers, No. 16, *Middle Eastern Affairs,* No. 3 (London, Chatto and Windus, Ltd., 1963), pp. 9–11, 20–40. Reprinted by permission of the author and courtesy of the publisher.

few years of rigged elections, musical-chair cabinets, suspended constitutions, arbitrary arrests, playboy monarchs, and absence of reform legislation should have been quite enough to convince the Arabs that they should give all this up and try something else—anything else. This was particularly the case after 1948, when it suddenly became clear that their governments were not only corrupt but, what was worse, that they were weak.

But this explanation does not take us very far. On the one hand, it unjustly implies an extraordinary naïveté on the part of Arabs as to the cultural and moral basis of Western institutions. In actual fact there has been no lack of Arab thinkers and statesmen who have told their people that to have constitutional democracy it was necessary to develop certain qualities of citizenship, a certain attitude toward science, a spirit of tolerance, a concept of secularism, and so forth. These preachings can be traced well back into the nineteenth century. On the other hand, the above explanation tells us nothing of the nature or background of the particular new ideas that have now begun to take hold. Not only has constitutional liberalism receded into the background, but another more radical concept of democracy has risen in its place. This concept has taken its most extreme form in Egypt, where it has been forcefully promoted by the government. But in a subtler fashion, it has influenced the mentality of a growing class of Arabs elsewhere who are anxious for reform. The idea is not—as is sometimes supposed—simply to strengthen the economic and social foundations for constitutional democracy, if necessary even by temporary authoritarian means. For not only is social and economic reform an extremely long-term and revolutionary proposition, but already in the course of organizing these reforms new political ideals have begun to take shape. It is not a question of a transition period by which Arab society would be led through a detour back again in the end to some Western model of constitutional liberalism. It is irrelevant to argue that the longer the detour the less likely it is to lead back to the main road. For the so-called transition period creates its own goals appropriate to itself. The detour has become the main road, not by miscalculation but quite deliberately, leading straight to a newly accepted destination, on the assumption that its surface will become smoother as one follows it along. Revolutionary government is looked upon by its enthusiasts not as a path back to liberalism, but on to a radically different form of democracy.

The radical conception of democracy is not really new, either in the West or in the Arab world. But it has reemerged in recent years in a new form and amid new conditions. Essentially the conception is that described by J. L. Talmon as "totalitarian democracy" and typified for him in the excesses of the French Revolution and in the ideological tradition of Rousseau and Marx as opposed to Montesquieu, Locke and Bentham. It is characterized by a moral preference—not just a tactical preference—for maintaining the maximum degree of unity of purpose and action at all political and social levels; by an emphasis upon the virtues of group solidarity and the evils of individual self-absorption and self-seeking; by a mistrust of competition, bargaining, and the promotion of special interests; and by a vision of strong government as a liberator rather than a danger to liberty. The free individual is not primarily a man who is left alone to do as he sees fit, but one whose usefulness and security in society are assured. Therefore it is not privacy but sociability that must be promoted. The role of government is not to maintain respect for a disparate mass of private individual purposes, but to take the lead in formulating and pursuing great national ideals which all can enthusiastically share. Individualism is criticized as a narrow, constricting, negative concept with which the Western world is obsessed and by which it is blinded to the problems of African and Asian countries, if not, indeed, to some of the ills of its own society.

Thus the Arab radical rejects the familiar Western assumption that the division of power and initiative in society among competing groups is inherently desirable, and that too much concentration of power in the hands of the state is a natural threat to private right. For him, the essence of democracy is found not in the existence of a parliamentary opposition, but in the creation of a socialist program and the enlistment of mass support in implementing it.

What are the forces which press the Arab radical to reject ideas of pluralism and decentralization of power? Are there historical roots or precedents for this rejection? Is it legitimate to consider the history of Arab thought at all, or is the Arab radical so completely cut off from his Islamic intellectual heritage that the conceptions of the latter are irrelevant?

A case can be made that certain forms of traditional Islamic thought, though not others, do provide some significant points of

similarity to present-day radicalism. The link between the two is
found in those Islamic modernists of the early twentieth century
who took as their ideological starting point a doctrine of the
Caliphate that had been elaborated in the later centuries of the
Abbasid Empire. They interpreted it in a manner suitable to
their own concerns and purposes, which were in some ways
closer to those of today's radicals than to those of their medieval
forbears. Indeed the modernists were, in their own odd way,
among the radicals of their time. Yet the Abbasid doctrine was a
well-chosen model which naturally lent itself to the particular
adaptations of the modernists, for it was based on similar
assumptions about the organization of power in a morally
purposeful society. And on the question of the organization of
power, the radicalism of the 1950's represents a revival of those
assumptions and a break with the liberal constitutional philosophy of the West. . . .

Without going into any detail on ideas and movements of the
1930's and 1940's, it may briefly be remarked that during these
years in a number of Arab countries, while western-style constitutional systems were in force (though frequently suspended),
and while parliaments were dominated by parties which at least
nominally subscribed to secular liberal ideas, a growing disenchantment gnawed continuously at their foundations. Large
numbers of angry young men grasped in desperation at a variety
of militant ideologies, from the Muslim Brethren to fascism and
communism, or merely strident expressions of nationalism. Like
many present-day Arab radicals, they were, as Jamal Ahmed
aptly puts it, "barely educated but emotionally exalted and heroic in an uncalculating way." [22] Even in the early 1930's, in an
Iraq that had barely gained its independence, such groupings as
the supernationalist *al-Ikha al-watani* gave evidence of disillusion with constitutional liberalism, as did such leaders as Antun
Saadeh in Lebanon and Ahmed Husain in Egypt, out of impatience with its emphasis on moderation and tolerance.

It is also notable that the Muslim Brethren, quite apart from
the religious question which they reintroduced into Arab politics, offered a political doctrine which (though hazy on many
points) shared the militant and revolutionary spirit of the secular
radicals, and in fact far outdid them by spelling out so frankly
the totalitarian nature of its program, from "eliminating political parties and orienting the political forces of the nation in a

single direction and in a single bloc" to "organizing the summer resorts in such a way as to eliminate the disorder and license which negate the fundamental purpose of summer vacationing." [23]

But it should not be supposed that religious puritanism is the only basis of the totalitarian mentality. For one thing, after the abrupt disappearance of the Brethren from the political stage in 1954, there were other symbols to which "emotional exaltation" and "uncalculating heroism" could readily attach themselves. For another, one may very well ask whether, in the Arab world of the 1950's, *any* reform-minded thinker determined to get to the bottom of existing social and economic problems and put them right by prompt and energetic political action, was not prone, wittingly or not, to encourage totalitarian methods and ideas. There is, then, potentially a double entrée to totalitarianism: first the emotional excesses of the nationalist mystique, and secondly the relentless logic of a socialist program, unimpeded by any lasting social barriers from reforming and reorganizing society down to the smallest detail. Nationalism without any social content, if it tries to compensate for the lack by still more nationalism, presents the danger of an irrational tyranny; socialism (or any other systematic principle of social reconstruction) may lead to a rational one.

It is true, of course, that many Arab socialists are moderate men who believe not only in parliamentary democracy but in the encouragement of diversity, voluntary social organizations, free individual expression of opinion, and so forth, and that their only aim is to establish economic and social justice in order to make these things possible on a wider scale. A case in point is the widely popular book by the Jordanian Ba'th writer Munif al-Razzaz, *Ma'alim al-hayat al-arabiya al-jadida (Outlines of the New Arab Life).* [24] Written on the eve of the Egyptian Revolution in 1952 and now in its fourth printing, the book presents a comprehensive statement of political, economic and social principles and proposals, which for the most part seem like a combination of English utilitarian and Fabian ideas. On the political plane the keynote is respect for free individual self-expression and for the diversity of individual tastes and interests. Tracing his ideas deductively from axioms reminiscent of the Declaration of the Rights of Man, Razzaz insists without qualification on freedom of speech, of political activity and party life, parliamentary elections, and so forth. He dwells at length on the need for more modern political parties based on programs rather than personalities, and is sharply critical of the existing (1952) party systems in the Arab world, but rejects appeals for the establishment of dictatorial reform governments to suspend party life or for the establishment of a single-party system, on the grounds that there can be no progress without a continuous process of conflicting interests, whose free expression dictatorships suppress. Dictatorship "tries to dye all the thoughts of the people in a single color . . . and to produce individuals who are really only copies of one another and who lack the spirit of innovation and creativity and independent thought, and are no more than cogs in this great complicated apparatus of the state." Furthermore, "as Nehru has said [sic], 'Power tends to corrupt, and absolute power tends to corrupt absolutely'." [25]

In economics, while accepting a general Marxist criticism of the evils of capitalism (e.g. that as the machine age progresses, the middle class is squeezed out, and only the very rich and the growing class of the poor remain),[26] he finds dangers and excesses in Marxist solutions. Excessive nationalization would cast too heavy an administrative burden on the state and turn the whole population into a government bureaucracy; it would create "an atmosphere of dreary and monotonous routine in which there was no pleasure, no novelty, no satisfaction of the appetites and no room for change." People should not all live in identical houses with identical furniture all manufactured by the same state company, and wear identical clothing.[27]

A number of Razzaz's specific economic proposals closely anticipate the program of the Nasser regime up to 1959, such as the creation of corporations jointly owned by private and government capital but under government direction, the encouragement of producers' and consumers' cooperatives, and the construction of the Aswan High Dam. But despite his constant defense of diversity and individualism, and his general tone of moderation and good sense, very different implications creep in at other points of his program. Razzaz is sickened by the material greed of Arab society: "The primary characteristic of the present system is that of exploitation. Its ideal is that of acquisition, which is the sole controlling element in the present society." [28] No real reform is possible until lust for money is removed as the basis of the economy. Money today buys power and prestige; it creates hatreds and resentments; it spoils the spirit of public service; it is wasted on luxuries. "Whatever system we propose must aim at making money the means of serving all society, not just certain individuals, and making the right of any individual to own property conditional on this wealth being used for the benefit of all." The government must "supervise production and consumption"; it must assume complete control of foreign trade, ensuring that "not one piastre" is spent on imported luxuries as long as mass-consumption commodities and capital equipment are needed.[29] All "heavy and medium" industry, if not fully nationalized, must be "fully supervised" by the government. Private enterprise may be left free to produce "jewelry, children's toys, and sweets" subject to government supervision of the use of capital and profits and prevention of "exploitation" by the owner; this measure of private enterprise (such as it is) should be preserved as a means of allowing the individual to "assert his own personality and inclinations, and develop himself in the way he desires." [30] The poor cannot afford the means of raising their children properly, and the state should therefore assume the task of rearing them, "since it is these children who in the near future will become the men of the sound society we wish to create." [31]

Razzaz's concern is to eliminate the social tyrannies and injustices practiced by privileged against deprived individuals. The state in Arab countries has been a political tyrant as well, but only as a reflection of the economic and social interests of the classes controlling it; and no constitutional provision for political liberty will be of any use to the masses until their economic misery is alleviated.[32] On these points one could scarcely disagree with Razzaz, given the facts of social and economic life in the Arab world in 1952 or, for that matter, today. But in reading Razzaz's economic and social chapters, one suspects that his liberal political ideals have become irrelevant even for Razzaz himself. He writes that his economic proposals are not ends in themselves but only prerequisite conditions for the development of individual initiative and liberal democracy.[33] But is this really so, or has he become so absorbed with the need for radical economic solutions that they are no longer judged in the light of the political conditions they are likely to produce? One might wonder what measure of latitude for personal taste and enterprise, for the competing interests of private associations, for the right of political dissent, and for a multi-party parliamentary system could be expected to thrive under a regime which organizes all economic enterprise above the level of the manufacture of sweets, prohibits all importation of luxuries, "supervises and directs a centralized national organization of cooperatives," [34] and "undertakes the exploitation" of the funds of the rich, as "this money is the property of society, not theirs." [35] Razzaz does not argue the point; he simply ignores it. There is, of course, a case to be made for his program on purely economic and social-welfare grounds, and he appears satisfied with that. Unconsciously, he has made his choice between pluralist politics and collectivist economics. Other thinkers were to make the same choice more consciously and consistently, introducing collectivist political ideas as well.

The springboard for such ideas on the political level has been the question of the class struggle, of which Razzaz made no specific mention, but which other writers, including Razzaz's fellow-Ba'thists, have treated with increasing emphasis. Thus Abdullah Abd al-Da'im, a professor in the University of Damascus, while making general statements about the democratic virtues of individualism and tolerance of diversity rather similar to those of Razzaz, is more explicit in defining their limits. We cannot speak of democracy in a given society, he writes, without considering the social conditions peculiar to it. Freedom cannot exist in the abstract *(mujarrad)* but must be "embodied" *(mushakhkhas)* in concrete forms.

> Democracy, in essence, is an attempt to reconcile the demands of the individual with those of society. It is a type of accommodation between individual liberty and social compulsion. The concrete expression of this is found in the line we draw in making this accommodation. Consequently we cannot accuse a society of being undemocratic except after determining, by a study of its conditions, that it could have been brought to a greater degree of harmony between the freedoms of society and those of individuals. . . . The liberty of the individual, as it is often said, ends where the liberty of the group begins. . . . This means that for every society there is a limit to the liberty it can permit to its individuals, but that the least restrictive possible interpretation of that limit, and the effort to push the line ever forward, are the criteria of the democratic character of that society. [36]

What, then, are the limits he recognizes? In principle, the "fundamental limit which may not be exceeded, is the prohibition of those creeds which call for change by means of violent armed revolution." [37] But in practice he is prepared to go far beyond this. Despite the need to preserve a united national front in the face of imperialism, and to "substitute national cooperation for the class struggle and to try progressively to dissolve this struggle in pursuit of the greater national goals," this should not lead us to

> . . . make a truce with the exploiters and to make undue concessions in our socialist approach. . . . To be a truly revolutionary truce [*sic*] it must constantly carry within itself the features and form of the socialist society which is progressively achieved. Everyone must realize that this truce is only a transitional policy aiming at the piecemeal absorption of capitalist life, always assuring the progressive gains of socialism and the ultimate achievement of a socialist society.

The truce, then, must rest on the clear understanding that it is really an arrangement under which the reactionaries and capitalists will quietly be done in.

> For the capitalists can only accept a gradual surrender in favor of the national interest by virtue of two combined factors: first, belief in the national objective . . . , and second, awareness of the existence of a tremendous popular current, and of popular forces of production [i.e. means of economic pressure] to which they are compelled to yield, as otherwise they would be forced to make an even greater surrender. This second factor is important. For it is this which makes the capitalist class fear that its gains may be entirely lost, and consequently feel impelled to accept gradual surrenders. These two complementary prerequisites will be achieved when a popular regime representing the popular class is established, in which the people are the moving force behind the regime.[38]

In these passages the transition in Abd al-Da'im's thoughts emerges. From signifying individual liberties and the tolerance of all dissent short of armed violence, democracy has come to denote the supremacy of that mystical and featureless entity called the "popular class," whose only common identity lies in their lack of identity, but whose organic unity of will is nevertheless so readily assumed by radical nationalist writers in the Arab world and elsewhere. Abd al-Da'im makes this transition explicit by proceeding directly from the above-quoted remarks to a fulsome account of the principles of Sukarno's "guided democracy," in which "leadership is qualified by the process of consultation, but this consultation is guided by wisdom, not by debates and maneuvers which end in trials of strength and the counting of votes," and in which freedom of speech is assured "within certain limits" to protect "the safety of the state" and public welfare.[39]

Whether it is more important to preserve a front of national unity, comprising all social groups, against presumed outside dangers, or to promote "popular" solidarity against domestic "reactionaries" in the name of future progress and a more lasting form of social cohesion, is a dilemma that has concerned a number of writers (although in either case, of course, in the end it is "unity" that is considered to be at stake). But it is the second alternative which tends to have the last word. Thus Michel Aflaq, while rejecting the pure Marxian view of the class struggle for its exaggerated internationalism and for its disregard of nationalism as a focal point of loyalty for the working class in a given country, recognizes that within national boundaries the economic class factor is fundamental. The Arabs, he argues, cannot afford a national partnership between exploiters and exploited, because that would remove all positive significance from nationalism itself: "Nationalism is nothing more than words and phrases if coupled with oppression, poverty, and deprivation."[40] Arabs must beware of those exploiters who, in order to save their own skins, claim that they, too, are nationalists. "We are not afraid to use force against all those who prevent this progress and growth. The people must conduct a violent and determined struggle against those rulers and others who with their material and moral interests are obstructing the unity of the nation."[41]

Arab unity assumes the proportions of an apocalyptic vision in the mind of Aflaq. Within the Ba'th's almost theological trinity of "liberty, socialism, and unity" it holds first place, on the grounds (as Aflaq explains) that socialism and liberty cannot be truly achieved except on its basis. And in contrast to the superficial unity of the Arab League, the Ba'th version of unity is "fundamental, living, having its own theory as liberty and socialism have theirs, and, like them, having its own daily organized and continuous struggle of principle."[42] The cause of unity is bound up with that of socialism, for, although unity is the primary goal, "it cannot be achieved by governments, nor foreign states, nor politicians, nor thinkers, but only by the people alone"; but "the people" will play this part only if assured of social and economic justice. Socialism is the "body," unity the "spirit." Socialism is "only a means and a step toward a greater goal, namely the unification of the Arab homeland; and this unification is not the final goal, but is in its turn a means whereby the Arab nation may play its part in life. This mixture of the two goals, this incarnation of an idea in a body, is something fundamental which we always insist on." [43]

Unity—whether between the Arab states or within the ranks of the nationalist movement or of Arab society as a whole—is the symbol of militancy, of the mobilization of energy, enthusiasm and purpose. The Ba'thist writer and politician Abdullah al-Rimawi, asking whether "revolutionary Arab Nationalism" has progressed with the speed demanded of it by the "new logic" of the "battle" in which it is engaged, poses the following criterion of success:

> That in the Arab homeland the modern Arab nationalist movement become the one revolutionary movement with the one clear doctrine, relying on the oneness and clarity of its doctrine to provide the Arab nation with unity in its organization and unity in its struggle, and to provide it in its battle with unity of leadership and unity of revolutionary practical planning and tactics, so as to mobilize the nation's masses and harness its energies in a rising, conscious historic tide, on which this nation can proceed with the requisite speed toward the realization of its goals and the performance of its mission.[44]

Similar ideas were expressed in simpler and more coherent language by Fayez Sayegh, who in 1955 criticized the divisive effect of political party life on Arab politics. Partisanship, he wrote,

> . . . splits the nation into blocs, when it is in dire need of the cooperation of all its sons to the utmost limit. Partisanship puts party interests in place of public interests, and substitutes short-sighted conceptions for far-sighted ones. Partisanship means a predisposition to enmity not because

of differences in final aims or discrepancies in degrees of sincerity but because of differences in party membership and enrollment. Finally, partisanship destroys objectivity in judging movements and individuals, intentions and ideas and actions. The partisan judges matters not according to the extent of their affinity or usefulness to the national interest, but according to the extent of their affinity to the interest of the party.[45]

Similarly, the Lebanese socialist writer Clovis Maqsud laments the fact that many of the left-wing Arab nationalist parties have tended to devote more energy and attention to their own organizational strength than to the development—in common with one another—of a coherent ideology, and even to be jealous and critical of one another's ideological achievements. The result is that Arab socialism lacks the "oneness and clarity of doctrine" which Maqsud, like Rimawi, desires:

> Socialism has come to have various connotations, and is no longer a radical revolutionary doctrine, but rather is characterized in many cases by the middle or opportune solution between reaction and communism. As a consequence of losing the theoretical outlines of socialism, these party groupings which arose in the Arab nation within the ranks of the Arab elite designated themselves as socialist, without being prepared to achieve socialism—that is, to achieve the ideal society—because of their lack of serious, sound, conscious commitment to socialism and their lack of an intellectual apparatus capable of embracing its content. And this in turn causes the Arab elite to lack a plan for the Arab struggle by which to progress constantly toward the socialist society to which they aspire.[46]

But despite Sayegh's and Maqsud's common distaste for factionalism and their common desire for ideological coherence, they are poles apart on a more fundamental issue. Maqsud, like Rimawi, Aflaq, and some others, is consumed with devotion to the cause of transforming Arab society. If the precise outlines of the cause are not entirely clear, that is not said to reflect on its validity but only on the present degree of understanding on the part of its adherents. Not only must they organize their ranks, unify their leadership, mobilize their energies, and draw up their plan of battle, but they must clarify and elaborate their vision of the great transformation lying just over the horizon. What is its nature? It cannot be the ideal Islamic society imagined by the Rashid Ridas and Hasan al-Bannas only a few years earlier in Egypt, nor is it communism. It must take the form either of nationalism or socialism, or both, for these are now the only effective rallying points. But it must carry within itself some all-embracing principle of social morality comparable to that of the Islamic and the communist utopias.

It is this implicitly totalitarian tendency against which Sayegh very sharply reacts. In a pair of short articles in 1959, he discussed the question of the "limits" of the nationalist ideology he wished to see developed. There is a danger (he wrote) that to counteract the challenge of communism, Arabs will be tempted to create against it an ideology of equally comprehensive proportions. Communism "passes judgment . . . on all human activities, including creative activities in the fields of science, art and philosophy, and on such human values as freedom and morality. It is a system which anchors the bases of all these things in itself, and no part of human life, individual or collective, escapes its judgment." Some Arabs think they must have a nationalist answer to communism on every one of these points. But this is a mistake. Nationalism, if it presumes to judge all aspects of human life, will become tyrannical. Nationalism should therefore aim at evolving an ideology which is not "totalitarian" (*kulli*) but only "adequate" (*wafi*).

Sayegh's concern is to preserve what he defines as "secularism" (*ilmaniya*), by which he means the distinction between personal and social affairs. Secularism is destroyed either when a religious or philosophical creed, dealing with personal and private matters as well as social questions, asserts its control over the state and thus establishes a theocracy, or when a social doctrine such as communism, socialism, or for that matter nationalism, asserts its sovereignty in personal affairs. Secularism means not only keeping the religious establishment out of politics but, conversely, isolating the social authority from personal and spiritual life. Totalitarian social ideologies tend to make religion, philosophy, art, etc. the servants of their own desired social system, on the assumption that the whole existence of man is of purely social significance.[47]

To these points Maqsud replies with two arguments. In the first place, he says, nationalism itself should not be allowed to become an ideology. Nationalism is only a loyalty to a certain concept of identity, and should be no more than a prerequisite to domestic social and political action. Those who attempt to make an ideology out of nationalism alone are likely to end in an irrational totalitarianism.

In the second place, Maqsud distinguishes between what he calls "total" *(kulli)* and "totalitarian" *(jama'i)* ideology, inserting the English terms in his text to make his meaning clear. His own socialist ideology, which is "total," does not rest on common ground with communism, nor is it a response to the communist challenge, but is simply a comprehensive and systematically integrated view of life. Therefore,

> Dr. Sayegh is correct in concluding that the nationalist ideology, if it becomes total, will become tyrannical and will strip the nationalist movement of its positive values. But this does not apply to the "totalness" of the socialist ideology. The chief difference between us is that Dr. Sayegh insists upon a nationalist ideology, and in order to lighten its inevitable tyranny, takes refuge in making it "adequate" *(wafi)*. The mistake lies in his commitment to the ideological character of nationalism, instead of being satisfied with the nationalist movement as a preliminary stage . . . . This major difficulty confronts many of our Arab thinkers who hesitate to commit themselves to socialism as a programme and as an image of the society they want to create . . . . The appeal to an "adequate" ideology, in my view, does not stem from a conviction of its soundness, but from the desire to reconcile one's hesitation to commit oneself to socialism as an ideology on the one hand, with a deep consciousness and fear of the danger of nationalism as an ideology on the other . . . .
>
> The political position of socialism toward non-socialist ideologies might cause it for tactical reasons to welcome their being "adequate," but this does not at all mean that it agrees that an adequate ideology of socialism would be sound by virtue of being adequate; on the contrary, making socialism adequate would mean making it indeterminate, incomplete, and incapable of shouldering the comprehensive revolutionary responsibility that is thrust upon it. Hence the necessity of defining the total quality of socialism. . . .[48]

Those who share Sayegh's apprehensions may well ask why

socialism, if it purports to be a comprehensive doctrine of life as Maqsud says, is any freer than other ideologies of the danger of totalitarianism. What guarantees of individual liberty does "total" socialism provide? On these points Maqsud offers a characteristically verbose and vague, yet revealing, explanation. True socialism holds that

> . . . man's freedom consists in his ability to expand the scope and horizons of his active participation in life so that he may give to life and to society something of value from his own being, and take in return something that will help him achieve his own happiness. It is the "total" nature of socialism that organizes the social framework in a form that embraces individual initiative, and assures a system of public relationships that will not alienate sections of the people from actively exercising their initiative under guise of preserving liberty. In practice, liberty is exercised only as the result of liberating oneself, and will only be complete if the liberation has been complete. If we decide that man's problem is a totality, and that socialism is the doctrine capable of solving the problem in a manner compatible with the needs of evolution and equality, then socialism must be total . . . . Socialism is not socialism at all unless it is total: that is, unless it comprises the totality of human experience and takes a stand on all issues in conformity with the assumptions in which it believes and the values stemming from them. If on the other hand we content ourselves with an "adequate" doctrine of socialism, we will have condemned Arab thought to a dissipation of its potentialities and to reliance on what is fragmentary and only immediately necessary, and we will have exposed it to the frightful contradictions and the distorted and false positions into which many of the right-wing socialist leaderships in Europe have fallen.[49]

Perhaps the key phrase in the above passage is "if we decide that man's problem is a totality," from which it follows that "socialism . . . [must] take a stand on all issues." Maqsud nimbly sidesteps Sayegh's point by making *kulli* mean "total" as opposed to *jama'i* or "totalitarian" (though "collective" would be a more natural translation of the latter term). But by *kulli*, Sayegh clearly meant "totalitarian," and it is difficult to see that

Maqsud's ideas, as he himself describes them, escape the substance of Sayegh's argument.

Recent political writing in Egypt is of a very different quality from that of radicals in the Fertile Crescent countries. The latter are critics of existing regimes; they are individuals, not committed to any established line, and they carry on a genuine debate among themselves. They have not deliberately turned their backs on western liberal thought, but have gradually drifted away from it. Hence their critique of liberalism has generally been an indirect and implied one, and many of them would no doubt protest against some of the conclusions drawn in the foregoing discussion.

In Egypt, on the other hand, while there is no real debate, the trend of ideology is more explicit, under the stimulus of an authoritarian regime that has made a point of scrapping Western constitutional forms and erecting new experimental institutions in their place. It is natural, therefore, that it should be in Egypt that the frontal attack on liberal traditions has been made, in a manner that substitutes bluntness for sophistication.

In Egypt, where a government dedicated to sweeping reform has been in power for a decade, a curiously ambiguous attitude to ideological questions has developed. On the one hand, the men in power have continued over the years to insist on their aversion to theoretical speculation and their preference for an empirical and *ad hoc* approach to individual problems. At the same time, the very pace of government action, its determination to reach the masses effectively and to cut through the fog of their tradition-bound mentality, its enthusiasm for large-scale construction and reorganization, has increased the need for a systematic framework of explanations and exhortations to the public. Demagoguery might be sufficient to communicate a spirit of nationalist emotion, but not to justify and guide a calculated social revolution. President Nasser himself showed some signs in 1961 of recognizing that such a need might exist. His speeches on the occasion of the sweeping socialist decrees of July 1961 referred to the class struggle and to the exploitive nature of capitalism; in October he spoke of the incompatibility of the people's interests with those of their enemies, and the need to establish a criterion for "isolating" the latter from public affairs. Still he was reluctant to set himself up as an official ideologist. In an address to the Preparatory Committee of the National

Congress of Popular Forces, he reproved Egypt's intellectuals:

> At the Law College you teach political economy—Adam
> Smith's theory of supply and demand—and you say that
> such talk is the best in the world, and that such theories are
> ideal. People would then look at us in surprise and say:
> What we have learned at the Law Faculty differs from
> what is being applied here. I say: No, the process is not one
> of supply and demand. We are forging a new system. To
> achieve a social revolution we should write books. Some
> authors have written books on economics which were sim-
> ply copied from other countries. Who has written a book
> on the economy we are now dealing with? When we have
> written such a book we can say we have written a theory.
>
> But we cannot say that we have produced a theory when
> we refer to books on well-known economic systems . . . .
> There are thousands of such books available. We cannot
> say: O Jamal Abd al-Nasser, produce a theory for us! I shall
> not be able to produce a theory; you must produce the
> theory. The intellectuals must produce the theory. When I
> find a suitable book on the nature of our economy, on our
> experience, then I will feel that this book constitutes a large
> part of the theory, and that we have actually begun to lay
> the foundations. But when I realize that these economics
> books are merely a repetition of what we were taught at
> the Law Faculty in 1936, then I am filled with endless
> disappointment.[50]

The difficulty is that the atmosphere in Egypt in the past decade has scarcely been conducive to the publication of very
original, creative, or sober books, even if Nasser himself might
welcome them. Each new step the government has taken has
produced in its wake a rash of hastily written popular justifica-
tions. The creation of the National Union led to attacks on political parties; the nationalization of the press in 1960 led to
attacks on private publishers who distort or suppress the news;
the socialist decrees of 1961 led to attacks on capitalism and
to cheap versions of the theory of surplus value. An ideology had begun to emerge, but whether Nasser intended it or
not, it was inevitably his own creation.

In the deluge of second-rate books and articles inspired by
each new action taken by the regime, a sort of Gresham's Law
takes effect whereby sycophantic propaganda drives serious

discussion out of sight. Even on those occasions when notice is taken of the isolated and demoralized condition of Egyptian intellectuals, such notice takes a form likely to discourage creativity and independence even more. Thus the editor of *al-Ahram*, while drawing attention to "the crisis of the intellectuals" in a series of feature articles, identified the crisis as a long-standing conflict "between the force of revolutionary impetus and the intellectuals," as if to brand the latter as a group of reactionaries. He went on to contrast "experts" (as a category of intellectuals) with "trustworthy people" (i.e. army officers) and to explain why it was the latter to whom political power must be confided.[51] Another journalist attributed the crisis to the fact that "every word that an intellectual says, every phrase or idea he expresses, makes him, according to the interpretations of certain groups, an outlaw."[52]

In these circumstances one cannot judge from recent Egyptian political literature what the mood of educated opinion really is. One might therefore be tempted to dismiss what is written as unworthy of attention, were it not for the fact that however tedious much of it might be, it does indicate what sort of ideological pattern Egyptian publicists find it advisable to conform to, and what sort of arguments are open to elaboration. The gradual development of an official political ideology, while it may have closed the door to controversy on certain questions, has certainly not cut down the flow of publications; quite the contrary.

Within established limits there has been room for a certain variety of emphasis and degree in ideas. Thus since the promulgation of the 1956 Constitution it has been understood that a multi-party system was unacceptable, and that the National Union, as a nationwide popular organization, was above the level of parties and a more truly democratic means of representation. Yet it was possible, in the autumn of 1961, for a prominent journalist to criticize the loose organization and ideological open-endedness of the National Union and to demand the creation of a single tightly knit political party in its place, not representing all classes but only those elements of the population having a vested interest in socialism.[53]

Likewise, although by the end of 1961 there had been no particular tendency in the Egyptian President's speeches to suggest that Western democracy in the West itself rested on false principles (it being said only that Western institutions were inappropriate to the Arab countries), it was open to individual writers to apply the full range of Marxist and other criticisms to Western practice and to denounce it as a fraud perpetrated by the exploiting capitalist classes. Thus one writer, for example, asserts that American politics, as well as those of Britain and France, have fallen under the domination of capital, and affairs of state have come to be directed by "monopolists and the owners of factories and oil companies." The two American parties, which are instruments of the moneyed interests, have "taken over" the Congress and local government, "interfering in the elections and working with capital to falsify them, and—after succeeding in the elections—controlling the Congress, the municipal councils, the police, and the local courts without any reference to the people." This perversion of the true purposes of democracy is due to the historical circumstances in which Western democracy first arose, namely, the intrusion of the capitalist middle class into affairs of state to protect themselves against the feudal nobility, but without reference to the great majority of the people. "Thus the present domination of capital over the western democracies is only the expression of a status quo that has existed from the time when this democracy first arose until the present."[54]

Elections are rigged (the same writer continues) by local officials and police who are bribed by the capitalist-dominated parties. The government works only for the interest of the party rather than the people; appointments to public office are made on the basis of the spoils system without regard to competence. "And this is not all, for monopoly capitalism has set itself up as the ultimate authority in supervising government officials, by means of a special law called the Hatch Act, whereby it gets rid of any official whose loyalty to the party which finances him is in doubt, through special committees which fix the accusation of communism on such officials."[55]

The National Union system, by contrast, reflects "the will of the whole people, which is of the will of God. . . . The people are not limited by partisan principles but are gathered together around their national goals to achieve the mission of Arab nationalism and to stimulate their efforts for the sound political, social, and economic construction of the nation."[56]

This writer's interpretation of American politics is a crude and somewhat extreme, but by no means untypical, example of recent Egyptian literature. Such an attitude is, after all, a logical extension of the very widespread Arab view that the essence of democracy consists in the triumph of the will of the masses over the selfishness and privilege of a small group of individuals, and that a system that perpetuates and institutionalizes conflicts of interest is obstructing the emergence of the true popular consensus and is therefore not fully democratic. Democracy is a process of uniting the people rather than dividing them, of emphasizing their points of agreement rather than their disagreements.

One is reminded of the notion, familiar in a long series of social philosophers in Europe, of "rational self-realization," according to which individuals (or whole societies) must be liberated from their own blindness, selfishness, or passion by those who possess true insight into the dictates of objective reason. The interests of all citizens, when properly understood, can only be harmonious because they are rational. "To compel men to adopt the right form of government, to impose Right on them by force, is not only the right, but the sacred duty of every man who has both the insight and the power to do so." [57]

Thus it was explained that the reason Nasser had simply issued the July 1961 social legislation by presidential decree, without submitting it to the National Assembly as required by the Constitution,[58] was that "it could not have obtained the Assembly's consent, despite the necessity [for such legislation] in order to begin the social revolution." [59] It scarcely seemed necessary for anyone to argue the point further than this, for clearly the promotion of socialism could not yield precedence to parliamentary procedure. This was not a sacrifice of democracy for the sake of welfare, but an affirmation of democracy. Being in the rational interest of the masses, the socialist program must be assumed to have their implicit support, which would be made explicit once they were enlightened.

"The [local] committees of the National Union must make their members apostles to spread the gospel of socialism while explaining the obstacles and pointing out the difficulties as every true apostle must do, and drawing a picture of the glorious future," wrote a journalist. "Within these committees the scope of the discussion and debate must be widened, until the whole people sense their role in the construction of their future. And when all the people are engaged in this work, they will all feel it spontaneously

and enthusiastically, and they will look to the future with
pleasant anticipations." [60]

From such assumptions it was but a short step to the adoption
of a doctrine of class conflict and to the view that those who did
not share in what was identified as the general will, or who at a
given stage of history did not fully support what was presumed
to be the national cause, simply did not belong to "the people."
As Nasser declared on November 25, 1961:

> The word "people," of course, varies according to circum-
> stances and ideologies. . . . In the current stage of socialist
> construction, the people are all the groups and classes who
> support and contribute to it. So these are the ones to whom
> we have given full freedom and democracy. The rest, those
> who are against social justice and the social revolution,
> those who are against liberation from political, economic,
> and social exploitation, those who want to rule, or who in
> the past represented the influential class and the
> minority—are these the people? In my view they do not
> represent the people, but represent something else.

A press commentator added that there is a vital difference
between conflicts between the people and their enemies, on the
one hand, and among different elements of the people on the
other. The first is "a conflict of enmity which may not be
susceptible of resolution by peaceful means, so that the people
may be compelled to resort to other means to break the power
of their enemies, such as arrests, sequestration of property, and
deprivation of political rights." The second class of conflicts are
"natural, non-antagonistic" ones that can be resolved by "debate, exchange of views, and persuasion." [61]

Freedom, then, could only exist when the enemies had been
overcome and only the non-antagonistic conflicts remained, and
when the harmony of true interests could rise to the surface
unimpeded by the unnatural selfishness and hostility of an earlier, lower stage of history. "The enemies of the social revolution must be swept aside so that the masses thereafter can
exercise their full and unconditional freedom. The uncongenial
mixture of the minority who do not desire the social revolution
with the great majority who desire it was the main obstacle
which impeded the course of freedom." [62]

The Westerner who sits comfortably amidst his own liberal axioms is apt to look aghast at much of this radical ideology, and at the monolithic shape that one or two Arab regimes have been taking, and conclude either that Arab radicals are blind and naive, or that some evil genius has taken them by the hand and is deliberately leading them down the path to totalitarianism.

It would be more to the point to bear in mind that many recent Arab thinkers, though well schooled in Western liberal teachings and by no means attracted in any conscious way by totalitarianism as such, chafe at the exclusive pretensions of the liberal system, just as an earlier generation, faced with the claims of traditional Islamic doctrine, felt suffocated and anxious to break out of its closed circle. Western liberalism in the nineteenth and early twentieth centuries was a breath of fresh air to those Arabs who wished to introduce a principle of movement and creativity into their society. It was a challenge to the monopolistic pretensions of Islamic traditions, and a means of facing new problems that had begun to arise. Today liberalism is believed to be similarly outmoded. The communist system is not particularly attractive to Arabs in certain respects, but Marxism is at least relevant to their concerns in many ways. Separated from the example set by the particular countries in which they have been applied, and freed from the irritating dogmatism and arrogance of orthodox communists, many aspects of Marxism have a natural and powerful appeal, particularly when disguised by another name, such as "Arab socialism."

It might be argued that the new radicalism is not so much a rejection of liberalism as the extension of a certain form of it. To a great extent, the liberalism in which many Arabs were schooled one and two generations ago, particularly in Egypt and Syria, was of a rather idyllic type. Arab liberals owed more to the universalism of the French Enlightenment and to nineteenth-century French Romanticism than to the English constitutionalists or utilitarians, and far more to the inspiration of the French Revolution than to the English Revolution of 1689. The skepticism and sense of limits of a writer like Burke, which might usefully have tempered some of the euphoric exaggerations of liberal mythology, never made a strong impression. Thus the Egyptian writer Khaled Muhammad Khaled, who in recent years has stood out in his country as a continuing and fervent believer in parliamentary democracy and civil liberties, is typical not only of many past and present Arab liberals, but of radicals, too, in reacting with disgust and incomprehension to Disraeli's statement: "I prefer the liberty that we now enjoy to the principles that the Liberals promise us; and I prefer the rights of Englishmen to the Rights of Man." [63]

Nevertheless even Khaled himself, despite his interest in social reform, was shown to be out of step with the new radicalism by the debates in the Preparatory Committee for the Congress of Popular Forces, which met in Cairo in the autumn of 1961; and it would be wrong to suppose that the radicalism in Cairo and elsewhere is something less than radical, and that it does not signify a departure from previous ideological conventions. It is, perhaps, the Arab radical's conception of the nature of his society's problems that has changed, rather than his understanding of what liberal ideas mean, or his esteem for the liberal virtues in themselves. These have simply ceased to have practical meaning to him. But while the virtues seem irrelevant in the abstract, in practice they often appear as outright vices, for they conflict with what *is* considered relevant: the need to pull together the scattered fragments of Arab society and to instill in its members an awareness of common moral bonds and a sense of citizenship; to hasten the end of an outdated stratification, immobility, and quiescent spirit in what remains of traditional society, which foster resigned acceptance of weakness and injustice; and to overcome the alienation and rootlessness of the new classes, which alternately promote opportunism and despair. And overlaid on the radical's preoccupation with all these problems is the humiliating sense of national impotence that continues to fester after several generations.

In these circumstances the desire for a government that is strong and determined (whatever else it might be) is overwhelming. John Stuart Mill would find widespread agreement with his view that "many a people has gradually emerged from this condition [of passiveness and submissiveness] by the aid of a central authority, whose position has made it the rival, and had ended by making it the master, of the local despots, and which, above all, has been single." [64]

No Arab writer has yet produced a comprehensive, relevant, and sophisticated theory of social, economic, and political development that can effectively compete with the great world ideologies of communism and democratic liberalism. Nor has anyone made a satisfactory attempt to make liberal principles applicable in any systematic way to contemporary Arab problems. The radical ideas described in this article indicate that the search for principles is on, but that often it takes the form either of a fragmentary rejection of outmoded or inappropriate doctrines, or an unattributed but uncritical borrowing of other ones. There are a great many unanswered and even unrecognized questions about the political implications of economic development. A great gap exists between ideologues and economists: Where are the Arab Fabians? If ideas are not available to shape events, then by default events will shape ideas, in keeping with their own unplanned and, perhaps, grotesque course.

2. The Transformation of Ideology in the Arab World BY HISHAM SHARABI

THE RADICAL CHANGES taking place today in the political and economic systems of the Arab world represent, *au fond,* an ideological rebellion against Europe and Western social and political values. This fact cannot be properly understood simply by analyzing the political and social developments which took place during the last two decades. These represent only the terminal phase of a long process of transformation and change that has its origin in the last part of the nineteenth century—a process which extends over the life and experience of three generations (*ca.* 1875–1950), roughly the pre-World War I generation, the interwar generation, and the postwar generation. The first generation saw Europe's political pressure and economic exploitation gradually transformed into colonial expansion and imperial domination; the interwar generation experienced the full brunt of Europe, as exercised primarily by England and France after the First World War; the postwar generation witnessed the internal disintegration of Europe during World War II and the end of its world hegemony in the years immediately following the end of the war.

Moreover, to describe and analyze the relationship of these three generations with Europe only in terms of the impact which Western ideas and institutions exercised in social and intellectual life, or in terms solely of political resistance against European rule, would hardly be enough to account for these radical transformations. For at the same time that the move-

Reprinted from *The Middle East Journal,* Vol. 19, No. 4 (Washington, D.C., 1955), pp. 471–86, by permission of the editor.

ment of "westernization" began to take root, the inner rejection
of the West also began; the more firmly European ideas and institutions implanted themselves, the more hostile and negative
the reaction to Europe became. The process is difficult to analyze. However, this much is clear: The rejection of Europe was
not confined to the conservative and traditionalist elements of
the Muslim elite but was to be found in the "westernized" elite
as well. This expressed itself in an obdurate, repressed hostility
which apparently became stronger and more articulate as "westernization" spread and increased; in its early stages its strongest
manifestation was an attitude of ambivalence, which at one and
the same time coveted and detested Europe, respected and de-
spised it, wanted and rejected it, imitated and spurned it.

The double view which the educated and professional classes
had of Europe was itself reflected in their view of themselves
and their social reality. Inevitably, the moral and psychological
tension resulting from this duality could resolve itself in the end
only by either complete identification with Europe or total
repudiation of it. For the urban educated Turks as well as for
the Christians and Levantines of the coastal cities, the first
course seemed possible, but not to the vast majority of the
Muslim elite of the Arab world.

From this standpoint the relationship to Europe seemed hap-
piest and most secure at the beginning, when Europe was seen
through the eyes of the generation of Tahtawi (d. 1883) and
Khayr al-din (1889) and Bustani (1873).[1] Europe then was a
promise discovered with joy and excitement; there was still no
cause for alarm (the occupation of Algeria in 1830 was still a
remote incident which had passed almost unnoticed in the
Muslim world); the good things it had to offer were to be
adopted without question, and the bad things simply discarded.
Europe, in short, was something to be used and exploited.

In the eyes of the young revolutionary elite of nearly a
century later, there seemed something almost adulterous in the
relationship with Europe. Thus the final and most serious revolt
was not political, for it took place after political liberation had
been achieved. Hence the positions of nonalignment and positive neutrality are proclamations that signify the end of sub-
servience and humiliation as much as they do national independence and sovereignty. In this light, it is not enough to keep the
West *politically* at bay; the West must again be reduced to an
alien entity, to be made wholly *other.* In order that genuine

autonomy be restored, the West must be extricated from the roots; it must be put on an equal level with the other cultural entities of the world. These are the preconditions of the true renascence.

Beneath the political convulsions and social transformations of the last three quarters of a century, there is to be seen then this concealed, furtive struggle whose first results have only now become apparent. Neither compromise nor moderation nor any purely utilitarian consideration can seriously influence the course which the midcentury revolution has already taken. From the first blind repudiation of the traditionalists of the first generation seventy-five years ago to the rebellion of the revolutionary elite of the present generation, a full circle has been completed. The West, as a pattern of evaluation and thought—a cultural edifice rooted in the Graeco-Christian tradition—is again being opposed in the name of other values and independent systems of thought. Westernized intellectuals no longer enjoy position and prestige; they are now suspect.

Neoimperialism, reactionism, feudalism, antirevolutionism, are concepts that have concrete and clear meaning in this context. Thus "Bourguibism" can have as little future in the Arab world as the Western-oriented attitudes advocated by Charles Malik and other Christian intellectuals in Lebanon. These and similar tendencies cannot really coexist for long with "Nasserism" or with "Algerian socialism"; the revolt has captured society and seized the undisputed intellectual initiative.

In order to gain insight into this revolt, we have to start with the late nineteenth century and work our way back through the intervening generations to the revolutionary situation of the present. But first let us underline the principal political turning points.

(1) The Russo-Ottoman war of 1877–78 brought home to the first generation the fact that the Ottoman Empire could be penetrated militarily and made to surrender [2] (Treaty of San Stefano, 1878), and that the fate of the most powerful Muslim state would henceforth be decided in Europe (Congress of Berlin, 1878) [3]; the occupation of Tunisia by France in 1881 and of Egypt by England in the following year provided the proof of Europe's determination to conquer the East and subjugate Islam. This was the first generation for which Europe became a concrete presence: It was no longer merely a "civilization," but a challenge and a threat; *imperialism* was added to the image which the Near East now had of Europe. [4]

(2) The great war of 1914–18 brought about the collapse of the Ottoman empire and the spread of European imperialism in the Near East. The second generation thus saw the overthrow of Islamic hegemony and the rise of the European-dominated nation-states. Turkey and Persia, the two countries to defy European domination, established their independence on the basis of westernized dictatorial systems. The years following the rise of facism in Italy and Germany and communism in Russia, added another dimension to the image of Europe: a centralized, anti-democratic system potentially more powerful than that represented by the colonialist democracies of Britain and France.

(3) The Second World War and its aftermath effected a radical change in the relationship to Europe: The fall of France in 1940 sealed the end of French supremacy; the defeat of Italy and Germany put an end to the allure of fascism; and the emergence of Soviet Russia as a world power provided a new source of influence and attraction. The East-West division of the postwar world marked the beginning of Britain's decline and the end of European supremacy in the Near East.

THE PRE-WORLD WAR I GENERATION

For the first generation, that which came to maturity in the years before the First World War, Europe's challenge no longer evoked strictly religious reactions; the monopoly of the *ulama*—through whom alone Tahtawi had seen European knowledge channeled into Muslim society[5]—had been contested and already secular elements (lawyers, journalists, army officers, teachers) had begun to come to the intellectual fore.

For both the *ulama* and the new secular elite, however, Europe's prosperity and might still had two basic explanations: scientific knowledge and constitutional government. For this intelligentsia, science was not method or technique, but rather a key for unlocking nature's secrets and gaining mastery over man and society. Constitutional government meant the triumph of liberty and the end of despotic government through universal suffrage. Education was approached as a discipline and system of transmission, as a means through which the individual gained success and society prosperity and strength. Indeed, though never fully thought out or articulated, the system of thought which animated the intelligentsia of this generation was basically utilitarian and pragmatic.

Lacking scientific training and the tools of objective criticism, the secular as well as the religious intellectuals lent themselves to a method of approach which aimed more at softening the impact of the increasingly complex problems confronting society than at directly solving these problems or overcoming them. Underlying this approach were three principal assertions:

The first—which first appeared with Tahtawi in Egypt, Khayr al-din in Tunis, and Bustani in Syria, and which later became the basis of a standard argument—held that Arab civilization had once been the greatest in the world, that Europe had adopted the basic elements of this civilization, and was thus able to reach its height.[6] This approach was useful in two ways. It justified the principle of borrowing and affirmed the Arabs' inborn capacity not only to partake of modern civilization but also to excel in it.[7] Though at the moment Muslim society appeared backward and politically weak, this was an ephemeral condition, an accident of history which could and would be corrected.

Another assertion, advanced a little later, postulated the distinction between the realms of religion and society without directly confronting the problem of drawing the line separating the two. The vagueness thus created made it progressively feasible to advocate ideas and practices that were not clearly sanctioned by religious tradition and, more important, made possible the establishment of a foothold for social and political action that implicitly lay outside direct religious jurisdiction.

The third element of this approach consisted in positing two basic premises that served as safety valves in confronting the problems brought about by Westernization. The first simply stated that Islam *rightly understood* was always found to include everything which modern civilization approved or had to offer; and the second, that whenever a contradiction occurred between "true" Islam and modern civilization, the cause of the contradiction was not in Islam but in *false* civilization, that is, in civilization *inadequately understood.*[8] Thus Islamic validity was safeguarded at the same time that the intrinsic worth of civilization was affirmed.

It is perhaps chiefly due to this pattern of approach that formal disavowal by Muslim secularists was rendered unnecessary and superfluous, and that for a later generation, no longer seriously committed to these problems, silent indifference became the easy alternative.

In its political ideas, the prewar intelligentsia adhered fully to the basic tenets of the liberalism of nineteenth century Europe.[9] Writers such as Farah Antun (d. 1922), Shibli al-Shumayyil (d. 1917), and Ahmad Lutfi al-Sayyid (1963) gave full expression to this.[10] Despite their one-sidedness, these intellectuals reacted to Europe's most elevated ideals with an openness and magnanimity of which the following generation seemed incapable. Though they were blind to economic and social problems, they earnestly believed in the possibility of a just society.[11] Influenced more by the ideas of the French Revolution and the democratic individualism of the British utilitarians than by the authoritarian philosophers of Germany and Italy, they upheld individual freedom and the freedom of speech to be the two most essential attributes of political justice. In their nationalism, they stressed, as did Mazzini, the concept of the fatherland *(watan)* more than they did that of the state. Indeed, the state symbolized not so much power as it did national freedom; for without freedom, that is, without political independence, there could be no state. Independence, whether from British or Ottoman domination, signified not only political freedom but also progress, enlightenment, justice, prosperity. This was the generation in the modern awakening whose political preoccupation was concerned more with ideas and moral values than with the realities of power and the problems of social control. Their climate was still heavy with the arguments of the *ulama,* and their ideas were still rooted in the formalism of religion and morality. It is not surprising that they assumed virtue to be fundamentally a social attribute, a condition less of inwardness than of action. In this sense virtuous conduct was the ground of progress and the final guarantor of both political freedom and social well-being.

THE INTERWAR GENERATION AND EUROPEAN DOMINATION

The Great World War of 1914–18 changed the world, and for the Arab Near East the most important change was the triumph of European imperialism. The period between the two wars saw not only the transformation of Europe's image but also the rapid change in the composition and orientation of the new elite. This change was marked by four major developments.

(1) Until 1918 political life had been the monopoly of a small

urban Sunni aristocracy; with the end of the First World War, the masses entered the political arena. The "revolutions" of the postwar years—1919 in Egypt, 1919–22 in Turkey, 1920 in Iraq, 1925–27 in Syria—by engaging the masses of the population in the political struggle, subjected political leadership to pressures and influences that changed its character and direction. It marked the end of the period of the religious reformers, of the literary societies and the conspiritorial cells, and ushered in the period of *mass leadership* and *nationalist political parties*.

(2) Islam and the problems centering around it were now no longer the chief concerns of political action. It can perhaps be safely said that with the death of Muhammad Rashid Rida and the closing down of *al-Manar* in 1935, the Islamic controversy which began with Afghani and 'Abduh finally died down.[12] Islam was now absorbed into nationalist dogma, defended and upheld as part of the national legacy. The last apologetic works of the older intelligentsia which appeared in the late 1930's and early 1940's—Haykal's *hayat Muhammad*, Aqqad's *Abqariyyat Muhammad*, Taha Husayn's *Ala hamish al-sirah*—raised none of the old problems and advanced no solutions to the new ones.[13]

(3) The interwar generation, which may be described as the last "liberal" generation, adhered to ideas which had been cherished before the war and which were embodied after the war in the parliamentary institutions and legal systems of most of the countries of the Arab Near East. The failure of interwar democratic government did not engender enough serious doubt to lead to open repudiation of parliamentary democracy. But the liberal Europe of Taha Husayn—the last important spokesman of liberalism of the last generation (particularly in his *Mustaqbal al-thaqafah fi misr*)[14]—was beginning to lose its meaning for the rising generation. By 1945 this new generation had already turned away from the ideas and convictions of its fathers.

(4) The new generation, more at home than the previous one in the Europe-dominated world, had been ready even before the outbreak of the Second World War to challenge and in some instances to take over leadership from the older generation. In the 1930's the young intellectuals of the Destour party took over the leadership from the old conservatives in Tunisia, and in Algeria the young nationalists led by Misali (PPA) replaced the Muslim-oriented "Society of Algerian *Ulama* of Bin Badis; in Egypt and the countries of the Fertile Crescents, though the old guard nationalists maintained their grip on political control,

they were the target of the attacks by the doctrinal parties which became the rallying points of the younger generation.

THE YOUNGER GENERATION AND THE DOCTRINAL PARTIES

In analyzing social and intellectual developments during and immediately after the Second World War, we have to keep certain factors in mind which were making for rapid change and which here can only be briefly touched upon.

In the first place, it should be recalled that the Second World War directly contributed to vast expansion in urban population. Trade unionism, already established in North Africa before the war, makes its entry in a large scale into the countries of the Arab Near East. The oil industry comes into its own, creating a new source of power and wealth; large numbers of workers, technicians, doctors and teachers from surrounding Arab countries flock to Iraq, Saudi Arabia, Kuwait and other Persian Gulf shaykhdoms. Movement within the Arab world increases to a degree unknown since the Middle Ages.

The gates of Europe and America are open as they were never open before. Thousands of students now travel to Europe and America to return in a few years with advanced training in various fields of the physical and social sciences as well as the humanities.

Simultaneously the emancipation of women is accelerated and the veil all but disappears in most of the cities and larger towns. The press and radio, and later, television, multiply the means of communication and control; universal military service and compulsory elementary education end the isolation of the countryside and create the first generation of mass readers.

In the postwar period these and similar changes in the social environment were accompanied by two crucial phenomena: the emergence of "mass" society and the rise of military dictatorship.

At the end of the war, the masses were still outside the pale of organized political life, but from the standpoint of the internal struggle for power, they constituted an important though mostly negative force which within a few years became considerable. Lacking articulation and leadership, the urban mass constituted the city mob, which by demonstration and street violence gradually began to achieve awareness of itself as an effective political force. It remained, however, only vaguely conscious of itself as a separate class, and as such, was incapable of acting in terms of class interest. The failure of the Communist Party to make serious headway among the masses and the inability of any of the doctrinal parties to build a genuine following from its ranks left the masses basically open to only two types of leadership and control, that of the local city *za'ims* ("bosses") and that of the charismatic military leader.

The old nationalist leadership, which since the 1920's had monopolized power and developed an intricate system for the distribution of privilege and prestige within the closed circle of its own ranks, had already begun to disintegrate before the outbreak of the war; after the war it was removed from power by violence in one country after another. The cycle of *coups d'état* which began in 1949 resulted in the prevalence of military dictatorship and the paralysis of parliamentary government.

The postwar intelligentsia was radically different from that of the two preceding generations in its social origin as well as in psychology and outlook. No longer restricted to small closed-in circles, it grew to include a large body of men from various walks of life with varied backgrounds and training. The great families of the big cities, though still enjoying the privileges of wealth and position in certain countries, were no more the sole source of power and influence in society.

This younger intelligentsia broke away from the world of the older generation partly by conscious will, but also partly as a result of the final disintegration of the traditional framework. On the intellectual level, the problems which the older generation had raised were no longer real or meaningful. The challenge which before 1918 Islamic society had to rouse itself in order to confront, had in the intervening decades been transformed into a different kind of challenge; and, moreover, official Islam had meantime learned to adjust itself to *de facto* situations without too much agony of self-examination. In this sense, this is the first Muslim generation to find itself—and to have full awareness of the fact—deprived of inherited certainties. For it, Islam, as a truly sustaining force, had collapsed, and more importantly, the family, the strongest and most abiding social institution in Muslim society, had begun to break down. The tasks with which this generation was now confronted involved not merely social or political reform but the total reconstruction of society and the state and the reestablishment of a meaningful view of life.

The character and orientation of the new elite has to a great degree been molded by the new system of education which was established in most Near Eastern countries after World War I. In terms of its structure and underlying philosophy, this system of education may be divided into two types, "national" and "foreign." National education encompasses primarily the government-controlled primary and secondary school systems and institutions of higher learning; foreign education is comprised of private schools and colleges controlled by European or American administrations based on European or American systems of education.

The national schools and universities have generally produced the highly nationalistic elements of the elite, well trained in the humanities, particularly in national history and in Arabic language and literature, but deficient in the physical sciences and foreign languages. Education in the foreign system, especially on the college or university levels—e.g. at the American University of Cairo, the American University of Beirut, Université de St. Joseph, Aleppo College—did not mean that students received antinational or even an exclusively Western type of education. Indeed, the breeding ground of Arab nationalism was for a long time the American University of Beirut. The foreign system differed from the national one in two important respects: in providing thorough training in a foreign language, so that graduates of foreign institutions were usually fully at home in English or French (often both) and therefore had easier access to Western culture and thought; and in giving more attention to methodological training in the disciplines of the various fields, so that the graduates of these colleges and universities had a firmer grasp of their materials and were better equipped to pursue further work abroad.

THE NEW FOUNDATIONS OF POLITICAL ACTION

For the new generation, both the search for identity and the rebuilding of the new social and political order were to be accomplished through the only effective type of action, political action: To be committed now meant to be *politically* committed.

The doctrinal parties through which the elite of the younger generation channeled its energies and organized its activities had these basic qualities in common: All these parties rejected the principles and convictions of the political groupings of the older generation and set up totalitarian ideologies as the basis of action; they all based their doctrines on comprehensive philosophies of man and society; they all had as their final goal the capture of political power and the total transformation of the social order. Of more significance perhaps is the fact that for all the doctrinal parties the sources of inspiration and belief lay outside the realm of both traditionalism and westernization. From their standpoint, both the traditionalists and the secularists had failed. The myth to which they now reverted was that of history, the glorious past and nationalism, the sources and guides of the new resurgence.

Two examples of the leading doctrinal parties, the Syrian National Party (PPS) and the Muslim Brotherhood, will provide a closer look at the new type of political thinking that now develops. Though diametrically opposed in philosophies and goals, these two parties have many basic characteristics in common. The ideas of their founders, Antun Sa'adah and Hasan al-Banna, respectively, are the logical conclusions of the main streams of thought of the late nineteenth and early twentieth centuries, particularly those of Islamic reformism and secular nationalism.

Sa'adah removed religion altogether from the realm of national action and based his social philosophy on evolution and culture. He relegated Islam and Christianity to the background by reducing them to a common origin and by characterizing all religious belief as submission *(Islam)* to a metaphysical reality which is beyond the realm of rational discourse.[15] As such, he considered religious belief a matter of individual conscience, falling outside the sphere of social action and political life. Sa'adah was perhaps the first intellectual to proclaim publicly that what was desirable from the standpoint of religion was not always or necessarily so from that of national interest. He was a positivist and a skeptic; and in constructing his political doctrine he did not hesitate to carry his arguments to the end. His influence on the younger generation, like Banna's, was profound. Himself greatly influenced by German and Italian thought of the nineteenth and early twentieth centuries—the nationalist German historians, Mosca, Pareto—he infused contemporary political thinking with new ideas and values that gave vitality and color to his teachings. Sa'adah's thought was revolutionary not only because of the methods he advocated in political action—military discipline, violence—but in his attack on the philosophy of individualism and the political system in which it was embodied. He viewed the parliamentary system with mistrust: Political democracy was wasteful luxury, corrupt, decadent; it left no room for discipline and diluted the sense of responsibility. Individualism meant class interest on the political plane and unbridled egoism in economic life. Society is the final reality, higher and more important than the individual. "Individuals come and go; they live out their lives then fall off like autumn leaves; what is real [and permanent] does not disappear, it lives on [in society]. . . ."[16]

Sa'adah maintained, as did Banna, that his ideas derived not from any foreign source, but from history and the national heritage. While present weakness and decline are attributed to the disasters of the recent past, the remote past emerges as the source of strength and inspiration, evidence and symbol of national greatness which can and must be recaptured.

Put Sa'adah's militant philosophy into Islamic terms and you have the activism of the Muslim Brothers. In Banna we have the radical ideas of Islamic revisionism—first encountered in Afghani and 'Abduh—reaching full circle. In order that Muslim society be able to face up to the challenge of the modern world and restore its past glory, it is not enough to reform Islam. Muslim society must purify its beliefs and practices, but it must also enter the political struggle and seize political control. In order to be able to do this it must first modernize itself. Thus Banna did not hesitate to approve borrowing from the West. Indeed, modernization to him meant borrowing all technical and scientific aspects of Western civilization that are useful to the revival of Islam. The institutional and ideological content of the "West" meant little to him. European democracy was but a pale reflection of the pure and genuine egalitarianism of genuine Islam. The two sources, the Quran and the Sunnah of Muhammad contained all that was needed to build the just and prosperous society. In the final analysis every innovation, every borrowed idea was good or bad according to whether it conformed with the Word of God and the teachings of His Apostle. The kind of Islam which Banna wanted to restore was the early Islam of Muhammad's time. Pristine Islam forms the core of the Muslim Brothers' revivalist doctrine. For Banna the separation of church and state, of the secular and the spiritual, are inadmissible. Islam comprises the entirety of man's life; it is at once "religion and state, contemplation and work, holy book and sword."[16]

For Banna, as it is for Sa'adah, European liberalism and the principles of Western parliamentary democracy do not constitute the central problem of political life. Indeed, Europe is no longer a superior culture to be warded off or imitated. Europe's technological and scientific progress is a fact which conceals no secrets peculiar to European civilization. The whole world has entered upon the European legacy and now shares with it the instruments for conquering nature and controlling society. But each society, each people, will build its own future in the light of its own traditions, values, and interests.

THE REVOLT

In 1949 Hasan al-Banna and Antun Sa'adah were killed, the first by an assassin's bullet in Cairo and the second before a firing squad in a suburb of Beirut. Their death symbolizes the turning point in the political life of the third younger generation. The years following their death witnessed the disintegration of the doctrinal political parties and the rise of the army to power.

The phenomenon of "revolutionism" *(al-thawriyyah)*, which now develops into a theory of political and economic dynamism, represents the final stage in the breakdown of the socio-political system which was introduced into the Near East under the influence and guidance of England and France. The center of attention now shifts from the doctrinal and philosophical concepts of nation and nationalism to the class structure and economic organization of the national community. The object of political concern now becomes the mass of the population, which since the beginning of history had been outside the system of power and control and perpetually the instrument and means of the ascendency and well-being of a small ruling group. It is significant that as parliamentary democracy had been established without a middle class, revolutionary socialism under army control is now instituted without the firm base of a working class or proletariat.

For the revolution the ideological content no longer has the same significance which it had for the doctrinal parties. Not truly Marxist, the revolution nevertheless has its intellectual source in the European left which is the heir of Marx.

Democracy as an ideal of political organization has not, however, been abandoned but viewed in a new light. *True* democracy is impossible to achieve without social and economic liberation. It is defined not in terms of individual freedom and traditional parliamentary structures, but in terms of social and economic justice. In order to establish this justice, political life has to be centralized and regimented. Thus in the revolutionary regime the single party becomes the instrument of political control, the state the repository of total power. Though elections and representative bodies are not renounced, they are subjected to strict procedures that put them fully under the control of the party and the state. Parliamentary democracy gives way to guided democracy, and laissez-faire economy to state control under an Arab type of socialism.

Though it is the most pragmatic and least violent in approach, Egypt's socialist system has spearheaded the socialist revolution in the Arab world. Syria's Ba'th party and Algeria's Front for National Liberation, however, have given the more systematic expression of the goals and social and political structures of the socialist revolution. To understand the ideas and goals of the contemporary revolution, it is necessary to study carefully three important documents: Egypt's "National Charter" (1962), "The FLN Program" (1962), and the "General Resolutions of the Sixth National Congress of the Arab Ba'th Party (1963)." [18] Here, however, we can only quote a few excerpts from each of these documents to illustrate some of the points mentioned above and to give a few examples of the new valuation structure.

According to the Egyptian National Charter,

> Political democracy cannot be separated from social democracy. Nobody can be regarded as free to vote without three guarantees: freedom from exploitation in all its forms; equal opportunity for a fair share of the national wealth; and freedom from all anxiety concerning future security.
>
> Political democracy cannot exist under the domination of any one class. Class strife always exists in some measure, but peaceful solutions are possible within the framework of national unity. Democratic interaction between the various working forces, namely, peasants, workers, soldiers, intellectuals, and national capital, is alone capable of replacing reactionary democracy by true democracy. [19]

Socialism, however, does not mean the elimination of private property. "Control over all the tools of production does not mean the nationalization of all the means of production, the abolition of private ownership, or interference with rights of inheritance. . . ."[20] Freedom, in its social sense is the condition of political freedom:

> For the individual, freedom is the greatest stimulus to all good exertion and is the basis of faith. . . . The individual must be free to shape his destiny, determine his position in society, express his opinion, and take an active part in his society's evolution. Law must be subservient to freedom. But no individual can be free unless he is saved from exploitation—hence, social freedom is the only way to political freedom:[21]

For the Ba'th party the foundation of the socialist revolution is the masses.

> The process of socialization in Syria and Iraq is to continue on a democratic basis and in cooperation with the masses . . . the mass basis for the democratic and revolutionary experiment in the two regions would reflect the revolution not only in Syria and Iraq, but would also generate repercussions in all the countries of the Arab homeland. . . .[22]

As in Egypt, the bourgeoisie is completely removed from the picture, for it

> is no longer capable of playing a positive part in economic life; [politically] it is an opportunistic class and constitutes a natural ally of neo-imperialism. . . . The socialist revolution in its first stages should be accomplished by the workers, peasants, the educated revolutionaries (both military and civilian), and the *small* bourgeoisie. . . .[23]

The FLN resolutions taken at the eve of the independence set forth for the first time in a systematic fashion the revolution's socialist principles and goals. The foundations of the FLN are declared to consist of:

> First, the poverty-stricken peasants . . . the agricultural laborers (permanent and seasonal), the share-croppers, the small land agents, and the poorer landholders.

Two, the working class, which is relatively small, the "half-workers" *(ansaf al-ummal),* who are more numerous, and the "near-workers" *(shibh al-ummal),* who are becoming more numerous in the cities and consist mostly of peasants whose lands were confiscated. . . .

Three, a middle social group which includes small manufacturers, professionals, civil servants, small merchants, and a segment of those engaged in free enterprise—a social group which can be called the *small* bourgeoisie. . . .[24]

The vanguard of the revolution, however, consists only of "the awakened elements of the peasants, workers, tenant groups, and the educated revolutionary youth."[25]

Democracy, as in the Egyptian *mithaq,* is not defined in terms of individual freedom: "Since the lot of the individual is indissolubly linked with that of society, democracy cannot be restricted to individual freedom but should be the collective expression of the people's responsibility."[26]

In revolutionary action, the Algerians, perhaps more so than the Egyptians and the Syrians, tend toward taking a Marxist position.

One must be careful not to trust the preachings of the naive idealists who want to transform society and solve its problems by means of ethical values alone. This is a false and misleading approach. The moralistic idealism which some proclaim is nothing but the cloak which hides inability to cope with social reality and the power to control it positively.

Revolutionary action does not consist of good intentions, however sincere these may be; it must employ objective means. Individual morality, though its values may be valid and worthy in themselves, is neither essential nor decisive in the process of rebuilding society. It is social progress that provides the climate for social prosperity.[27]

"Liberal" parliamentary democracy in the Arab world has survived to some extent in the republics of Lebanon and Tunisia. In both countries, however, the system has been maintained under special conditions. In Lebanon the parliamentary system has been preserved mostly because of the sectarian substructure of Lebanese political life, which renders parliamentary representation eminently suited for the division of spoils among the various sects. As such, Lebanese democracy is not a typical phenomenon and cannot be accurately cited as an example of successful democracy in the Near East. Tunisia, on the other hand, is a single-party regime with a good deal of state control in economic life. The president, who is also the head of the party, enjoys extensive powers. The liberal character of Tunisia's parliamentary system derives mostly from the fact that the dominant Socialist Destour party reflects in its composition and orientation the various classes and groups that make up Tunisian society. Though the party is nonauthoritarian in structure and the leadership theoretically elective, Tunisia's political regime remains closer to Max Weber's *Führerdemokratie* than to a Western-type parliamentary democracy.

CONCLUSION

The failure of liberalism is, however, not so much the failure of a political system as it is of the values which have animated that system. Anyway, for the mass of society, representative government has never meant much in terms of political freedom or civil rights. And to the educated stratum of society, particularly to those who belonged to the doctrinal parties, it symbolized monopoly of power and the ascendancy of a corrupt ruling class.

The chief transformation that has taken place in the Arab Middle East and North Africa since the Second World War—the transformation of the elite from an elite of ideas to an elite of power—has its source in the withdrawal of European civilization from world leadership. For the Western-oriented intellectuals, the cause of Europe's failure lay in the sickness which has gripped the entire West in the twentieth century. Thus, for Charles Malik as for many Western-oriented intellectuals today, it is only "when [Western] culture mends its own spiritual fences, [that] all will be well with the Near East."[28] For these intellectuals, reconciliation still seems possible, but not on the transient plane of nationalist or revolutionary action: "East and West can come together in peace only if they repent together under transcendent judgement."[29]

To the revolutionary elite this position is reactionary, the remnant of bourgeois moralistic intellectualism. The Graeco-Christian tradition no longer has meaning or relevance. In the midst of the starved and illiterate millions, the only true values are those of bread, dignity and power. Truth is a human not a transcendental value.

Frantz Fanon, the philosopher of the Algerian revolution, put it thus:

> Toutes les valeurs méditerranéenes, triomphe de la personne humaine, de la clarté et du beau, deviennent des bibelots sans vie et sans couleur. Tous ces discours apparaissent comme des assemblages de mots morts . . . Le fellah, le chômeur, l'affamé, ne prétend pas à la vérité. Il ne dit pas qu'il est la vérité, car il l'est dans son être même. [30]

3. Democracy and Military Regimes

BY CLOVIS MAQSUD

THE MILITARY REVOLTS which have taken place in a number of Asian countries in the last few years indicate that democracy is passing through a severe crisis. In this study, we must treat this matter with precision and objectivity if we are to arrive at radical solutions through which democracy can acquire firm foundations and answer the needs of the Afro-Asian masses. In our view, democracy implies a form of organization and a definition of the relations between the individual and society through which the people have an active participation in all fields of life. The crisis of democracy in Asia, and to a certain extent also in Africa, undoubtedly affects democracy in the rest of the world and consequently also its very theory and practice.

Before beginning a study of the future of democracy in Africa and Asia, and particularly in the Arab states, we must define the principal words we shall use in order to understand the theoretical concepts in the light of which we have reached our conclusions.

The term "military," as used in this study, means the armed forces and their attached organizations. Although in Asian and some African countries, the army plays the principal role in the armed forces, and through its power, provides their motive force in politics, we are not excluding air, naval and other forces. In Asian and some African countries these play a secondary role, unlike in the advanced industrial countries where the air force has become the center of both offensive and defensive strategy and international policy and where the land forces play a com-

Excerpts reprinted from the *Middle East Forum*, Vol. XXXVI, No. 4 (Beirut, 1960), pp. 32–36, by permission of the editor. The complete version of the same article appeared as a chapter in the author's *The Crisis of the Arab Left*, published in 1960 by Dar al-Ilm (Beirut).

paratively auxiliary role. In the underdeveloped countries the
land forces form the basis of international and defense policy.
This explains the difference between the influence of the army
in underdeveloped and advanced countries, and is of great importance in defining the army's power to exert pressure in both
types of country. In the underdeveloped countries, the army can
exercise political power either directly or indirectly.

Because they are not totally absorbed by purely military affairs
—especially now that the struggle for leadership between the
great military powers has forced the armies in underdeveloped
countries to take a secondary role in the development of international relations—some of the military in the underdeveloped
countries have tended to concern themselves with nonmilitary
affairs. The army and its leaders are prepared to concentrate on
military matters to the extent that they have access to material
resources and modern techniques. Because the armed forces in
advanced countries possess the most modern equipment, they are
aware of the importance of the role they are playing in the life
of the state to which they belong. In underdeveloped countries
they have neither the knowledge of the latest military theory
nor modern equipment, and to make up for this deficiency, they
conceive themselves, not as a specialized instrument of the state
but as the mainstay of the state itself. When this reassessment
takes place, the army becomes sensitive to the fact that it is
not advanced in its special field. This leads to its involvement in
politics in an effort to transform the state in such a way that it
can play the same role as the armies of advanced nations. This
restlessness and search for new horizons forms an important part
of the thought and conduct of the army in underdeveloped
countries.

These features are not characteristic of all sections of the
army. We usually find the discontent with the state of backwardness is also directed against the high command which has
helped to perpetuate it. Thus, this revolutionary feeling is usually
found in the second rank of officers, supported by the younger
officers. It is the officers of the second rank who are usually more
conscious of the weakness of the high command and the most
ready to take revolutionary action.

Before going on to make further definitions, we must mention
certain differences between the military classes in different underdeveloped countries. Although they all have certain characteristics in common which distinguish them from their counterparts
in advanced countries, they themselves vary in important details

which can only be understood through extensive study of the
way in which the army developed in each of them. . . .

ARMIES' SEPARATE GROWTH

Although a number of Afro-Asian countries achieved their
independence through liberation movements, the position of the
military is not always comparable. In . . . countries . . . such
as Indonesia and Burma, we find that the military emerged out
of the political liberation movement. In other countries, in spite
of the existence of such a movement and a deep-rooted political
heritage in the nationalist tradition, the armies did not necessarily grow from within it. This was especially so in countries
where the colonizing power established native armies under the
command of its own officers. This was the case in underdeveloped
countries which were so large that they could only be controlled
by locally recruited armies commanded by foreign senior officers.
When these countries gained their independence and control over
their own development, they inherited armies which, through
their disciplined organization, were a vital defensive arm for the
country. However, these armies did not have any direct link
with the nationalist liberation movements which achieved independence. The lack of this historical and political link meant
that the army confined itself to its professional task of defense.
But this detachment does not last if the army finds that the civil
authorities are not only obstructing the development of the nation but also the military classes' specific defense tasks. This is
in fact what happened in many Arab countries after the disastrous
war in Palestine against the Zionist aggression. The Palestine war
would have been an opportunity for the Arab armies to prove
their military potentialities if they had been given clear political
direction, free from the contamination of outside interests. When
the fight with Zionism failed, the military command realized
their defeat was due not so much to deficiencies in their own
technique and organization as to chaotic political planning and
the fact that the civil leaders themselves were not exerting all
their efforts to defeat the Zionist aggression.

The Arab military classes were created independently of the
popular movement and hence were entirely unconnected with the
civil power at that time, as was the case in Indonesia and Burma
and other countries . . . . One result of this noninvolvement was
that the army's idea of its own role, especially after the Palestine

tragedy, was that it should take the initiative in assuming political control. Discontent came to a head, and action was taken to remove the civil authorities whom they held responsible for the military failure in Palestine. The army was thus involved in politics. Although the army is usually imbued with the same national feeling as the people, this is not enough to drive it to revolution, unless it is forced into it through a feeling that the army itself has been defeated in its own field as a consequence of misdirection from outside. The army then breaks not only with its own leaders but with the whole system that made it possible for such leaders to develop. The army is then neither an instrument for democratic or economic reform nor something that will instill democracy with a healthy discipline. It rejects democracy as a means of solving problems of underdeveloped nations.

The progressive motives which drive the army to revolt will not always continue to exist, however much it may wish to remain an expression of the popular and progressive movement. It is not enough for the army to know what it wants to get rid of. It must also have a clear and positive idea of what it wants. In an underdeveloped country this is impossible, because the circumstances in which the army was created have left it psychologically ill-equipped to build a new state to replace the one it has destroyed. Through its absorption in "putschist" activities, the army breaks also with the popular movement which is the basis of all authority and government. The army begins to show that it regards itself as the framework within which the future of the nation and the principles on which the state will be based can be decided.

ISOLATED FROM CIVIL LIFE

It is to be feared that the army's lack of contact with the civil authorities, against which it is revolting, will lead to its complete isolation from all civil life. If this happens, the military revolutionaries are free from the popular restraints which could transform them into a true revolutionary expression of the popular will. Such a transformation only takes place if the revolutionaries are imbued with the popular spirit. If this process fails, the military not only becomes detached from the nationalist movement but is diverted from the very goals for which it revolted, and the military revolution entirely loses its *raison d'etre*. Con-

sequently, there reverts to the popular movement the right to
return to its note [sic] as a corrective force which it abandoned
temporarily in the belief that it was opening the way to reorganizing itself and recovering its original revolutionary impulse.
When the popular movement finds that the military revolution
has not, as it imagined, initiated a period of reform, it can fight
against it. It will realize that its previous support for, or failure
to oppose, the military revolution was a lapse which can be re-
deemed by a popular counterrevolution.

This brings us to an important fact, which is that military
revolutions are in most cases destined to deny popular participation in public life. But even when the military revolt comes to
express the popular revolutionary movement, it cannot do so
completely until it has ceased to be militaristic and become
completely civilianized. This is the standard by which we must
judge military revolts.

Consequently, it is of the essence of the sort of democratic
state that we want, that the military—or rather its
leaders—should split up into a military cadre which confines itself to military matters, and a progressive civil group which
understands that its power cannot be exercised except in an
atmosphere of democratic freedom and with the genuine participation of the people.

We therefore can distinguish between the various army
revolts in recent years. The only real way in which we can
judge them is in how far they serve to establish true democratic
principles. In Egypt, the political atmosphere before 1952 was
favorable to revolution. The ruling authorities were a provocation to both the military and civilians. The military were driven
to revolt because of the inadequacy of the popular movement
both in theory and practice. Because the popular movement was
unequal to the provocation of reaction, the military decided to
intervene to enable the people to answer the challenge
effectively. In demanding that the political parties should purge
themselves of the elements which had corrupted the government and prevented the people from having any influence on it,
the military accepted certain assumptions. It admitted the fact
that its power was transitional and planted the seeds of its own
maturity and readiness to comply with the aspirations of the
people. In other words, the army began that qualitative change
which enables the basis of a democratic state to be established.
But there is no reason for complacency or indifference. The

development toward a true democratic state will only take
place through the popular will expressed by the people themselves with courage and insistence. If the popular movement
hesitates to further this development and lets it remain as it is,
the progressive civilian elements will not influence the various
branches of the state.

POPULAR IRAQI REVOLUTION

In Iraq the military revolution through its destructive action,
acquired a positive character, particularly because it did not
hesitate to have full popular participation in its planning and
was ready to accept the guidance of the popular will. The military gave expression to a popular revolution which had been
fermenting but which lacked the force to pass into action. From
the beginning it was serving democracy. Broadly its experience
was comparable with those in Indonesia and Burma where the
military, in spite of a few technical indications to the contrary,
was cooperating with the popular movement and trying to give
expression to it. But the popular movement in Iraq, in spite of
the historic opportunity it had been granted, failed in this matter because the unity between the various popular forces which
had been involved in the struggle against the prerevolutionary
regime did not last. Each current in the movement regarded the
military revolution as an extension of itself and not as an expression of the whole popular front. This would have been natural if
each of these ideological forces had formed a precise estimate of
its own strength and had deduced that it was the truest expression of the popular movement. If they had done this, they
would have realized that the popular movement was committed
to the aims of the popular front as a whole and not to the sum
of the objectives of each of its constituent elements. In Iraq,
when these different currents came into conflict, the army also
was affected and became incapable of playing an independent
role as an arbiter. The army was affected not only by the broad
aspirations of the popular movement, but also by its contradictions. The popular movement had to lead without the revolutionary discipline needed for sound guidance. Instead of satis-
fying the elementary requirements of the revolution, the
different elements in the popular movement sought to break it,
thinking they would assume the leadership.

A PREMATURE STRUGGLE

This struggle was premature, and bad timing in declaring all the aims of the various elements in the revolutionary movement meant that it was impossible to begin fullfilling the people's basic wishes. Nonideological opportunism was able to recover its strength. It benefited from the premature struggle because it did not want the popular movement to be the focus of power in Iraq. Opportunism is now the only single disciplined force capable of ruling in Iraq, although the various conflicting currents in the country do not for a moment want it to play this role. Opportunism in Iraq has roots in the Iraqi polity which enables it to adapt itself to the general atmosphere. It is consistent in only one thing, and that is its fundamental opposition to democracy because the circumstances of its growth during the previous regime make it the sole beneficiary of the destruction of democratic freedoms in Iraq. When opportunism became the ruling power in Iraq, the revolution began to decline from a proper revolution to a mere *coup*. This does not mean to say that the transformation will stop where it is. There will be a persistent revision of ideas on the insistence of the various ideological elements in declaring themselves as the sole vanguard of the popular movement while, objectively speaking, none can claim to be.

We shall take the Sudan as our model of the possible case of the military taking action without there being any sound reasons for it. This is what we mean by a state of permanent "putschism," mentioned above. Parliamentary life was proceeding soundly and maturely, in spite of certain deficiencies in national life, due to the Sudan's special historical circumstances. The military's aim was not to remedy the deficiencies in the state. The army thought it had a right to take power and that it was capable of ruling. The Sudanese revolution was not in response to the desire of the masses because, from their point of view, there was insufficient provocation to justify it. Thus the revolt became stultified and never matured into a true revolution. This does not mean that there were no deficiencies in Sudanese policy before the revolution but neither does it contradict our thesis that the means of remedying these deficiencies existed, had democracy been able to develop naturally.

We see therefore that there are certain characteristics of the military we must consider if we are to have a clear picture of the general political development of the underdeveloped countries of Afro-Asia. The principle characteristics of the military in underdeveloped countries arise from the key position of the land forces in the state. This is in contrast to the advanced countries, where it is becoming increasingly clear that these play a secondary role. The reason why the military is of such importance in the political revolutionary movement is that most of its branches are organized and disciplined, which enables it to carry out its responsibilities speedily when the opportunity arises. Because these are certain immediate problems which require quick solutions, there is a lack of desire to resist the military movement at that stage.

But the military movement does not embrace all the officers. In most cases it is directed not only against the established authorities but also against a section of the army command itself which is connected with them. The revolutionary military movement finds a youthful generation of officers which is closer to popular feeling and is consequently more ready to understand and represent it. This is the difference between the military revolt which is carried out by the whole army, as in the Sudan and Pakistan, and the revolution directed against part of the army connected with the corrupt politicians. The difference is greater or less depending on the degree of corruption of the existing government and the extent to which the government is prepared to organize itself on the basis of a program.

Our definition of the form, behaviors and ideas of the military class would be incomplete without a definition of what we mean by democracy, especially in Asian countries.

We are not going to give a complete definition of democracy here. What we shall do is to try to define it within the context of the military classes in the backward countries. This will give democracy a special meaning some will agree with and others will dispute. We must not necessarily have an academic definition which everyone will agree on, although I think a considerable majority will accept it.

DEMOCRACY'S TWO ELEMENTS

Democracy has two fundamental elements: Consent and Participation. These two elements must be present. The institutions through which they operate have evolved with the passage of time but they are not all the same owing to the different historical circumstances of the societies in which they arise, which led to variations in the degree of participation in public life and to a difference in the degree of emphasis on certain aspects. This difference only appears when certain people want to associate democracy with certain institutions and to base it solely on them. When a certain type of institution comes to be regarded as the substance of democracy, and hence form is given precedence over reality, democracy loses one of its most important elements, i.e., the participation of the people not only in general political life but also in the creation of the institutions which are suited to the particular circumstances of their society. Thus, if the institutions insure the growth and development of the elements of participation and consent, they will be suited to the conditions in which they have evolved and there will be democracy in its total sense.

By the element of consent, we mean the acceptance by the individual of the rules of authority. This consent is an essential condition of the authority's legality. This approval must be unanimous—an expression of the general will of the people. It also implies the right to dissent so that, if it is the majority that differs, it is the dissenting view which represents the will of the nation from which the government's authority derives.

Dissent is not always the contradiction of consent. In fact, it is inherent in it. It is used when the authorities deviate from the policy for which they have received prior consent. The right of dissent gives the element of popular consent in democracy its quality of freedom, and through it the changes both in principle and detail are made consistent with continuous progress.

This right to dissent can only operate properly if there is agreement on the basic principles of the state. When the dissenting view is incompatible with the agreed foundations of the state it becomes subversion and subversion, when it succeeds, violates the general will and destroys democracy. We do not deny the difficulty involved in distinguishing between dissent and subversion but, where there is doubt, we should call it dissent. This is not to say that subversion is not a potential danger, especially in countries which are aiming to progress out of their state of backwardness.

By participation we mean bringing the mass of the people into active involvement in all aspects of public life. This is not only achieved through participation through representative institutions but also in the liberation struggle against imperialism.

When liberation movements clash with the imperialists, they are democratic because they require the broad and continuous participation of the people.

This national action in the struggle for independence creates a nucleus of public opinion on which backward countries can build a democratic society. In our view, participation should not be confined to politics but should include the economic, social and cultural fields. It is therefore more comprehensive than the classical western concept of democracy.

For democracy in the Afro-Asian countries to fulfill all its essential conditions, it must pass through stages which differ from those in the West. Before what is understood as political liberty can exist, these countries must achieve national liberation. Thus demands for some of the forms of democracy, such as the immediate proliferation of political parties, before full sovereignty is achieved, dissipate the popular will and harm the liberation movement.

Democracy in its full sense also means participation of all the people in economic life, which must be so organized that there is no exploitation but sharing in the means of production, a just distribution of products and equality of opportunity. This concept of democracy means that there is no individual liberty without national freedom, no genuine democracy without equality, no active popular participation without social and economic guarantees, and no consent to an authority which does not accept these precepts. The crisis through which democracy in Asian countries is passing is due to the fact that nationalist movements, in the period of the direct clash with imperialism, comprised all the class interests of the nation. When these countries obtained their independence, the nationalist movements tried to maintain unity and dissolve the class conflict without solving its problems.

WHERE DEMOCRACY FAILED

National movements in most cases yielded to pressure from the most influential classes. Except in India, the nationalist leaders failed to understand the full meaning of democracy and consequently relied on the forms of democracy without its substance. The government became an instrument serving the interests of a narrow exploiting class, cut off from the people, whom it failed to give a share in ruling. The result has been corruption in the government, the growth of opportunism in the administration, the use of the security forces to fix elections, and the limitation of freedom. Essential problems remain unsolved and without hope of solution. The people turn increasingly to radical revolutionary movements, if such exist—as one did in China—or they become hopelessly apathetic and give their silent consent to the revolutionary trend in the army. The people come to want a government which they will accept but not share in.

In this semi-democracy, i.e., consent without participation, an atmosphere is created which is favorable to military rule. The military class is characterized by its nonradical outlook and its liking for authoritarian government. This gains for them the approval of the ruling economic classes who see in them a protection against the radical demands of the people. At the same time, the people regard a military revolt as a step forward and as something preferable to the previous regime. It is thus possible for military rule in an underdeveloped country to paralyze political life for a period in which it enjoys temporary approval to strengthen its position but fails to put down the permanent roots which it can only acquire through the active participation of the people.

The crisis of democracy in underdeveloped countries arises from its imprisonment within the narrow classical concept and the fact that the democratic potential has not insisted on its socialist element and the revolutionary values which are essential to it. Only insofar as the democratic potential in national movements is committed to socialism, will democracy realize itself.

AN ATTITUDE OF MIND

Democracy rests in institutions, but it is also an attitude of mind. It starts with the premise that man is the center of existence and that human activity is ultimately aimed at his happiness and not merely his satisfaction. Social legislation can insure man's satisfaction, but freedom and equality alone can insure his happiness. In the underdeveloped countries we see no hope of any speedy achievement of general welfare—let alone happiness. Faced with this fact, our conception of democracy must be total. It must comprise radical solutions for man's problems. It must insure a society in which human satisfaction is only the first and not the final goal. We must realize that military revolutions, in spite of their justification in certain circumstances, are the penalty of our failure to think clearly and empirically in the early stages of democracy in underdeveloped countries—rather than a solution to man's problems.

What we have to insure is that this price we have paid shall not destroy the socialist democratic movement, but act as a stimulant for it.

4. Beginnings of Socialist Zionism

BY NACHMAN SYRKIN

FROM THE DAYS of the famous "Cultural Clubs" of Berlin during the twenties of the eighteenth century, till Moses Hess, and later Aaron Lieberman, Jewish radicals did not stop trying to merge the vision of a better world with that of the renaissance of the Jewish people. But a genuine socialist Zionism could not arise till the independent development of political Zionism and the formation of a Jewish socialist movement. The latter stimulated Jewish revolutionary energy which, in turn, was deepened by a specific Jewish protest and by Jewish idealism.

As far back as the Hoveve-Zion period, an intimate contact between the national and socialist movements already existed. Despite the antagonism between the respective organizations, their ideologies touched and completed each other. Both Jewish movements were engaged in perpetual literary polemics and political debates, and a steady stream of converts and penitents flowed back and forth between Zionism and socialism. But Zionism and socialism were still viewed as antithetic instead of as the components of a natural synthesis.

A socialist-Zionist ideology began to take shape immediately after the First Zionist Congress in 1897. In Basle there already appeared a group of intellectuals who sought to create a new synthesis between their Zionist sentiments and their socialist consciousness. However, since at the First Congress Zionism

Reprinted from the *Jewish Frontier*, XVII, no. 6(182), by permission of the editor, pp. 7–12. This historical account by the founder and theoretician of the socialist-Zionist movement appears for the first time in English translation. It was reprinted in the *Jewish Frontier* on the occasion of the 45th anniversary of the Poale Zion in America as part of the basic literature of the movement.

assumed a reactionary bourgeois character in keeping with the social group which was its protagonist, these rudimentary and ill-defined attempts at a union between socialism and Zionism disappeared.

Between 1898 and 1900, only one voice was raised for such a synthesis. In 1898, in a German magazine, there appeared "The Jewish Question" (by Nachman Syrkin, *Ed.*) which offered the following theses: that the Jewish people is viewed as alien everywhere in the Diaspora; that the Jewish bourgeoisie invented the deception of assimilation to promote its power of exploitation; that a profound moral contradiction exists between the bourgeois lie of assimilation and the revolutionary truth of socialism; that the Jewish socialist is dutybound to aid the Jewish people and to accept Zionism as the instrument for the emancipation of the Jewish people and the spiritual redemption of the individual Jew.

This article in enlarged form appeared later as a pamphlet under the name of "The Jewish Question and the Socialist Jewish State" (Bern, 1898). It became the starting point for a furious discussion in the Zionist and Jewish Socialist press.

In 1901 a Russian pamphlet entitled "Call to Jewish Youth" (by Nachman Syrkin, *Ed.*), issued by the Socialist-Zionist Party, appeared in Berlin. The author argued that the social and political needs of the constantly wandering Jewish masses could not be met by socialism alone. Hand in hand with the struggle for socialism, the Jewish proletariat had to fight for a Jewish homeland in Palestine, not as a holy land but as a territory. The author criticized bourgeois Zionism for its reactionary political tendencies and its conception of the Jewish state as a class state, and he called for a cooperative society in the Jewish homeland.

These writings were still the expression of a solitary literary voice and lacked the weight of an organized movement. However, from 1900 on, the first sproutings of a socialist-Zionist movement began to appear in Russia under the name of Poale Zion (Workers of Zion). The first group of Poale Zion was organized in Minsk; at the same time, other groups were formed in Ekaterinoslav (South Russia), where the Jewish workers had as yet not been organized in the "Bund." More groups soon appeared in various cities of Lithuania such as Vilna, Dvinsk and Vitebsk. Later, the movement penetrated into Russian Poland. As a result of emigration to America, Poale Zion groups began to be established in the new world.

The first scattered Poale Zion groups consisted of various elements and lacked central unity. To begin with, many of the groups under the leadership of the Minsk Poale Zion were merely Zionist workers. Their name "Poale Zion," (Workers of Zion) in part indicated an occupational difference and in part was simply a traditional designation, one of the various names used by Zionist groups, such as "Lovers of Zion," etc. The founders of these Poale Zion units merely sought to introduce Zionism among Jewish workers, and tried to combine cultural work among the Jewish masses with Zionist propaganda. They were indifferent to socialism and to the revolutionary struggle, and they still opposed Zionism to socialism. Exactly like the bourgeois Zionists, these first Poale Zion groups of the Minsk type ignored the relationship between the Jewish people and the revolutionary movements and ideas of the time. In the Diaspora they strove to localize the attention of Jewish workers on their immediate elementary economic needs. They reasoned as follows: Since even a revolution in Russia and a free political regime could not wipe out Jewish need which springs from *Galuth* [exile], and since the Jewish working class cannot be the agent of the Russian Revolution, the Jewish workers must stand apart from the Russian revolutionary movement, even though they have a revolutionary awareness and expect help from non-Jewish progressives for the Jewish people and proletariat. The Minsk Poale Zion rejected every advanced concept of a socialist society, and only gradually began to emphasize the social character of Zionist colonization (the nationalization of land).

But parallel with these Zionist groups of the Minsk variety, other Zionist labor groups of a more radical and intellectual cast came into being. Such groups already existed in Ekaterinoslav and other cities of South Russia where the influence of B. Borochov was felt. These Poale Zion groups, followers of the ideology of Russian social democracy, were educated in the ideals of revolutionary struggle and socialism, and sought to base Zionism on Marxist principles. A type of socialist and revolutionary Poale Zion developed which aimed frankly at the synthesis of socialism and Zionism. But unfortunately, all these groups were scattered, independent units which differed both in their theoretical concepts and their practical activities. They had no party literature and were cemented by no common bond. During this formative period, only their genuine enthusiasm was able to overcome their theoretical and practical helplessness.

At this debating-society stage, the first socialist-Zionist organization, *Heirut,* was formed in Berlin. It included the Zionist socialists who had published the "Call to Jewish Youth" (in Russian in 1910). *Heirut* set itself the goal of becoming a socialist-Zionist organization which would arouse the Jewish masses to struggle for a Jewish homeland and a new society.

Heirut attempted to formulate the theoretical basis of socialist Zionism in two publications which appeared in 1903: *Hamon* (Yiddish) and *Hashachar* (Hebrew). The following arguments were presented:

The Jewish proletarian masses, constantly under the pressure of Jewish political and economic need and migration from land to land, are the natural fulfillers of the Zionist idea; they are driven to Zionism by necessity. Their historic redemption depends on the establishment of a free Jewish land of labor and socialism. The acquisition of civil rights by the Jews of Eastern Europe and emigration to America result in the transformation of the Jewish working class into a middle class. A productive working class is created in the Diaspora only under the pressure of necessity; the productive class changes into a nonproductive one as soon as this pressure is released. Zionism is therefore the complement and requisite of Jewish socialism, and becomes the ideology of the conscious Jewish socialist. Similarly, assimilation becomes the concern of the Jewish bourgeoisie, and the ideology of Jewish defeatists, escapists and traitors.

The Zionism of the Jewish masses is more than the colonization projects of Hoveve-Zion with its bourgeois limitations; it is more than the longing for a "spiritual center" which is the national ideology of the *maskil* [enlightened]; it is more than the philanthropic Zionism of the West Europeans. The Zionism of the Jewish masses is *social,* and bound up with the ideal of a new *society.* Only through such a tie can the Jewish masses be won for Zionism and become its inspired disciples and champions. Through the organization of the Jewish masses, their criticism of the Jewish bourgeoisie, their fight for the national funds controlled by the middle class, and their demand that the assimilated Jewish middle class give national capital for Zionist purposes, can the idea of a Jewish homeland be realized.

On the basis of this platform, *Heirut* started a movement among Jewish workers in London to fight ICA for the colonization fund which the representatives of the Jewish bourgeoisie controlled, contrary to the Zionist will of the Jewish people.

In 1903, the year when the Uganda project had such a dispiriting effect on the entire course of Zionism, the influence of socialist Zionism was already felt among the Jewish masses but differences of practice and principle rent the various groups. It was a period of theoretical chaos. The majority of these groups still called themselves Poale Zion, but only a few more radical elements had assumed the name "Socialist Zionists." These groups were united by strong Zionist sentiment, a recognition of the abnormal character of the Jewish economic situation, and a realization of the limitations of the class struggle in *Galuth* economy. They were divided by varying degrees of revolutionary conviction, socialist education and maturity; and, as was natural for all Jewish movements, they were diversely drawn by the rainbow-shimmer of Russian socialism in all its shades.

In this period of theoretical confusion, Zionism itself went through a serious crisis which deepened the differences among the socialist Zionists. To the Sixth Congress in Basle (1903) was brought the British government's offer to establish a Jewish national home with local autonomy in Uganda. On the one hand, the wave of pogroms and on the other, the apparent hopelessness of getting a charter from the Sultan by diplomatic means, had caused Herzl to bring the Uganda plan to the Congress, and loosened the complex of motives which had constituted Zionism. The romantic-traditional element, with the *maskilim* [enlightened ones] and the Hoveve-Zion at the head, remained true to the primacy of Palestine; the avowed political Zionists, whose first objective was a Jewish state—not necessarily the specific Jewish land with its historic romanticism, but their own land—declared themselves for Uganda. Because of this practical problem the Zionist movement split into various groups: "Palestinians" on principle, "Zion Zionists" who saw in the diversion of Zionism to any other country not only a practical error but a betrayal of the Jewish national idea; territorialists, "anti-Palestinians" who saw in the Palestine fixation a hindrance to a Jewish state, and less marked groups of "Ugandists" who included orthodox and political Zionists, and combined Palestine and Uganda in the sense of Herzl's Uganda proposal.

At the Seventh Congress (1905), after Herzl's death, the Uganda proposal led to the formation of a territorialist fraction, which organized itself as a "Jewish Territorialist Society" under the leadership of Israel Zangwill with a center in London.

The territorialist crisis affected Poale Zionism even more

crucially and destructively than general Zionism. The Uganda
project, by giving Zionism a more practical aspect, had attracted wide circles of Jewish workers to socialist Zionism. But
together with the increased interest of the masses in a Jewish
homeland, there came greater intellectual chaos as to the
substance of socialist Zionism. If previously there had existed
confusion in regard to the extent of the revolutionary struggle,
now there were differences as to the realization of
Zionism—Uganda or Palestine. However, since Uganda or any
other territory was only apparently "realistic" and, if one considers Jewish actualities and national energies of that period,
even less realistic than Palestine, territorialism lacked the concrete strength to go beyond theorizing. All the Poale Zion clubs
regrouped themselves according to a fresh dividing line.
Previously, Poale Zon groups which accepted the idea of political struggle had begun to call themselves socialist-Zionists, and
the groups of the original Minsk type had kept the name of
"Poale Zion." Now both blocs divided again along the question
of Palestine or territorialism. There were groups of the Minsk
type who were indifferent to political struggle, yet sided with
the territorialists. In South Russia, on the other hand, there
arose socialist Poale Zion groups who were "Palestinian." The
largest number, however, were the socialist-Zionists who had
first accepted the concept of political struggle, and now turned
to territorialism.

Soon another tendency arose in socialist Zionism which began
to play an important part in the entire Jewish national
movement—the *Voroshdenye* (renaissance). *Heirut* had been
characterized by its strong socialist-Zionist sentiment, its desire
for a Jewish state, and the central role it accorded to Zionism
in the Jewish national-revolutionary renaissance. There was bound
to arise another group of socialist-Zionist intellectuals who
placed the center of gravity of the Jewish renaissance not
on Zionism but on Jewish nationalism in the Diaspora. In 1904
(London), appeared a Russian publication, *Voroshdenye*, concen-
trating around itself a significant number of young intellectuals
who sought to find a new content for socialist Zionism. The
leading article, "Our Task," struck the keynote for the future of
the movement. The author (Ratner) criticized the indifference of
the Jewish socialists to the Jewish people and its fate; at the
same time, he strictured the one-sidedness of the Zionists who
concentrated on a Jewish land in the future, and ignored present

Jewish needs and contemporary Jewish national impulses. He proposed developing a Jewish national-revolutionary movement in the Diaspora, with a Jewish homeland as its historic goal. But despite the *Voroshdenye* group's repeated declarations of faith in the holy tie between national renaissance in the *Galuth* and a Jewish homeland, they actually thrust the idea of a Jewish homeland into the theoretical mists of the future and by so doing deprived even Diaspora nationalism of its vital sap.

But before socialist Zionism had a real opportunity to crystallize as an idea and a movement, a process of dissolution set in. The deepest crisis this fruitful idea was to encounter came in 1905, a year which was to have a decisive effect on the further development of socialist Zionism. The Russian Revolution (1905) opened a free field of political activity for the Jewish working class and aroused new hopes for the Jewish people in Russia. Theoretically at any rate, the *Galuth* had ceased to be the dark, hopeless vale of tears which the Zionist "deniers of the *Galuth*" had painted. A dazzling prospect for Jewish economic and political independence unfolded.

In addition, the Zionist organization split the same year, though neither the old Zionist organization, nor the new territorialist movement had any realistic expectations. The Zionist organization again called for small settlement projects in Palestine, a call which could in no way provide the impetus for a national movement. And the territorialist idea met with cold indifference among the people, and remained the responsibility of the early groups of territorialist Zionist socialists.

The as yet unformed socialist-Zionist movement did not waver in its theoretical recognition of the need of a Jewish homeland. But the program and tactics of Zionism became uncertain and imitative, and no longer bore their original absolute character. Because of the unfavorable climate for Zionism, a tendency arose in the socialist-Zionist movement to argue that the attainment of a Jewish homeland was a historic process of the future and that the chief value of a homeland for the Jewish working class was its role in the class struggle. In this sterile and apathetic atmosphere and under the influence of a social-democratic ideology which thrust every social phenomenon into the all-inclusive grab-bag of historic determinism, the Zionism of the socialist-Zionists became foolishly scientific. It became fatalistically dependent on the "redemptive future," and lost its true spirit of free creativeness.

At the conventions of the then existent four socialist-Zionist parties which took place during the winter of 1905–06, this failure of will was already apparent. The Poale Zion groups of the Minsk type, which in revolutionary spirit had been left far behind by other socialist-Zionist groups, had remained the most conservative element in the movement. Though they paid their respects to socialism as a theory, they fought shy of any ideological involvement or practical inference.

A different and more radical approach was developed by the SS (the Socialist-Zionist Party of territorialist persuasion) after the Uganda offer. By Marxist formulas they sought to interpret the disabilities of the Jewish working class, its "nonproletarianization." The inability of the Jewish masses to enter basic industries because of persecution leads to emigration; since emigration becomes a historical necessity it must be turned into colonization or territorialism. The attempt to reduce territorialism merely to a phase of the proletarian class struggle indicates how the radical Zionist intelligentsia sought to adapt Zionism to the social-democratic ideology in fashion among Jewish proletarian circles. Through this attempt territorialism became impoverished as a national idea and socialist ideal, and crippled in its struggles against the assimilationist bourgeoisie.

Socialist territorialism was a fresh nuance in socialism, a new and extraordinary moment in the development of the *Galuth* proletariat and not merely an episode in the class struggle. The Jewish proletariat should have viewed it as an instrument of human and cultural liberation and the starting point for the creation of a new socialist society. The impoverishment of the territorialist conception was particularly to be seen in its debasement to a "historical necessity," the last step of the *stychic* process of Jewish emigration which inevitably becomes transformed into concentration and colonization. This entire approach was merely a copy of the Marxist formula for the development of capitalism. Small production develops into great production, but at a certain stage of capitalist development the forces of production clash with the existing relations of production, and socialism arises. The Marxist formula was applied to territorialism. At a certain stage contradictions develop within the emigration tide and it is transformed into colonization. This unconscious emigration and colonization process becomes conscious and turns into "territorialism."

The movement sank to such a caricature when it lost the

courage to think and act independently, and feared to shake off
the influence and the phraseology of the reigning intellectual
style. The leaders of the movement wanted to present territorialism as a rectilinear development of Jewish reality, just as
socialism was the final conclusion of the capitalist process. Actually, territorialism was not a continuation but a conscious opposition, a conscious free creation which sought to overcome the
mad chaos of Jewish *Galuth.*

The inner timidity and slavish imitativeness of the socialist-
territorialist movement proved to be its undoing. It never
had the strength for any territorialist undertaking, either a territorialist organization or territorialist colonization institutions. To
maintain its proletarian purity, it kept clear of any contact with
the wider territorialist movement; nevertheless, it too soon fell
victim to the general territorialist apathy. Finally, the social-
ist-territorialist party joined a philanthropic enterprise in
America which sought to transport Jewish immigrants not to
New York but to the Harbor of Galveston so as to spread Jewish
immigrants throughout the United States and prevent their concentration in the industrial centers of the eastern states. The
"Galveston Plan," subsidized by some American Jewish philan-
thropists, thus became that inevitable *stychic* emigration and
colonization process which socialist territorialism was supposed
to elevate to conscious activity.

The same spirit which animated the program of the socialist
territorialists could be seen in the "Jewish Social-Democratic
Workers Party—Poale Zion." There was the same Marxist phraseology, the same dependence on historic determinism, the same
tendency to designate the longing of the Jewish working class
for a homeland as a "moment in its class struggle." The chief
theoretical tenets of the party were formulated in the party
publication, "The Jewish Workers' Chronicle" (1906) by B.
Borochov.

These were as follows: The positive basis of national life is a
land. A landless people cannot develop its powers of production;
therefore, in order to exist it must penetrate into alien economies. But a landless people is isolated and thrust out of the alien
economy. The essence of the Jewish problem lies in the fact that
the Jewish people is extra-territorial. Besides, the Jewish problem assumes various forms among different social classes. The
Jewish great bourgeoisie, which does not suffer from isolation, is
fundamentally assimilationist. Though for this class alone there

is no Jewish question, it fears anti-Semitism, which is stimulated by the immigration of poor Jewish masses. Consequently, Jewish capitalists concern themselves reluctantly with the Jewish problem and try to aid their unhappy East European brothers by philanthropic means.

The Jewish middle bourgeoisie suffers more directly from anti-Semitism and therefore has a sharper national consciousness. It would like to have a national market and an independent political existence in a Jewish state. But its nationalism is bourgeois-cultural. Its national energy is feeble because its main interests still lie in the *Galuth*. The Jewish petite bourgeoisie, from whom the "proletariazing" masses emerge, suffers most from competition and emigrates. In the fresh countries of immigration, it again suffers from competition and discrimination. But since this class is only the passive object of a national process, it lacks the power to solve the Jewish question. These declassed workers are the most unfortunate element among the wandering Jewish masses because all they seek is a place of employment. They do not even dream of a territory.

The Jewish proletariat, however, is the class which will solve the Jewish question through the class struggle. It has a national interest in a territory because among alien surroundings it lacks the possibility for developing its powers for the class struggle. The national question of the Jewish proletariat consists in the abnormal character of its stategic base, which renders it politically and economically strengthless. Often its economic struggle is illusory because it is employed in backward branches of production and is not engaged in heavy industry. Because the class contradictions in Jewish society are so weak, the Jewish proletariat is tragically helpless and must drag after the surrounding political movements. Since the Jewish class struggle is sterile, the Jewish proletariat is prone to an exaggerated revolutionary phraseology. "Prometheus bound, who in impotent fury would tear with his teeth the feathers of the vulture picking at his heart—that is the symbol of the Jewish proletariat."

The tragic situation of the Jewish proletariat makes territorialism necessary. The more the waves of emigration increase, the more essential it will be to find new lands. The tendency of Jewish emigration is toward concentration in a definite territory. This concentration cannot take place in a completely undeveloped land. Immigration into new countries is only possible on the basis of a wide agricultural colonization, which sends its products to an industrial market. But Jews are an urban people separated for centuries from the land; they cannot go over to agriculture suddenly; the process must be gradual. A land suitable for Jewish concentration must be one adapted to a gradual change from an urban to an agricultural economy. Such a land is Palestine which has for the present [a] semi-agricultural economy. Therefore Palestine is to be the land where the process of *stychic* concentration will take place.

There are no obstacles to Jewish immigration to Palestine, argued Borochov in 1906. The decrees of the Sultan against immigration will be overcome as soon as democratic regimes will be introduced into Russia and Austria. Through diplomatic means the Jews will secure free immigration into Palestine. More and more Jews will enter Palestine and develop it into a capitalist country. In this fashion an independent Jewish society will be created. Simultaneously, there will develop a desire for political independence and for territorial autonomy. Such territorial autonomy will be won through a political struggle led by the Jewish proletariat. The class struggle between the Jewish proletariat and the bourgeoisie will involve the opposition of the Turkish bureaucracy. Then the struggle of the proletariat for the political independence of Palestine will commence. The Jewish independence movement in Palestine will be supported by the Diaspora and by the intervention of the Great Powers, who will want to find a solution for the Jewish problem and will be eager to secure the peace of the Middle East. Finally, therefore, Turkey will accede to demands for Jewish independence.

Borochov's arguments for a territorial solution differ little from those of the SS. Instead of an abstract territory, Palestine is introduced for the sole reason that it is a half-capitalist country and therefore suited for a Jewish urban population. This entire theory, like that of the SS, is fitted into the framework of the reigning social-democratic ideology. An even weirder application of Marxist ideas is to be found in the additional argument which proves why Palestine is the most suitable territory. Both movements agreed in subordinating Zionist activity to the fashionable ideology of historic determinism. In this lack of national courage and independent thought lay one of the reasons for the social impotence of the Poale Zion in Russia.

In 1905–06, socialist-Zionist ideas began to take root in the United States. In America, where the Jewish working class was not subject to a particular school of thought and where every theory was measured by its practical results and possibilities, there was no room for the airy abstractions of Russian Poale Zionism. The theoretical program of the American Poale Zion could not go against the dictates of sound common sense. The absence of vague theorizing in American life and the impulse for practical accomplishment had a refreshing and revitalizing effect on American socialist Zionism, which assumed a concrete, active character.

At a conference held in Philadelphia in May 1905, various American Poale Zion groups united in one organization. At first the Party consisted of both pro-Palestine and territorialist elements, but such a combination could not last. At a later conference (December 1905) in Baltimore, a pro-Palestine Poale Zion Party was formed. Its declaration of principles was marked by simplicity and a readiness for practical activity:

> Since the development of mankind expresses itself through the development of individual nations, since the normal social-economic, political and cultural development of every people requires a majority status in some land, and since such a development can only be realized in the historical homeland of a given people, we attest our belief in Zionism which strives for an openly secured homeland for the Jewish people in Palestine.
>
> Since we consider a society based on private ownership as a society in which a minority owns the means of production and lives on the labor of the majority, we will strive to alter unjust social forms and to introduce a socialist society. As socialists, we will take part in every activity tending to emancipate the working class and we will work jointly with all socialist organizations insofar as these do not conflict with our national aspirations.
>
> We want the future Jewish state to be established insofar as possible on socialist principles.
>
> "Although the complete solution of the Jewish question can only take place in Palestine, we fight for the full equality of the Jewish people in all the lands of the Diaspora. (*Yiddisher Kemfer* 1906)

PART 2

The Transformation of Society

Like many of his friends . . . he envisaged himself as a hero, a savior, a conspirator of the people, who would consciously merge in them, who would turn all their wild noise into a hymn of joy for an age of love and justice. . . .

Our people can now flare up. They can unglue their rears from seats and walk down the streets in hordes and actually crack their throats with shouting. It means we're no longer dead. It doesn't matter whom we're rising up against. Sooner or later we'll hit on the right thing, the right person.

But the injury, the suffering, the blood incurred in such an uprising—they're all wasted?

Nothing is wasted. It is part of the exercise of will power. For eight hundred years we've been cowed and kicked about. A little more and nothing of the sort will happen. But we must exercise our limbs, we must hurry, we must learn to face the gunfire. . . .

Every country east of the Mediterranean is torn to bits by ever-competing jealous politicos coming to power by some kind of inheritance. . . . But I can envisage the day when these countries will be even worse, torn by degree-holders more self-interested and sycophantic than their predecessors, and far, far less charitable. If you think the sheikh grinds the faces of his tribesmen you should wait and see the Ph.D. grind the faces of all and sundry, without even a touch of the magnanimity we pride ourselves on.

Jabra I. Jabra, *Hunters in a Narrow Street* (London, 1960).

1. In Search of a Doctrine:
A Study of the Ideology of the
Egyptian Revolution BY DON PERETZ

AMONG most Afro-Asian leaders, there has grown during the past decade an increasing awareness of the importance of fundamental social and economic change. Most have espoused programs which envisage total social and political reorganization of their nations. Throughout the Afro-Asian world, there are common aspirations to unify society, raise living standards, increase productivity, and to effect drastic social revolutions.

In the Arab world, the efforts of Jamal Abd al-Nasser to achieve these aspirations are most significant since it is the Egyptian Revolution led by him which has come to symbolize among most Arab nationalists the fulfillment of their yearnings for social and economic progress. The Egyptian Revolutionary government was the first successful neo-Arab nationalist venture in the Middle East to attempt, on a large scale, the realization of a democratic, socialist and cooperative Arab society.

When the Revolutionary Command Council (RCC) came to power in Egypt in 1952, its stated aim was to act merely as a "caretaker" until competent and trustworthy civilians would take over the government and effect the changes in society on behalf of which the revolution was staged.

There was no comprehensive social and economic program or doctrine by which to measure the progress and success of the Revolution. None of the officers who led the Revolution had either the theoretical knowledge or the practical experience prerequisite to efficient and effective management of govern-

Reprinted from *Middle East Forum*, Vol. XXXV, No. 6 (Beirut, 1959), pp. 13–17, 33; by permission of the editor.

ment. Most were from lower-middle-class backgrounds educated
in Egypt's military academy where they acquired little knowledge of the social and economic problems of their country. Few
had delved into the complications of political, social and economic theory. At best, they were only vaguely familiar with concepts like socialism, fascism, communism, planned economy,
nationalization of the means of production, and the like. What
awareness there was of such theoretical concepts was more of
symbols and slogans than of the substance of ideology.

Within the original RCC, only two officers had any clear-cut
political ideologies, both of leftist orientation. Colonel Yussuf
Sadiq was removed from his position in the early months of the
regime because of close identification with, if not actual membership in, the MDLN, a Communist front organization. Major
Khaled Mohieddin, who, although not an out-and-out Communist, was an ardent admirer of that doctrine, broke with the
remaining RCC members in 1954 and has since become the editor of *al-Masa*, a left-wing Cairo daily.

NATIONALISM COMES FIRST

Neither in their clandestinely published prerevolutionary
tracts, nor in the early speeches, writings or pronouncements of
the RCC leaders was there any direct reference to a clear-cut
doctrine or comprehensive economic and social program. Nasser's *Philosophy of the Revolution* makes no mention of economic or social ideology and little of social reform.

The circulars of the Free Officers Society, secretly distributed
before July 1952, emphasized nationalist, not reformist slogans.
A lesser emphasis was on the campaign against corruption. But
even this was secondary in importance to "national aspirations."
A 1952 prerevolution circular stated that: "Among the objectives of the Free Officers is the launching of a campaign against
corruption in all its aspects, against bribery, favoritism and
abuse of influence; but we should not combat such evils unless
we have been completely freed from imperialism. Any other
step would be tantamount to unpardonable treachery to the
fatherland."

As in so many other Afro-Asian nations, it was not until after
the military came to power that they began any extensive
discussion of economic and social reform. In this respect the situation much resembles that in Pakistan, Burma, Thailand and

other Asian nations where military men took over corrupt or
ineffective governments initially as a transitory measure until competent civilians would reestablish normal civil administrations.

It was disagreement and disillusionment with civilian politicians and administrators over the extent and pace of reform
which decided the officers to remain in power. Upon consulting
Egypt's experienced leaders, "we were not able to obtain very
much," comments Nasser. "Every man we questioned had nothing to recommend except to kill someone else. Every idea we
listened to was nothing but an attack on some other idea. If we
had gone along with everything we heard, we would have killed
off all the people and torn down every idea, and there would
have been nothing left for us to do but sit down among the
corpses and ruins, bewailing our evil fortune and cursing our
wretched fate."

The RCC was no more enthusiastic about the masses which it
had come to redeem. The crowds that assembled to pay the
young officers homage "were disunited, divided groups of strag-
glers . . . we needed order, but we found nothing behind us but
chaos. We needed unity, but we found nothing behind us but
dissension. We needed work, but we found behind us only indo-
lence and sloth."

Although the desire for and intention to carry out basic economic and social reform was present among the revolutionary
leaders, the means of implementing it were far from adequate.
The young officers were at best regimental commanders without
experience in managing a civil bureaucracy of tens of thousands
of nonmilitary workers, or in balancing budgets of tens of millions of pounds.

Various political trends were formed among the early RCC
members. They ranged from those strongly favoring a government similar to the Eastern European People's Democracies
through support of the corporate state idea. The common cement which prevented political fragmentation was the all-
powerful nationalist sentiment stronger than any of the borrowed
ideologies. Its binding element was an ardent Egypt-consciousness
stronger than even the Pan-Arab sentiment which in many of
the neighboring countries seemed more potent than individual
national loyalties.

Out of the hodgepodge of ideology there emerges a rather
crazy-quilt pattern of approach to the country's complicated
economic and social problems; an experimentation in various

methods—some often contradictory—for dealing with the morass into which Egypt had fallen during the previous half century.

A major issue, one which precipitated overt seizure of government control by the army, was land reform. Within the RCC, there were various points of view about the kind of reform and methods to attain it. The most radical wanted outright confiscation of all estates over fifty feddans. But a more moderate approach prevailed. Although the decision to undertake land reform was announced at the time of the initial *coup d'état* in July 1952, the law was not enacted until September because of attempts to work out compromises with the old civilian politicians. When it became apparent that the civilians, led by Ali Maher, were dragging their feet, if not actually opposing land reform, the RCC decided to take over the government outright. On the next day, the Agrarian Reform Law was enacted.

DESTRUCTION OF FEUDALISM

The land reform has been successful to the extent that it ended political domination of Egypt by a small feudal oligarchy. The political power of the old regime, based on large land holdings, has been irrevocably destroyed. The relationship between wealth—which in Egypt was based primarily on land—and political control has ended. For all practical purposes, the country is now controlled by officers who are from the middle and lower middle classes; and is administered by a corps of technicians and officers from the managerial middle class.

A second aim of the agrarian reform, as stated in the preamble of the Law, was to induce those from whom land was expropriated to invest their compensation in industry and land reclamation. This goal has not been realized because of practical obstacles and the reluctance of Egyptian capitalists to participate in venture investments.

The law also sought to reduce rents and to raise agricultural wages, but the country's land shortages and huge labor surplus have made extensive implementation of these provisions impossible to date. The total economic effect of the law on the Egyptian peasant has not been at all startling. It has done little to increase productivity or to raise living standards. But it has been a major deterrent in checking a continuing downward spiral of peasant living standards to the extent that it has stopped exploitation. Doreen Warriner summarizes the effect on the fellah:

What is new is the idea of a fair deal for the fellahin, or at any rate a fairer deal. The real change is that the cultivator has a recognized legal status; that, in itself, is an immense change for the better, outweighing any criticism. If the reform can maintain this position, that is the greatest measure of success. The Government has done as much as was practicable, and far more than might have been expected.°

A far less successful experiment was Liberation Province. There, under the direction of Major Muhammad Magdi Hassanein, it was hoped to found a collective settlement intended to "accustom our people to the desert, to make the young intellectuals practicably active in reclamation . . . Humanity is to be the keynote." With the traditions of ancient Egypt as the inspiration, a new liberated life would be established, with sport and music—not technical education—as the influences. No foreign experts would be employed. Women would participate fully. Settlers to populate the new desert-province villages would be handpicked. They would have to pass social, medical and psychological tests.

Life in the project was to be controlled strictly—down to uniformity in clothing, setting-up exercises in the morning and, of course, the work schedule.

But Egyptian society was not ready for such rigid centralization and control of family life. The plans for collectivization were impracticable even on an experimental basis. More important, the project was not economically feasible. After pouring many more times the amount of money than originally intended into the reclamation work, the results were meager, causing a national scandal. The charges, discussed in the National Assembly, were waste and maladministration rather than corruption or malfeasance. It was clear that the young major's vision was not based on the realities of Egypt's present social and economic structure. His plan was scaled down and revamped in an attempt to save what was possible from its ruins.

EXPERIMENTATION

Initial contact of the RCC with Egyptian political realities, its disillusionment with the nation's political leaders and with the masses, soon led the group to experiment with various political

°*Land Reform and Development in the Middle East,* p. 48.

forms. Democracy was de-emphasized and a regime devoted to "order, unity, and work" was established. Demands for return to parliamentary government and civilian administration were brushed aside. Those both within and outside the government who kept up their insistence on a hasty return to democratic government were removed from positions of influence and power. Government became more and more centralized in the hands of the RCC until all of the old politicians were removed. The only civilians who today hold top posts are professional administrators, technicians, and other specialists whose services are indispensable. Army officers or ex-officers who before the Revolution were either colonels or of lower grades, now command strategic positions throughout the administration.

Although creation of a democratic society is among the stated objectives of the Revolution, attempts to reconstitute parliamentary government have been periodically deferred in the interest of attaining national unity. The revolutionary leaders have feared that removal of the ban on political parties, the end of censorship, and the lifting of rigid police controls is still premature. Nasser has frequently told visitors that he aspires to the creation of a "free life" not in parliamentary institutions or slogans, but in "the life of the people."

Among the revolutionary leaders, there is no clearly articulated concept of what democracy means; no realization of the relationship between parliamentary institutions, civil liberties, freedom of thought, and a free and truly progressive society. The military do not seem to comprehend the inherent paradox of "controlled democracy."

Although their intentions are above reproach, methods of attaining aspirations are often heavy handed and maladroit. This is evident in the reaction of many Egyptian intellectuals to attempts by the government to revamp the educational system. Many claim that youth is not being educated but militarized.

On the university level the passion for national unity has already weeded out a number of leading intellectuals who were considered undesirable. Creative intellectual life in the realms of political thought and philosophy is under wraps for the time being because of the ubiquitous threat of censure.

But sentiment for establishment of democratic political institutions has not been completely disregarded. Attempts to broaden the base of popular participation in the Revolution began with the abortive establishment of the Liberation Rally. It aroused little enthusiasm among intellectuals and no wide popular acclaim. It was replaced in 1957 by the National Union.

GRADUAL DEMOCRACY

Both the 1956 Egyptian and 1958 UAR constitutions provide for parliaments controlled by a strong executive. In both cases, the National Union, headed by the President of the Republic and his former RCC associates, could veto candidates for parliament. In 1957 a committee headed by three former RCC officers rejected 1,210 of the 2,528 applicants for candidacy in the election of National Assembly members.

Although there is no official censorship of the local press, government controls are effective if indirect. All employees of any Egyptian publication must be on the rolls of the government-managed Press Syndicate according to a 1955 decree. Only foreign correspondents serving Egyptian publications abroad are exempted. The purpose of the Syndicate, according to the government, is "to raise the efficiency of the profession, safeguard its dignity, defend its rights and interests, promote a spirit of cooperation among its members and raise their moral and material standards."

An even more effective method of control is government ownership of newspaper shares. Of the five large Cairo Arabic dailies, the regime now owns shares in three. An editor of one of the other two Arabic papers told me that although there is no censorship, the government "assumes" that all publications support it wholeheartedly on certain matters such as foreign policy and the form of government.

"Of course, you westerners have different standards about these things," I've been told frequently by those who rationalize the limitations on civil liberties and the restraints on parliamentary institutions within the present regime. "Egypt is not ready for the freedom you enjoy in the United States. We are still too underdeveloped," runs the argument.

These are to a large extent the sentiments of President Nasser, who maintains that "intellectual freedom" and civil liberties were in the past mere mirages which the masses never enjoyed, and therefore have not lost. His emphasis, like that of so many other Asian leaders, is on a system of government in which a trusted leadership portions out democracy bit by bit to those who deserve it, earn it, and have proven themselves capable of managing it. Social and economic democracy, in this view, must precede political freedom. The latter will come only after the standards of the nation have been raised to a point where full political freedom can be a useful tool in developing the national interests.

SOCIALIST TERMINOLOGY

After 1956 there began to be much greater use of the term "socialist" to characterize the Egyptian Revolution. This was the trend throughout the revolutionary governments of the Afro-Asian world. At the Bandung Conference, Nasser probably had his first contact with other nationalist leaders who were making extensive use of the term and attempting to create social revolutions in their lands. In 1957, when the National Union was formed to replace political parties, its stated program was "to realize the objectives of the 1952 revolution and to promote efforts to build up the nation on good foundations by establishment of a socialist, democratic, cooperative society, free from political, social and economic exploitation."

But there are many obstacles to realization of a socialist program in Egypt. The country lacks both adequate theoretical and technical planners to work out an extensive program. The population is not yet attuned to thinking along such ideological lines. Although the term "socialist" is used, a socialist doctrine does not exist, but there is experimentation in various individual "socialistic" projects.

Efforts to effect a planned economy have, to date, been largely experimental. A planning commission headed by President Nasser was established in 1957 by amalgamating the National Production and Social Service Councils set up in 1953. The commission has produced blueprints for pilot projects rather than schemes for revolutionizing the nation's economy such as those being carried out in India or in China. Shortages of capital and of qualified personnel have stymied more rapid progress.

Although progressive social legislation has been introduced, it has not been pervasive enough to alter the economy and social structure of Egypt. Difficulty in enforcing labor legislation and agrarian rent controls, lack of proper administrative and technical personnel, and a rural population which has not yet reached the stage of development or sophistication where it can take advantage of such reforms make thorny the path of progress. Traditional resistance to taxation and government fiscal controls block a fundamental alteration in the distribution of national income through reforms such as revising the tax structure. Inheritance, personal income, company and corporation levies are still relatively low if compared with those of most western, even nonsocialist, nations.

The most extensive phase of a socialist program is the nationalization of property which had developed from the sequestration measures following the British, French and Israeli attack on Egypt in 1956. The original purpose of the sequestration legislation was to speed up the "Egyptianization" of the economy. This process, which otherwise might have taken many more decades, was telescoped into a period of a few weeks as a direct result of the tri-power attack. Since private Egyptian capital was unprepared to take over most of the sequestered businesses, the government itself set up machinery to absorb them.

The original decrees, proclaimed two days after the attack, placed under custodians all properties of British and French citizens, and that of "internees, suspects and other persons or organizations." In January, further decrees ordered all foreign banks, insurance companies and sales agencies to become Egyptian limited companies within five years. "Enemy" concerns were to Egyptianize immediately. Thus some sixty-four insurance companies, including Lloyds of London in Egypt, were taken over. The total value of the French and British property affected was estimated to be in the neighborhood of $500,000,000.

ECONOMIC PLANNING

Simultaneously the government set up the Economic Organization to take over sequestered property not purchased by Egyptians. By May, the Economic Organization had received from the custodians shares in a wide variety of formerly foreign-owned plants. Today the Organization, which has since become the Economic Corporation, is active in pharmaceutical, banking, insurance, mineral and oil exploitation, fertilizer, cement, tire, textile, paper, sugar, importing, exporting and shipping businesses. As a result of the Corporation's activities, it has become possible for the government to direct the movement of finance, facilitate and control credit, encourage investments and savings, control national imports and exports, and widen its influence in numerous private industrial and agricultural companies which are dependent in various degrees upon the government-operated firms.

The activities of the Economic Corporation did not develop out of an overall plan, nor were they the result of an ideological or theoretical approach to relationships between government and business. The organization sprang up almost overnight as a practical method of coping with circumstances which are not foreseen.

The revolutionary government's attitude toward capital and labor has also evolved as a result of circumstances. Initially there was a desire to work closely and on friendly terms with capitalists, but since 1952 relations between private businessmen and the young officers have frequently been strained. The capitalists were often reluctant to invest in "productive" enterprises with the result that the army has increasingly attempted to "guide" them along "progressive" lines. Nasser's attitude toward capitalists was expressed in a talk with the US socialist Norman Thomas in November 1957. There is only one productive capitalist in Egypt, the President stated. That was Ahmed Abboud, the nation's leading industrialist. "All the others are speculators."

The President's reaction to speculators was expressed in a speech to an annual cooperative conference in 1956. These "men of substance," he announced, "are only interested in building luxurious apartment buildings which they rent at exorbitant rates—they are not interested in building apartment houses for the middle class or the working class."

The relationship of government to business would be to "guide it with the intent of promoting the social interest and to prevent capitalism from exploiting both the individual and the society." The state would participate with the people "because it has trusteeship over the people. This trusteeship is aimed at protecting small capitalists and small savers from other capitalists."

PATERNALISM

Labor unions in Egypt today are under government control and supervision. Strikes are unlikely unless approved by the government, as were those of the various labor syndicates which supported Nasser in the conflict with General Neguib in 1954. Then the strike was organized for a political purpose by the

RCC-controlled Liberation Rally, and had nothing to do with wages or labor conditions. In 1957 the government created a large federation bringing some 250,000 members of the loosely organized labor movement under direct supervision of the Minister of Social and Labor Affairs, Colonel Hussein Shafei. The stated objective of the new organization was to "direct the activities of the labor syndicates and to protect the principles and philosophy of the Revolution."

The cooperative aspect of the Egyptian Revolution has been one of its most successful. Greatest progress has been made in rural rather than urban cooperation. Even before July 1952, Egypt was in the vanguard of the Arab cooperative movement which began there before World War I. By the eve of the Revolution, there were 2,103 societies with nearly 750,000 members. Within three years an additional 480 societies were formed with 120,000 new members. Legislation regulating the movement has been progressive, and attempts to implement it have been effective in contrast to other social measures, such as those regulating minimum agricultural wages and maximum land rents.

One of the most important provisions of the agrarian reform was the establishment of cooperatives which each peasant who received land must join. The agrarian-reform cooperatives and their managers have in effect replaced the former landlords and their agents in villages where land was subdivided. The farmers look to the government officials not only for agricultural advice and guidance, but for direction on political and social matters as well. In many cases, the new cooperatives are the only direct link between the regime in Cairo and the peasants. It is they who transmit the ideas and ideals of the Revolution to the grass roots.

By mid-1958 there were 272 agrarian-reform cooperatives with 82,000 members. They offered about £E5,000,000 [Egyptian pounds] worth of agricultural services. In addition to organizing the cultivation and exploitation of the subdivided estates and marketing their crops, the co-ops offer a wide variety of other services. Agricultural supplies, seeds, fertilizers and machinery can be purchased through them. They grant loans from funds obtained through the Agricultural and Cooperative Credit Bank. Recently they began to experiment in cooperative rural housing.

When the cooperatives were first organized in land-reform

areas, it was difficult to convince farmers to turn over their crops. But when they discovered that their produce was sold at better prices through the cooperatives, they welcomed the new organizations.

THE POPULATION PROBLEM

No doctrine or ideology has been able to answer Egypt's most pressing problem—the population explosion. At present, the more than 23,000,000 Egyptians are supported on an area of approximately 6,000,000 acres, making Egypt among the most densely populated nations. Its vital statistics—birth, death and disease rates—compare with those in prewar India and China. Population is continuing to outstrip the meager resources available to sustain it. Instead of rising, the nation's standard of living has been in a constant downward spiral for decades. Although productivity has increased, it has not done so at a rate anywhere nearly as rapid as necessary to sustain even the present abysmally low standard of living. So far, there is no answer to the problem either within Egypt's borders or beyond. It plagues the country's leaders, who are keenly aware of the urgent dilemmas it presents.

A variety of proposals have been presented, but no comprehensive plan has yet crystallized to cope with the problem. At present, emphasis is on increasing national production, and the cornerstone of such a program is the Aswan High Dam. It has been estimated that successful completion of the project would enable the country to increase its agricultural production by about a third and to multiply its industrial potential several times. Yet within the score of years required to complete the project, it would just barely enable the economy to keep up present living standards for the increasing population.

To help with plans for national development, President Nasser has set up a number of advisory councils in which are concentrated the country's best civilian technicians. They are charged with formulating long-term plans to increase productivity, rationalize industry, and coordinate national resources. Although they have put forward a five-year plan, it does not compare in its scope with similar projects in India or China. The first five-year plan was merely a pilot program to determine long-term project needs.

At this point in its history, it is still too early to determine the future course of the Egyptian Revolution. The number of variable factors, both within the newly formed UAR and on the world scene, which can effect the outcome is so large that only pseudo-social science can speculate about the future. Scientific innovations such as distillation of sea water, solar energy, atomic power, and better birth control methods may change the area's whole pattern of economic productivity and demography.

The present thinking of the dynamic, youthful new nationalism is still so inchoate and in such a state of flux that it could be influenced constructively by evocative western political thought in its search for a democratic society suitable to its own social structure and environment. On the other hand, the new nationalism could produce a Peronist corporative-type state in which there is greater concentration of power in the hands of a totalitarian military clique influenced by admiration for sheer physical power.

In most modern revolutions which aspire to reconstruct the social and economic framework of society, permanent positive accomplishment is difficult. It often takes decades before the negative phases of the revolution—the uprooting of anachronistic political and social forms—are achieved and progress is made in building society anew. In Egypt, the negative political phases of the Revolution have been accomplished. The old regime which based its political power on great landholdings has been irrevocably destroyed, and the Egyptian peasant and urban laborer now have a self-respect which they never had before.

The question now is whether or not the leaders of the Revolution will be able to galvanize intellectuals, students, the professional classes, progressive capitalists, and most important of all, the fellah of the Nile Valley for the constructive work and the great sacrifice required if Egypt is to cope with its internal problems, which at this point in history seem almost insurmountable. Will President Nasser be able to organize the nation's meager resources and scarce technical and administrative abilities for the best possible use? Will he be able to evolve a doctrine suitable to the outlook of the Egyptian masses which will guide the Revolution along those paths which he and those who made the Revolution so desire?

2. The Crisis in Nasser's Egypt

BY ANOUAR ABDEL-MALEK

DURING SEPTEMBER 1966, there was a significant governmental shift in Egypt. Zakariyya Mohieddin, for long the regime's strong man, was replaced by a colonel of engineers, Sidky Soliman, who had for several years been Minister responsible for the Aswan High Dam. Interpretations of this shift differed; but in any case, the transition was cut short. After a period of mounting tension on the Arab frontiers in the spring of 1967, Israel launched an all-out war, bombing airfields in Egypt, Syria, Jordan and Iraq, and capturing within a week the West Bank of Jordan, Sinai, Jerusalem and the Golan Heights. The overall consequences of this crushing military defeat are not yet fully manifest. But as far as Egypt is concerned, it constitutes a major crisis in the development of the nation.

To situate these events and determine their exact nature, some accurate study has to be made of the role of the army in Egyptian political life since the Free Officers organization seized power in the early hours of July 23, 1952. The word "political" is to be understood literally: involving every aspect of policy throughout the entire country, and not merely in the limited sense of the struggle for power and the various vicissitudes which inevitably accompany this in every country at any epoch.

I. INDEPENDENCE

First we must be clear about what the Egyptian army was in

Reprinted from *New Left Review*, No. 45 (London, 1967), pp. 67–81; by permission of the editor.

1952. Unlike almost all the other armies in the so-called Third World, it was a *national army*, historically allied to the national movement—in the revolution of 1881–82, which broke out with a military insurrection by the entire army led by Colonel Ahmed Arabi and his comrades; in the Secret Organization of the Wafd, which was the work of radical patriotic officers led by Colonel Abdel Rahman Fahmi (1919–23); in the passive resistance on the part of the army against British pressures during the Second World War; in the participation by the military in the guerrilla committees *(fida'iyyin)* against the British base in the Suez Canal Zone (1950–51); in the Palestine war (1948–49); and finally, from 1948 onwards, in the setting up of the clandestine Free Officers organization which took power on July 23, 1952.[1]

Right from the start of the British occupation in 1882, the Sepoy forces repressing the national movement were concentrated in the police, and particularly in its two active branches, the political and the criminal police. The army was held in reserve, neutralized because practically unarmed, though a support for the regime. It was linked to the Occupation-Palace coalition by the privileges granted the officer corps, entry to which was confined to the sons of the elite until 1936 when the Wafd widened entry to include the sons of the middle classes and the petite bourgeoisie. The army was ineffective—indeed it was deliberately made ineffective by the coalition in power. Yet it was attuned to the "national elite," and from 1936 onwards, very close to the populist and radical trends which sprang up at almost every point in the spectrum of the Egyptian national movement.

The army was in the first place an officer corps, where the Free Officers were recruited. The officer corps was at the time composed of two groups: the sons of the propertied classes (in particular the landowning aristocracy) on the one hand, and members of the middle classes and the petite bourgeoisie on the other. The first group made up the whole of the General Staff and the great majority of the higher officers; the second group, naturally, made up the mass of the officers on active service, as well as the elite of the young officers at General Staff Headquarters who by 1952 had reached the rank of major, lieutenant colonel, or in very rare cases, even colonel. But there was also the British influence, manifested in the extraordinary importance given to NCO's. Their specific weight was enormous in the years preceding the 1952 coup, and many of them later joined Communist organizations or the Muslim Brothers. After the coup they were relegated to the role of mere agents; they were not institutionally part of the Free Officers organization, which was confined exclusively to officers. As for the troops, until 1952 they were mainly *fellahin* and poor townsfolk who could not afford the money to buy themselves off military service; to a certain extent they were an army of the poor, a mass which was bound to respond *en bloc*, as in 1881–82, to the call of their leaders.

Initially the Free Officers worked with the technocratic help of the industrial big bourgeoisie—the leading agents of the Egyptian Federation of Industry and the Misr group, all those who had been the least affected by the liberal democratic ideology of the Wafd at the time. However, lacking any real program, the Free Officers merely upheld "six principles":

(1) Faced with the British armies stationed in the Suez Canal Zone, the first principle was to liquidate colonialism and the Egyptian traitors supporting it.

(2) Faced with the despotism of feudalism which ruled arbitrarily over vast territories, the second principle was to liquidate feudalism.

(3) Faced with an attempt to exploit the Revolution's sources of energy in the interests of a group of capitalists, the third principle was to put an end to the domination of capital over the government.

(4) Faced with exploitation and despotism, which were the inevitable consequence of all that had gone before, the fourth principle was to install social equity.

(5) Faced with the plots aimed at weakening the army and utilizing what little force it had left to threaten the domestic front, which was ready to revolt, the fifth principle was to set up a powerful national army.

(6) Faced with crooked politics which deformed national realities, the sixth principle was to establish a sound democratic life.[2]

The problem was how to put through such a program with political groups which had done their best for the past thirty years to smash the majority party, the Wafd, by alternately allying with the occupying power and the palace, or more often with both together.

"Realists" like Ali Maher could, of course, "understand" points (5) and (6), and numerous reformists were quite happy to accept the utterly theoretical notion of "social equity" (principle 4). However, there was a real problem with the first three principles. Application of the principle of liquidating colonialism and the Egyptian traitors who supported it surely meant breaking with these political groups, even those which had backed the new regime for a while.

Early illusions had swiftly to be abandoned. The defection of short-lived allies, backward-looking or "modernist," culminated in a crisis in the spring of 1954. Now confronted by a heterogeneous coalition embracing the right, the left and the Wafd—the latter two forces pressing for the restoration of parliamentarianism—the Free Officer group decided to monopolize state power. General Muhammad Neguib was displaced, as were Colonel Abdel-Moneim Abdel-Raouf, the representative of the Muslim Brothers on the Revolutionary Council, Colonels Yussef Sadiq and Ahmed Shawki, and Major Khaled Mohieddin, who represented the left. Less than two years after the *coup d'état*, Lieutenant Colonel Jamal Abd al-Nasser, combining the offices of President of the Revolutionary Steering Committee and President of the Council of Ministers of the Republic, had emerged as unchallenged leader of the Egyptian National Revolution. At this point, the dominating consideration for the national movement was the evacuation from Egyptian territory of the British occupation troops—80,000 men highly equipped—who were concentrated in the Suez Canal base. From spring 1953 to October 1954, guerrilla attacks and negotiations succeeded one another in an effort to dislodge the British; finally, an Anglo-Egyptian treaty providing for the evacuation of the base was signed on October 19, 1954.[3]

With this obstacle overcome, efforts could now be focused on the promotion of an industrial revolution; an appeal for foreign capital investments; repeated invitations to the Egyptian bourgeoisie; the floating of five domestic loans between 1954 and 1956, and so on. But the redirection of capital toward industrialization met with many difficulties. The preference of the landholding aristocracy (i.e. the agrarian wing of the upper bourgeoisie), following the first agrarian reform of 1952, was property investments, not the creation of new industries.[4]

However, it was urgent that some advance be made. So the government, following the advice of technocratic ministers, notably Drs. Abdel-Jelil al-Amari and Abdel-Moneim al-Kaissouni, and of the Egyptian Federation of Industry, made approaches to the United States and the International Bank. The objectives were to obtain both the military equipment necessary for the modernization of the Egyptian armed forces and also credits for the construction of the Aswan High Dam. This project occupied an important place in the thinking of the military rulers; it would simultaneously permit an expansion by one third of the area of cultivable land, and above all, provide the power needed for the creation of a heavy industrial base for the economy. The outcome is well known: the creation of the Baghdad Pact (November 1954), the supervision of the Egyptian budget by the World Bank, and a ban on further borrowing in accordance with the "preconditions" of Eugene Black; finally, the sudden *volte-face* by John Foster Dulles, who announced on July 19, 1956, that the USA would not participate in the financing of the Aswan High Dam, a decision followed the next day by Britain. The nationalization of the Suez Canal Company on July 26, 1956, was utilized as an alibi for the military action against Egypt between October 29 and November 6, when the combined pressure of international opinion, the action of the Soviet Union and the mediation of the United States put a stop to the military operations. On December 22, Port Said was evacuated.

We may summarize the political action of the officer corps in this first phase in the following way:

(1) Complete seizure of the state apparatus (armed forces, police, prisions, and in lesser degree, the courts) from the very first hours of the *coup d'état*. It was then that Jamal Abd al-Nasser became Minister of the Interior and that Colonel Zakariyya Mohieddin took over both the political police and the intelligence services, thus inaugurating his long proconsulate of the state and repressive machinery.

(2) Formulation of the elements of a radical national program, whose economic and social constituents remained sketchy at this stage, the main accent being put on the objective of independence and the reconstitution of a sovereign state endowed with genuine autonomous power.

(3) However, considerable ambiguity and imprecision were evident in the definition of an overall political line, both internally and in foreign relations. This has been variously attributed either to the political inexperience of the new leadership or to their machiavellianism. Both elements were involved, though it is difficult to assess which predominated.

(4) Important shifts in the structure of political power and decision-making as a result of two new elements: the hegemony exercised by the Executive Council of the Revolution, the real center of political life, and the creation on January 23, 1953, of the first unified political party, named the Congress of Liberation, of which Jamal Abd al-Nasser was named Secretary General on February 6.

II. SOCIAL POLICY AND IDEOLOGY

From the outset, the Suez affair conferred on the state and military regime considerable economic resources. The banks, companies and foreign enterprises nationalized in reprisal now joined the banks and insurance companies with foreign majority shareholdings which were "Egyptianized." This whole complex was placed under the Economic Board, the first link in what was to be the public sector of the economy, whose activity, along with that of the whole Egyptian economy, was to be oriented by a Higher National Planning Committee. From January 13, 1957, when these two organs were set up, until the summer and autumn of 1961, the government tried to interest the big combines of Misr and Abboud in the program of industrial development. A second single party, the National Union was created on May 28, 1957, as a preliminary to the legislative elections for the first National Council; and the results of this election, announced on July 15, gave considerable room to the various sections of the bourgeoisie. Again, the unification of Syria and Egypt within the United Arab Republic on February 1, 1958, provided a very profitable and advantageous zone of operations in the new Northern Province for the big bourgeoisie allied to the State Economic Board.

Nevertheless, this alliance was in crisis. The reason was that while the Free Officers were anxious to have the industrial and financial wing of the big bourgeoisie in Egypt involved in the gains of economic expansion, they were not prepared for any sharing of the key decision-making powers. Despite the repression of the left launched during the autumn of 1952 at Kafr-el-Dawar, continued in the period 1954–56, and intensified from January 1, 1959; despite the muzzling of the trade-union movement; despite the economic profits from "positive neutralism" for the country as a whole; despite the expansion of the market, and consequently of profits, to Arab dimensions—despite all these facts, state control of financing and of the distribution of dividends worried the Egyptian bourgeois class. For while it was ideed associated with power on the parliamentary plane, it was scarcely consulted in the exercise of political decision-making. The major representatives of the bourgeoisie challenged the central thesis of the Five Year Plan (August 2, 1960) which aimed at "doubling national revenue in ten years." The political leadership, on its side, could not afford any slowdown, given the demographic upsurge and the exigencies of national construction. On February 11, 1960, the National Bank of Egypt and the Misr Bank were nationalized, and the aftermath showed clearly that what remained of the bourgeoisie's powers of decision in the economic and social field was now being withdrawn and power finally concentrated in the hands of the military leadership.

The decisive blows were contained in a long series of laws (June to September 1961) which nationalized the major heavy and medium industries, key elements of foreign trade, all banks, insurance companies, shipping companies and major public-transport businesses. Agrarian real estate, domestic trade and small-scale industry were left in the hands of the bourgeoisie.

All this took place against a background of crisis; on the one hand, a crisis in the communist and Marxist left, "guilty" of rejecting Arab unity in its nonfederal and centralizing form—a rejection implicitly adopted by Jamal Abd al-Nasser in his self-criticism of October 16, 1961, after the breakup of the UAR, and formulated by him repeatedly in various ways since that date. This tragic crisis of the left crippled a movement which since the Second World War had won over the central core of the Egyptian intelligentsia and trade-union movement. Its crisis merged into the "crisis of the intellectuals" (1961), guilty, by implicit solidarity with the left, of failing to provide the regime with its ideology and social philosophy. Finally, a crisis within the state power itself, since the UAR was itself to disintegrate on September 28, 1961, at the initiative of the Syrian army and political forces which had themselves demanded of the union three and a half years earlier.[5]

The whole problem of the search for a specific ideology is beyond the scope of this essay. The key factor to bear in mind is that the military leadership had somehow or other to synthesize "Islamic fundamentalism" in its radical variant, that is, hostile to the ideology of the Muslim Brothers, with the principles of freedom and social justice which derived from the revolutionary tradition of the industrial era. This ideology was to be in turn defined as "democratic and cooperativist socialism," "Arab socialism," even "Muslim" socialism, and finally, but only in the Charter of National Action (May 1962), as "scientific socialism." [6]

We can now sum up the political action of the officer corps during this second phase in the following terms:

a. conquest of the totality of political power of decision, and not merely the control of the state apparatus;

b. assertion of hegemony over decision-making in the economic, social and ideological fields, accompanied by a tighter grip on the whole of public life;

c. a striking retrenchment in the conception of political alliances, notably a rupture in the front with the industrial and banking sectors of the upper bourgeoisie which had long been maintained at any cost;

d. confrontation with the communist and Marxist left with the objective of reducing it psychologically and politically, and then, in the second repressive wave, of destroying its organization and cadres. By this act, the state and its military leadership were left alone to face the only political force which had been tolerated by the regime since 1954: the Muslim Brothers, with their anachronistic ideology and their "secret organization," which was geared to direct action.

III. FROM THE "NATIONAL" REVOLUTION TO THE "SOCIAL" REVOLUTION

The breakup of the UAR in October 1961 was the prelude to a general overhaul. The governing center was henceforth Egypt. Its problems were to be set within the context of the Arab world (shortly to be differentiated by President Nasser into reactionary and revolutionary states), of the African continent and, more generally, of the Afro-Asian and Tricontinental Conferences.

The National Congress of Popular Forces, which met through-out the spring of 1962, drew up a Charter of National Action, which was promulgated on June 30, 1962. The document has ten sections, of which several are worthy of attention. The second section, "On the Necessity of the Revolution," defines its objectives as "freedom, socialism and unity." Sections 3 and 4 for the first time since 1952 examine "The Roots of the Egyptian Struggle," and then "The Study of The Regression." The national history of modern Egypt, from Mohamed Ali to the Wafd, re-emerges, still strongly tinged by the subjectivist interpretations of the military leadership; but at least not placed under a ban of silence as before. But it is Section 6, "On the necessity of a Socialist Solution," which shows up the pragmatic character of the political line adopted by the military rulers, graduated as it were "ineluctably" to socialism:

> Socialism is the path to social liberty . . . Socialism's solution to Egypt's economic and social underdevelopment is a revolutionary march towards progress. It does not constitute a hypothesis based on a detailed choice, but is rather an ineluctable historical fact dictated by reality, by the great hopes of the peoples and the unstable nature of the world in the second half of the twentieth century . . . Scientific socialism is the form which is suited to the realization of a real plan to ensure progress . . . One can reach (socialism) through two processes:

> 1. Creation of an efficient public sector, to direct progress in all domains and above all the development plan.

> 2. The existence of a private sector which contributes to development, within the overall plan, devoid of any inclination towards exploitation.

> But the two sectors must be controlled and dominated by the people . . . . Socialist planning is the sole means of guaranteeing exploitation of all resources, material, natural and human.[7]

The National Union was dissolved on the grounds that it had been "taken over by reaction," and was replaced by the new single party, the Arab Socialist Union, whose leading core was a "political organization" of cadres. At the same time, Muhammad Hassanein Haykal, editor of *Al-Ahram*, defined the role of the army within the framework of the "new socio-political theory." The revolutionary movement of the people could not but lean upon the army to clear the path of the revolution. In this he resumed the thesis of Jamal Abd al-Nasser: "We do not want politicians in the ranks of the army. But the army as a whole itself constitutes a force within the national political process." [8]

To this end Jamal Abd al-Nasser, who now combined supreme power in his dual capacity as President of the Republic and President of the Executive Committee of the Arab Socialist Union, divided the military cadres into two categories:

(1) Officers in political activity. They had to quit their uniforms and abandon all prerogatives of rank, but in return received key posts in the state providing: the very great majority of senior diplomatic personnel; a considerable proportion of presidents, directors and members of the boards of public corporations, etc; a very considerable number of ministers, undersecretaries of state, director generals and directors of the various ministries; the quasi-totality of the senior personnel and administration of the security services; and a very significant proportion of the key posts in culture, the press, radio and television.

(2) Officers continuing their military career. These were to receive training far superior to that prevailing before 1952: creation of an Institute of Higher Studies of National Defense and of a military polytechnic faculty; creation of a new rank, that of *fariq awwal* (army general) following the Yemeni War—permitting a considerable increase in promotions to the ranks of brigade general, division general and general of army corps—in other words, an inflation of the caste of generals. The corps of staff officers were to be given greater weight in military and political decisions, and the better qualifications of senior officers were to make them into a group of technocratic cadres capable of challenging their civilian counterparts quite effectively.

Progressively, the role of the officer corps has become more clearly defined, exactly along the lines envisaged by some of the activist wing of the old Free Officers organization. Not only the highest state position, in the person of the President of the Republic, but also the whole of the overall direction of the state apparatus (notably the Ministries of War and of the Interior) and of the government is in military hands. In the government of Sidki Soliman, which was installed on September 10, 1966, the Prime Minister himself was an engineering colonel of great competence, three of the four vice-presidents of the Council were senior engineering General Staff officers (Abdel-Mohsen Aboul Nour, Mahmoud Yunes and Sarwat Okasha, who was also a Doctor in Literature from the Sorbonne), and the fourth, Dr. Mahmoud Fawzi (Foreign Affairs) had a counterpart on the strictly ministerial plane—another officer, Mahmoud Riad. Half the Council of Ministers was composed of senior and staff officers. Furthermore, this domination and control over the power of decision extended to the key area of the public sector and of the two linked zones of culture and information.

The principal characteristic of the reshuffle installing the Sidki Soliman government lay in the fact that, for the first time since the seizure of power in 1952, it was the *radical wing* of the Free Officer group and of the attached civilian cadres which obtained governmental power, once the pro-Western superministers were dislodged (A.M. al-Kaissouni for Economics and Finance; Abdel-Qader Hatem, Culture and Information; A. Sharabassi, Social and Religious Affairs, etc). Certainly several ministers representing this tendency kept their place. But the center of decision—at the governmental level—shifted into the hands of a new group. "At the governmental level"—a necessary qualification because state power remained the apanage of the President of the Republic.

Furthermore, the Arab Socialist Union itself, conceived as the crucible of all socialist forces,[9] was basically run by dominant members of the officer corps, former members of the old Council of the Revolution or simply functionaries in the ruling politico-military apparatus. Out of an executive committee of one hundred, it is possible to discover two who belonged to the "historical" noncommunist left. All the others have been named by the ruling nucleus of officers, in particular by Ali Sabry, the current secretary general, the leading proponent of a dialogue with the West and notably with the Americans in 1952. Sabry has been radically opposed to any alliance with the Marxists, and it was he who succeeded in isolating the chief representative of the left current of Nasserite socialism, Kamal Eddin Rifaat, member of the Secretariat for Ideological Affairs, while Major Khaled Mohieddin was restricted to the Movement for Peace. This tendency naturally reproduced itself at all levels in provincial and urban committees, section committees, committees at cell or base level, and so on; but it has been the leading committees which experienced to the greatest extent this invasion of the military into the political process.

Everything proceeded as if the political cadres drawn from the military were applying to their civilian opposites the rule which the state leadership applied to the Marxist left: "Collaborate with them, absorb them, but at all costs keep every decision-making power in our own hands." On the political level, the Arab Socialist Union, unwieldy and inflated (five million members out of thirty million population), is inevitably afflicted by paralysis, given its lack of cadres and effective powers, since communists, Marxists and socialists historically known as such have been pushed aside. Elsewhere, in the other domains of public life, the domination of political elements from the officer corps has generally made for greater efficiency (Suez Canal Company, Aswan High Dam), although it remains difficult to predict the long-term effects this structure of management may have on social life.

In the last analysis, *everything* in Egypt will depend on the creation of a genuinely popular socialist party, equipped not only with proper means of action but also with the power of critical reflection—not just in the cultural and aesthetic field but above all in the domain of social science and political theory.

There are numerous examples to prompt thought. Most notably, that of Ataturk. In Turkey, a national revolution precipitated by an independence war which lasted four years and mobilized an entire nation with millenial traditions around new slogans of liberty, modernity and renaissance, nevertheless was less than a generation later caught in the vice of religious reaction—pushed back but still tolerated and, in fact, deeply entrenched in the countryside—and of the bureaucracy, but above all of the military apparatus itself, resolutely hostile to any further social transformation. The renovation set in motion by Ataturk affected culture and daily life in the countryside, but without any ulterior socialist project. This process was halted in the absence of any effective instruments for mobilizing the people around the military leader and national hero.[10] Evidently, there is a critical difference, that of the epochs themselves, as the Charter notes, with regard to the espousal of socialism. Yet the *central* problem is identical: How can the "national" revolution be transformed into a "social" revolution? How can the social dialectic be renewed, both at the level of ideas and of practice?

In Egypt, the process of national revolution has attained the most advanced stage experienced in the present history of the "Three Continents." Its originality resides basically in its initiation of a genuine and deep transformation of the economic and social structure of the country, including the countryside. To effect this transformation, two instruments have been deployed: first, the officer corps, "this national radical and inter-sectoral force," [11] whose social roots lie in the petite bourgeoisie, and which has converted itself, along with its fringe of technocratic personnel, into a new class—at least in the socio-political, rather than economic, sense of the term. Secondly, an empirical and dirigiste ideology has been developed, reinforcing the ancient traditions of Egyptian pyramidal centralism, endowed with the label of socialism.[12]

The critical factor—namely, the "popular masses" in whose name all this functions—still remain distanced from the political power of decision, even if called on as a participant in the discussion. The fact is that the process of transformation of social life now makes possible a rapid and genuine takeoff, not merely on the "developmental" plane, but in the creation of a socialism which is authentically Egyptian in style and form. Hence the coordinated resistance from the governing apparatus and the bureaucracy—the ruling class, in short. Egypt's multiple problems and their inevitable consequences stem from this situation.

At present, solutions are still being sought within the old framework: via state action, through the apparatus and the administration—and through a party which exercises no real power. The Soliman regime which came to power in autumn 1966 was on the whole adapted technically and, to some extent, politically to operate this transition.

THE WAR AND ITS CONSEQUENCES

On the morning of June 5, 1967, Israel launched a war against the Arab countries and obtained a lightning military victory. No doubt we will have to wait for some time to learn the true details of this campaign, in particular the exact role of the Sixth Fleet, and more generally the extent of strategic and logistic support given by the United States and, in a more limited if still effective way, by other Western countries.[13]

For our purposes it is useful to situate this somewhat dazzling military aspect within the wider setting of political and sociological analysis. The September 1966 Cabinet revealed very clearly to the ruling groups that Jamal Abd al-Nasser was determined to promote radicalization of the Egyptian national revolution—without, however, establishing the indispensable vehicle for this: an instrument of reflection, organization, mobilization and execution that was committed to socialism. It is from this point that there began to take shape a process which it may soon be possible to call a conspiracy of generals and elements of the "new class" against the independent national state. The general line is clear enough: to urge on Jamal Abd al-Nasser, as in the period 1958–61, policies that would carry him down the slope, to overextend his resources on all frontiers of the Arab revolution, from Syria to Yemen. Then, when the inevitable confrontation with the United States materialized,[14] whether directly or through an incident with Israel, the object was to immobilize the military striking force, notably the air force, so as to break Nasser, the soldier who had aspired to be what his people demanded, the leader of an Egyptian revolution. In the moment of defeat, a rightist pro-imperialist coalition could be installed, supported by or allied to the Muslim Brothers; the massed financial, economic and diplomatic assistance of the United States would be sought, after the denunciation of the whole Nasserite strategy for compromising Egypt's future by allying her too closely with the wrong power, the Soviet Union; and the "liberation" of Sinai could be obtained to cover the campaign against the left, a halt to nationalizations, and the return of the privileged.

By Friday, June 9, this whole scenario seemed to be coming true: While Jamal Abd al-Nasser was making his dramatic speech announcing his resignation and naming Zakariyya Mohieddin as his successor, batteries of anti-aircraft guns lit up the

Cairo sky to discourage demonstrations, and several hundred members of the paramilitary formations of the Arab Socialist Youth were sent into action against the Soviet embassy by Dr. Hussein Kamal Baha, secretary of the Youth and right hand of Ali Sabry.

However, simultaneously, the Egyptian people made a counterattack: The whole population of Cairo and vast masses of people from other towns, such as Port Said and Tanta, marched to join the demonstrations in the capital; all the cities and smaller towns were in turmoil throughout the night [15] until the next morning, when the apparatus was compelled to announce Nasser's decision to remain at his post "until the elimination of the consequences of aggression."

Thus the political objective—the overthrow of the Nasserite regime and the ensuing removal of the Syrian regime—was not achieved. Analysis of the present conjuncture enables us to highlight the key elements in the struggle that is a consequence of the aggression:

> a. The pretension of the *army*, as a corporate force, to occupy a hegemonic position in Egyptian politics is now profoundly rejected by all popular classes and groups. In his July 23 speech, Jamal Abd al-Nasser gave indications that the whole High Command, notably the Commander in Chief of the air force, refused to follow political directives. At the same time, however, he made a balanced and firm rehabilitation of the people's army; the aim was to try to rally the middle and lower cadres against the generals, and to reconcile them with popular feeling as a whole.

> b. The *apparatus* has been deeply shaken. Its military wing is thoroughly discredited and now undergoing a complete reorganization. Its political wing—which is much more important (influence of Salah Nasr)—seems to have opted for the maintenance of the status quo; but as already mentioned, there are active influences working for an opening to the right. The ex-War Minister, Shams Eddin Badran—who was responsible for the exclusion of all the officers trained in the Soviet Union from operational commands (given instead to "safe" officers, whose loyalty was secured by favors received . . .)—was replaced first by A. W. al-Bishri, then, on July 21—two days prior to the speech

marking President Nasser's apparent personal takeover—by Amin Hameh Houweidi, whose task is to reestablish the political loyalty of the armed forces. At the same time, another ascendant name is that of Abdel-Mohsen Aboul Nour: Minister for Agrarian Reform (after having been one of the vice-premiers in the Cabinet of September 1966), he was named commandant of the Popular Resistance movement (June 21), then assistant secretary general of the Arab Socialist Union (July 9), the secretary general no longer being Ali Sabry, but the President of the Republic himself.

c. The *party* is incapable of functioning, according to the best qualified observers. A new central committee has to be chosen, and its precise composition will enable some assessment of the position of the left in the leadership of a party which aims to be socialist. But in any event, it is hard to see how the center of gravity of state power can be shifted from the ruling apparatus, which has evolved in the direction of a markedly anti-Marxist nationalitarian ideology, toward a socialist party led by socialist cadres. The party organization installed by Ali Sabry at present remains in place: functionless local organizations; a "political organization" (cadres) whose time is spent in discussion and the drawing up of reports; the paramilitary Arab Socialist Youth Organization, some 300,000 youths trained for street action, and the real tool of Ali Sabry, who publicly declared his differences of view with the theses of Abd al-Nasser in April 1967.[16]

d. The *government* which was formed on June 19 appears to be a right center formation: The leading position is given to Zakariyya Mohieddin; A.-M. al-Kaissouni, the most competent of the liberal technocrats, has returned. But real power is elsewhere in any case.

e. The *popular masses,* whose action on June 7 and 8 was decisive not only in keeping Jamal Abd al-Nasser in power but also in imposing the establishment under his authority of an armed people's resistance organization, have now been neutralized by the apparatus. Instead of forming popular militias which could protect the country, back up the political power against any plots, and in so doing promote the advance of new political cadres from the base, the

apparatus—led directly by Zakariyya Mohieddin—refused to
distribute arms, except in a grudging way to certain key
factories at night. The presidential address of July 23 stated
that the country did not have the means to arm the people.
From this witholding of arms, to demobilization, to disaffection—the way has been opened for a consolidation of
the rightist apparatus, neutralization of the radical and
left-wing tendency, and ultimately for a renewal of the
political operation checked *in extremis* by popular action
on June 7–8.

The kernel of the crisis which affects the Egyptian national
revolution and inhibits its development may now be formulated
in two propositions:

*(1) It is impossible to build a modern state in the absence
of a "political class" in the Gramscian sense of the term;
yet this is precisely what the military regime has been concerned to eliminate since 1952.*
*(2) It is impossible to initiate a socialist revolution and to
build a popular state in the absence of socialists, without a
mobilization of the popular masses, rural and urban, and
the revolutionary intelligentsia; certainly not by relying on
a political apparatus committed to a fight against the left,
and by that fact open to all forms of penetration.*

To speak of "renewal" after the discrediting of the military
leadership means little—unless its content is specified in the
sense mentioned. But the most important thing to recognize is
that the thesis which explains everything in terms of the retardation and lack of development of Egyptian economy, society
and technology is *fundamentally* erroneous. Vietnam, where the
most modern military machine in the world is bogged down, is
there to prove the contrary. A country that is much more backward in many respects than Egypt can maintain its independence,
can strengthen its position and advance along an authentically
national and socialist path *on condition that* it has a political
force, a genuine political leadership, armed with a radical and
scientific social philosophy wielded boldly and creatively.

Egypt's future is at this price.

3. Syria on the Move:
Ascendancy of the Left Wing

BY WALTER LAQUEUR

RECENT developments in Syria have attracted general attention throughout the world and caused concern both among Syria's neighbors and in the Western capitals. The present article sets out to review the emergence of the new forces in Syria in whose hands political power is now concentrated. Whether they are indeed "left wing" is a moot point; the very title of the present study is a concession to time-honored usage rather than a precise definition. Ever since the appearance of fascism and communism on the international scene, the European political landscape has frequently defied the traditional classification into left, right, and center. In the Middle Eastern context, "left" and "right" are meaningless to an even larger degree. The "left" in the Arab countries opposes the social and political setup at home, favors domestic reforms, combats the "feudal" forces. But it certainly does not conform to the established Western left-wing pattern of radical democracy, humanism, internationalism, and so on. The situation is further complicated by the fact that even the newer totalitarian categories do not exactly apply. The Arab Socialist Renaissance Party, probably the most important political factor in Syria now, used to be called

This article originally appeared in the January 1957 issue of *The World Today* (pp. 17–26), the monthly journal published by the Royal Institute of International Affairs, London. It is reprinted here by permission of the author and editor.

"semi-fascist" by outside observers only a few years back. More recently this party has usually been called "left wing." It has been an oversimplification of a rather complex issue in both cases, and this goes for the assessment of many other political groupings in the Arab world as well.

The rise of "leftist" forces in Syria has to be viewed in the wider context of Syrian domestic politics during the last twenty years, the failure of parliamentary democracy there, the disintegration of the old parties, and an almost permanent economic crisis. When the country gained full political independence in 1944–45, one of the old political parties, the one headed by Dr. Shahbandar up to his assassination, had already ceased to exist as an important political factor. Its rival, the National Bloc, led by Shukri al Quwatly and others, was in power after 1943, but failed to give the country efficient leadership. Torn by factional strife, the party was identified with the rule of individual and economic vested interests and the many affairs of corruption which came to public knowledge. The since defunct Republican Party (founded by Jamil Mardam in 1947) and the People's Party (which came into existence after the fusion of some dissidents from the National Bloc and a group of Aleppo politicians) promised radical changes while in opposition. But after they entered the government, they proved to be no better qualified than their predecessors to provide efficient administration and carry out long-overdue political, social and economic reforms.

From 1949 to 1954, Syria was ruled by military dictators. The Palestine war of 1948 had precipitated these *coups d'état*. But public opinion was, for some time at least, not unsympathetic to the colonels who had taken over the government; it was believed, apparently, that military dictatorship could hardly be worse than the rule of the old discredited parties. Shishakli's regime was overthrown early in 1954, and since then Syria has until very recently been a parliamentary democracy once more. However, the old tensions and the old discontent have not been overcome. During most of this time the country has been ruled by a coalition of the old Nationalists and the People's Party, which, it soon appeared, had not learned much since its debacle in the late forties. As a result, the influence of various leftist oppositionist groups has greatly increased over the last two years: first in the streets of the Syrian cities and among the peasants of certain regions, and later also among the army officer corps and eventually in the government itself.

THE ARAB SOCIALIST RENAISSANCE PARTY

The most interesting of the parties and, in view of its many sympathizers in the Syrian army command, probably the most important at present, is the Arab Socialist Renaissance Party. In view of its close contacts with parties in other Arab countries and its efforts to establish an alliance of Arab socialist parties, its emergence is of more than local significance. It came into being as the result of the merger, in September 1953, of two separate groups, the Arab Renaissance Party (*Al Ba'th*) and the Arab (or Republican) Socialist Party. The history of the Renaissance group goes back to the late 1940's. It was headed by Michel Aflaq (a leading member of the Syrian Communists up to 1943), and its Secretary General was Salah al-Din Bitar, who is now Syrian Foreign Minister. The party was based mainly on a group of young intellectuals in Damascus, Deir az Zur, and a few other centers. It was strongly oppositionist, demanded neutralism in world politics, and stood for a socialist program at home. Aflaq's demands for equality for women and the disestablishment of Islam brought him into sharp conflict with all the authorities. *Al Ba'th* never attained much political importance; in the 1949 elections for parliament only one of its members was elected. The party executive thereupon decided to act as an "educational association" for the propagation of its political theories rather than as a political party. Aflaq himself has not been entirely free from opportunist deviations: he agreed for a time in 1949 to serve as Minister of Education in a "feudal" government, and he promised, under some pressure apparently, to collaborate with Colonel Husni Za'im and later with Shishakli. But on the whole his policy has been based on left-wing principles and not on that expediency which was presumably the cause of the relative failure of his group.

Akram al Hawrani, the head of the Arab Socialists, is a very different type of political leader. A brilliant speaker and dynamic personality, his political career is distinguished by determined efforts to achieve political power rather than by close adherence to socialist (or any other) principles. His party was originally founded as an "anti-feudalist" group of young intellectuals in Hama, his native city, and in Homs, during the winter of 1949–50. His group organized and actively supported the peasant movement in the northern districts of Syria, and from the very beginning took great care to establish close contacts with certain sections of the officer corps. Hawrani also organized small storm troops which frequently clashed with the members of the old parties and the feudal families. In its program everything was promised to everybody: The party was to be "national-socialist-popular-progressive," standing for reforms in all walks of life, raising of the living standard, destruction of feudalism, nationalization of physical resources, and a republican, parliamentary regime. However, when Hawrani's relative, Colonel Shishakli, took over, he became one of the main supporters of military dictatorship and for some time served as Minister of Defense. It was only toward the end of Shishakli's rule that the two quarreled, and for a brief period Hawrani became a political refugee.

After the restoration of the parliamentary regime in 1954, the united party remained at first in opposition. Within the party, Hawrani with his extremist nationalist slogans gained the upper hand over Aflaq, who put the main emphasis on a socialist, reformist program. (There were other points of discord between them: Aflaq, who had some considerable first-hand experience of communism, opposed cooperation with that party, whereas Hawrani, a man of less experience but more ambition, favored close collaboration.) While in opposition the party strengthened its influence among the urban intelligentsia and the students and intensified its "anti-feudal" propaganda among the peasants. It made considerable headway in the elections of September 1954, when sixteen of its members were elected. There is some reason to assume that well-wishers within the officer corps had a hand in this success: the party's election campaign had been financed in part from unspecified army funds. In this campaign the party appeared in favor of Arab unity and as the most rabid anti-Western group, outstripping even the local Communists, who were somewhat impeded by the Moscow "peaceful co-existence" strategy. It also came out as the most militant Arab nationalist party, attacking even Colonel Nasser for compromising with the British over Suez.

Shortly after the elections the party agreed to enter a government coalition with the nationalist right wing. In January 1955 the party council was convened for the first time in several years, and details were given about the establishment of a common leadership of all Arab socialist parties, to be sponsored by the Syrian party. The parties referred to were the Jordan *Ba'th*, the Iraqi National Democrats (now National Congress), and the

Lebanese Progressive Socialists. There have been close relations ever since with the first two, whereas the Lebanese party came gradually to dissociate itself from the nationalist-extremist demands and the pro-Soviet orientation of their Syrian comrades.

Meanwhile the internal tug of war continued: Hawrani insisted that the aim of the party was to gain power with whatever allies it could find on the way, while Aflaq said that the main target should be to propagate the ideals of socialism and Arab nationalism throughout the Middle East. This dissension led to a split in September 1955, when several leading party members and parliamentary deputies, among them Jalal al-Sayyid, secretary of Al Jezira district, left the party. Nevertheless, the growing internal crisis in the country and the mounting tension in the Middle East prevented a general split. Hawrani, never at a loss for a revolutionary slogan at a critical moment, put out a new one: "The establishment of a revolutionary government for the mobilization of all forces for the coming war against Israel." [1] The party tried to absorb the remnants of Shishakli's movement (the Arab Liberation Movement), while its collaboration with the Communists became very close indeed. But above all, its alliance with sections of the army General Staff had by the autumn of 1956 become one of the crucial facts in Syrian domestic politics.

THE COMMUNISTS

The Syrian Communist Party, illegal up to 1954 and semi-legal until recent months, has now come into the open. The party publishes several newspapers of its own (*al-Nur, al-Tali'a,* etc.) and has been behind the publication of several other ostensibly unaffiliated organs (e.g. *al Ra'i al am, Barada*). Its leader, Khaled Bagdash, has been to Egypt and has talked freely about his own and his party's activities. Many details hitherto unknown have been revealed—including even the type of classical music that Bagdash prefers (his favorites are Borodin and Tchaikovsky). Broadly speaking, however, these revelations hardly call for a modification of the general picture of the Syrian Communist Party that had already emerged during the past few years: that of a small but extremely active and well-organized party with a capable leadership, which puts much stress on its patriotic convictions and works largely through a variety of front organizations. Khaled Bagdash has been at great pains to emphasize (in interviews with Egyptian newspapers) that his political biography is not really different from the life and tribulations of any other radical Arab patriot, and he has with rare consistency played down the anti-religious character of his party. He has even blamed the Syrian Socialists for putting undue stress on their anti-clerical opinions at a time when all the efforts should be directed towards the establishment of a wide national front—recalling in this respect the period of the "popular front" in Europe, when the Communists sometimes blamed the Socialists for their over-intransigeance toward Catholic and right-wing parties.

The Syrian Communists met with some setbacks in 1956. Early in the year Bagdash was elected a member of the Foreign Affairs Committee of the Damascus Parliament, but later he was removed in view of certain suspicions on the part of members of the other parties. The Syrian Muslim Brotherhood, which five or six years ago was inclined to be pro-Soviet, has of late become rather anti-Communist. This presumably has something to do with the fact that in 1950 the Communists were not yet a real rival to the Brotherhood, whereas at present their influence in the cities constitutes a serious challenge. On the whole, however, Bagdash has been quite successful in neutralizing public opinion, and the accusations directed against his party (on account of his meetings with Israeli Communist leaders in Moscow, and in view of allegations about "communism being a Jewish invention") have fallen flat.

Indeed, this concentration of anti-Communist propaganda on religious and racial factors may even have helped Syrian communism. Wide sections of the public have thus been led to believe that a Communist is easily recognizable as a man fighting Islam. But as the Syrian Communists profess to be tolerant in this respect, people argue that they are obviously bona fide Arab nationalists rather than real Communists, and so there is no reason to worry about an imaginary "Communist danger" in Syria. Recent declarations made by leading Syrian politicians, denying the existence of any such danger in Syria, have to be explained against this background, which is a direct outcome of the unsuccessful attempt to pin down communism exclusively to the religious issue. It may also be mentioned in passing that the Syrian communists have enlisted the support of quite a number of influential Damascus *ulama* in their front organizations, who are willing and able to defend them against accusations from the Muslim orthodox camp.

During the past years, Communist speakers have drawn the largest crowds at political meetings. The party is also said to have considerable funds at its disposal. It has paid much attention to front organizations such as, for example, the Syrian Students' Union (affiliated to the communist IUS) or the newly founded League of Arab Writers. The contacts between the party leadership and its sympathizers among the officer corps have been less publicized, but during the past year much progress has been made there, too. (Some of the officers originally belonging to the Hawrani wing of the Socialists have apparently been won over by the party. It is of some interest to note that the army High Command "recognized" the Communist Party even before it had been legalized by the government. There was an official exchange of letters between the army High Command and the party leadership after the assassination of Colonel Maliki.[2]) In Arab politics, the Syrian Communists have come out in favor of the Egypt-Syria-Jordan treaty; their stand has been welcomed by the Egyptian press which went to some lengths to demonstrate that though there was no room for a communist party in Egypt herself, it could fulfill a useful function in other Arab countries.

The Syrian Communist Party is now the largest and best organized Communist Party in the Arab world[3] and one of the leading forces in the country. It could not rule the country alone, and short of direct Soviet intervention it does not intend to do so. But as a guide and mentor behind the Socialists, the pro-Soviet elements among the Nationalists and Independents (Khalid al Azm), and above all the army officer corps, it has already decisively influenced the course of events.

THE ARMY

The Syrian officer corps has, with only short interruptions, played a decisive role in Syrian politics throughout the last seven years. Such intervention has taken place at times in many other countries; when other institutions broke down or became discredited, ambitious young soldier-politicians have stepped in with or without invitation. In Syria, as in other Arab countries, the officer corps has shown a passionate interest in politics, though it has hardly ever been united in its purpose. The Syrian army is small: It numbered 10,000 men in 1948, and today has about six brigades with 42,000 men. The few hundred officers with the rank of captain or above who constitute the backbone of the army have quarreled among themselves in the past not only (and perhaps not mainly) on political lines. They have frequently been divided on personal grounds in the struggle for power, and other considerations, such as the interests of the community or clan they represented, have also been important.

The Maliki affair may serve as an illustration of the enormously complicated relations existing between various factions of officers, and between them and the political parties. Adnan al Maliki, Deputy Chief of Staff and a leading supporter of the Socialists in the army, was assassinated early in 1955; the trial of the murderers and their accomplices lasted for many months and became the most important domestic issue. On the face of it, this was just another battle in the struggle between the Socialists and Antun Sa'adah's Syrian Nationalists. But during the trial it appeared that personal reasons were also involved: Maliki had offended several brother officers by not promoting them, and at least one of them, Ghassan Jadid, subsequently sentenced to death *in contumaciam,* became involved in the affair.

The whole maze of relations between various groups of officers, and between them and the parties, is far too complex to be described in detail. Suffice it to mention that Shishakli's overthrow in 1954 was brought about by a junta headed by Colonels Faisal al Atassi and Amin Abu Asaf (a Druze), subsequently joined by Colonel Mahmoud Shawkat, Lieutenant Colonel Omar Kabani, and the Chief of Staff, Shawkat Shuqair. They promised at the time that the army would return to the barracks and cease to meddle in politics. But this interlude did not last for long. A group of young and ambitious officers, friends of Akram al Hawrani and supporters of the Socialists, thought that a far more active role should be played by the army in view of the inefficiency of the parliamentarians. They succeeded in removing many of their rivals and opponents from key positions. The most important of them, the *deuxième bureau,* headed for a long time by Mahmoud Shatra, was taken over by one of this group, Ra'is Hamdani, who in his turn handed it over to the leader of the group, Captain Abdul Hamid Saraj. Saraj brought about the downfall of the Chief of Staff, Shawkat Shuqair, in the summer of 1956. (One of the unofficial reasons given was that Shuqair, a Lebanese by origin, had adopted Syrian nationality only a few years previously and was therefore unacceptable to Syrian patriots.) The new man, Tawfiq Nizam al-Din, was a rather colorless officer without military experience and political ambitions, who had, however, faithfully served the various Syrian regimes during the last decade.

The group headed by Saraj is at present in full control of the Syrian army and, according to most reports, of the country in general. Their political convictions are radical: They want a change in Syrian politics and in the Arab world as a whole, in accordance with the lead given by Colonel Nasser, the Socialists, and the Communists. This radicalism is admittedly of a vague character, and their pro-Nasser, pro-Soviet orientation has less to do with Marxism-Leninism (or any other ideology) than with a general feeling that these are dynamic, purposeful movements which somehow "get things done." Back in the thirties the same officers would almost certainly have become pro-fascist (as so many Iraqi officers did at the time). Their anti-Western attitude has similar reasons: the West stands for the status quo in the Middle East, and has been allied with the "old forces" in Syria, Iraq and Jordan which these officers want to replace. Saraj seems to be firmly in the saddle at present; an attempt by the government to remove him last September by appointing him military attaché in Paris failed. Nevertheless, it would be a mistake to identify Saraj and his junta with the entire Syrian officer corps and the army. The old rivalries, political and private, continue to exist; by the appointment of the Saraj group's own members to key positions, many other officers have been antagonized and would probably be only too eager to square accounts with the present ruling faction. The source of strength of the Saraj junta is its close contacts with important political forces (the Socialists and the Communists) inside the country and, even more, its alliance with Nasser and, of late, the Soviet Union. Previous military juntas in Syria had not such strong international support.

SYRIA ON THE MOVE

Syria has for long been regarded by Soviet observers as the most promising country in the Middle East. Recent events have shown that these hopes have not been misplaced. In view of the news blackout imposed by the Syrian army in early November, it is difficult to assess exactly how close Syria has moved toward Moscow. The news published by the Syrian press and radio since then has been based mostly on the Soviet and Egyptian news agencies. Syrian political leaders have been brought to the microphones of Damascus radio and have declared that the reports about the progressive "satellization" of the country are mere hostile inventions. But the Soviet military buildup in Syria and the Communist propaganda monopoly are obviously not inventions. Nor is it known to what degree the Syrian government continues to be a free agent. According to some observers, it was only to be expected that the growth of Communist and Soviet influence in Syria would be played down, for those behind it are undoubtedly afraid that too sudden a development of this kind would arouse contrary forces in the other Arab countries.

It would be mistaken to attribute in retrospect the growth of Soviet influence in Syria entirely to left-wing activities in that country. Some sections of the right-wing parties have contributed equally, if not more, to the rapprochement with Russia which has now reached its climax. They include Shukri al Quwatli, the President of Syria, who went on a state visit to Moscow in late October 1956, and Sabri al Asali, who tried to ban the publication of news critical of the Soviet Union even before the army introduced political control on the satellite pattern. As far as the right wing is concerned, these were concessions of minor importance made to a restive public opinion. In any case, these forces felt they had no other alternative: They felt their support slipping away. They could either have come out in favor of a radical domestic reform program, which for many reasons they were unable to do, or decided to follow a "radical" foreign policy. The dilemma facing these circles (not only in Syria) has been fittingly described by Sir H.A.R. Gibb: [4]

> Inevitably, as the nationalist leaders felt mass support slipping away they made ever more violent efforts to regain it by continuing to harp on the continued presence of European forces or enterprises or controls, or on the hidden hand of Western diplomacy and on Western support of Zionism. When accused of neglecting social issues, they insisted that those were secondary and controversial, and must not disrupt the nation's united determination to achieve its national aims. However genuinely the politicians desired national independence, they did not know what to do with it. Concentrating on its negative aspect as freedom

from foreign interference, and without positive program, they could only try to fill the void of policy by propaganda.

This propaganda led almost inevitably toward a pro-Soviet orientation as the way of lesser resistance. This is still frequently combined with a naive but sincerely held belief that no lasting harm can possibly ensue from close collaboration with the Soviet Union, and that those who endorse it are perfectly able to take care of themselves.

But the old nationalist forces are now very much on the way out. Among those who now rule Syria from behind the scenes, some are Communist or pro-Communist and want Syria to become part of the Soviet orbit. The others view current events only in the framework of local politics, and do not greatly care about the international implications one way or another.

4. The Syrian Enigma:
What Is the Ba'th? BY ERIC ROULEAU

A FEW WEEKS before the Israeli-Arab conflict last June, an uncharitable commentator compared the Ba'th to Samson. Blinded and weakened like the biblical hero, he wrote, the party in power in Syria was doing its best to pull down the pillars of the temple which would kill it. Samson did not fail in his suicide. He also succeeded in burying his enemy, the Philistines. The Ba'th however, by no means destroyed the Israelis and their imperialist allies; on the other hand, it emerged very much alive from the ruins of military defeat.

Those who sought—and doubtless still seek—its death were nevertheless numerous. Since last autumn, the Israeli leaders have proclaimed their intention of overthrowing the Damascus regime, made solely responsible for the commando raids on Israeli territory. Since the seizure of power by the left of the Ba'th in February 1966, the Americans have shown their disapproval of the Syrian leaders, whose political options seemed to lie midway between those of Moscow and Peking. In a talk to the businessmen of Latakia, the American Ambassador reassured them with the following words: "Do not worry. In the near future there will be major changes in Syria. Free enterprise and democracy will triumph." [1]

The British, deprived overnight of important contracts; the oil companies, who were forced to pay higher royalties under threat of nationalization; the conservative regimes of the Arab world, sapped by agitation sponsored by the Ba'th; not to speak of "friendly" countries such as Iraq, embarrassed by propaganda

Reprinted from *New Left Review*, No. 45 (London, 1967) pp. 53–65; by permission of the editor.

from Damascus, do not nourish much affection for these left-wing, "semi-anarchist" and "romantic" socialists, whose revolutionary zeal—even if it lacks commensurate means of action—disrupts established order and the status quo.

ISOLATION AND SECRECY

If the Ba'th has many enemies, it has also won very few allies. One of the founders of the party recently said to me, somewhat bitterly: "The Ba'th leaders, it must be admitted, have an extraordinary gift for turning even potential friends into allies." On the eve of Israeli-Arab hostilities, neutral observers were unanimous in thinking that the Syrian regime had only limited popular support, in spite of the social measures it has taken in favor of the dispossessed classes. It was confronted with the hostility of the mercantile petite bourgeoisie of the towns, the indifference of a part of the peasantry, restrained criticisms by the working class, and the distrust of numerous intellectuals. The Muslim Brothers, the followers of the former leadership of the Ba'th (Michel Aflaq, Salah al-Bitar and Munif al-Razzaz) and even some small left-wing groupings were plotting against it, while Nasserites and Communists were supporting it almost against their will. The Soviet Union was giving it aid more from necessity than from sympathy.

One might, of course, explain the relative isolation of the Damascus regime at home and abroad in terms of its policies in recent months. Any such explanation, however, risks being superficial if it does not take account of the origins of the party and its leaders, of its past and present ideology, its organization, its activities, and its very special role in the Arab world.

The Ba'th is a very elusive party. It has a number of faces. Its general physiognomy has changed over the years. It has reached its majority, without acquiring the definitive traits of maturity. A quarter of a century of clandestine life has made it secretive and obsessively distrustful. Even in power, it continues to behave more like an occult sect than a political party aspiring to popularity among the Arab masses.

There are very few studies devoted to the Ba'th. This is what makes the book which Kamel S. Abu Jaber has recently published in the United States such an important contribution.[2] The author, an American of Jordanian origin, who is a professor at the University of Tennessee, has made extensive use of Arabic materials and has interviewed leaders of the Ba'th and observers of the Arab political scene. By talking mainly to Michel Aflaq and Salah al-Bitar, who are certainly the two best-known personalities of the party, but are also the leaders of only one of the three factions which constitute the Ba'th, he has left the other founders of the party in the shade: Zaki al-Arsouzi, Wahib al-Ghanem, Slimane Issa, Darwiche Zouni, Ali Mohsen, Sedky Ismail and Yousef Chakra who formed the Arab Ba'th in 1940, not to speak of Akram Hawrani, leader of an organization which joined the Ba'th in 1954 and left it again in 1961. To omit these two political currents is necessarily to limit our understanding of the ideology of the Ba'th and the influences which it underwent.

On the other hand, by entitling the first chapter of his book *"The Beginnings of Arab Socialism,"* Kamel Abu Jaber risks lending credence to the thesis that the early founders of the Ba'th were descendants of the humanist and utopian socialist thinkers who appeared in the Arab world in the nineteenth and above all the beginning of the twentieth century. In fact, the preoccupations and the ideology of a Michel Aflaq or a Zaki al-Arsouzi were, and still are, in essence purely nationalist. It is significant that the party called itself from 1943 to 1954 Party of Arab Resurrection (Ba'th), and only adopted the designation "Socialist" after its fusion with the Arab Socialist Party of Akram Hawrani, whose aspirations to social justice themselves were based on no socialist doctrine whatsoever.

AFLAQ AND ARSOUZI

It is true that Michel Aflaq and Salah al-Bitar showed a certain leaning toward the left during their studies at the Sorbonne between 1928 and 1932. But this ephemeral attraction was nationalist in its motivation, just as were their apparent sympathies for Nazism in the early years of the Second World War. The refusal of Leon Blum's government, in which there was Communist participation, to grant Syria independence in 1936 ended the influence which the European left exercised over them. In the course of an interview in 1963, Aflaq told me that he had not been influenced by any Western philosopher or writer. He added: "Besides, I have lost contact with the currents of Western thought since the beginning of the Second World War, devoting most of my time to the practical tasks of my party."[3]

The political initiation of Michel Aflaq is strikingly similar to that of Zaki-Arsouzi, the other "spiritual father" of the Ba'th. Both studied in Paris, in the same epoch. Both taught at Damascus, where they formed separate groups of nationalist students, before creating political organizations whose main aim was to expel the French from Syria and to work for the "reunification of the Arab nation" and its liberation from the grip of imperialism. Professors of history, they both borrowed the names of their respective organizations from the Italian Renaissance. Aflaq initially called his movement: "Al Ihya al Arabi" (Arab Revival); Arsouzi called his "Al Baas al Arabi" (Arab Rebirth). The two organizations fused into a single party in 1947, at the First Congress of the Ba'th, in which Arsouzi refused to participate personally—less because of deep political differences than personal dislike for a man whom he calls in private a "screech-owl."

Zaki al-Arsouzi at the age of sixty-seven is a picturesque personality who continues to expound his ideas to circles of admirers in a well-known Damascus cafe. He explained to me his aversion to Michel Aflaq as follows:

> Aflaq is an opportunist. He came back to Damascus professing allegedly progressive ideas. But when the pro-Axis rebellion of Rachid Ali Gailani erupted at the beginning of the war in Iraq, he formed a support committee for it in Syria, with the encouragement of the Vichy administration. I, on the other hand, actively opposed the strike in support of the German cause which was called in Damascus, and was rewarded with the persecution of the French authorities.

Born in Alexandretta, Arsouzi had led the movement against France's cession of the Sandjak to Turkey. But his nationalism did not yield to the temptation of Nazism. He observed: "The Arabs are the only human group who have remained faithful to the spiritual values bequeathed by Adam. Hence they could only hope for the victory of the Allies."

Deeply influenced by the work of Bergson, whom he has "reread ten times," Arsouzi recounts how in 1928 he had "a metaphysical experience." "I was at the entrance to the Sorbonne, plunged in thought," he told me, "when I was suddenly invaded by a feeling of ecstasy. My soul was metamorphosed and my way of seeing the world completely transformed."

To his numerous disciples, who included General Salah Jedid, the present Syrian strong man, and General Hafez Assad, Minister of Defense, Arsouzi explained that "The white race is divided into two branches, one Semitic (of Arab origin) and turned towards spiritual affairs, the other Greco-Germanic and oriented towards the sciences of domination." The regenerated Arab nation thus had the mission of "inundating humanity with the light of the soul."

It is not known whether Aflaq also had a "metaphysical experience." But the message which he sought to convey to the new generation was equally saturated with mysticism and Arab chauvinism. The speech which he gave on April 5, 1943, in the great amphitheatre of Damascus University, which marked his debut in the political scene and won him a certain notoriety, is considered in this respect one of the texts most representative of his thought.

NATIONALISM AND ISLAM

To the Memory of the Arab Prophet, which his followers still quote with fervor, confers a capital role on Islam in the "eternal mission" of the Arab nation; for Aflaq, Islam is a manifestation of the Arab genius, a superior form of its civilization. Himself a Greek Orthodox, Aflaq did not hesitate to assert:

> Islam is the motor which sets in motion the latent forces of the Arab nation; this nation then overflows with warm life, sweeping away the obstacles of tradition and convention to renew its bond with the universe. It is overcome with wonder and enthusiasm; it begins to express its wonder and enthusiasm with new words and splendid actions, and unable to contain itself, under the impulse of its ecstasy, overflows into other nations by its thought and by its action. In this manner it attains universality. . . . The duty of Arabs is to spread through the world their qualities and their virtues until other peoples can grow to resemble them or raise themselves up to their level.

The founder of the Ba'th hastens to add that this must not be interpreted as any form of will to conquest, but simply the desire to accomplish "a divine duty full of truth, conviction, pity, justice and sacrifice." "It is obvious," he continues, "that the Arabs can only accomplish this duty if they are a strong and reborn nation . . ."

In the name of this triumphant nationalism, Aflaq invited his own co-religionists to range themselves under the banner of Islamicizing Arabism:

> Christian Arabs will become aware, when nationalism fully awakes in them, that Islam is a national culture for them which they must assimilate until they understand and love it. They will then be devoted to Islam as to the dearest aspect of their Arabism. If this aspiration has still to be achieved, the new generation of Christian Arabs is called to achieve it with audacity and disinterest, sacrificing pride and egoism, for there is no honor equal to that of belonging to it.

For the hundreds of thousands of Arabs of Jewish faith, Aflaq had no word, whether of friendship or hostility. He ignored them. They were excluded from the Islamo-Christian Arab nation which he wanted to place under the sign of the Prophet Mahomet.

One of his companions of that time, today a professor at the University of Damascus, wrote to me recently: "In 1937, Michel Aflaq spent his holidays in France, with Salah al-Bitar. He came back to Syria full of admiration for the works of Alfred Rosenberg, the theorist of Nazi racism, and in particular for *The Myth of the Twentieth Century*, which he had read in Grosclaude's translation. He thought at the time that Hitler's Germany, by contrast with the communist countries, had succeeded in achieving the perfect synthesis of nationalism and socialism." However, in his speech *To the Memory of the Arab Prophet*, Aflaq never refers to socialism. His text, written in a lyrical and passionate style, is a hymn to the Arab nation whose every line expresses his will to restore its former magnificence to it.

Several years later, Kamel Abu Jaber tells us,[4] Michel Aflaq had to correct his statement that Arabs were morally and intellectually superior to other nations, in the following manner: "We do not say that we are better, only different from others." But the legacy of national-socialist ideology is a tenacious one. As late as 1960, his inseparable friend Salah al-Bitar was writing: "The greatness of nations is not measured by the size of their populations but by the number of geniuses and leaders they produce."[5]

CLASS BASIS

The emphasis on the notion of the leader is not accidental. The founders of the Ba'th, whether of Arsouzi's or Aflaq's current, addressed themselves exclusively to an elite: students, professors, intellectuals and country teachers, who were expected in their turn to carry the good tidings to the people. In effect, the great majority of recruits to the Ba'th belonged to the small and middle bourgeoisie. Their natural milieu was that which produced the leaders of nationalism throughout the Arab world. The ideas of an Aflaq, however shocking to a westerner living in an advanced industrial society, answered a psychological need. At the time, the Arab peoples were living under the shadow of colonialism and were profoundly humiliated by it. The leaders of the traditional parties were in eclipse or were collaborating with the occupier. The prospects of an Allied victory over the Axis powers afforded little hope for liberation. A feeling of impotence, disillusion and discouragement overcame those who had hoped for the military defeat of the colonial powers.

The Ba'th had the merit, despite its nationalist verbiage, of reviving hope and restoring confidence to certain elites in disarray. By exalting the golden age of the Arabs, their past conquests and achievements, and telling their descendants that they were a "nation not like others" endowed with a "mission" to humanity, the Ba'th nourished a new optimism and spirit of resistance, even if it was essentially xenophobic. Ba'thist ideology seemed equally attractive to the middle classes, who were sincerely nationalist but hostile both to the traditional political formations in Syria, dominated by the large landowning and merchant bourgeoisie, and to the Communist Party.

Towards the end of the Second World War, the extreme left in Syria had the wind in its sails. The epic of Stalingrad had strongly impressed Arab opinion, which began to turn its attention from Nazi Germany and to "discover" the Soviet Union. The USSR proclaimed itself, moreover, anti-imperialist and a champion of the right to self-determination and equality between peoples. The Communist Party, led by Khaled Bagdash, had acquired a solid experience of political action in its twenty years of existence. It had enjoyed the opportunity to organize and extend its influence in conditions of legality from 1936 to 1938, thanks to the Popular Front government in France, and had forged militants steeled in the wartime underground. The entry of the Free French Forces into Syria allowed it to re-emerge into the open, to launch its propaganda on a large scale and to reestablish its relations with the fraternal parties, especially with the Soviet party. The Communist Party thus appeared to the Ba'th a potential political power and henceforward a formidable rival.

ANTI-COMMUNISM

Michel Aflaq and Salah al-Bitar devoted their first political manifesto, written in 1940–41, to a denunciation of the "anti-national character of communism." [6] From 1944 onwards, Aflaq set about the task of refuting Marxism.[7] He began by attacking it for being "a Western ideology, foreign to everything that is Arab," into which Marx "has breathed something of his vengeful Jewish spirit." Moreover, he wrote, "The Arab nation is not a small nation of secondary importance which can adopt any other message than its own, or follow in the path of another nation and feed on its scraps." He went on to claim that communism "denies the spiritual bases of the nation" and "establishes between the Arabs and the world a dangerous, party-based relationship." Aflaq rejected the economic and historical determinism of Marxism, the class struggle, the dictatorship of the proletariat and the internationalist character of the working-class movement. "If they free themselves from the nightmare of communism," Aflaq ended by promising, "the Arabs will have no difficulty in pursuing the path of Arab socialism . . ."

"ARAB SOCIALISM"

The formula was born: "Arab Socialism." It was to be authentically national, having no roots or connections with Western socialism, still less with the "pseudo-socialism" of the communist East. Kamel Abu Jaber states that Aflaq considered European socialists disguised imperialists who pursued the policies of conservatives when they were in power. However, Ba'th socialism in the 1940's was merely a variant of social-democratic doctrine. It promised to combine individual freedom with limitation of private property, ensure the welfare of the unprivileged classes while protecting the legitimate interest of the possessing classes, and install social justice while respecting "spiritual values." Above all, socialism was to be subordinated to the interests of the nation and become the instrument of its unity and development. It was by the reeducation of the Arab citizen that the society in which he lived would be improved. Rejecting "sterile abstractions," Aflaq believed that socialism should not rest on any dogma or doctrine, but be the fruit of lived experience and pragmatic action.

If we are to believe Dr. Wahib al-Ghanem, one of the founders of the Ba'th, neither Aflaq nor Bitar originally wanted to include socialist objectives in the party's program. "At the beginning of 1947," he told me, "Aflaq and Bitar came to see me in Latakia to negotiate the fusion of their movement with that of Zaki al-Arsouzi to which I belonged. I professed socialist ideas at the time, influenced by Marxism which I began to study after the Soviet victory of Stalingrad, and I insisted that the unified party be oriented to the left. My two interlocutors, above all Bitar, were firmly opposed to this, arguing that the Ba'th should be an exclusively nationalist formation. After forty hours of discussion, Michel Aflaq, who was mainly anxious to unify the two organizations into a single party, yielded. This was what made possible the founding congress of the party in the Luna Park cafe of Damascus, in April 1947."

The program which was adopted, and which may be read as an annex in Kamel Abu Jaber's study, was the fruit of this compromise. It presents a curious mélange of an exacerbated nationalism and a socialism that was audacious, almost revolutionary for the epoch.

The "Arab Nation, one and indivisible," endowed with an "eternal mission," is characterized by its "vitality and creative genius." Class struggle is "banished" from its midst, but the interests of the collectivity predominate over those of the individual. The Ba'th undertakes to nationalize large industry including public utilities, natural resources and means of transport; to limit agrarian property, control internal and external commerce, introduce planning into the economy, industrialize the country, ensure the workers participation in the profits of enterprises and encourage the establishment of a "welfare state" similar to that advocated at the time by the British Labor Party. However, in contrast to the Labor Party, the Ba'th declared that socialism would triumph only by "revolution and struggle." On the other hand, it said nothing about the right to strike and abstained from defining the regime—monarchical or republican—with which it intended to endow the Arab state.

"The contradictions and lacunae in the program," Dr. Wahib al Ghanem told me, "are explained by the heterogeneous character of the participants to the Congress. We were 247 intellectuals from countries as different as Syria and Morocco, Iraq and the Lebanon, Palestine and Transjordania. There were rightists and leftists; conservatives and socialists, monarchists and republicans. It was inevitable that a compromise was forced on the Congress arbitrarily. Unfortunately, none of us could endorse entirely the objectives that we were supposed to defend to the Arab masses. This was the origin of the incoherence, the internal struggles and the weaknesses of the Ba'th."

CONSEQUENCES OF THE PALESTINIAN WAR

However, by making the Palestinian conflict its battle-charger, the Ba'th succeeded in safeguarding its unity, extending its influence and bidding for power. The nationalist platform of the party was also its safety plank. The Arab world was going through a period of acute crisis: Humiliated by the Zionist victories, infuriated by the installation of a Jewish state in the Holy Land, and indignant at the impotence of its governments, public opinion sought new solutions. The wave of nationalism which swept the region tried to dislodge bourgeois or feudal regimes, now completely discredited. The Communists were not in position to fill the political vacuum. Having supported the partition of Palestine, following the example of the socialist camp, they were isolated or actually consigned to popular opprobrium. The Ba'th, intransigently nationalist and socialist to boot, offered an attractive alternative.

Its leaders returned from the front, where they had fought with the irregular Palestinian forces, invested with the prestige of *mujahiddine*. Three months before the outbreak of hostilities, Salah al-Bitar had denounced the UN in the party's daily newspaper, *Al Baas* (February 16, 1948), as an "instrument of Zionism and the Western powers," and added: "The Palestinian problem will be solved on the spot, and not at the United Nations." If the Arabs had lost the war, explained Dr. Munif al-Razzaz, the future secretary general of the Ba'th, it was the fault of anachronistic governments which should never have been in power in the middle of the twentieth century.[8]

In effect, governments and regimes were crumbling, one after the other, in the Arab world. Before the fall of the Iraqi and Egyptian monarchies, King Abdullah of Jordan and the Lebanese Prime Minister Riad al-Solh were assassinated. In Syria, a cascade of military coups followed one after the other. The Army, now the only organized force left in the country, profited by popular anger to replace the traditional elites. The Ba'th, like all the other political formations, was not strong enough to seize power.

In the vortex of events, the party radicalized. In 1949, it pronounced in favor of republican government. Its conception of Arab unity evolved: Henceforward it sought to regroup the countries with progressive regimes, while waiting to overthrow the corrupt monarchies. It denounced the supporters of the "Fertile Crescent" and "Greater Syria" (a plan for uniting Syria and Jordan) as agents of British imperialism and launched a resolute struggle against the extreme right Syrian People's Party. In opposition to the dictatorship of General Shishakly at the end of 1951, the Ba'th was led to a *rapprochement* with the other parties engaged in the same resistance, particularly the Communist Party. From 1954 to 1958, comments Kamel Abu Jaber, there was a "slide to the left," not only in Syria but in the whole of the Arab world, where the Ba'th numbered several "regional" organizations.[9]

In fact, the projects for "common defense" such as the Bagdad Pact which the British and Americans tried to impose on the Arab countries contributed to refueling the anti-Western struggle with greater intensity, this time actively supported by the Soviet Union. Nasserite Egypt resisted the pressures from Washington and London by accepting Soviet arms and Soviet funds to build the High Dam at Aswan. The nationalization of the Suez Canal marked the high point of its anti-imperialist policies. In Jordan, King Hussein refused to join the Bagdad Pact under pressure of public opinion, sacked Glubb Pasha, the English commander of the Arab Legion, permitted elections which produced a genuinely nationalist government, and denounced the Anglo-Jordanian Treaty. In the Lebanon, Iraq, Saudi Arabia and Libya, the nationalist movement—often inspired by Ba'thist elements—gained a new *élan*. Meanwhile, in the Maghreb, the Algerian people were fighting heroically against France under the leadership of the FLN.

The Ba'th, temporarily abandoning its anti-Communist policies, began to collaborate with the Arab Communist parties, particularly in Jordan against the British presence there, in Iraq against the Hashemite monarchy, and in Syria against the traditional parties. After the delivery of Soviet arms to Egypt in 1955, it played down its anti-Soviet propaganda, "forgot" that Moscow had voted for the creation of a Jewish state at the United Nations, and advocated, especially after the Suez crisis, close co-operation with the USSR.

This apparent metamorphosis was not only due to the anti-imperialist climate which dominated the country. The Ba'th had absorbed new blood when it fused in March 1954 with Akram Hawrani's Arab Socialist Party. Entrenched in the rural zones, especially the poverty-stricken region of Hama, Hawrani's organization provided a contingent of militants from the poor peasantry who were much more radical than the urban petite-bourgeois who made up Aflaq's party. Moreover, the Syrian Army, purged of its conservative leaders after the overthrow of Shishakly, had been taken over by younger officers who had not been chosen and trained under the French Mandate. Most of them, whether Ba'thists, Socialists, progressives or Communists, were markedly to the left of Aflaq's apparatus.

UNION WITH EGYPT

Syria, it was said at the time, was in danger of "sliding into the socialist camp." In fact, there was no chance of the Communist Party seizing power, but it was expanding rapidly. After the overthrow of the dictatorship of Shishakly in 1954, Khaled Bagdash was elected deputy for Damascus with a huge majority. A brilliant orator, he made great use of the Chamber and pursued a policy of alliance with the "national bourgeoisie," for whom he increasingly became a moderate reformist inspired by the best anti-imperialist sentiments. His party became a pole of attraction for the very middle classes which provided the clientele of the Ba'th. The latter now risked being thrown into the shade by its formidable competitor or being dragged along in its wake, as it tried to outbid it in a path it had not chosen.

Confronted with this dilemma, Aflaq and his friends found an unexpected exit: unity with Nasser's Egypt, whose popularity had been constantly increasing since the Soviet arms deal of 1955. Previously they had had nothing but contempt for the Egyptian colonel, who in their eyes completely lacked "Arab consciousness," knew nothing of socialism, and had "made concessions to British imperialism." They had, in fact, violently criticized the Anglo-Egyptian Agreement of 1954. But the Nasser of 1955 and above all of 1956 was a revelation to them. He had "broken the arms monopoly of the West" and nationalized the Suez Canal, one of the largest prizes of imperialism. He had, above all, showed that one could be simultaneously anti-imperialist, pro-Soviet and anti-communist. Leader of the most powerful country in the Arab world, he deserved to become the leader of the whole Arab nation from the Atlantic to the Persian Gulf, beginning with the "Syrian region."

To this effect, the Ba'th was willing to show self-denial and a spirit of self-sacrifice. Nasser demanded as a condition of unity the dissolution of all the Syrian political formations. The Ba'th decided to scuttle itself. The operation, however, was only to be a simulated suicide. The leadership of the party thought that Nasser would undertake to eliminate the Communists from the Syrian political scene. After that, the Ba'thist leaders and militants were the obvious candidates to organize and lead the single party of the new United Arab Republic. Aflaq and his friends thought, in effect, that they were changing one steed for another, stronger and faster one.

Their calculations, however, proved partly incorrect. Nasser certainly unleashed a massive repression against the Syrian left, but he also did not delay in getting rid of his Ba'thist "friends" who had thought that they would control him.

THE EMERGENCE OF THE LEFT

The Syrian-Egyptian Union, which lasted from 1958 to 1961, resulted in a failure which helped to aggravate the contradictions within the Ba'th. A left wing, which challenged the content of Aflaq's Pan-Arabism, now emerged. Its members, mostly a younger generation who had joined the party since 1950, wanted priority to be given henceforward to socialism, whose installation would hasten the era of Arab unity. Clandestinity under the Nasserite regime favored the crystallization of numerous groups and factions within the party, and above all of a military "clan." By a reflex of self-defense, young officers—among them Salah Jedid, the present Syrian "strong man"—formed their own autonomous organization, which was later to eliminate the historic leaders from power, on February 23, 1966.

The path of those who are today called "Neo-Ba'thists" was not an easy one. It took them five years, from 1961 to 1966, to achieve their aims. The national (i.e. Inter-Arab) leadership of the Ba'th, inspired by the Aflaq-Bitar tandem, controlled the party machines—a control which allowed them to engineer successful coups in Iraq on February 8, 1963, and Syria on March 8 of the same year.

Apparently strengthened by this double triumph, the Aflaqist wing of the party soon, however, began to experience the boomerang effects of its own policies. In Iraq, it approved the massacre of some 5,000 Communists and the atrocious war against the Kurds. In Syria, it showed its inability to make clear political and social choices, and earned the hostility of both the middle and the laboring classes.

The hour of truth came in October 1963. At the Sixth Party Congress, the Aflaqist group was outvoted, and the left faction gained dominance of the party. Resolutions inspired by Marxism, amounting to a new program replacing that of 1947, were passed: The ideas of scientific socialism, class struggle and international solidarity were subtly introduced into a text whose nationalist character was still not in doubt. The expression, "the eternal mission of the Arab nation," in particular, subsists. In spite of this, at the end of the Congress, Michel Aflaq cried: "I no longer recognize my party!"

The right, nevertheless, did not renounce its leadership of the party. Allying itself with the group of Salah Jedid, which was temporarily distanced from the left, and conducting numerous maneuvers, Aflaq and his followers managed to put their adversaries in a minority at the Seventh Congress. The struggle between the two surviving clans continued for two years before being decided in favor of Salah Jedid. The latter now took over the aims and slogans of the Marxisant wing of the Ba'th, to whose elimination he had contributed.

SOCIAL UPHEAVAL IN SYRIA

The Neo-Ba'thists now in power have multiplied bids to win the support of the socialist camp and the dispossessed classes.

The authenticity of their radicalism need not be doubted. In the past three years, Syria has undergone a major social upheaval. The Ba'th government has decreed an agrarian reform with ceilings of 15 to 55 hectares for irrigated, and 50 to 300 hectares for unirrigated land. Uncultivated estates have been expropriated without further ado. In a country where, as late as 1958, 45 per cent of all irrigated land and 30 per cent of nonirrigated land was owned by only 2 per cent of the population, while 70 per cent of the population owned no land at all, this is a very drastic change. The reform has not yet been fully implemented, although the Ba'th claimed to have redistributed 2,500,000 hectares out of the national total of 6,000,000 by early 1967. Simultaneously, the signing of an agreement with the USSR for the construction of the Euphrates Dam ultimately promises a huge leap forward for agriculture; the Dam will double the area of irrigated soil in Syria. In the industrial sector, the Neo-Ba'thists have been no less intransigent. The lightning decrees of January 1965 nationalized 80 per cent of Syrian industry. Foreign trade was effectively made a state monopoly. The scope of these measures can be gauged from the fact that they instantly led to a general strike and shutdown of all business and trade in the great urban centers and bazaars, while mullahs preached open revolt against the government from their muezzins. In an armed social conflict, the Ba'th regime, aided by workers' militias, trade unions and Communist militants, succeeding in crushing bourgeois resistance to the new order. This unfolding of a mass social crisis and violent armed clashes distinguishes the Syrian experience sharply from the tranquilly bureaucratic Egyptian nationalizations of 1958. It led to waves of emigration among the once prosperous Syrian bourgeoisie: There are now 200,000 exiles in the Lebanon. Beirut has become the Miami of this class.

POLITICAL PROSPECTS

The Ba'th regime, however, despite these sweeping measures and the new support of the USSR, has not yet succeeded in winning a wide popular base. Its architect is General Salah Jedid, an Alawite from Latakia who is forced to remain an *éminence grise* because he belongs to a religious minority. The army has been transformed in recent years, after the massive purges of 1963 when hundreds of "separatist" officers of bourgeois origin were cashiered. The new officers who dominate the army are now predominantly of poor peasant origin, but are heavily recruited from the Alawite and Druze minorities. The Ba'th never possessed a large cadre of militants. Indeed, in 1963 it had only

four hundred active members in the whole country. Hence the
zeal of the Neo-Ba'thists to monopolize power in Syria is a
source of weakness. They are to some extent aware of this, as
the inclusion of one Communist and two independent Marxists
in the Cabinet indicates. But the regime is still somewhat fragile. The other leftist groups, meanwhile, call for the widening
of the government in a national revolutionary front.

As in the decade of the 1940's, the new Ba'th leaders have
decided in recent months to make the Palestinian problem their
main issue. But it is not certain that their slogan of a "people's
war of liberation" has brought them many political dividends,
especially after the military defeat of June. Confronted with an
impasse which has now lasted twenty years, the Arabs are, in
effect, showing a growing skepticism about the promises of their
leaders. On the other hand, the Ba'th has undoubtedly weathered the Israeli-Arab war better than Nasser in Egypt—partly
because it has allowed such popular initiatives as the formation
of workers' militias. But there is still much to be done. The
Ba'th, like every other Arab political formation, is now at the
crossroads. All the present Arab governments risk disappearing
from the political scene as did the elites who ruled the Arab
World on the eve of the first Palestinian conflict in 1948. The
seismic effects of the second Palestinian war have yet to come.
The Ba'th will have to renovate itself to survive.

5 Iraq Under General Nuri

BY DR. MOHAMMAD FADHEL JAMALI

AMBASSADOR GALLMAN has done history a great service by writing his recollections of Iraq under Nuri al-Said, for recent events in the Arab world and the work of immense propaganda machines have distorted or obliterated facts to such a degree that it is difficult to appreciate the great services rendered to their nations by the leaders of the past generation.

This book is especially important because it is written by an outsider who looked at Nuri objectively. Ambassador Gallman was a career diplomat who had to deal with the men in office and to know them as well as possible. His contacts with Nuri himself were direct and frequent, and this book is valuable insofar as it deals with firsthand experiences and personal reporting. When it gives secondhand information and reports it is sometimes inaccurate.

Had Gallman established adequate contact with politicians other than those in office, he could have provided a clearer picture of the forces around Nuri, whether forces of construction or destruction, whether Iraqi or non-Iraqi, whether in opposition or in alliance with Nuri. He might even have foreseen the tragic end of Nuri.

Still, this book is an excellent record, and I agree with its general outlook and its appreciation of Nuri's work. I shall, however, make a few comments and add my own explanations of some of the points raised by the author.

Reprinted from *Middle East Forum*, Vol. XL, No. 7 (Beirut, 1964), pp. 13–24; by permission of the editor. This article is a review by Dr. Jamali of Waldemar J. Gallman's book, *Iraq Under General Nuri, My Recollection of Nuri al-Said, 1954–58* (Baltimore, 1964). All page references in the article are to this book.

Ambassador Gallman opens the first chapter by describing the resignation of my Cabinet in 1954, my refusal to join Nuri's proposed Cabinet, and Nuri's coming to power later in the same year. Gallman was not in Iraq at the time, and his information is inaccurate.

I did not resign my office because of matters related to the flood relief, as stated in the book. My Cabinet had the full support of the Parliament and the people of Iraq in its dealing with the flood affairs. As a matter of fact, Iraq has rarely seen a unity of purpose and action, national and international, as strong as that which arose to face the flood tragedy. The praise my Cabinet colleagues received on the handling of flood affairs was overwhelming. No one minded the few dissident voices whose criticism was known to be based on personal feelings rather than facts. The reasons for my resignation and my refusal to join Nuri in a succeeding government were not openly stated, for we, as collaborators, did not publicly divulge our differences. However, had Gallman asked me about them I would have told him.

My differences with Nuri were as follows:

(1) I refused to undertake legislation which he suggested regarding the restriction of parties and the press, and the withdrawal of Iraqi nationality from subversive elements. (This legislation Nuri carried out later by ordinance.)

(2) I wanted to pass laws for land reform and social welfare to which Nuri objected. (He later adopted some of my points and legislated them in a diluted form.)

(3) The immediate cause for my resignation was my disagreement with Nuri on the policy of federation with Syria.

It is a well-known fact that, during my premiership, I, with the help of my friend, ex-Prime Minister Saleh Jabr, assisted the nationalist Syrians, who had the federation of Iraq and Syria at heart, to cause the downfall of the Syrian dictator, Adib al-Shishakly. The next step after the fall of Shishakly was to take constitutional steps toward the federation. I decided to go ahead. Development of the policy would have incurred some expenditure which would have had to be legislated. Nuri objected to the expense, and since the parliamentary majority belonged to him, I decided to resign.

The question may logically be raised why and how I undertook the premiership if the parliamentary majority was Nuri's. The answer, which is another little-known fact, is as follows.

When Prime Minister Jamil Madfai resigned, I was President of the Parliament (Speaker of the House). The people consulted about the formation of a new Cabinet were of the opinion that the Parliament should be dissolved if any premier, other than Nuri, was to come to power. I was the only exception. I advised H.M. King Faisal II not to dissolve Parliament. Nuri gave me his support, and I formed my Cabinet. Nuri's eventual withdrawal of support showed itself by the absence of some of the members of Nuri's party from Parliament, thus preventing a quorum. I considered this as lack of cooperation from a Parliament which I had helped to uphold.

Subsequently, when Nuri asked me to join him as Foreign Minister, I declined because I did not want to deal with a Parliament which had not cooperated with my Cabinet. I also enumerated to Nuri our points of difference on internal policies as well as on the question of Syria. Nuri failed to form a new Cabinet at that time, and Arshad al-Umari succeeded me as premier. I joined him as Foreign Minister on two conditions: first, that Parliament should be dissolved; and second, that the policy of federation with Syria should be implemented.

The Parliament was dissolved, and Arshad carried out elections. In the new Parliament Nuri had no absolute majority, although he had the largest bloc of members. This Parliament was more representative of the people than the previous one. Of the 135 seats, it provided Nuri's party with 56, Saleh Jabr's party with 24, and other parties with 12. The rest were independent members, some of whom cooperated with me.

In the meantime, Nuri had gone to England for a major surgical operation, and I was making plans to visit the United States. Before leaving, I was asked by H.M the King and his uncle to see Nuri in London and ask him to return and form a new Cabinet.

I saw Nuri in London. He was suffering and in pain. When I conveyed the King's message to him, he was furious. He recalled that when Parliament was controlled by his supporters he was not wanted as premier. He said that he could not accept responsibility for governing with the new Parliament and that those who had made the mess should bear the consequences. Furthermore he said that he would never enter a Parliament which included men like Kamel Chaderji. I reported Nuri's views to Baghdad and sailed for New York. During my absence, the Regent went to Paris to meet Nuri and convince him to come back and form a government.

As Gallman reports, Nuri came, formed his new Cabinet, and dissolved the Parliament. Some think this was one of his most serious mistakes, for the Parliament then elected seriously reduced the number of the opposition. Had Nuri faced the members of the Parliament elected when Arshad was prime minister; had he carried the majority of the diversified elements of that Parliament with him to pass progressive legislation, the whole history of Iraq might have been different, and Iraq might never have suffered the shocks of the next few years.

I have elaborated on these events because of their importance in Nuri's later political life.

Another point which needs correction in the first chapter is the statement, " . . . for Jamali was close to the Crown Prince, Abdul-Ilah, who occasionally entrusted Jamali with missions of personal interest." (p. 2) I wonder where Gallman collected this mistaken information.

As for Nuri's "real attitude toward Jamali, and estimate of him," (p. 3) the truth is that Nuri depended on me in matters of foreign affairs. After we attended the United Nations together in 1947, he told me that he had written a personal letter to the Crown Prince telling him that he had complete confidence in Jamali's stand on Iraq's foreign policy, and that if he (Nuri) were to die, he would be comfortable [knowing] that Iraq had a man like Jamali to look after foreign affairs.

It is a fact that we agreed on most issues of foreign policy. We differed only on the handling of Arab affairs, for example, the federation of Iraq with Syria. I usually went much farther than he did in developing Iraq's role in Arab affairs.

Nuri entrusted me with major political missions. I acted on his behalf at the Bandung Conference and the Conference of Arab Prime Ministers in Cairo, 1955, not to speak of my leading the Iraqi delegation to the United Nations many times. In all these missions, he never issued any instructions. He trusted my judgment completely. He also gave me great help and encouragement during my successful negotiations with the United States for the Arms Agreement.

In Chapter II, Gallman deals with Nuri's background. He was an Iraqi and a loyal Arab nationalist. Arab nationalism, however, is not a racist nationalism. It is a matter of language, culture and history, and in that sense Nuri was a true. Arab nationalist. An Arab may have descended from any race.

Nuri was well brought up in typical Baghdadi culture and mannerisms. This means a generous spirit, a hearty reception of fellowmen, a clever wit, a sense of humor, and a tendency to go to excess in one's reactions. His military background and his experience in the Arab Revolt taught him courage and realism.

Then, he was schooled in practical political life under King Faisal I and his British advisers and friends. He was a great disciple of King Faisal I, and a great admirer of British methods. He believed in British wisdom, their concept of social evolution, and their philosophy of fair play. He often mentioned Mr. Nehru as a model of oriental wisdom who had been able to keep his country within the Commonwealth and who followed the British parliamentary method of government.

Nuri's relations with the British were based, not on a blind following, or selfish interests, or the paying of political debts, but on his faith in the British methods of government and his belief that it was important for a rising young country like Iraq to learn British ways. Nor was he likely to forget Britain's help to Iraq after World War I, when the vilayet of Mosul was included in Iraq, for without British help at that time, it would have gone to Turkey.

It is no wonder, then, that Nuri became Britain's most trusted friend in Iraq and that he utilized his friendship to get the best possible help from Britain for Iraq. It was he who signed the 1930 treaty with Britain, after which Iraq joined the League of Nations in 1932 as an independent state; it was he who saw the end of that treaty with Britain in 1955; and it was he who signed the Oil Agreement in 1952 with the Iraq Petroleum Company, the agreement which still provides the main source of revenue for Iraq.

In Chapter III, Ambassador Gallman describes his first meeting with Nuri and rightly speaks of Nuri's great interest in getting US arms help according to the Aid Agreement which I had signed. Nuri considered the army's strength a cornerstone in internal peace and order as well as a great card to play in promoting and protecting national and international peace and security. He thought that Iraq's standing nationally and internationally depended on the strength of its army. On account of his military background, Nuri had the welfare and strength of the army very close to his heart.

Ambassador Gallman rightly gives the Baghdad Pact an important place in his book. Chapters IV and V deal adequately with the Pact and Nuri's role therein. This is the main contribution of the book as far as the history of the last years of Nuri's life go.

I was an active supporter and collaborator in Nuri's efforts concerning the Baghdad Pact. At the time I agreed completely with all his arguments in favor of the Pact and worked for it wholeheartedly. Nuri found in the Baghdad Pact the answer to all his international problems. Some of his arguments ran as follows:

(a) A small country like Iraq needs strong support from great powers. It needs great friends for its defense and for its economic development. It needs arms and it needs economic development through the exploitation of its oil and other natural resources. Nuri thought that Iraq and the Arab world should rely on Western friendship and, following King Faisal I's method, learn to get the best from the West. The Baghdad Pact would insure the friendship and alliance of two great Western powers, the United Kingdom and the United States. These two countries would help to build Iraq's defenses and its economic system.

(b) Iraq's geographical and strategic position imposes on it a double responsibility. The one is national (Arab), the other Islamic. Iraq is the east wing of the Arab world, yet Iraq is the heart of the Islamic world. It is bound to Turkey, Iran, Afghanistan and Pakistan by historical, cultural, religious and strategic ties. Their destiny is interconnected. There is no doubt that whatever happens in Iran and Turkey affects Iraq immediately, and vice versa. A pact which might bring the Arab world and the Moslem world together would be an ideal achievement in international relations.

(c) Iraq had to rid itself of the 1930 Anglo-Iraqi Treaty, and it had to regulate its relations with Britain on a basis of equality and collaboration. A multilateral arrangement would be the best way out. The Baghdad Pact provided this arrangement.

(d) Communism to Nuri was anathema. He could not tolerate it. Its dangers to oil-rich Iraq both from within and without were apparent. Iraq and the Arab world needed defense arrangements for their security. The Baghdad Pact was a defensive arrangement based on Article 51 of the United Nations Charter. It was the legitimate right of any member of the United Nations to enter such defense arrangements if it was necessary for its safety.

Nuri's thinking on the Pact was clear, realistic and constructive. He hoped that the Arab states, with their Muslim neighbors, would align together as a great defense force for peace and get the military support of the West and Western help in economic development.

Before embarking on the Pact negotiations, Nuri was already familiar with the neutralist policy of Mr. Nehru of India. During my premiership in 1954, Nuri suggested that he should go and see Mr. Nehru, for whose opinions he had a great respect. My Cabinet decided to send him to India accompanied by Dr. Dhia Ja'afar, one of his trusted colleagues. Nuri had lengthy talks with Mr. Nehru, which he reported to us on his return. The gist of his report, as I remember, was that a neutralist policy which might hold good for India would not necessarily apply to Iraq.

In one of the secret sessions of the Bandung Conference, Mr. Nehru attacked military pacts and alliances and pleaded for coexistence. I asked for a definition of the word "coexistence." Then I asked if Mr. Nehru was willing to organize a neutralist third bloc. This he was not inclined to do. I then asked how a responsible statesman could leave the safety of his country in the air by not belonging to a group for self-defense. After a lengthy debate, Mr. Nehru conceded the right of any state to enter a pact for self-defense.

It was most unfortunate that our Egyptian brethren did not see eye to eye with us at the time. They were passing through a period of trial and error in international affairs. Gallman has faithfully narrated what he heard about Egypt's attitude before and after the Baghdad Pact.

I wish to relate here some of my firsthand experiences in the matter, which may corroborate Gallman's statements. In the summer of 1954, after my visit to the United States, I returned to Iraq. On my way back I heard that Nuri had formed the Cabinet and that Major Salah Salem, Egypt's Minister of National Guidance, had visited him in Sarsank in northern Iraq. Before I reached home, Salah Salem had returned to Egypt.

I went to Sarsank to pay my respects to His Majesty King Faisal II and to report on my trip. There I met Nuri, who related to me in detail his discussions with Salah Salem, stating that they had agreed that the Arab defense pact should be fortified by Western, that is, United States and United Kingdom support, and that it would be open for neighboring countries to join. It was agreed, Nuri told me, that Egypt should approach both the United States and the United Kingdom on the matter. He asked me on my return to Baghdad to call at the two embassies to find out if they had heard from Washington and London about the Egyptian overture. I did this when I returned to Baghdad and found out that no move had been made by Egypt.

When Nuri returned to Baghdad, I was preparing to leave for New York at the head of the Iraqi delegation to the United Nations. I was to go via Cairo, where the Arab League was to hold a meeting to plan for United Arab action at the UN. Nuri gave me a personal letter to deliver to Salah Salem in Cairo. When I arrived in Cairo, Salah Salem was not there. He had gone, I was told, into retirement in a village. I heard in Cairo that he had been rebuked in the Council of Ministers for the steps he had taken in Sarsank. I met with Foreign Minister Mahmud Fawzi and learned that Egypt could not go along with the Sarsank plan.

Later on, Nuri visited Cairo, London and Ankara. He told me that President Nasser had agreed to enter the defense arrangement, but due to internal troubles with the Muslim Brotherhood, the proposed visit of Turkish Prime Minister Adnan Menderes to Cairo had to be postponed. Nuri also told me that, while Egypt was not ready to enter the defense arrangement, President Nasser had told him that Iraq might go ahead. That was what Nuri understood. Later, however, President Nasser denied that his language meant what Nuri thought it meant. It seems that a misunderstanding had taken place between the two leaders.

Instead of going to Cairo first, Prime Minister Menderes came to Baghdad, and the mutual cooperation agreement between Iraq and Turkey was announced. This upset Cairo and the storm began.

I was asked by Nuri to go to Lebanon and Syria to explain our point of view to President Chamoun of Lebanon and President Atassi of Syria, which I did.

President Nasser called for a meeting of Arab Prime Ministers. Nuri, being unwilling to attend such a meeting, asked me to head the Iraqi delegation, which included Acting Foreign Minister Burhanaddin Bashayan, the Director General of Information and Guidance, Khalil Ibrahim, and the Iraqi Ambassador to Egypt, Najib al-Rawi. I presented the Iraqi point of view as calmly, clearly and logically as I could. I thought I carried the meeting with me that night. Our Egyptian brethren wavered in their attitude. At first they showed some leniency. Salah Salem made me understand that the matter was much simpler than it seemed. Some heads of delegations told me that the issue had not been clear before, and that now Iraq's stand seemed quite reasonable. Prince Faisal of Saudi Arabia and Prime Minister Faris al-Khouri of Syria made me understand that the issue was now clear and that Iraq's action was quite legitimate and correct.

The next morning, however, our Egyptian brethren came to the meeting prepared to attack. President Abd al-Nasser, Salah Salem and Mahmoud Fawzi all spoke in a tense mood. I answered each of them calmly. Salem put the Prime Ministers in an embarrassing situation when he asked them to express their views. He apparently expected them to condemn Iraq's action. None of them committed himself. Only Prince Faisal said, "We stand with Egypt on whatever stand she takes."

To find a way out of the impasse, I spoke to President Jamal Abd al-Nasser during the recess, emphasizing to him that he should not cut all ropes with Nuri Pasha, and that it might be wise if he would agree that the meeting should send a delegation to Baghdad. He agreed. When the meeting was resumed, I made the proposal to send a delegation to Baghdad to see Nuri Pasha. The proposal was accepted. I returned to Baghdad, and the delegation arrived.

A meeting was held in Nuri's house because of his indisposition. He was rough with Salah Salem. Shouting at him, Nuri said that he was in no position to yield to their command! The delegation returned to Cairo having failed in their mission to bridge the difference between the Egyptian and Iraqi points of view. I did not return to Cairo, but Acting Foreign Minister Burhanaddin Bashayan did, with no fruitful results.

From that day until Nuri's death, the wound in the relations between him and our brethren in Egypt never healed. It is a great pity, for Nuri loved Egypt and the Egyptians. He had rendered Egypt great services in its political struggle.

I remember the days when he worked hard to influence Sir Anthony Eden to bring about the British evacuation of Egypt. We must also remember Nuri's great effort to convince the Egyptians to join the Arab League and to help promote Arabism in Cairo, for Egypt had not considered itself Arab before World War II. Nuri was, for a time, Iraqi minister to Cairo during the Second World War. Our young brethren in Cairo probably knew little or nothing about all his services to Egypt. They tried to dictate policies in a terse manner coupled with attacks from *Sawt al Arab* radio. Nuri had to preserve his self-respect and the self-respect of Iraq as an independent state. Iraq was not an Egyptian satellite. Egypt and Iraq parted ways, to the detriment of Arab interests in the area.

Iraq took an active part in the Baghdad Pact. Nuri was very enthusiastic about the promotion of its aims and purposes. I did not attend the opening session of the Pact in Baghdad, for I was at the United Nations. Nuri insisted, however, that I attend with him all the subsequent meetings in Teheran, Karachi and Ankara.

The meetings dealt chiefly with self-defense against Communist infiltration, subversion from within and pressure from without, but Nuri always seized the opportunity of bringing home to the member states, Muslim and Western alike, that communism was fed in the Middle East (Arab world) on the tragedies of Palestine and the harsh measures of the French in North Africa (Algeria). He constantly emphasized the importance of settling these issues in order to face communism with greater strength.

In Chapter VI, Ambassador Gallman deals with Nuri's domestic policy. It is a very fair and enlightening picture of things as they appeared in those days. I wish to make the following additions and comments thereon.

It is to Nuri's credit in domestic policy that he could achieve order and stability in Iraq for many years. Iraq is not an easy country to rule. Its people vary in stages of development from nomad to ultramodern. There are diverse racial and religious elements. In the days of the Ottoman Empire, before World War I, many tribes and the bulk of the population were left in ignorance and were in frequent defiance of the government's authority. Nuri, with his firm hand, charming personality, and the prestige gained from experience and frequent undertaking of responsibility, could achieve order and tranquility whenever he took office. Ordinary people feared as well as loved him. He was like a kind, old-style schoolmaster who was loved by his students—who knew, however, that he had the cane. He was feared and respected and therefore rarely used the cane.

He was certainly devoted to the material development of the country, and flood control and irrigation projects rated first with him, as with most prime ministers who governed Iraq before 1958. In social legislation and land reform he was very conservative and slow.

Nuri believed in western democracy in theory. In practice he
felt that Iraq needed a special kind of government. Iraqis are
ultraindividualists and very eruptive. Their individualism made
cooperative political work very difficult. Party discipline would
be hard to apply. The eruptive nature of Iraqis required frequent changes of government. Nuri had to adapt himself to conditions, but he did not think of fundamentally changing these
conditions, nor was it in his power to do so alone.

His government, though benevolent and constructive materially, was not consonant with the changes of the times. He had
no new ideology or doctrines to offer the people. He did not
care to explain the good policies that he cherished or sell them
to the masses who were invaded by communism, by Ba'thism,
and by adverse propaganda from Cairo. The intellectual group,
which was ever increasing in number, the youth, labor and peasantry all needed organization and leadership in ideology.
Unfortunately they did not find it under Nuri. He certainly
fought communism with all his might, but his policy was
mainly one of repression.

I remember one day when he called on me in my home. We
were talking about the danger of communism to Iraq, and Nuri
was telling me about the vigilance of the police in checking the
communist danger. I told him, "Pasha, communism cannot be
met with repression alone. You need four measures for dealing
with commumism:

(1) An ideology which is higher and more appealing to our
people than that of communism;
(2) Social reform and the correction of social and moral
corruption;
(3) Basic economic development and a quick rise in the
standard of living of the masses;
(4) Vigilance and strictness in applying security measures."
I said, "Pasha, you emphasize point (4) and do not do much
about points (1), (2), and (3)."

He jokingly answered, "I know you are against Point 4." He
was referring to American economic aid in Iraq, of which I was
very critical. This was characteristic of Nuri Pasha. He turned
aside a serious argument with a joke.

His individualistic nature made him suspicious of some of his
most sincere and loyal collaborators in Iraqi politics. Take for

example, Saleh Jabr, who was his devoted friend and colleague. They carried together the burden of seeing Iraq through the hard days of the Second World War. They took together many harsh measures with great courage and at the risk of their lives. They came out after the war as the two strong men in Iraqi politics. Saleh Jabr formed the Cabinet in 1947, but he was always a devoted friend and supporter of Nuri.

When they came to form a political party, they disagreed on the choice of members. Saleh wanted no elements whose politics had been questioned in the past. This disagreement led to a parting of the ways. Saleh formed the Nation's Socialist Party vis-à-vis Nuri's Constitutional Union Party. The two parties were supposed to alternate in ruling the country, but their relations turned into bitterness. This was the great break in Nuri's political house.

When Nuri came to power, he dissolved all the parties, including his own, although his followers actually became the ruling group. As an independent and friend of both Nuri and Saleh, I worked hard to alleviate their personal differences, but such efforts had no lasting effects. The matter had gone deep with Nuri, and he felt that Saleh Jabr intended to become his competitor for the leadership of Iraq. Actually Saleh Jabr, who had acquired great political stature through merit, never questioned Nuri's priority and leadership, and it must be put on record that in the most critical times of Nuri's rule, 1955–56, Saleh supported him with magnanimity and devotion.

Saleh was watching the internal deterioration of affairs under Nuri's rule. In June 1957 when I went to say good-by to Saleh before leaving with Nuri to attend the Baghdad Pact meeting in Karachi, Saleh said to me, "Fadhel, what have you got to do with the Pact? Why do you bear responsibility when you are not in office? I must tell you that things are not going well in the army. There is going to be a coup and the King and the Crown Prince and Nuri are going to be killed." I asked, "Have you informed them?" He said, "Yes, but they do not listen." I replied, "I am going to Karachi because I believe in the idea of the Baghdad Pact, and I am ready to serve my idea at any cost.'

On the day that I returned from Karachi, I went straight from the airport to the funeral of Saleh Jabr, who had fallen dead with a heart attack in the Senate the day before.

I have recorded here the Nuri-Saleh affair in order to give an example of Nuri's complacency and individualism in internal affairs, which, added to his neglect of the political and ideological education of the people, contributed to the downfall of the regime.

I was one of those who experienced Nuri's restrictions. In 1956 I felt the urgent need to start a political party and publish a newspaper. I prepared the platform of the party, The People's Progress Party, and submitted it to His Majesty the King. I also prepared an application for permission to start a newspaper. Nuri hugged me in a most friendly way and begged me to drop the idea for the time being. He argued that if he were to open the door for a party and a newspaper, he would not be able to withstand the pressure from others wanting the same thing. I had to yield.

In 1957, when Ali Jowdat was Prime Minister, I applied for a license to publish my newspaper, *Al-Amal (Action)*, which appeared from December 14, 1957, to July 14, 1958. When Nuri saw the newspaper, he told me he regretted not having given his permission when I first asked for it.

Nuri was not a theoretician, and he was not an intellectual leader. He was a father, a well-meaning ruler, and a keeper of order. His repressive measures regarding the parties, the press and the Communists were all negative measures. He was very slow and late to acknowledge the importance of propaganda and the effect of the radio and the press.

The following quotation from Gallman's book points out this weakness in Nuri's domestic policy: "The public, however, did not enter into his day-to-day calculations. He was blind to the need for good public relations."

It is only fair to point out, however, that Nuri's impatience with the press, the political parties, Communists, etc., was only partially due to his individualistic nature. It was due in some part to the international circumstances which were imposed on him.

He was a staunch believer in a pro-Western policy and a deadly enemy of communism. But how could he win the masses to such a policy? Wasn't the United States of America the close friend and main supporter of Israel at the expense of Arab rights to their homes? Wasn't Britain the attacker of Egypt, as well as the first cause of the Palestine tragedy? Wasn't France the attacker of Egypt as well as the killer of hundreds of thousands of Arabs in North Africa? Free political activity and a free press in Iraq would, in most cases, have turned anti-Western and not anti-Communist. Nuri's job was a thankless one. He fell, in a sense, as a victim of Western policies in the Arab world.

Nuri's domestic policy received blessings from the West in the form of oil revenues which made possible the Development Board. But it suffered impossible handicaps from the West over Palestine, Suez and Algeria. The balance tilted against the West. The harm done was greater than the benefits received.

In Chapter VII, Ambassador Gallman starts by pointing out that aspersions have been cast on Nuri's Arab nationalism because he made Iraq join the Baghdad Pact. That is true, but it was unjust, as Gallman goes on to say.

I have already pointed out that Nuri used the Baghdad Pact not only as a defense measure against communism, but that he also used it as a platform to defend Arab interests, especially the questions of Palestine and Algeria. This is no place to go into the details of the efforts expended in the Baghdad Pact's secret meetings on behalf of Palestine and Algeria.

Nuri's record is rich with his struggles for the Arab nationalist cause. As a young man, he escaped from the Ottomans and joined the Arab Revolt. He then served under King Faisal I in Syria, and later came to Iraq and helped in organizing the new state of Iraq and in leading it to independence. In foreign affairs he served the cause of Syria and Palestine. In 1939 he attended the Round Table Conference in London which produced the White Paper on Palestine. During World War II, he served the cause of the independence of Syria and Lebanon and worked for Palestine. At this time he produced his so-called Fertile Crescent scheme for federating Iraq, Syria, Lebanon, Palestine and Transjordan. He helped found the Arab League and was one of its chief architects. He worked hard for British withdrawal from the Suez Canal Zone in order to achieve complete Egyptian freedom. He gave moral and material support to the struggle of our brethren in North Africa, Tunisia, Morocco and Algeria. I remember the planes loaded with arms which used to go from Iraq to Libya to be delivered to our Algerian brethren. How many Arab nationalists are there who can boast of a record of national service like that of Nuri's? Nay, Nuri's record on Arab nationalism cannot be denied or impugned.

Gallman rightly refers to Nuri's part in achieving the union of Jordan and Iraq. Nuri was not overly enthusiastic about unions at that time. He thought that the Arab states should first build themselves from within and that union would come in time. He also preferred to build a strong Iraq, thinking that union would be much easier if Iraq was strong and stable. That is why he was against early union with Syria, an idea which I cherished. When Syria amalgamated with Egypt, he had to go ahead with the union of Iraq and Jordan, a union for which he had no great enthusiasm. Iraq could not carry the financial burdens of Jordan, and that is one reason why Nuri worked hard for Kuwait to join the Union so that it might contribute to the financial needs of Jordan.

When Mr. Selwyn Lloyd, the United Kingdom's Foreign Minister, passed through Baghdad in the spring of 1958, we met at Qasr al-Rihab. Present were H.M. King Faisal II, the Crown Prince, Prime Minister Nuri, Vice-Premier Tawfiq al-Suweidi and myself as Foreign Minister. The question of union with Kuwait was raised in detail. It was my suggestion that the first step should be the independence of Kuwait and the raising of the Sheikh's status to that of a King. Mr. Selwyn Lloyd said that this matter would need a decision on Cabinet level.

In the first days of July 1958, on my way to Iraq from the United States, I called on Mr. Selwyn Lloyd at No. 1 Carlton Gardens. He told me that Nuri had been to see him about several matters, including Lebanon and Kuwait. He had been most impatient and excited about British procrastination on the

It was planned to hold an Anglo-Iraqi Conference on July 20, immediately preceding the Baghdad Pact meeting, to discuss matters of mutual interest to the two countries, including Kuwait. I, as a member of the Arab Union Council, was to attend that Conference with Nuri, Prime Minister of the Arab Union, and Suweidi, Foreign Minister of the Arab Union. The collapse of the regime on July 14 put an end to all Nuri's worries about the Union.

Regarding Syria, I have already intimated that Nuri stopped my efforts to go ahead on the federation of Iraq and Syria. He would not consent to spend any money for that purpose. A few years later, during the Anglo-French-Israeli attack on Suez, the Syrians destroyed the Iraqi oil pipeline that went through Syria. The Communist infiltration of Syria became obvious, culminating in a Communist, Afif al-Bizri, being chief of the General Staff.

If Syria goes Communist, who will save Iraq from the Communist danger? The River Euphrates, on whose water half of Iraq's life depends, passes through Syria. If an unfriendly regime dominates Syria, how can Iraq survive? Also, Iraq's access to the Mediterranean is through Syria.

Nuri had objected to my Cabinet's intention to spend one quarter of a million dinars for the federation project, but Iraq lost some fifty million dinars when the pipeline was cut.

In 1956 Nuri was at last convinced that something should be done to bring about a federation with Syria. He did not discuss the matter with me. I was at the United Nations when I read that a secret move to federate Syria and Iraq had been discovered and crushed. Nuri had bet on the wrong horse. He had depended on Colonel Shishakly, the former dictator of Syria, to execute the plan.

With all other Arab states, Nuri cherished friendship and good relations. He had nothing but good will towards Yemen, Saudi Arabia, Egypt and Lebanon. All he hoped for was that each country would be free to develop its own affairs without interference and without encroaching on one another. Unfortunately, Saudi Arabian money was spent in Jordan, Syria, Lebanon and Iraq itself to obstruct Iraq's constructive policies. This came to an end after a friendly *rapprochement* between the two ruling families.

Toward Egypt Nuri harbored the sincerest best wishes, but he could not see any justification for Egypt's desire to dictate Iraq's foreign policy. Egypt never consulted Iraq when formulating foreign policy. The Egyptian radio and press attacks on Nuri and the ruling family of Iraq could not be justified among brother states. They were suited to a state that is an enemy in an antagonistic camp. Still, Nuri was shocked by the British collusion with Israel in the attack on Egypt.

As for Lebanon, he always supported the idea of an independent Lebanon to be a neutral state among the Arab states. He deplored the interference in the affairs of Lebanon which led to the disturbances of 1958. He wanted to support the legally established authority there by all means, and he strongly advised King Faisal II to bring personal pressure on me to go the Security Council to defend the case of Lebanon.

In short, Nuri was one of the great Arab nationalists of the first half of this century. He was well known as such to the older generation, but toward the end of his life he lost touch with the new currents in Arab nationalism and with the younger generation. This does not in any way minimize the greatness of his contribution in his time.

In Chapter VII, Ambassador Gallman deals with Nuri's attitude toward Israel. His remark that "Nuri's public statements on
Israel differed sharply from what he had to say in private"
shows complete misunderstanding and misjudgment of Nuri.

Nuri hated the existence of Israel as much as any other Arab
nationalist, and he stated his feelings both publicly and privately. I know this from my personal experience with him.

However, Nuri distinguished clearly between Judaism as a religion and Zionism, between the Jews as a people of a faith and
Zionists. He had nothing against the Jews, but he certainly opposed Zionist aggression and domination.

On the question of Palestine, Nuri had a sense of realism and
the art of practical policies. He was in favor of the Arabs accepting the 1939 White Paper. When they rejected it, he
thought they had lost an opportunity. Later he felt that the
Arabs should have accepted the Bevin plan or the minority plan
of the United Nations Commission of Inquiry which advised
cantonization of Palestine. Having missed that chance also, he
took the stand accepted by the Arab League and the Bandung
Conference, namely, that the UN resolutions on Palestine should
be implemented. To him politics meant realism and the art of
the possible.

A point of importance in his policy on Palestine was his
knowledge that the Palestine issue is the most sensitive one in
the Arab world. The Arabs may be divided on other issues, but
never about their rights in Palestine. That is why Nuri was always careful not to back a solution or a policy which had not
been agreed upon by all the Arab states unanimously. Even then
he would not make a move before asking the Palestinians to
express their views and to bear the responsibility for the step to
be taken.

In Chapter IX, Ambassador Gallman speaks of Nuri's "loyalty" to the British. I do not think that the word "loyalty" should
be understood in any sense other than friendship. He certainly
was a loyal friend of the British. But, if the word "loyalty" were
to convey political allegiance, it would be unfair and incorrect.

Gallman is also incorrect in saying that the King and Crown
Prince owed "everything they had, position and substance, to
the British." The royal Hashemite family was not foisted upon
the Iraqi people. King Faisal I ascended the throne after the
Iraqis revolted against British rule in 1920. It was decided that
one of the sons of King Hussein would be asked to become King

of an independent Iraq. A delegation consisting of the leaders of the Iraqi Revolution went to Hejaz to invite Faisal to come to Iraq. A referendum was held in which the overwhelming majority of the people of Iraq asked Faisal I to become their king. The British could not have imposed an undesired king. The King and the Crown Prince owed what they had to the Iraqi people, and not to the British.

The fact that the British tried to hold as tenaciously as they could to their old position and privileges in Iraq was only natural. Actually, when it came to business we find that the British in 1958 had no great interests in Iraq other than their shares in the oil. The other two important issues which affected their interests directly were the contracts of the Development Board and the voting in the United Nations.

As far as the contracts of the Development Board go, they were usually given to the lowest bidder. In the year 1958, the British had no important share of the contracts.

As for the voting in the UN, the Iraqi delegation consistently voted supporting the liberation of the colonies and quite often aroused the friendly displeasure of the British delegation.

There is no doubt that the British yielded ground in Iraq very substantially, and Nuri had much to his credit in gaining Iraqi rights from the British in a friendly manner. Had Gallman been acquainted with previous conditions in Iraq, he would have been convinced that Iraq had moved from occupation to practically complete liberation after the Second World War.

When I came to the Ministry of Foreign Affairs in 1946, there was only one ambassador accredited to Iraq—the British Ambassador. The Anglo-Iraq Treaty of 1930 made it impossible for Iraq to accept ambassadors from other nations. It was through friendly negotiations that this particular article of the Treaty was abrogated that year so that Iraq as a sovereign state could have whatever ambassadors she chose, including an American.

As for the Anglo-American rivalries in Iraq, that is a matter between London and Washington, and Nuri, in the years under study, was certainly as cordial with the United States as he was with the United Kingdom. He showed no partiality so far as I know.

The case of Mr. Nelson which Gallman describes is a good example of this point. Mr. Nelson, an American member of the Development Board, seems to have displeased the British, who, through their Ambassador, influenced Nuri not to renew Nelson's contract. Several Iraqis, including myself, were greatly disturbed. I went to the British Ambassador and expressed my displeasure at his personal intervention to prevent the renewal of Nelson's contract. The Ambassador answered that he had had nothing to do with the matter, since the affair was entirely the concern of the Iraqi government. I went to Nuri and he said that he was not going to renew the contract of either foreign members of the Board, neither the British nor the American. Actually when the term of the British member, Mr. Ionides, was over, it was not renewed either, in spite of the British Ambassador's desire and request for its renewal.

Nuri was one of the best bargainers I have ever met. He used his charm and friendship to gain as much as he could for his country.

The residue of anti-British propaganda, which remained from the days of the occupation, greatly exaggerated the extent of the actual British influence in Iraq before 1958. Much of "the-British-run-Iraq" propaganda was out of touch with the realities. Iraqis ran their own affairs as freely internally and externally as any other independent state in the world.

Ambassador Gallman is at his best in Chapter X, dealing with the Americans in Iraq. He is very sincere and honest in emphasizing the importance of America's cultural contribution. As a graduate of American universities both in Beirut and the United States, I wholeheartedly underscore Gallman's emphasis. In the long run, nothing leaves a lasting impression on the hearts and minds of a people like education.

Nuri welcomed and encouraged any educational contribution which America could make to Iraq. There is no doubt that fine work was done by Americans in other fields of life such as defense, medicine, argiculture, engineering, etc., but nothing has a lasting effect like education.

My chief criticism of nonmilitary American aid, which was called the Point Four Program, was that it spread over too vast an area and too thinly. It left hardly any lasting impression on the life of the country. American aid often came "too little and too late."

Mr. Gallman's criticism of his own government is quite constructive. Nuri's attempt to buy powerful radio equipment through the United States government is an excellent example of how Americans missed a good opportunity to help. (pp. 49–50) Iraq struggled hard to get a 100 kw. radio station.

In June 1958 when I went to Washington, Nuri asked me to see Secretary of State John Foster Dulles about Iraq's desire to purchase equipment for a very powerful radio station. I saw Dulles, and he gave the matter his attention. As soon as I got back to my hotel, the Counsellor of the British Embassy rang asking to see me. He came to inquire about our radio requirements. It seems that Mr. Dulles had relegated the matter to the British again.

My pet project was an American university for Iraq, emphasizing agriculture and mechanics side by side with the humanities. Nuri gave his support to the idea. The State Department could not find the ways and means to establish such an institution, and the project was never realized. I am sure that this kind of university would have been a bridge between America and Iraq and would have served their interests more than defense aid or Point 4.

In Chapter XI, Ambassador Gallman deals with the 1958 Coup and its aftermath. I have nothing to say on the chapter more than to underline its concluding sentence: "To destroy is easy. To build is difficult."

In Chapter XII, Ambassador Gallman gives a very fair picture of Nuri as a statesman and as a noble human being with points of strength and weakness. There is no doubt that Nuri was a great Arab nationalist. He started as a revolutionary and he helped Iraq achieve the revolutionary objectives of the nationalists of the epoch—political liberation and independence.

In the social and economic field, he rose from the level of the medieval Iraq in which he was born and brought up to the level of a twentieth-century conservative. When great new social trends in the world became apparent, he definitely sided with the West and had nothing to do with the East.

I think history will prove that Nuri and his school were, on the whole, moving on the right track, in spite of their several mistakes and weaknesses. Iraqis today are yearning for security, stability and prosperity. I believe that this can be achieved only by democracy based on personal freedom and absolute moral standards.

The book contains several printing errors, especially in the spelling of proper names, and a few errors of fact. In the footnote on p. 38, speaking of the Portsmouth Treaty, Gallman states, "Nuri advised against signing until political leaders in Iraq had been consulted. Jabr rejected the advice, signed, and was then faced with the riots . . ." I was present at the time, and I do not remember such advice from Nuri. The political leaders were consulted before the delegation went to London. Nuri himself signed the Treaty. So did I, and so did Tawfiq al-Suweidi and Shakir al-Wadi as well as Saleh Jabr.

According to the footnote on p. 204, Baba Ali, Minister of Communications, and Muhammad Hadid, Minister of Finance, had had previous experience on the Cabinet level; Ibrahim Kubba, Minister of Economics and Siddiq Shanshal, Minister of News and Guidance had not.

In closing I wish to repeat that Ambassador Gallman should be congratulated for having produced a fine book. It should be read by all those interested in the affairs of the Middle East in general and the Arab world in particular.

6. The Iraqi Revolution of July 14, 1958

BY KHALDUN AL-HUSRI

PART I*

DR. FADHEL JAMALI'S REVIEW of Ambassador Waldemar J. Gallman's book *Iraq Under General Nuri* is an apologia for the *ancien régime* overthrown by the Iraqi Revolution of July 14, 1958. As a historical document, it is a mixture of truths, half-truths, and falsehoods. That it should be so can to some degree be both understood and expected; the apologias of defeated politicians are seldom otherwise. Even the writings in exile of that great historian Trotsky lack something of the breadth, depth, and objectivity of his earlier works. On this point we must be charitable with the document under consideration. We must also not dwell too long on the numerous instances of self-laudation: Jamali convincing Mr. Nehru "after a lengthy debate" in a secret session of the Bandung Conference of the right of states to enter into military pacts for self-defense; Jamali recalling his meetings with President Nasser—"I presented the Iraqi point of view as calmly, clearly, and logically as I could . . . Our Egyptian brethren wavered in their attitude . . . President Abd al-Nasser, Salah Salem and Mahmoud Fawzi all spoke in a tense mood. I answered each of them calmly"—Prince Faisal of Saudi Arabia, who attended these meetings, recalled in 1955 that Jamali was far from calm; [1] this is only a minor point.

We must also not attempt to pick up and examine each single

*Reprinted from *Middle East Forum*, Vol. XL, No. 8 (Beirut, 1964), pp. 25–27; by permission of the editor.

thread that has gone to make up the whole tissue of Jamali's apologia, distinguishing the false from the true and the true from the half-true. This would be too easy, and we could miss the forest for the trees. The secret archives of the Iraqi Government have been opened by the revolution, and the documents they contained, many of them in Jamali's own handwriting, have been freely used by The People's Court.

We shall examine instead Jamali's document *in toto*. Jamali does not regard the Revolution of July 14 as an indigenous act of the Iraqi people springing from their discontents and grievances. The Iraqi masses, according to him, were "invaded *(sic)* by Communism, Ba'thism, and by the adverse propaganda from Cairo." This claim, even at this late date, does not greatly surprise us. Throughout history the enemies of this or that revolution have claimed to the last that they were overthrown by this or that diabolical foreign force or element—Jews, Germans, Freemasons, Communists. Jamali's particular villains are Communists, Ba'thists and *Sawt al Arab* radio. In reality the Revolution of July 14 was an indigenous Iraqi movement, with roots extending deep into Iraqi soil, fed by discontents and grievances that existed long before President Nasser or the spread of communism and Ba'thism. We must now examine these roots briefly.

The overwhelming majority of those who have studied the phenomenon of revolution find it intimately connected with war. Revolutions, from those of ancient Athens to those of Russia in 1905 and 1917, down to those of our own times, have followed unsuccessful wars. Rarely does a ruling class survive defeat in war. Its weaknesses and corruptions are laid bare by defeat, leading to the loss of whatever loyalty it had previously condemned [sic] among the ruled.

The Iraqi people had suffered defeat not in one, but in three wars—The Anglo-Iraqi War of 1941, the Palestine War of 1948, and the Suez War of 1956. In two of these wars, that of 1941 and 1956, their rulers were openly on the side of their enemies; their rulers were in fact their enemies. To understand the Revolution of July, it is essential to know these facts.

The earliest of the three wars, the Anglo-Iraqi War of 1941, had in many ways left the deepest and ugliest scars in the hearts and minds of the people. What, briefly, was this war? Professor George Kirk, in the Chatham House volume *The Middle East in War*, surveys it under the title of "The Iraqi Bid for Independence." To the Iraqi people that war was indeed their war of independence; and its loss was to be one of their most bitter experiences. Abdul Illah and Nuri al-Said were to fight this war on the side of the British and to enter Baghdad after the collapse of armed resistance protected by British bayonets. That war was to be followed with what is generally known in Iraq as "the second British occupation," the first being that of 1917. What happened in that war and in "the second British occupation" that followed, profoundly touched the emotions of the people. Those who saw the black RAF Wellington bombers fly over Baghdad were always to remember them as gigantic ugly birds seen in a nightmare. The small town of Falluja, which had changed hands twice in the course of the month-long war, was bombed and strafed by British planes and became the Guernica of the nationalists' mythology. Iraq's greatest modern poet, Marouf al-Rissafi, wrote a forceful poem, *The Day of Falluja*.[2] But in 1956 Iraqi audiences were to watch with repulsion in newsreels and illustrated magazines King Faisal II in the uniform of an RAF vice-marshal inspect and visit Odiham Air Force Station and Harrow School.[3] Following the defeat of 1941, concentration camps in Iraq were filled with those who supported this war, "the one great corporate action of modern Iraq,"[4] and the leaders of this bid for independence were hanged like ordinary criminals. One of them, Salah al-Din al-Sabagh, was to be hanged in public in 1945, having been handed over by Turkey to Abdul Illah, although no extradition treaty existed between the two countries. Al-Rissafi, in another poem on those who were hanged, was to write:

> Let manliness and chivalry disown us,
> If we forget the day on which you were hanged.[5]

That day was in fact not forgotten; and the mob on July 14 was to hang Abdul Illah's corpse at the very same spot at which Salah al-Din al-Sabagh had been hanged, and a man was to climb up a pole and start stabbing the lifeless corpse, shouting, "Take this for Salah al-Din al-Sabagh! and this! and this!" Today public squares in Baghdad are named after the leaders who were hanged, and the revolutionary government has created a special order that is given to all those who have participated in the war of 1941. Recently both President Abdul Salaam Arif and Premier Tahir Yahya declared that the

Revolution of July was the continuation of the Revolution of 1941—the terms "revolution" and "war" being interchangeably used in Iraq to describe the Anglo-Iraqi armed clash of 1941.[6] Jamali, who never mentions this war, objects to Ambassador Gallman's statement that the King and the Crown Prince owed "everything they had, position and substance, to the British." Writes Jamali: "The Royal Hashemite family was not foisted upon the Iraqi people." He then goes on to explain how Faisal I became the king of Iraq. It cannot, of course, be said that the majority of Iraqis objected to Faisal I becoming their king, although it is equally true that it was the British who had put him up as the candidate to the throne of Iraq and supported him energetically in the referendum of 1921.[7] But Gallman is clearly writing not of Faisal I and 1921, but of Faisal II and the post-1941 Iraq. In that Iraq, people had come to believe that the King and the Crown Prince owed their power to the British, and in the light of this belief, to reconsider the past and then regard the whole royal family as an alien family imported and imposed on them by the British.

There seem to have been some men on the British side, like General Wavell, who had advised their government at the time to come to terms with the nationalists of Iraq. The distinguished Iraqi historian Majid Khadduri is of the opinion that "a political settlement with the nationalists might have proved more beneficial for future friendship and cooperation between Great Britain and the Middle Eastern countries." [8] With this I am in full agreement. I also believe that Great Britain, by not removing Abdul Illah after the end of the World War (to an ambassadorship in London or some other European capital) lost a second opportunity to reach some *modus vivendi* with the Iraqi nationalists. Most roads leading to revolutions are strewn with lost opportunities.

Public opinion in Iraq had passionately supported the cause of the Arabs of Palestine since the twenties. Thus the visit to Baghdad in 1928 of Sir Alfred Monde, a leader of British Zionism, had caused violent anti-Zionist demonstrations in which 20,000 people had taken part,[9] and disagreement with British policy in Palestine had been one of the principal causes of the war of 1941.[10] It was, therefore, only natural that Arab failure in Palestine should touch the Iraqis as deeply and painfully as other Arabs. The ruling class was held directly responsible for the humiliation in Palestine. Public opinion was to note the Regent's unwillingness to stand up to his uncle, Prince Abdullah of Transjordan, who had gone into the war not to prevent the creation of a Jewish state in Palestine but to annex those parts of it allotted to the Arabs by the UN resolution on partition. They also strongly resented the withdrawal of the Iraqi army in 1949 from the triangle of Nablus-Tulkaram-Jenin. Furthermore, Iraqis had been aware that after 1941, Major General Renton, head of the British military mission, and his successors had systematically worked to weaken the Iraqi army. Thus, Major Mahmoud al-Durra, a military expert, estimates that between 1941 and 1948, 2,879 officers, many of them staff officers, had been dismissed from the army, and he finds that the pursual of an "arms without ammunition policy" was responsible for the shortages of the army in Palestine, particularly in the firepower of its artillery.[11]

By the end of the Second World War and in the years immediately following, it was apparent that a sharp polarization of ideology and policy had taken place within Iraqi society. Longrigg and Stoaks, who know Iraq well, observe in the history of postwar Iraq "a new political division within Iraq herself, no longer so significantly within the ministerial group (i.e. the ruling group) as between that group and upholders of a new form of nationalism opposed to many of that group's policies. [12] This "new form of nationalism" was in reality not so new; this, not Nasser's propaganda or anything else, explains its great hold on the minds and the emotions of the politically conscious Iraqis. Iraq had been the standard-bearer of pan-Arabism since the twenties, and anti-Zionism had been the declared official policy of successive Iraq cabinets. The desire to get rid of all British domination had been an aim of the Iraqi nationalist movement from 1921 to 1941. In addition, a desire for nonalignment and neutrality in international affairs had been conspicuous among the nationalists in Iraq since the thirties, and of this desire Longrigg and Stoaks themselves write: "Between the two European blocs of that period many nationalists favored what was later to be called positive neutralism." [13] The desire to strengthen the armed forces was in turn to cause the nationalists to try to break Iraq's exclusive reliance on Britain for armaments; the Iraqi government, in 1936, was to buy planes from Italy and to conclude an "arms deal" with Germany for £25,500,000, payable over a period of fifteen years in cash or bartered raw materials.[14] (Was there any need for radio Cairo to make Nasser's 1955 arms deal popular with the Iraqi nationalists?) And finally, a deep concern with social justice and the reform of Iraqi society had been apparent in Iraqi politics since the thirties.

A desire for social justice, and all the other elements of this "new form of nationalism," were long popular with the Iraqi masses. It was not the siren songs of Cairo radio which made them so, as Jamali claims. Jamali blames Nuri al-Said for not having waged an energetic war of propaganda against Nasser's ideas and finds that Nuri's "neglect of the political and ideological education of the people [had] contributed to the downfall of the regime." Anybody who today goes over the transcripts of Radio Baghdad broadcasts and the Iraqi newspapers of the period, including Jamali's own *al-Amal*, as well as the official proceedings of the Iraqi Chamber of Deputies and Senate, cannot say that Nuri al-Said and the Iraqi *ancien régime* neglected the use of propaganda or left their policies unexplained to the people. And that this propaganda was doomed to fail should not have surprised anyone with passing knowledge of the history of modern Iraq.

PART II°

In an address to the Senate in 1955, Nuri al-Said claimed that "99.75 per cent" of the Iraqi people supported the Baghdad Pact. In fact, however, the overwhelming majority of Iraqis were clearly and bitterly opposed to it. Ambassador Gallman, himself in favor of the Pact, admits that "the pact never enjoyed wide popular support" and that "the pact did not have the backing of the Iraqi people." [1] The people resented the fact that the pact estranged Iraq from the rest of the Arab world and aligned it with non-Arab powers that had never been popular with Iraqis. Turkey, the ex-overlord, was not liked; its irredentist intentions, of which an example was the claim it advanced for Mosul after the First World War, were suspect; and its annexation of Alexandretta was strongly resented. An earlier attempt by Nuri al-Said, in 1946, to conclude a treaty of friendship with Turkey had run into considerable opposition. Gallman himself tells us of eggs thrown at the Turkish delegation when it arrived in Iraq to negotiate the Baghdad Pact and of street demonstrations in the holy city of Najaf that forced the government to cancel the Turkish President's visit there. [2]

°Reprinted from *Middle East Forum*, Vol. XLI, No. 1 (Beirut, 1965), pp. 24–29; by permission of the editor.

Iraq's relations with Persia had always been strained by the dispute over the Shatt al-Arab waterway and by frequent frontier incidents. Pakistan's stand over Palestine was fully appreciated, but Iraqis reserved their admiration for nonaligned India, its great leader Nehru, and "Bandungism."

The Pact was furthermore criticized by politically conscious Iraqis for involving Iraq in the power struggles of the two world blocs and for preventing her from pursuing a truly independent foreign policy based exclusively on Iraq's national interests, which had been an aim of the nationalist movement since the thirties. It was also feared that the Pact averted Iraq's eyes from the real enemy—Israel. That there were some grounds for this fear cannot be denied. As Anthony Nutting was to write: "Ambassador Ebba Eban admitted to me two years ago at the UN, that the Baghdad Pact is in no sense a threat to Israel, rather the contrary, in so far as it averts the Arab gaze from the struggles within the Middle East and directs it towards the far greater menace from without."[3]

Nuri always argued that the danger of "international" Communism was greater than of Israel, but Nuri had finally to admit it was difficult to sell this idea to the people.[4] It was also argued, as Jamali still does in his apologia, that the Baghdad Pact gained friends for the Arab point of view on Israel. This, however, was not convincing, as Britain disassociated herself from the Iraqi-Turkish exchange of letters on the implementation of the UN resolutions concerning Palestine, while Turkey itself continued its cordial relations with Israel.

Finally a fantastic attempt was made to correlate Zionism and communism. Thus Jamali was to declare in Parliament: "We must not differentiate between the two, because Zionism is the daughter of communism and communism is the mother of Zionism";[5] but how this feat was achieved and what, if anything at all, in Zionism and communism could be correlated, Jamali never explained in this or in any other of his speeches.

In 1955 Britain joined the Baghdad Pact and concluded with Iraq a special agreement. This agreement was resented by the nationalists as much as the Baghdad Pact itself, for they saw it as nothing but a continuation of the treaties of 1948 and of 1930—the last officially known as the Treaty of Preferential Alliance between Iraq and Great Britain. All previous Anglo-Iraqi treaties, those of 1922, 1926, 1927 and 1930, were ratified with difficulty by Iraq because of stiff and vociferous nationalist opposition. The 1930 treaty had terminated the mandate and admitted Iraq into the League of Nations, but it did not satisfy the nationalists, who demanded nothing short of *al-Istiqlal al-tamm*—complete or absolute independence; they objected to the privileges which the 1930 treaty reserved for Britain, and to the two airbases of Habbaniya and Shuayba which Britain retained on Iraqi soil.

In 1948, Britain concluded with Saleh Jabr a new treaty of alliance, which again allowed Britain the use of the two airbases; but the treaty caused the bloody uprising of 1948 known as *Al-Wathba,* which cost the lives of between 50 and 100 Iraqis, with four times that number injured.[6] Abdul Illah was forced to repudiate the treaty, and *Saleh Jabr* himself had to flee Baghdad.

By 1955 time was running out for Britain, and it was clear to her that a new formula had to be devised to ensure Britain's occupation of the airbases. As Eden puts it: "There was another reason why we should support and maybe join the pact. The Anglo-Iraqi treaty of 1930 would expire in 1957 and we had to take account of nationalist feeling, even in the most friendly countries. It was important to get rid of any taint of patron and pupil. An attempt by the Labor Government to negotiate a new treaty had ended in riots and disappointment."[7] By placing the new treaty within the wider context of the Baghdad Pact, Britain and the Iraqi ruling class sought to avoid nationalist opposition; but nationalist public opinion was not won over. It clearly saw that the new special agreement was nothing but the old one of 1948 against which they had risen. Eden at the time openly declared in Parliament: "The engagement they (the Labor Party) entered into is precisely the same kind of engagement that we are entering into."[8] And indeed it was, for Britain continued to occupy the two bases under a somewhat new and ingenious formula. Anthony Nutting, then Minister of State for Foreign Affairs, explained this new formula to Parliament: The bases reverted to the ownership of the Iraqi government to use jointly with Britain. RAF squadrons would, under the new arrangement, visit Iraq for joint training with Iraqi squadrons, *"at all times,"* to quote the terms of the agreement. "They will be looked after by our own ground staff, who will still be permanently stationed there."[9] And later Nutting was to write tersely and more succinctly: "Iraq has solved the problem of British bases. She owns the airfields, and Britain uses them."[10]

Nuri al-Said and the ruling class, using all the repressive

measures at their disposal, were able to ratify the Baghdad Pact and the Special Agreement of April 1955. But Iraqis were not to forget or forgive them the fact that a new treaty of alliance with Britain was forced on them only eighteen months before the hated 1930 treaty was to have expired of itself.

In the quarrel between Egypt and Iraq's ruling class over the Baghdad Pact (and earlier still over Syria), the emotions of the Iraqi people were squarely on the side of Egypt. This was because Egypt and Nasser had become for most Iraqis the repository of that "new form" of Arab nationalism whose constituent elements had first appeared in Iraq, but had been frustrated in the defeat of 1941 and in the "second British occupation" which followed. Jamali, in one of his anti-Nasser articles, was to write that those who supported Nasser in Iraq were the very same people who had earlier supported the war of 1941; and in this he was absolutely right.

Nuri and the ruling class, engaged in what they considered a mortal struggle with Nasser which could only end in the destruction of one side or the other, constantly urged their Western allies to "do something about Nasser." And this undoubtedly contributed to the withdrawal of the American offer to finance the Aswan Dam. Eden writes: "Already at the beginning of the year (1956) the Iraqi Government were complaining that the Egyptians had done better out of the West by bullying them than they had by co-operating. The Iraqis had got £3,000,000 and a few tanks, the Egyptians seemed about to get the Aswan Dam . . . They could hardly be expected to view with enthusiasm the advance of large sums for an Egyptian project. . . ." [11] Dulles in explaining his action was to say: "The Egyptians, in a sense, forced upon us an issue to which I think there was only one proper response. That issue was, do nations which play both sides get better treatment than nations which are stalwart and work with us?" [12]

THE SUEZ CRISIS

When Nasser nationalized the Suez Canal, Nuri and the ruling class found in this act their golden opportunity and urged the immediate bringing down of Nasser. On July 26, 1956, when news of nationalization was brought to Eden, King Faisal, Crown Prince Abdul Illah, and Nuri were dining with him. Eden writes: "I told my guests [the news]. They saw clearly that

here was an event which' changed all perspectives, and
understood at once how much [the] world depends upon the
resolution with which the act of defiance was met." [13] Lord
Birdwood, Nuri's friend and admiring biographer, is even more
explicit. He writes:

> On the evening of 26th July, he [the King] and Pasha took
> dinner with the Prime Minister and Mr. Selwyn Lloyd, and
> learnt of colonel Nasser's seizure of the Suez Canal; it may
> be assumed that their views and the terms in which they
> were expressed were not very different from those of their
> hosts. Certainly the Pasha in the following days left no
> room for doubt in the minds of his friends in London . . .
>
> In many interests it is wise to refrain from moralizing and
> keep silence on many aspects of a desperate occasion. It is,
> however, legitimate to infer this much. Within the Foreign
> Office there had been a growing recognition that somehow
> and at some time Nasser would have to be restricted,
> isolated and brought down, perhaps by his own people
> through his own follies. More particularly after his personal
> reaction to the Baghdad Pact did a mere understanding
> become a set policy. It seems only sensible to assume that
> Iraq's Prime Minister would have been kept informed of
> each development and intention as it emerged. [14]

Gerald de Gaury, Abdul Illah's great friend, is no less explicit:

> From then [the moment they heard of the nationalization
> of the Suez Canal] Nuri al-Said desperately and constantly
> pressed for action against Egypt. The Crown Prince told
> me that he did not know if he would be seeing Sir Anthony
> again before he left England, but he wished it made known
> in Government circles that it was his strong view that, if
> immediate military action had been impossible because the
> British Army had not been ready, then as soon as it were
> ready some pretext must be found for action. He realized
> that once public indignation in England and France had
> died down strong action would present greater difficulty;
> but surely an incident could be arranged—perhaps some-
> thing to do with a ship going through the Canal?

Abdul Illah also advocated "that a kingdom should be

restored in Egypt. King Farouk, however, should not be allowed to return, nor his direct heir. Prince Abdul Munim is the best man. . . . The mob in Cairo is ultra-volatile and would cheer anything new. The bourgeoisie and much of the army is against Nasser." [15] After Suez, Nasser actually made public that the Egyptian authorities had in fact discovered during the aggression a secret plot to put Prince Abdul Munim on the throne of Egypt after getting rid of Nasser. [16]

Thus it is clear that Nuri, Abdul Illah and the ruling class had advocated and supported the attack on Egypt. But Jamali claims that Nuri was taken by surprise when Egypt was attacked. And what about Jamali himself? Was he also surprised? Jamali writes in a book he recently published that in August 1956, Nuri told him in Rome of Britain's intention to attack Egypt and asked him to return to Baghdad for discussions of problems that might arise inside Iraq when that attack was mounted; he says that he had in fact returned to Baghdad when he received an urgent cable from Nuri and found that Tawfik al-Swaydi had also been recalled by Nuri from Lebanon to take part in the same discussion. [17] Jamali maintains in his book that he advised the British ambassador in Baghdad against attacking Egypt. Clearly an Arab patriot's first duty was to warn the Egyptian Ambassador in Baghdad of Britain's intentions—but this Jamali seems not to have done.

We cannot yet determine Nuri's ideas on the role that Israel was or was not to play in any British attack on Egypt. Those of Nuri's friends who admit his foreknowledge of the attack on Egypt maintain that, when it came, he was really shocked by Israel's participation; and Lord Birdwood states that Nuri had categorically advised the British against the involvement of Israel in any attack on Egypt. [18] But Eden tells us that early in 1956, Nuri "suggested that we 'should make it clear to Egypt that, if she persisted (in opposing the Baghdad Pact), we should no longer consider the protection afforded by the Tripartite Declaration as applying to Egypt.'" [19] Thus it is clear that previous to Suez, Nuri had advised the British to employ the threat of Israeli aggression against Egypt. At present we do not know more than that.

Public opinion, enraged by British aggression against Egypt, demanded Iraq's withdrawal from the Baghdad Pact and the stopping of the flow of Iraqi oil to Britain; but Nuri resisted both demands. He only broke off diplomatic relations with

France and declared that Britain was to be excluded from the deliberations of the Baghdad Pact "in view of current circumstances"; the British, however, were allowed to attend all the Pact committees that met at the time in Baghdad. The nationalists' *amour-propre* was touched to the quick when it was the Syrians who had to carry out what Iraqi nationalists regarded as their own duty: the stopping of Iraq's flow of oil to Britain. (But Jamali argues in his apologia that Nuri, by refusing him the amount of one quarter of a million dinars to bring about unity with Syria, lost Iraq some fifty million dinars in oil money when the pipelines were cut off by the Syrians.) Nuri had, furthermore, continued to supply Britain with Iraqi oil from the south all through the Anglo-French-Israeli aggression against Egypt.[20] Nutting spoke of the formula whereby "Iraq owns the airfields, and Britain uses them." Iraqis learned from copies of the *Times* of London, sold in the bookshops of Baghdad, that the British garrison in Jordan, boycotted and virtually cut off from outside contact, was being supplied by RAF planes from Habbaniya.[21]

"The Suez crises," correctly observes Gallman, "came close to being Nuri's undoing." Nuri, in fact, weathered the storm with difficulty. He declared martial law, jailed the nationalists, suspended Parliament, closed down schools and colleges (when they were finally opened, 300 students were expelled and inducted into special camps in the north, "to do their military duty"). There were bloody riots and demonstrations almost all over the country: Baghdad, Najaf, Mosul, Kut, Kirkuk, Samawa, Samaara. Suez was to be the last storm that Nuri and the ruling class were able to ride; from then on it was only a matter of time before they were brought down by their own people. Abdul Illah was to tell his doctor in London, when he tried to persuade him to stay longer to avoid political trouble in Baghdad: "Ah, well—I suppose they'll get me in the end."[22]

Jamali maintains that Iraqis are today hankering after "security, stability and prosperity," suggesting that they are yearning for a return to the status quo ante. What actually was this prerevolutionary Iraq? Iraqis most certainly did not "run their own affairs as freely internally and externally as any other independent state in the world," as Jamali writes in his apologia. Gallman, the US Ambassador to Iraq between 1954–58, observes that: "The King ostensibly made and broke prime ministers, but behind the scenes the British were present, directing the plays." [23] This, of course, was the sad truth, and one wonders how Jamali can deny it. Jamali writes of heading Iraqi missions to the Bandung Conference, the Conference of Arab Prime Ministers, UN and Security Council sessions: "In all these missions he [Nuri] never issued any instructions." But Jamali continued to claim before the revolutionary court, both as accused and witness under oath, that he acted under instructions, even saying: "The truth is, I did not represent in the Security Council my personal opinion; I was not responsible because I was not the foreign minister, neither the prime minister, nor a member of the government." [24] In no way does this absolve him from his responsibility, but Jamali's claim to have acted under instructions seems to be supported by the official documents.

We cannot, for the sake of brevity, go here at length into each and all of these meetings, but we will just take two documents concerning the Bandung Conference. The first is a cable from Nuri to Jamali dated April 13, 1955, in which Nuri informs Jamali that the American Ambassador has conveyed to him Mr. Dulles' wishes that the Iraqi delegation to Bandung stand firmly against Communist China and instructs him to do so. [25] In the second cable, dated April 20, 1955, Nuri tells Jamali that Archbishop Makarios will be going to Bandung to put before the conference the case for *Enosis* and informs him that the British government [does] not want this case discussed at the conference and instructs him to oppose its being raised. [26] The Iraqi Foreign Ministry's correspondence with the Iraqi Embassy in Washington was carried by the British diplomatic pouch, [27] and the Ministry of Interior's plans for putting down public demonstrations were drawn up by Mr. MacIntosh, the "adviser" on internal security at this ministry. A state which entrusts its confidential correspondence to the diplomatic pouch of another or its plans for internal security to a foreign "adviser" is surely not internally and externally as free "as any independent state in the world."

"DEMOCRACY AND DEVELOPMENT"

Prerevolutionary Iraq did not practice the parliamentary democracy it preached and was supposed to champion in the Arab world. Toward the end of that era, there wasn't even much serious pretense of going through the motions; thus in the elections of 1954, only 23 seats were contested; all the rest of the 135 members were returned unchallenged—*bil-tazkia*. Earlier Nuri had challenged in Parliament any member who claimed to have been elected to it by the people "to resign immediately and leave Parliament" and stand for reelection, with the government not putting his name on its lists, and see whether he could be thus reelected.[28] No member of Parliament took Nuri's challenge. On April 8, 1958, Jamali sent the following cable to one of his collaborators: "Please inform me immediately if you prefer membership of Parliament or ambassadorship to Beirut," and had received this answer on the same day: "Thanks I prefer ambassadorship to Beirut." [29] But Jamali claims to have disagreed with Nuri on democracy, freedom of the press, and party life. He maintains in his apologia that he was a great supporter of party life for Iraq and criticizes Nuri for dissolving Saleh Jabr's party, which was "supposed to alternate in ruling the country" with Nuri's party. The documents tell us differently. Jamali had sent Nuri a letter, in his own handwriting, telling him that he had been trying hard to convince Saleh Jabr to dissolve his party.[30] It is, of course, evident that the ruling class, even if it really wanted to, could not afford to practice any form of democracy. As Jamali writes: "Free political activity and a free press in Iraq would, in most cases have turned anti-Western and not anti-Communist."

Jamali also writes of the devotion of Nuri and of most other prime ministers who governed Iraq before 1958 to the material development of the country, to flood control and irrigation projects. This had been from an early date the stock defense of all those who set themselves to defend the Iraqi *ancien régime*. When Mr. Crossman said in Parliament: "Nuri al-Said is in power because he has served Western imperialism faithfully over the last fifteen years," Sir Anthony Eden was to answer him: "Iraq, more than any other country in the Middle East, has spent money on developments in an endeavor to improve the conditions of her people." To this Mr. Crossman retorted: "I am sorry that the Right Hon. Gentleman should have adverted to a quite different subject. What I said . . . has nothing to do with development at all." [31] It was paradoxical to hear the Conservative Eden stress material development to the Socialist Crossman. But what Eden did not then understand, Jamali still does not grasp. No material development could substitute for a sense of dignity, both personal and national, that Iraqis were deprived of by their rulers. As a personal illustration, once in

1956 a well-to-do officer broke into tears when he learned of the blowing up of pipelines in Syria. *"We should have done it,"* he kept on repeating between sobs.

Furthermore, how successful was this "endeavor of Iraq to improve the conditions of the people," to use Eden's words? With no limit to landownership, no taxation on land, no income or inheritance tax, it was obvious that the projects of irrigation and flood control were to make the rich richer. And this is exactly what happened. As Doreen Warriner observed: "Money does not percolate downwards. Wealth accumulates and men decay." [32] This, historically, could be easily foreseen. Egypt in the nineteenth century had gone through rapid economic development; flood control and irrigation projects had been carried out, but, its political and social structure being what they were, only the rich benefitted. Although careful not to express political opinions, Lord Salter could not but raise in his masterly report in 1955 the question of who was to benefit from the water-control and irrigation projects on which Development Board money was spent.[33]

The effectiveness of the development projects in winning over the people was further diminished by the corruption that permeated the ruling class. Nuri, although personally not corrupt, was surrounded, as Gallman notes, with some corrupt people; [34] he did not only tolerate corruption but often used it to obtain his political ends. At the top of this corrupt ruling class stood Abdul Illah, with his insatiable lust for money. Writes de Gaury: "Participation in local enterprises and his encouragement of light industry [sic] merely led to more trouble for him. It was assumed by the critics that his own financial advantage was the prime reason in every case for his interests." [35]

But this ruling class professed, and some members of it must have genuinely believed, that the people could be won once the projects of the Development Board bore fruit and prosperity reigned in Iraq; all that they needed was time. De Gaury reports that near the end of the reign the Chamberlain Tahsin al-Qadri had told him: "If only the people of this country could go to sleep for ten years and then wake up." [36] That wish had been actually expressed earlier by Abdul Illah to the well-known American journalist Joseph Alsop, who used it in his syndicated column in *The New York Herald Tribune*. The ruling class did not realize that a people cannot be put to sleep at will—no matter how hard one tries. And hard they tried. The carrots of material development were constantly dangled before the eyes of the people and the stick of the police was generously used. "The police budget (£7.5 million) exceeded that of Education (£.6 million) by a sizeable sum." [37]

In the final years of their rule, there was something surrealistic and unreal about the ruling class in Iraq. They had managed to convince themselves and to convince some of their friends that all was well with them and with the Iraq they ruled. Nutting wrote less than a year before the Revolution, "By no means all other Arab regimes are as stable as Iraq." [38] Nuri earlier had told his enemies: "The house of the master [Iraq] is safe and secure." [39] Jamali himself, only four months before the Revolution, wrote in his paper that the few who were dissatisfied with conditions in Iraq had to be isolated, watched and treated. He advised the government "to provide a sufficient number of psychotherapists for the treatment of critics [of conditions in Iraq] who look at things through dark glasses." [40]

To the very end, Nuri kept on trying to bring down Nasser. In April 1957, he told Gallman: "Tell Dulles that up to now he has been working only on the tail and leaving the head, Nasser, intact." [41] He also believed that he could use the Iraqi army against Syria, and in London he called for an Anglo-American landing in the Lebanon and promised the British the support of the Iraqi army.[42] Jamali writes that Saleh Jabr informed him in January 1957: "I must tell you that things are not going well in the army. There is going to be a coup and the King and Crown Prince and Nuri are going to be killed." But this warning seems not to have affected Jamali's optimism, for the official documents show us that he kept on trying to use the army in Syria and Lebanon. And on June 21, 1958, less than two months before the Revolution, the Iraqi Ambassador to Lebanon reported to his government that he had discussed with President Chamoun a plan for sending Iraqi troops to Lebanon for the protection of its frontiers, but that Chamoun expressed to him his misgivings and doubts based on what was "commonly known": that the Iraqi army would not fight and open fire on other Arabs. Tawfik al-Swaydi cabled the Ambassador the very same day with instructions to meet Chamoun and correct his impressions about the Iraqi army.[43] Less than two months after this, the 19th and 20th Brigades of the Third Armored Division received orders to proceed to the

Jordanian frontier, in connection with the situation in the Lebanon. Both Brigades converged on Baghdad on the morning of July 14 and opened wide the floodgates of the Revolution which was to sweep away the whole Iraqi ruling class in a matter of hours.

There was ceratinly no tragic grandeur in the gradual decline and final collapse of the Iraqi *ancien régime*. There was instead something of Alice in Wonderland and the *opéra bouffe* about its last years—the King and the Crown Prince in plumed cocked hats, riding to open Parliament in a landau that belonged to Queen Victoria, bought by them from Hooper's in St. James, London, and the handpicked members of that Parliament dutifully listening to and applauding empty speeches.

W.H. Auden concluded his poem *Spain* with these lines:
History to the defeated
May say Alas but cannot help or pardon.

History may not even say "Alas" to the defeated *ancien régime* of Iraq and its apologists.

7. Histadrut and the State

BY DAVID BEN GURION

To REGARD the people of Israel today strictly in terms of the Marxian division into two classes, bourgeoisie and proletariat, is to inhabit a world of formulas totally unrelated to the world we live in. Labor in Israel has built up its own enterprises, industries and maritime transport . . . Israel is not a socialist state; yet neither can it be called capitalistic. Private enterprises exist in the country; and we must encourage the flow of outside private capital and private productive initiative. Israel has also worker-owned and state-controlled enterprises. These embrace the majority (over 70 per cent) of the wage-earning population. The Histadrut is not simply a labor federation similar to trade unions in other countries. In it are organized agricultural settlers who are responsible for most of the cultivated land in the state; transport cooperatives who conduct almost the entire intraurban and interurban transportation; producers' cooperatives on land and sea; great industrial plants established by Solel Boneh, T'nuva and Hamashbir. The railways, electric-power plant, Dead Sea enterprises, mines, and so on are state enterprises. Our economic and social structure is quite unique and cannot be compressed into a frame of outmoded and inapplicable formulas.

But the differences which present the most serious problems for us are those that exist between the old *yishuv* and the newcomers to Israel. Class distinctions existed even before the creation of the state; but then we were one people, one entity—not

Reprinted from *The Jewish Frontier*, Vol. XXIII, No. 5 (252) (New York, 1956), pp. 6–9; by permission of editor. These excerpts are taken from an address delivered at a Histadrut conference held in Israel in 1956.

only potentially, but actually—and this unity was strikingly demonstrated during our war of liberation. Today we are not one people actually, and the gulf between the old settlers together with those new settlers who have struck roots in the country and between the majority of the new immigrants who have not yet struck roots, contains a serious threat both to the security of the country and for the labor movement. From the economic and social standpoints, the people in the *ma'abarot°* and immigrant settlements fall into the laboring class, but that is no guarantee that they have a sense of solidarity as workers. . . .

In the days of the Second and Third Aliyah, the worker was bound to the Histadrut primarily by ideals; today, the bond is primarily one of "interests." Actually, there need be no absolute conflict between the two, provided that the latter are public, not individual interests. Nowadays, the Histadrut member's first concern is for his own economic betterment or, at best, that of his own circle, profession or locality. This is quite a far cry from—and frequently diametrically opposed to—the ideological approach of the worker of former days.

Israel has hundreds of agrarian settlements established by recent immigrants who have come to us from all corners of the globe. But unless we provide every immigrant settlement with an adequate complement of teachers, doctors, nurses and technical instructors experienced in agriculture, self-defense and communal organization, there is no guarantee that they can stand up in times of stress and no assurance that they will not fall easy prey to the rightist or leftist forces which are inimical to our government and fight labor.

Until now, people from *moshavim,*† including both veterans and young people, have accomplished something on behalf of the immigrant settlements. But for the moral and security reinforcement of these settlements, and for filling the gap between them and the old established community, it is necessary that thousands of our best young people, not only from the labor settlements—for we cannot cast this entire burden upon them alone—but also from the towns and large villages, accompanied

°*Ma'abarot:* workers' villages which were created by the government to facilitate absorption of immigrants.

†*Moshavim:* workers' settlements, agricultural villages, in which each family works on its own plot of land and is allowed to keep the income derived from this source. The land initially belongs to the Jewish National Fund.

by our best teachers, nurses and doctors, should go to settle in these immigrant settlements and live with the immigrants.

It is good for the city and town worker to spend some time with the new arrivals in their various border outposts. They undoubtedly gain more from these visits of a week or two than the newcomers, for they bring back with them the rich tang of the soil and the courage of the frontiersman. But such sporadic visits are no solution for the newcomers' problems. Only a strong and enduring bond between our rooted youth and the immigrants can bridge the gap which threatens the stability and security of our country.

We must not overlook the fact that thousands of new Histadrut members have never had any form of Jewish education. Some of them can neither read nor write. Whether this situation can be remedied for the people over fifty remains to be seen. But certainly the younger people can be taught. The army managed this very successfully. I appreciate the difference between the power of army discipline and the limits of the Histadrut's province, yet this difficulty must be overcome. Otherwise, the membership of an illiterate in the Histadrut will remain purely fictitious—if not worse.

I do not minimize the importance of routine and the machinery of membership dues. Without them the Histadrut could not exist. However, vital though they be, they are merely scaffolding. The real structure of Histadrut is composed of the souls of workingmen, their social conscience, their loyalty and identification with the aims of the working class and its historic mission.

And here we come to the relation of the man of scholarship and the scientist to our movement. More and more, we have come to rely upon the scientist and technologist for the development of our industries, agriculture, enterprises of all types and, finally, the very security of our land. During our own lifetime, developments in physics, chemistry and biology have improved conditions of life, health, natural increase and labor production.

It is the duty of the state, as well as of labor, to encourage scientific research and the training of young scientists. But in our zeal, we must not overlook other studies which are no less vital for the development of our country—history, literature, philosophy, sociology, the arts, etc. Too great a concentration on science alone can prove limiting and stultifying. The dedication of the scientific expert automatically narrows his field of activity. Without an equally firm cultural foundation, man is doomed to deteriorate. Therefore the state, and this means labor as well, must not content itself with the training of scientists and technologists, but must have an equal interest in nurturing the culture of our people and of the world at large. Above all, it must be remembered that unless there is a spiritual and social communion with the laboring class, no contribution on the part of the men of science and thought can raise the cultural level of a people. Only a closer rapport between them can foster our cultural and economic creativity.

Here again must be applied the principle of "population distribution." The desert expert cannot do his best work unless he lives in the Negev himself. Engineers and chemists who are working on the minerals of the Dead Sea and other finds in the Negev should live in Beersheba, Elat, or in any one of the many points springing up in the area.

More immigrants have entered Israel in the seven years of its existence than entered the country during the seventy years before that. The Histadrut has also increased its membership proportionately. But, though there has been a quantitative growth, a qualitative deterioration has evidenced itself, both in the country as well as in the Histadrut. Let us first review the changes which took place in the Histadrut. This is not entirely due to the great immigrant influx of recent years. We began to see signs of the change a number of years ago. The most significant of these was that personal, professional and economic interests were gradually replacing the idealism and vision of the old Halutz. The strength of the old standard-bearers has slowly waned in contrast with the strength of those forces and interests which first served as a means of attaining the goal of the working class and have now become the goal in themselves.

There is no clear conflict between vision and interests. On the other hand, they cannot be comfortable bedfellows. In the early days of our movement—down to the Third Aliyah—and during the early period when the workers of Eretz Israel emerged as the leading force in the Zionist movement, vision was the ruling spirit, and our movement achieved great things. In the first report (1923) delivered by the representative of the Vaad Hapoel on the activities of the Histadrut since its inception thirty-three years earlier, he made the following statement:

The Histadrut . . . is the heart of the liberation movement

of our people, the main artery of our national and social rehabilitation; the Jewish labor movement in Eretz Israel is the consolidated expression of a great national and social passion which has seized the Jews of our generation. Our movement is the concentrated expression through action and deeds of the yearnings of our generation and the hope for freedom and redemption which lives in tens of thousands of hearts and is called by various names.

Would such a formulation apply to the Histadrut today? My reply would be in the negative for two reasons:

(1) The light of vision has paled among the working classes; their unity is weakened; their pioneer spirit is no longer as keen; mutual responsibility has been weakened, and special interests, personal, professional, economic and partisan, have gained strength.

(2) On the other hand, with the creation of the state there emerged a better instrument because stronger and more comprehensive, than the Histadrut. It is up to us to draw the proper conclusions from these phenomena.

During the Mandate, the Histadrut assumed many quasi-governmental duties. The retention of these duties, now that we have a state, not only places an undue burden on the Histadrut, but it is an indictment against our government. The example of the labor exchange and the national water supply are cases in point. In order to ensure an equitable division of labor—essential both for the worker's as well as for the state's well-being—there should be a government labor exchange, working in close conjunction with both labor and employers. I believe it is not necessary for me to point out that the water supply of our land should be under the exclusive control of the government. Water is a most vital key to the development of our country, and the Histadrut may well be proud of having discovered and put into use hidden springs which now irrigate the land being developed by our people. But once the state came into being, this work should have become its exclusive province.

The object of the Histadrut is to aid the government, not to compete with it. There was a time when the Histadrut organized, equipped and directed the Haganah, fulfilling a great historic mission, just as did Hashomer. But with the establishment of the state, defense has passed into the hands of the government, and though the members of the Tsova Haganah L'Israel are for the most part workers and children of workers, it must recognize only one authority and that is the state and its authorized institutions.

Without going into further detail, I believe that one rule can be established: Any service which benefits the public at large should be under state control. When I say "state control," I do not mean specifically state machinery. Many services can be conducted better by consumer groups, as, for instance, health services. It would be a waste of energy and a loss to the public if health services would be directed only by the government, especially when the people themselves, with Histadrut in the vanguard, have so successfully developed medical services in our country. However, it is the duty of the government to make medical aid available to everyone, and to furnish government health service to those who do not belong to Kupat Cholim.

The concentration of all civic activities and enterprises in the hands of government is a fallacious socialist, or statist, concept. Just as the government should encourage self-rule in municipalities and local councils, it should also support the initiative of its citizens in all public concerns not confined to a particular locality. But all activities which are essentially a general governmental function, and which were undertaken by the Histadrut before the state was established simply because there was no Jewish governmental machinery during the Mandate period, should no longer be carried out by the Histadrut but handed over to the government.

We must look upon the Histadrut, even now, not merely as a combine of interests but as the agency of a historic mission, as the vanguard of a people that will eventually return to its fatherland. . . . The Histadrut can fulfill the historic mission of the worker only if, in addition to its professional duties and activities, it takes the lead as *an educational force with pioneering initiative* and places spiritual vision and physical labor in their proper place as the central forces which nurture a people, build its society, and strengthen its country.

We must honestly face the changes which have taken place over the years since the founding of the Histadrut and, more particularly, since the creation of the state of Israel. Both were the result of great vision, but they are no longer both led by the vision. With the change in the type of immigrant arriving today, changes have taken place in the motives which primarily actuate the workers. *Need and personal requirements have replaced vision and mission.* Not only is the character of today's immigration different from that of the Second and Third Aliyah, but even their economic, social and political backgrounds are new to the country. For the most part, they come from backward regions where the feudal system of the Middle Ages still prevails. They know little of national and social liberation movements and still less of modern Hebrew or any other culture which were the molds which fashioned the immigrants to Israel before the Second World War.

The immigrant of today has come to Israel out of desperation, although with vague messianic hopes, and he accepts the tasks given him because he must. This need does not detract from the dignity of colonization. Many of the early pioneers also came to the country out of need, and often this need is a blessing in disguise. Tens of thousands of the immigrants from backward countries have developed into a creative force, have adjusted themselves to their work and settled on the land, making the wastelands bloom in the south, in the Galilee and in the Jerusalem Corridor—and have helped to further the security of the country. But the materialist motives which lead to immigration may also lead to emigration. And the need which makes one a worker and a settler, if it is not enriched with new values of national and social significance associated with labor and colonization, may disappear when conditions are altered and cause the workers and settlers to move to the towns and become traders and peddlers.

For political, social and psychological reasons—foreign rule, lack of space, ingrained habits of a diaspora people—most of our population has crowded into the narrow strip of land along our coastline and into three cities. The only areas in our country that are wide open are the Galilee area and the south. Here are large stretches of unsettled land, and two-thirds of the south is completely unoccupied. We shall never attain economic independence nor be able to preserve our security if these areas are not settled and developed through our own industry and energy. In theory, the labor movement agrees that the wider the distribution of the population and the more extensive the colonization of our wastelands, the better it is for the stability and security of the country. But in practice, we have been doing just the opposite. The headquarters of the Colonization Office is in Tel Aviv, as is the central office of the Histadrut. Labor enterprises requiring financial assistance must come to Tel Aviv. All applications to the government must be made in Jerusalem or in Tel Aviv. Even the departments concerned with the development of the Negev are located in Tel Aviv. All of the Histadrut institutions are in this city, and it goes without saying, so are all the newspapers. The writers of our country, all our intellectuals, our best teachers, doctors, scientists, and our research institutions, as well as all our publishing houses, are concentrated in Jerusalem, Tel Aviv or Haifa. Only a small segment of our people—a handful of idealistic young men and women and a large portion of our newcomers—go to Galilee, to the south and the Negev.

There is a most gratifying trend "from city to village," and lately, a very successful movement "from ship to village." But if we are serious about distributing our population, we should distribute our institutions. The government should set up offices in Nazareth and Beersheba, in Safed and Elat; the Histadrut, the colonization offices and our various research bureaus should do the same. This would save time and energy for the treasurers and administrators who now have to make the long trip to Tel Aviv or Jerusalem every time they have to redeem a note, make a loan, discuss budgets, or get technical advice.

Let us not give way to nostalgic memories of "what once was." The days of vision and pioneering spirit are behind us. They will not return. We can no longer discount the importance of personal needs and interests which have become a strong and moving factor in the country and in the labor movement. We have been granted, in our lives, a colossal apparatus with which we can accomplish much and change the course of human lives—a thing which we could never do in the heroic pioneer days. We have a state of our own which can mobilize manpower and resources through the force of law, and launch undertakings which we never dreamed of in the "good old days." The state has become a force which educates, builds, colonizes, develops and initiates, beyond the power of any voluntary force of the early pre-state days. But the state is not all-knowing. Its structure is not preordained, and the hegemony of the worker is not assured; and the state will not inevitably apply its power to achieve those ends for which we struggled more than fifty years.

The supplementary task of the labor movement after the establishment of the state is accordingly a twofold one:

(1) to mold the character of the state and prepare it for the

full achievement of our aims of national and socialist liberation and also to educate and organize the workers for their role;

(2) to take a pioneering initiative in educational, economic, and social activities—activities which cannot be carried out under compulsion and law and solely through the governmental machinery.

8. Israel: A Society in Transition

BY DAN AVNI-SEGRE*

I

THE PURPOSE of this paper is to show some political consequences of the impact of industrialism on Israeli society, and the
influence of some of the original trends of agrarian Zionism on
Israel, a state increasingly relying on industrial power and
institutions.

Many aspects of the history of the Jewish national movement
in Palestine could be described in terms of the fight of an underdeveloped colonial territory and society for independence. What
is perhaps unusual in the Zionist struggle is that the will for the
development of a "just society" preceded the will for political
independence; and that the effort of industrialization was undertaken more as a result of unforeseen internal and external
pressures than as an expression of national self-assertion or as
the outcome of a specific ideology.[1]

This peculiar attitude of Jewish nationalism toward industrialism has its roots in both Jewish and European history of the
eighteenth and early nineteenth centuries and the absorption of
ideas of the Jewish and non-Jewish Enlightenment.

Jewish Enlightenment (Haskalah) is a much-studied phenomenon whose sociological and economic aspects are to this day less

Reprinted from *World Politics*, Vol. XXI, No. 3 (April 1969), pp. 345–365; by
permission of the author and editor.

*This paper is based on a lecture delivered for the Program in Near Eastern
Studies at Princeton University, in March 1968. I am grateful to Professor Mor-
roe Berger of Princeton University, Professor Joseph Agassi and Professor Robert
S. Cohen of Boston University for their suggestions during the preparation of
the original text; and to Dr. Meir Vereté of the Hebrew University of Jerusalem
for reading and generously helping me when rewriting the final draft. (Author's
note.)

clear than are its historical and cultural implications. It contained many Jewish biblical and post-biblical ideals, such as the equality of man, messianic harmony of nations, humanistic rationalism, which could easily fit into the thinking of the non-Jewish Enlightenment of the eighteenth century. At this same time, Judaism had always proclaimed the supreme duty of the Jews to resettle their ancestral land. Well before the rise of the Zionist movement, the idea of the return of the Jew to the land—not only the distant and for many almost mythical land of Israel, but to the land as an honorable source of livelihood—was popular in the still compact and very traditional Jewish society of Eastern Europe. By the nineteenth century the settlement of Jews on the land was considered a noble way to regenerate the pauper nation. It fitted well with the Russian idealization of agrarian values that had developed in the wake of and in reaction to the westernizing trend of Russian society, at that time shaken by the Napoleonic invasion.

These ideas of the Jewish Enlightenment had direct or indirect connections with the social ideals that the French soldiers had brought into the Jewish society of Eastern Europe. Central to them was the concept of the equality of man and of the emancipation of individuals and oppressed nations. It polarized the hopes and passions of both Jews and gentiles and contributed to the dephasing of the Jewish national movement in time and space. Zionism is a movement of emancipation born on European soil, nourished by the ideals of the Enlightenment, and, finally, realized in Asia in the middle of the twentieth century.

The consequences of its involuntary stretching in time and space are still traceable in contemporary Israeli society, most particularly in the ideological postures of some of its political elites.

II

As a political *movement*, Zionism was born after the Russian pogroms of 1881, which shattered whatever faith Jewish intelligentsia might have had in the capacity for liberalization of Tsarist society.[2] As a political *program*, Zionism was born fourteen years later, in 1895, when the Dreyfus trial shattered the faith of an Austrian Jewish journalist, Theodor Herzl,[3] in the civilizing mission of France.

The outcome of the first crisis was the organization of the settlement of Jewish pioneers in Turkish Palestine following the example of those "Lovers of Zion"[4] who had already left Eastern Europe to settle in the land of Israel, where they were generously helped by Baron Edmond de Rothschild.[5] The outcome of the second crisis was the appearance of Herzl's political pamphlet, "The Jewish State," which changed the course of Jewish national history.[6] This pamphlet became a public political Jewish manifesto almost by chance. Originally meant to serve a very small audience, it was written as a reasoned argument in favor of Jewish immigration to Palestine, to be presented by Herzl to the Jewish philanthropist Baron Maurice de Hirsch and to the Rothschild family—who took little notice of the Austrian journalist's proposal. Thus Zionism in its practical aspects was born at the end of the nineteenth century. But although it realized its aim, the creation of a Jewish state, only in the middle of the twentieth century, its intellectual origins go back to the eighteenth century and are firmly rooted in the conception of society, before the industrial revolution, in the minds of Europeans generally and of Jews in Eastern Europe.

Martin Buber has shown better than anybody else the French utopian origins of the Zionist collective settlement—the kibbutz—in his *Paths in Utopia*.[7] In general, it can safely be argued that Zionism got into trouble because its original belief in final human harmony—harmony within a Jewish people torn between traditionalism and assimilationist reform; harmony between the Jews and other peoples in a society torn between liberalism and anti-Semitism—clashed with the strife and competition of the modern world.

Zionism could have preserved some of its ideological logic if it had shared the minority view of Adam Smith, who believed that competition leads to harmony. But it did not, because its nineteenth-century leaders were already obsessed with Marxian and Hegelian belittlement of the idea of utopia. So from the very beginning Zionism suffered from the straitjacket of its own beliefs: It built in Palestine a society whose many symbols and institutions were founded on a utopian idea of harmony and whose daily life was carried out in Hegelian struggle.

Ideologically, it was a difficult situation, and it produced some remarkable theoretical twistings, especially for the Zionist-Marxists. Typical of them is the justification that Ber Borochov, a leading Zionist labor ideologist, gave for the return of the Jews to their homeland. Palestine, he said, was so poor that it was bypassed by big capitalism and thus gave the Jews the opportunity to develop it and build in it a better, more just society.[8]

In practice, however, the dichotomy between harmony and strife did not hinder the development of the Jewish community in Palestine. The ideological "monasteries" of the Jewish settlement—that is to say, the kibbutzim, the collective settlements—were utopian communities activated by continuous external military and economic strife. The ideological "church" of Jewish labor—the Histadrut, the Federation of Labor—went a long way toward the realization of a classless Jewish community in which the workers controlled labor, capital markets, social services, and culture and education.[9] Both were kept together and in movement less by utopian harmony than by continuous external struggle against the British administration and the Arab labor competition. They were also to have a lasting moral and material effect on the rest of the Jewish society of Palestine, and later on the Jewish state.

Things might have turned out differently if orthodox Jews had come to Palestine en masse, but in spite of the religious commandment to return and settle the land of Israel, they did not do so. This was the case for reasons that we shall not discuss here, ranging from social inertia of a traditional society to ideological opposition to Enlightenment. Enlightenment was after all an antireligious movement, and Zionism was Enlightenment, though it was Romanticism as well.[10]

Things might have been different also if Western European and American Jews had come in greater numbers to Palestine. They could have turned out differently if the masses of Arabized Jews had answered the call of Zionism. But they did not hear the call because Zionism as a political movement developed in Europe and was less interested in the "Jews of the colonies," partly because of ignorance but mostly out of necessity. The Jewish problem for which Zionism had to provide an immediate solution was the problem of the persecution and the assimilation of the Jew in Western European society, not in Asia or Africa where Jews were not persecuted nor in danger of losing their national religious identity through assimilation into Muslim theocratic society.

Thus only a tiny minority of forward-looking and revolution-minded East European Jews rose and went to rebuild Palestine. It was, naturally, a very select group, and for many years this selectness, born of common decision, provided a feeling of unity that was stronger than the already divided Zionist ideology. In this society, power and status became the affair of an even more select elite, the "collective aristocracy" of the land and the "cooperative aristocracy" of labor, who with great personal sacrifice upheld the belief in the possibility of a "perfect society" and in the regeneration of man through manual work. It was a very special and closely knit group that may best be referred to as the Zionist plantocracy, to use the term employed by W. H. Armytage[11] to distinguish the pre-industrial modernizing elite of the seventeenth and eighteenth centuries from the industrial elite of the nineteenth and twentieth.

Not all the Zionists who went to live in the land of Palestine believed in the mystical regenerative force of manual labor.[12] Under other conditions the early settlers might have turned into an agrarian society based on a conservative man-to-land relationship or into a "colon" society. And briefly, in the colonies financed by Baron de Rothschild and run with Arab labor, they did.[13] But soon the course changed under the growing pressure of Zionist socialism, of the kibbutz, of the cooperative workers' movement, of the labor federation, of the increased immigration, especially from Germany, and of the defensive situation in which the Jewish settlement found itself cornered because of divided British and solid Arab opposition to the establishment of a Jewish national "home" in Palestine.

This opposition—particularly to acquisition of land by Jews—combined with the necessities of immigration and military defense brought about some industrialization even in those very centers of agricultural purity that were the kibbutzim.[14] There were many objective reasons for this: mechanization of agriculture, need for autonomy in the maintenance of machinery, production of light weapons, etc. Private industrial enterprises in Palestine also often failed for lack of capital, lack of experience, lack of protected markets, and to a certain extent because of the British policy of laissez-faire, which in the colonies essentially meant laissez-faire to British firms. The collective and cooperative socialist groups of Palestine, being by their nature and structure the more secure and stable economic elements in a generally very poor colonial society, attracted and accepted the collaboration in capital and know-how of private investors. In spite of possible ideological divergence of opinions, both sides were also brought together by the common feeling of working for a superior Jewish national cause.

In terms of production, these efforts of agrarian and often joint private and socialist industrialization may have not meant much, and the cities remained the main centers[15] of industrial production in Palestine and in Israel. But in terms of national leadership, they permitted the collective and cooperative landed Zionist gentry to share and to keep abreast of all aspects of national economic development, thus extending to the whole community, agricultural and industrial alike, the social symbols and the code of behavior of its own select group. This certainly did not avert clashes of vested interests. But it helped to strengthen and make acceptable in all parts of the Jewish society those socialist agrarian values of puritanism and frugality that later proved vital to the economic development of the state of Israel. Puritanism allowed the industrial infrastructure to be established in Israel before the impact of rising expectations was felt. In this respect, the puritanism of the Zionist plantocracy played a role similar to that of Protestant and Communist puritanism in the industrialization of the Western, Russian and Chinese economies, and is also reminiscent of the military patriotic puritanism of the Meiji restoration, in the analysis of Masao Maruyama.[16]

The puritan contribution of Zionist plantocracy to Israel was the greatest moral achievement of the golden age of Zionism. Can it also be called a success? It probably cannot, for it is to the very weakness of Zionism as a utopian ideology that Israel owes its survival and its development.

III

The shortcomings of Zionism as a viable modern political ideology came to be felt as early as 1947. At that time the first Israeli war was being waged on two different levels—against the Arabs and against the British. For the British, it was a typical colonial struggle fought by Jewish settlers to obtain a measure of autonomy not very different from that which the American settlers had earlier claimed from Britain. It should be added parenthetically that the descriptive phrase "Jewish settlement" is seldom used in the literature. Its Hebrew equivalent, "Yishuv," makes it almost certain that no one will compare the Jewish and Kenyan settlers, Arab critics notwithstanding. In the colonial struggle against the British, the Jewish community of Palestine fought both for its own sake and for the sake of the Jews generally. Because of this dualism, it went a long way in compromise before resorting to violence.

In 1937 the Jews of Palestine had been deeply divided on the acceptance of a plan of partition—the Peel partition plan—that allotted to them the control of a very limited area around Tel Aviv and Haifa quite unsuitable for the establishment of a state whose national task was also to provide a home for the persecuted Jews of Europe.

In 1947 the Yishuv was ready to accept another plan for a partition of Palestine that would have allotted to the Jews a larger share of the country but would also have created a Jewish state economically dependent on its Arab neighbors and thus unfit to provide a solution to the Jewish problem.[17]

As to the Arabs of Palestine, the conflict between Arabism and Zionism remained for a long time as much a local, communal struggle as a nationalist confrontation, the Arab states and governments being considered by Arab opinion to be more capable of organizing the opposition to Zionism than were the Palestinians.

The solution was finally left by the British and the Arab governments to war. The outcome was the state of Israel controlling three-fifths of Palestine, the Kingdom of Jordan controlling the West Bank, Egypt controlling the Gaza strip, UN armistice agreements controlling nothing, and an Arab nation of refugees emerging as the most pressing political problems in the Middle East.

The emergence of a population of Jewish refugees in the heart of the middle East as a consequence of European anti-Semitism and of the Palestine conflict is probably the most momentous event of this century in that part of the world. It has had many consequences, some of them so recent that there are practically no documented studies of this phenomenon.[18] For twenty years, the two nations of refugees—Arabs and Jews—have been kept apart by the armistice frontiers established in 1948. The two sides followed their own lines of development, in two opposing directions. The Jewish refugees have been speedily integrated into the Israeli state and have mobilized for the future. The Arab refugees have remained, for political and economic reasons, turned toward the past, and only partly integrated into Arab society.

The 1967 war broke down the physical barriers between Arabs and Jews in Palestine, reconstructed the geographic unity of the country and of its historical capital, Jerusalem, and created, *de facto,* a bi-national Arab-Jewish society under Jewish control. This is an entirely new situation, never envisaged even by those Jewish political groups like Mapam and the Israeli Communist Party which advocated a bi-national state in Palestine. It is a very confused, tense situation that nobody in Israel had ever anticipated and for which nobody has so far put forward any clear plan. The result has been a very fluid coexistence of political hostility and practical day-to-day cooperation between the two nations of Palestine.

The Jewish side of the present population of the Holy Land is composed of a minority of Jewish immigrant refugees from Europe and a majority of Jewish immigrant refugees from the Arab states. The European refugees have of course had an extraordinary effect on the whole Palestine question. The atrocities of the Nazis, combined with the Hamletlike policy of the British makers of Palestine immigration laws, were responsible for the anguish that burst into terror and illegal immigration. They led also to the near-rebellion of the whole Jewish population against Britain, whom most of the Zionist leaders had deeply trusted and admired, and finally to the rise of the state of Israel and its passing of the Law of the Return as its first law. This law allows any Jew to enter the state of Israel as a citizen. It has become one of the main symbols of what the Arabs declare to be a European Jewish invasion of Palestine. In fact it has brought to Israel since 1948 only a limited number of European immigrants—about half a million, probably 100,000 of whom have since left the country permanently.[19] The Arab fears of a neo-colonialist Western Zionist invasion [20]—reasonable as they may have been—have not yet materialized. In spite of the appeals of Zionist leaders, the reluctance of Western Jews to migrate to Israel seems to indicate that the feared Zionist invasion will not materialize, at least for some time to come.

There has been, on the contrary, a massive Jewish immigration into Israel from the Arab states rather than from the West. Islamized Jews came in their myriads, from Yemen and Morocco, from Kurdistan and Lybia, without knowing who Theodor Herzl was and without ever having heard much about Zionism. They came spurred by fear of Arab violence and by the ancient traditional Jewish messianic hope of national redemption. They came without being called and without being indoctrinated in any ideology. They could not all be absorbed in agriculture, but instead found their place in industry. They were integrated not in harmony, but in strife. They were not impressed by the Western social and political ideas brought by Jewish immigrants from Europe, but were exalted by a still very religious form of Jewish patriotism. At the same time, they suffered from the sudden disruption of their patriarchic society. They did not put an end to any "Jewish problem" in the world from which they came; in fact, they brought new and acute tension to the Arab world and into the new society to which they immigrated. The immigration of the Islamized Jews represented a development quite contrary to the expectations of political and utopian Zionism.

The difficulties of economic adaptation and the ethnic sensitiveness of the Middle Eastern Jews created the problem of internal confrontation between the old Jewish residents and refugees of European extraction and the new Jewish refugees of Islamic background, currently known as the conflict between the "first" and the "second" Israel.

This conflict has been one of the major preoccupations of the state of Israel in the second decade of its existence. It is also one of the most widely analyzed problems in the Jewish state, since scores of specialists—Israeli and foreigners—have devoted very detailed studies to it.[21]

The Arabs—and many Communist or leftist specialists in Middle Eastern affairs—have equated the fight between the first and the second Israel with the stereotyped dichotomy of a Western, white, colonialist society against an Oriental, colored society. In doing so they were certainly led astray by some vociferous representations of ethnic strife in Israel and by the statements of usually self-appointed spokesmen[22] of the "Oriental Jews." It is possible that this inaccurate analysis of the internal situation in Israel contributed to the Russian and Arab miscalculation over the Jewish war potential in the 1967 war.[23]

On the Jewish side, also, the misunderstanding of the interplay of ideological and economic forces between the first and second Israel brought about some serious mishandling of the process of integration of the Jewish refugees from Arab countries into a society rapidly passing from an agrarian into an industrial stage. Two other factors may also be mentioned in this connection. One is the role played by the German personal compensations paid to the Jews who had been persecuted by the Nazis. The second is the social tension caused by the resumed immigration of European Jews into Israel from Communist countries in the years 1960–64.

It must be admitted that the Israeli authorities could do very little to control the effects on Israeli society of the German personal restitutions. In contrast to the German reparation payments paid to the state,[24] the restitutions were paid mainly by the German *Länder* to individual Jews or their legal heirs as compensation for the treatment suffered under the Nazis. In terms of Israeli society, this meant that only a part of the population, probably some 500,000 persons out of 3,000,000, benefitted from such payments, which by 1962 were already larger[25] than the total amount paid by Germany to the state of Israel, $750,000,000. But although not all the Jews of European origin received such economic restitutions, this fact did not diminish the feeling of economic discrimination of many Oriental Jews, who were in any case in a less advantageous economic and social situation than were the European-born Israelis. That they provided much of the labor force required by the practical implementation of the enjoyment of the German restitutions by many European Jews—the building of new luxury apartments, the maintenance of cars, the supply of domestic service—did not make the situation any better, but added to the Middle Eastern Jews' resentment of their lack of personal financial ability to provide for equal advantages for their usually larger families. At the same time, because of intensive government aid and increased salaries resulting from the rising investments (especially in the building sector) of the European-born Jews in Israel— themselves a direct result of German personal restitutions—the Middle Eastern Jews considerably improved their economic position without, however, bridging the social and economic gap that separated them from "old" Israel. Thus better conditions also contributed to increasing frustrations and demands for greater equality.

It was at this delicate moment, in 1962, that the immigration of European Jews from Eastern Europe was resumed. Details of this immigration from the Communist countries[26] are not available because of the censorship imposed on the whole subject by the Israeli government for fear of Arab pressure on the East European countries. But the numbers, however important, are really not very relevant to some of the psychological reasons for social and ethnic tension between the first and the second Israel.

One reason was that the new immigrants from Communist countries—because of their family relations with old-time Israeli settlers, because they were eligible for German personal compensations, and because they were usually highly trained in industrial, administrative, and academic skills—were almost immediately absorbed into the middle and upper social classes, thus filling many nonmanual jobs made available by the country's development.

Another reason for resentment was the emphasis placed by Israeli leaders on the importance of receiving more "educated" immigrants from Europe and America as a means of strengthening and accelerating the cultural and economic development of the state. They were of course right, because only the Jewish Western Diaspora, and possibly the Russian one, could offer the highly skilled manpower needed for rapid development.

However, the resentment created by this implied distinction between "more useful" and "less useful" Jews infuriated many leaders of the second Israel, who were conscious that they, more than the Western Jews, had responded en masse to the state of Israel's appeal for the Return.[27]

IV

It was against the background of this renewed social and ethnic pressure for rapid change of social structures that the third and main stage of the "Lavon affair" was fought in Israel. Its violence shook the very political foundation of the state and brought about the most dramatic political crisis in the history of modern Israel—the secession of Ben Gurion from his own party, the Mapai.

The Lavon affair[28] is a very complicated problem of Israeli internal politics that can be briefly summarized as follows. Originally it consisted merely of a controversy over the responsibility for an "intelligence mishap" in the high echelons of the army and the Ministry of Defense. As such, the matter could be quickly forgotten, and in fact Pinhas Lavon, who was forced to hand in his resignation as Defense Minister in February 1955, made a quick recovery and became secretary general of the powerful Federation of Labor—a post he occupied from 1957 to 1961. In the first stage of the affair, while Lavon—a powerful and controversial politician of exceptional intellectual abilities—was in control of the most powerful ministry in the government, strong animosity crystallized not only between opposing personalities but among politically still unarticulated bureaucratic and economic groups with growing vested interests in power.

The second phase of the Lavon affair began when Lavon, on the basis of newly discovered evidence, asked that his name be cleared of responsibility for the "intelligence mishap." What brought him into direct conflict with Ben Gurion was the fact that while the former Israeli Premier insisted that the whole affair be handled by a judicial court of inquiry, the Cabinet favored a government inquiry, which eventually cleared Lavon of all responsibility. The struggle over procedure was the "tip of the iceberg" of a much deeper battle for the succession to power between the old socialist guard and a new generation of leaders characterized less by age or ideology than by the fact that many of them had been formed outside the parties or outside the old bureaucracies. Overruled by his colleagues in the question of the court of inquiry, Ben Gurion had Lavon removed from the Histadrut leadership. For this he was openly accused of undemocratic methods.[29] The growing opposition he met inside and outside the Cabinet on the affair and on other problems, such as relations with Germany, induced him to abandon power in 1964.

At the time, his retreat was considered by many as a tactical step meant to prepare, if not his own return to power, at least his succession by the "new guard" of technocrats after an interim period of government by Ben Gurion's trusted colleague, Levi Eshkol. But the confrontation between the old guard and the new one had by then gone too far to be patched up by a compromise.

The third phase of the Lavon affair thus exploded into an open conflict between "Ben Gurionists" and "anti-Ben Gurionists," fought with verbal political ferocity in the general election of 1965.

We know the phases and outcome of this conflict. It caused the secession of Ben Gurion from his old party, Mapai; the formation of a "Ben Gurionist" party, RAFI,[30] which fought (and lost) the elections; the return of the parliamentary leader of RAFI, General Dayan, to power as a consequence of the war of June 1967; the subsequent reunion of the seccessionist parties with Mapai,[31] under the leadership of Premier Levi Eshkol; and the disappearance of Lavon and Ben Gurion from the Israeli political scene.

This curious dénouement of the Lavon affair is confusing for those who forget that both Ben Gurion and Lavon, in spite of their personal and political opposition, were in fact the product of the same old Zionist plantocracy that had found itself overcome by the industrialization of Israel. The real battle in the Lavon affair seems to have been waged not between two men nor between clear-cut ideological positions and factions. Because of the difficulties in the adaptation of the old Zionist elite and institutions to the needs of a new industrializing society, increasingly led by a new political technocratic elite, the Lavon affair became also the expression of the deep changes brought about by modernization and industrialization. Officially it was restricted to the Mapai party and some powerful groups in Israeli labor society. In fact, it was the expression of a tension that cut through all the parties and all the institutions of the state, irrespective of age groups or of political or ideological affiliations.

Pinhas Lavon, in an article [32] published in 1962, asserted that the traditional Zionist Socialist elite formed by "the pioneers, the laborers, and the disinterested civil service" had to retain its position at the top of the Israeli social pyramid if Israel was to remain a "chosen society." He said that it should also oppose the attempt of the parvenus to dislodge it, that parvenus being the "successful men" who had made their way up "without efforts" through the "opportunities offered by the military victories, by the development funds, or by the state apparatus"—in other words, the technocrats and bureaucrats, who believed that Israel must become a society like other societies in economic productivity instead of by ideological example. "I believe," wrote Lavon, "that the state of Israel requires additional dimensions, not in technology and not in numbers. . . . It is clear [that this dimension] cannot be expressed in the economic field. . . . If there is no serious about-turn . . . we shall be a completely normal society without any special attraction. We shall then be, in the last analysis, a *Levantine country.*"

Nothing could be more revealing than such a statement in connection with both the battle between the old and new elites and the contempt with which Lavon (but also Ben Gurion) regarded Middle Eastern–Levantine culture. The contradiction between him and the "successful men" becomes clearer, however, when we confront Lavon's ideological credo with that of Shimon Peres,[33] the secretary general of the short-lived "Ben Gurionist" party, the RAFI.

Peres and his group want, not a "chosen society," but an open and competitive one based on industry and science. They value the immense contribution of past Zionism and its utopian beliefs to the building of the state, but reject all types of "nostalgia." They want not promotion through ideology, but a meritocracy, with a minimum fair standard of living for all and equal opportunities for all to become meritocrats; they stress equal opportunity for education (the great demand of the Middle Eastern Jews) and an equal share in collective amenities: better and cleaner streets, shorter hours of more efficient work, more motor vehicles, less political rhetoric. Productivity, a higher standard of living, scientific challenges—these are their answer to the Western Jews' lack of enthusiasm for emigration to Israel. And productivity, not vague ideology, is obviously to be the remedy for the economic difficulties that developed in Israel in 1965 and made it a country of emigration.[34]

This last development could have been a critical one for the state. But then the Six Day War came. In its wake, emigration has almost stopped and the recession has been overcome. More permanent is one of its lessons. For the first time, the cure for economic troubles was sought and found not in inflation, but in deflation combined with rationalization of productivity, leading the trade-union movement to accept the inevitable outcome: dismissal of inefficient or redundant labor, in spite of the sacred principle of seniority.

This was but one indirect result of industrialization. Others were perhaps less dramatic, but much more durable and important.

Because of necessities of defense and nation-building, the Israeli army had been from the start the greatest educational organization in the country. One of Ben Gurion's services to the nation had been the suppression of all political and ideological trends in the army, so that it became a neutral, national body of civic education, deeply involved in the process of social integration of the Middle Eastern Jews who formed the largest mass of the enlisted soldiers. Ben Gurion also increased the efficiency and internal mobility in the army by allowing generals to retire at the age of forty-five—especially victorious ones. But the army also needed to face Arab pressure on the borders and the permanent danger of political embargo on its weapons by the great powers, and therefore requested and obtained a strong military industry, established in the quickest possible time. This industry became a major catalyst and accelerator for the industrialization of the country. For reasons of security, it set very high standards of production; it created a whole generation of technocrats and transformed thousands of unskilled Middle Eastern Jews into sophisticated technicians, much as the United States armed forces have been doing with Negro soldiers. More important, it pressed for industrial independence in fields like electronics, aviation, and nuclear energy. The men connected with military industrialization and organization were thus to be found in almost every important administration—public or private—of the state, probably equally divided between partisans of the old and the new guards in the Lavon crisis.[35]

Because of industrialization, the Middle Eastern Jews received special education through crash programs, and because of these crash programs, they became conscious of their positions and pressed for more education, more integration, and more responsibility. They were not the only ones. The Arab non-Jewish minority of Israel, 250,000 strong, followed close on the heels of the Middle Eastern Jews. It is significant that the first Arab mass public protest against what was defined as "political and social discrimination" took place in Nazareth, on the first of May, 1959,[36] two months before the first mass protest of Middle Eastern Jews in Haifa and other development towns of the country.[37] The motivations of the two groups were certainly different. But both public demonstrations were part of the new pattern of social tensions brought about by the transformation of Israeli society from an agrarian into an industrial one. It is interesting to note the change in the accusations of the Arab minority in Israel against the government in the course of the last twenty years. In the first ten years, the Arabs fought mainly to resist what they called "the unlawful expropriation of their remaining lands." After 1963, their hostility was directed against social and educational discrimination by the government.[38]

Land was no longer of primary importance, because an increasing number of Arabs now earned their living in industry and had broken away from the authority of their traditional agrarian society. Equality, then, became the persistent new demand. The Arab intellectual, even if he disliked the Jewish society and the Jewish state, wanted a place equal to that occupied by the Jewish intellectual in the administration and elsewhere. The Arab worker wanted—and the Histadrut encour-

aged him to ask for—social advantages and status equal to those
of the Jewish worker in urban society, into which the Arab
worker now commuted or which he had even begun to join.
And here again, it was modernization and industrialization, not
ideology, that brought tensions, changes and solutions. The most
significant step was perhaps the aboliton, in 1965, of military
government. Military government had been established for
security reasons, which were as valid as ever in 1965, but the
demands by growing industry for manpower called for greater
mobility and greater integration of the Arab worker into urban
(Jewish) society. The point was therefore reached at which economic considerations balanced those of security.

There was another even more striking indirect result of industrialization: An official Israeli source stated in 1967 that thousands of mixed marriages had taken place—usually between
Arab men and Jewish women. Their offspring, according to the
present Israeli ruling on nationhood, will technically be Jewish.
Thus while we may question the stability of these unions, which
are difficult to make official in a country in which civil marriage
does not exist, we may one day discover a quite unplanned and
rather non-Zionist "internal" Jewish immigration in Israel, due to
the social attraction of the Jewish majority in Israel's population.

On the other hand, the war in 1967 solidified the new privileged position of industry and caused Israel to move even
further away from the social structure of the old agrarian Zionism.

The war served, first of all, to provide a new framework of
unity centered on a community of interests, and on a more Jewish than Zionist national symbolism.[39] Contrary to their practice
during the two previous wars, this time even the most
anti-Zionist religious zealots volunteered to fight, sharing with
the rest of the Israeli population the feeling that this was a Jewish war, fought for Jewish survival (at least in the Middle East)
and for Jewish traditional symbols: the Temple, the tombs of the
Patriarchs, etc.

Together with renewing a general feeling of sympathy for religion and of solidarity with the Diaspora, the June war also
consolidated the supremacy of industry over agriculture. It was
the air force and advanced technology that won the war in the
first three hours of conflict. It was industry and technology that
proved they could assure the economic and political future of
the state. Productivism has thus become a widespread new idea
in Israel, brought about through a greater economic involve-

ment of the Jewish Diaspora in the development of the state. The hope is that it will provide for the integration of Israeli society through higher standards of living; that it will furnish the necessary financial and technical means for the quick solution of the problem of the Arab refugees under Israeli control; and that it will supply the necessary influence over the occupied areas for political neutrality, possibly even for cooperation.

Mobility, the vital condition for industrialization, is now encouraged whenever possible: mobility of goods among Israel, the West Bank, and Transjordan at a rate of exchange intentionally favorable to the Arabs; mobility of men; Israeli mass tourism into Arab zones; and free Arab movement from Gaza into the West Bank, Israel, and Transjordan. An economic entity, stretching from the Mediterranean to Iraq, is thus taking shape. Whether it will be followed by political cooperation or by renewed disruption and war, is of course an open question.

VI

Because of the inability of the ideals of the eighteenth-century Enlightenment to be adapted to nineteenth- and twentieth-century realities, Jewish national ideology, at least as expressed by the old agrarian Zionism, has become increasingly irrelevant to the situation today in the state of Israel. In the course of the realization of Jewish national aspirations, the Jewish settlement in the Holy Land has undergone an almost total transformation, in spite of the continuity of its social and political symbolism and of its institutions. An agrarian elite society directed by a westernized plantocracy has found itself changed into a non-European industrialized society increasingly run by a nonideological technocracy that after a long internal political and social struggle has, through the 1967 military victory, asserted its preeminent role.

The June war has brought together in an already realized territorial unity of economic exchange two nations of refugees, deeply hostile to one another but very close in the common cultural Islamic background of many of their members and in the recent experience of social uprooting.

The Palestinian refugees as individuals are powerless economically, socially and politically. As individuals, one of the main psychological differences between them and the Jewish refugees is that their outlook is turned toward the past, while the outlook of the Jews is directed toward the future, although in the case of some of them the pull of the past was strong enough to make them return even to Germany.

The communities of the Palestinian refugees, however, are very different from the rest of the Middle Eastern Arab communities in such matters as internal structure, town-and-village relations, and social and political identity. The Palestinian refugees or residents have become one of the most articulate, well-educated, and socially and politically most engaged group in the Arab world. They are, curiously enough, the only crystallized modern Moslem Arab Diaspora in the Arab world, which extends from Kuwait to Algeria. As such, they have become the community in the Middle East most open to innovation. They have become a new factor in Middle Eastern politics—a powerful social and economic force for acceleration in the Palestine complex. They now add their needs and pressures, in a conflicting way, to the needs and pressures the Jewish refugees and the Arab minority already exert on the Israeli state.

The consequences of such a momentous change are felt in the trend of negotiations for a settlement of the Middle East crisis. While the Jordanians, in the persons both of King Hussein and of some Palestinian leaders, do not reject the idea of a settlement, and in fact have already accepted economic cooperation with Israel, Egypt is much more inclined to be rigid in rejecting all forms of contact. National pride, internal instability, and possibly Russian influence are responsible for such a rigid position. But behind the Egyptian political decision, there seem to be deeper social and economic considerations linked with the competing industrial evolution of the Israeli and Egyptian societies. In terms of future development, Israel, the Palestinians, and the Transjordanians can be complementary; an industrial Jewish society would be dependent for its economic development and security on the good will and cooperation of its agrarian neighbors, although more for labor than for goods, since Israel is self-sufficient in agricultural production.

With Egypt, the picture is totally different. Here Israel is confronted with an ambitious, still agrarian but rapidly industrializing society, which considers the Jewish state a dangerous competitor for economic expansion within, and industrial development of, an agricultural area conceived of as a zone of natural Egyptian influence.[40] It is understandable that from the Egyptian point of view all agreement with Israel should be conditioned by the return of Israel to the status quo ante, a situation of economic as well as military and political vulnerability that would be a guarantee against the industrial development of the Jewish state and an obstacle to possible cooperation between the two segments of the Palestinian population, the Arabs and the Israelis.

But the Israeli industrial society and the emergence of the Palestinians as a distinct national group in the Middle East[41] are two realities that can no longer be dismissed. Whether they will eventually develop some form of stable cooperation or will continue their struggle is, of course, an open question. But whichever the case, it is by and around them, more than elsewhere in the Middle East, that the course of events in the region is going to be determined.

PART 3

Israeli Perspectives and Arab Unity

Discovery of problems, even discovery of the relative significance of problems, is sometimes a significant novelty. It follows immediately that declaring a known but unappreciated solution to a given problem to be important may change our view of the field in which the problem occurs and thus may lead to a series of major discoveries; it may then be itself considered a discovery which renders one of many given problems the central problem in that field.

Joseph Agassi, "The Novelty of Popper's Philosophy of Science," *International Philosophical Quarterly*, Vol. VIII, No. 3, p. 449.

1. Israeli Attitudes to the Arab World

BY NISSIM REJWAN

ISRAEL is a nation in the making about which no generalities can be made with any measure of certitude. Presenting a rich mosaic of ethnic groups, cultures, habits of thought and approaches, Israelis seem to speak with almost as many voices and react in widely divergent ways. This is perhaps nowhere more apparent than in their attitudes to the Arabs. What some Israelis consider "integration" into the Middle East, others may dread as "assimilation" and consequent loss of identity; what to some may sound like clumsy emotional outbursts and empty threats can strike others as "Arab anti-Semitism" and a thirst for real blood. In trying to examine Israel's attitudes to the Arab world, one thus has to distinguish between two sets of attitudes—that of the old, homogeneous, selective, idealistic and overwhelmingly European Yishuv of the pre-state days, and the culturally pluralist, heterogeneous, down-to-earth and increasingly Middle Eastern Israeli society of today.

For it is obvious that, like all men, an Israeli's attitude to the world around him is determined largely by the collective historical experience of his particular group. As a result of their long dispersion and the widely variegated natures of the peoples among whom they lived, the historical experiences and ultimately the worldviews of the various sections of Israel's present population vary accordingly. And so do the Israelis' attitudes to the Arab world. The prevailing view of the Arab in Israel today has, rather inevitably, been the one determined by the experi-

Reprinted from *New Outlook*, Vol. 9, No. 5 (Tel Aviv, 1966), pp. 24–28; by permission of the editor.

ence and worldview of that part of Jewry which has had the most decisive influence on the founding and development of the state, its cultural character, and its policies.

It does not take a great deal of research to discover which Jewish community this was. Professor Isaiah Berlin, a perceptive observer of Jewish and Zionist affairs, once wrote that it was "almost self-evident" that, if there had existed only the Jews of the Western world and those of the Eastern Muslim countries, "there would have been no Israel." Neither of these Jewries, he implied, had any influence on the building and early character of the state of Israel. The community, therefore that is to be considered as the most closely concerned with laying the early foundations of Israel are the Jews of Eastern Europe, specifically those of Russia and Russian Poland.

What may one infer from this fact as far as Israel's present attitude to the Arab world is concerned? To the Zionist cause the Jews of Eastern Europe brought many singular gifts and attributes: dynamism, idealism, a great singleness of purpose and uncommon devotion. But besides these qualities, this community possessed something which neither the Jews of the West nor those of the Middle East had. As a result of their own historical circumstances and experience, the Jews of Eastern Europe, unlike their brethren from farther to the west and southwest, had to maintain an independent existence of their own, and had thus grown to be a kind of a state within a state. As Professor Berlin sums it up: "The Jews of Russia and Poland, as a result of political and social persecution, had found themselves cooped up in a kind of single extended ghetto, called the Pale of Settlement . . . [where] they remained within their medieval shell and developed a kind of internal structure of their own." Within this fairly independent structure, these Jews developed a very powerful and extremely rich inner life, but in a certain sense, they "remained less touched by modern developments than any community of Jews in Europe"—or, one may add, in the Middle East.

The impact which this independent, somewhat exclusivist historical experience of Israel's founding fathers has had on the country's attitude to the Arabs can hardly be exaggerated. The lack of serious interest and concern on the part of the first Zionist settlers about the people, the region and the culture to which they had come (an unconcern often deplored by experts and historians) was no doubt a product of this legacy of exclusiveness and cultural self-sufficiency. So, too, is the prevailing belief that Israel is a specifically Jewish state in which no non-Jew could really feel at home.

These attitudes of mind are obviously fundamentally alien to the historical experience and outlook of both Western European and Middle Eastern Jews, who up to the establishment of the state, were neither numerically nor culturally an element to be reckoned with in the country. (Even the German element has had no influence here. To quote Professor Berlin once again: "For all the crucial contribution which the German settlers have made . . . to every walk of life . . . the heart of the national life is almost untouched by the values dearest to the German Jews. It is they who are expected to adjust to an outlook often alien to theirs."

PAN-ARABISM AS ZIONIST IMAGE

These, then, are the influences that have determined the attitude of the new state to the peoples and the cultures surrounding it. The ways in which these influences helped shape official Israel's view of the Arabs and of Arabism are many; but the most crucial and harmful of their manifestations has been that, in a very valid sense, the Zionists managed to create Arabism and Arab nationalism in their own exclusivist image. According to this image, the Arabs were, per se, a self-contained "nationality," an alien political and cultural entity standing in permanent and inevitable opposition to the Jews, who in turn constitute a separate, single "nationality."

A most striking illustration of this thesis has recently come to light with the publication of excerpts from the diary of Mr. David Ben Gurion in *Ma'ariv* under the heading, "An Effort that Failed." In these excerpts, he tells of a meeting he had in Jerusalem with George Antonius, the historian of the Arab nationalist movement, in which ways were discussed of reaching an understanding between the Zionists and the Palestine Arab leadership of the day. As was to be expected, Antonius' point of departure in these talks was that the whole problem was one which concerned the Arabs of Palestine and the Jewish settlers there—and that if an understanding were to be attained, both sides had to surrender part of their claims. Ben Gurion would have none of it; however, he told Antonius:

As a point of departure the proposition must be accepted that the issue is not one between the Jews of Palestine and the Arabs of Palestine: within this limited area there really is a conflict that it is difficult to surmount. Instead, we must view the Jews as one world entity and the Arabs as one world entity. I truly believe that between the national aspirations of the Jewish people and the national aspirations of the Arab people—which may perhaps not yet be clear and crystallized, but which will no doubt become clear and crystallized in the course of time—there is no inevitable contradiction. For we are interested only and solely in this country, while the Arabs are interested not only in this country—so that no matter what happens in this country it will not effect the world status of the Arab people. *(Ma'ariv,* February 25)

These rather extreme Pan-Arab sentiments were expressed by Ben Gurion in April 1936. . . . It is safe to suppose that even Antonius found himself bewildered by the vehemence of the Zionist leader's Arab nationalist views. For the plain fact is that not even the most visionary Arab nationalist of that day could possibly have formulated his doctrine in a more daring and "messianic" manner. Ben Gurion was not describing an existing state of affairs; he was engaging in prophecy, apparently elated at the prospect of the emergence and crystallization of the Arabs' nationalist (Pan-Arab) aspirations—and their appearance as a "world unit."

This Zionist concept of a tightly knit, united and homogeneous "Arab world" is a patently novel and drastically distorted one, as the experiences of the Arab nationalists during the past thirty years have shown. The fact is that, as Professor S. D. Goitein has written in his book *Jews and Arabs,* not a single independent state with Arabic as its official language was in existence before World War I. "If asked about his affiliations, an inhabitant of Arab Asia of that time would have described himself as a Muslim or a Christian, as a member of a certain tribe or clan, an inhabitant of one town or village, or another, or a subject of the Ottoman Sultan; but it would hardly have occurred to him to call himself an Arab."

NATIONALITIES AND NOT NATIONALITY

True, the countries of the area now commonly called "the

Arab World" have in the meantime secured an independent status. Arabic has become the official language in each of these independent entities. A "League of Arab States" was formed, and there has been endless talk about Arab unity and its imminence. All these, however, have not added up to a definable "Arab nationality"; in fact such an eventuality now seems farther than ever from materializing, and the Arabs in their different lands are coming to realize it. There is, to be sure, an Iraqi nationality, Syrian, Lebanese, Egyptian and Saudian nationalities; but between these and the materialization of an "Arab" nationality is a far cry. Similarly, there is an "Israeli" nationality—and instead of the artificial opposition of Arab and Jewish "nationalities," the Middle East seems destined to accommodate a mosaic of nationalities, cultures and ethnic groups: Syrians, Iraqis, Palestinians, Israelis, Muslims, Jews, Christians, Arabs, Kurds, Maronites, Armenians.

The part which Israel can play in creating and stabilizing such a pluralistic Middle East is considerable. For although the dominant view in Israel has so far tended to envisage the future of the area in exclusivist terms of Arabs and Jews, there are signs that a new approach is developing. These signs are discernible both on the official—elite—and the unofficial popular levels. In an article published in *The Jewish Observer* of London, for instance, Mr. Abba Eban, then Deputy Premier and now Foreign Minister of Israel, made the remarkable observation that the key to Arab-Israeli peace does not lie "in any of the conventional themes which the diplomats have agitated since 1948," but rather in a new and common understanding of the Middle Eastern structure: "The destiny of this region lies in a pluralistic interaction of Asia, Europe, Africa; of Judaism, Christianity and Islam" *(The Jewish Observer, September 11, 1964).* This is an observation worthy of serious contemplation, and if it truly represents the official Israeli view, it constitutes a radical departure from the old, monolithic opposition of Jew and Arab.

This new approach may well work, and at the same time be augmented, on a deeper cultural level. For, as has been indicated, there is an additional factor at work here—namely the introduction into Israel of an important Middle Eastern element in the form of mass immigration from the countries of the Middle East and North Africa. This new and in many ways unexpected development is fast changing the cultural face of the country, and will inevitably have a bearing on Israel's attitude to the Arabs. For the temperament of these Middle Easterners, their long experience of living side by side with the Arabs, their fundamentally different type of reaction to things not Jewish, are factors to be taken into consideration in any serious appraisal of future relations between Israel and her neighbors. For one thing: From what has been described as "just a patch of Europe transplanted to the eastern shore of the Mediterranean," Israel is bound to become increasingly "Oriental," a "normal Middle Eastern country at home with itself and its problems," as Dr. James Parkes, the well-known British historian and expert on Jewish-Gentile relations, has put it.

ORIENTAL JEWS AND THE ARABS

In what way is this development likely to affect the country's attitude to the Arabs? In general discussions in Israel on the state's relations with the Arabs, it is often argued that, far from having more understanding for the Arabs, the Orientals are actually more anti-Arab than the Europeans. There may appear to be some element of truth in this observation. In the first years of their immigration, the Oriental Jews were bound to feel resentment at having been victimized in their lands of birth, as well as at the first hardships they inevitably encountered in their new home, and they tended to vent their anger and resentment on the Arabs. Moreover, coming to a society whose mores, attitudes and sentiments were strongly slanted in favor of Europe and openly condescending toward the East, and in which the most observable prestige criterion was conformity to European ways and customs, many of these immigrants felt they had to go out of their way to dissociate themselves from their origin and culture, and often knew no better way to do this than to direct their resentment and contempt at their former compatriots. It was this phenomenon, understandable in the circumstances, that produced their anti-Arab attitudes and pronouncements and gave rise to the somewhat convenient view that the Orientals were anti-Arab. But this was bound to be a passing phase, and there is now reason to believe that these Arabic Jews are acquiring enough self-confidence and self-respect, and discovering more about themselves and their new surroundings, to have a more balanced and unprejudiced view of their fellow Middle Easterners.

There are endless possibilities in such a development. For one thing, the prevalent image of the Arab as another version of the

European anti-Semite—only a bit worse—is bound to disappear. Needless to say, this Israeli image of the Arab as a half-barbarian, murderously inclined neighbor (an image which, it must be added in fairness, has partly been the product of empty and thoughtless Arab propaganda and threats) has done much harm both to the future of Arab-Israeli relations and to the general psychological climate of the country.

One key to a better future undoubtedly lies with the Middle Eastern element in the Israeli setup. These Jews, whose historical circumstances spared them the experience of being cooped up in ghettolike enclaves, have had a long and firm tradition of dealing and discoursing with their Arab neighbors, and often took an active part in public affairs of the countries in which they dwelt. An Israel in which this important element gets its full share of responsibility and leadership will have a substantially different image of her neighbors and may thus be the better able to attain a meaningful coexistence and mutually beneficial cooperation with them.

2. Three Problems of Israel's Foreign Policy

BY SIMHA FLAPAN

The difficulty in securing a peaceful settlement between Israel and the Arab countries arises from the fact that, to complicate further the already complex objective problems which must be solved, a deep chasm of fear and mutual suspicion now yawns between them. Relations between the two peoples are characterized by distorted interpretations of the other side's policy, to which sinister designs are attributed. Anybody desirous of promoting the cause of peace must, therefore, devote himself not only to the actual conflicts between the two peoples, but to the imaginary ones as well.

On first analysis, those responsible for Israeli foreign policy are able to point out that ever since 1948 the state of Israel has been striving consistently for peace with the Arab states. The announcements of successive governments of Israel have expressed the sincere desire for peace cherished by the vast majority of the Israeli public. If this public was persuaded to support the preventive operation in the Sinai Peninsula, it was because it had come to view the existing security and political situation as one slowly and hopelessly deteriorating. There can be no doubt that this public would most willingly grasp any prospect of peace and would not only forego the advantages of a military victory, but would even agree to a compromise on controversial issues—if it could view this as a concrete prospect. The revisionist trend, which espouses territorial expansionism through mili-

Reprinted from *New Outlook*, Vol. 1, No. 1 (Tel Aviv, 1957), pp. 50–53; by permission of the editor.

tary conquests—and today its influence has increased owing to the despair that followed the withdrawal from Sinai and the Gaza Strip—would then shrink into an insignificant faction.

Those who shape Israel's foreign policy can, therefore, with a clear conscience, contend: "We aspired to peace. We proposed negotiations, but the hand proffered remained suspended in air." They can even point out that on the other side the Arab statesmen not only rejected the invitation to negotiate, but actually imposed an economic, political and social boycott against Israel, adopted guerrilla-warfare tactics, and went so far as to refuse to acknowledge Israel's very existence.

Hence, if the analysis of Israel's foreign policy were confined exclusively to subjective intentions, it could be exonerated.

The test of politics is its results, not its intentions, its efficacy rather than its desires. Declarations of peace, even the sincerest, do not in themselves constitute a policy of peace. Not even the antagonism of the opposing side can serve as an extenuating argument. The aim of Israeli policy should have been *to effect a change* in the attitude of the other side. The Arab world's hatred and animosity for Israel have been an established fact since 1948. The task of Israeli policy, therefore, should be to reduce this animosity, to drive a wedge into it, to arouse at least some measure of differentiation in Arab public opinion with regard to Israel.

The reasons for this failure are due not only to external factors but also to errors and fallacies of an internal nature. I propose, in the lines that follow, to dwell upon a number of problems in regard to which Israel's policy failed to anticipate developments and indicated a mistaken approach.

First of all, Israel's attitude toward the problems of the area must be analyzed. One may say that it did not take into account three central processes that have marked the area's development in recent years. These are:

(a) intensification of Great Power rivalry, in the wake of which has come the Soviet Union's tempestuous penetration into the area as a factor not to be ignored;
(b) the rise of an Arab national movement fighting for political independence, neutrality and unity of the Arab peoples;
(c) the retreat of colonialism and, first and foremost, the far-reaching contraction of British and French influence in the area.

Israel has reacted toward these processes, which evolved on the crest of a wave of stormy, dramatic events, by clinging conservatively to a political conception that accorded with the situation in the year 1948.

On the one hand, the Soviet Union was not at that time a factor of any influence in the Middle East. On the other hand, the Arab movement for neutrality and unity was in its infancy. The Western powers, headed by Great Britain, then constituted the decisive factor in the area.

Israel's chief aim was to secure Arab acknowledgement of its existence. Its efforts to achieve this were directed mainly to the Western powers, in the hope that the latter would urge the Arab governments to extend *de jure* recognition to a *de facto* situation. The result of this line was that Israel in her policy identified herself or openly sympathized with the Western viewpoint on all major problems of the area (the Persian oil crisis, British evacuation of the Suez Canal, the events in Algeria).

The Arab world interpreted this line as proof of Israel's opposition to national liberation and independence of the area's peoples; it strengthened the anti-Israel character of the Arab national movement, and this, in turn, intensified Israel's apprehensions with regard to the aim of the Arab nations to unite. This was a vicious circle par excellence.

The reciprocal influence between these two reactions led to a widening and deepening of the gulf between Israel and the Arab countries, a situation most dramatically expressed in the events of recent months, and the upshot was that Israel found herself linked to a declining force in the Middle East, associated in the eyes of all sections of the Arab national movement, and even in the eyes of the rest of the peoples of Asia, with colonial interests.

Such a state of affairs was not inevitable. There exists no real contradiction between Arab aspirations for liberation, independence and unity, on the one hand, and the existence of an independent, sovereign Israel integrated into the Middle East area, on the other. The independence and unity of the area's nations is a determinate historical process that will be consummated even though the tide of events has its ebb and flow. Any attempts to obstruct it by foreign or domestic agencies are foredoomed to ultimate failure despite temporary successes they may achieve.

Israel has nothing to gain by linking her interests with the obstructing factors and relying exclusively upon them. In doing so, she will only thrust aside the one prospect for mutual understanding and condemn herself to isolation.

On the other hand, so is the Arab national movement's attempt to view the struggle against Israel as a necessary phase in its anticolonial struggle doomed to failure.

Unlike Great Britain, France or the United States, Israel cannot be forced "to pack its belongings," get out of the area, and "go home." Because Israel *is* home, the home to which the masses of the Jewish people in capitalist and socialist countries alike are returning in an ever-widening flow at an increasingly rapid pace. The sooner the two national movements come to acknowledge the necessity for coexistence, the easier will they find the consummation of their national aspirations.

A second problem urgently requiring a new evaluation is the fate of the Palestine Arab people, victims of the Arab war against Israel in 1948 and today the principal victims of the absence of peace.

The Palestine Arabs had enjoyed a unique development owing to their joint existence with the Jewish community under the Mandate. The processes of economic and social transition amongst them were accelerated, and they had undergone a consolidation of national consciousness. At its very beginning, however, this national consciousness was diverted into anti-Jewish channels, despite the fact that the Zionist movement had attempted time and again to achieve a *modus vivendi* with the Arab national movement.

The United Nations General Assembly Resolution of November 29, 1947, accorded recognition to the right of self-determination and recommended the establishment of an Arab state economically linked to Israel. The war of 1948, which aimed to destroy the state of Israel, ended in calamity for the Palestine Arabs. The majority of them became refugees, bereft of home and country, dispersed throughout the Arab states. The problem of hundreds of thousands of refugees presents today the chief objective obstacle to peace.

The refugee camps, with the stagnation, poverty, idleness and hopelessness for the future that characterize them, are a hotbed of hatred, a veritable reserve force for *Feddayun* formations, a convenient and effective instrument for fomenting tension, conducting guerrilla warfare, and applying political pressure. Indeed, refugees everywhere have provided a never-failing source of interference with the normalization of relations between peoples and states. Their presence renders uncertain the stability of boundaries and the validity of treaties.

Israel may contend that the moral responsibility for the existence of the Arab refugee problem rests squarely upon the Arab governments. Since they sought to prevent by violence implementation of the UN resolutions, it is their duty to assume responsibility for the fate of the refugees.

The unbroken, unsolved existence of this problem, however, serves neither the cause of peace nor Israel's interests. It plays into the hands of those selfsame elements in the Arab states that refuse to reconcile themselves to the existence of the state of Israel.

Israel cannot ignore the tragedy of hundreds of thousands of refugees, nor can she ignore its negative effect on the prospects for peace. She must take the following facts into consideration:

> (1) The existence of the refugee problem is to the detriment of Israel.
>
> (2) Just as there can be no peace settlement based on any cessation of Jewish immigration to Israel, so there can be no peace without a solution of the refugee problem.

Even those forces among the Arabs who regard a settlement with Israel as imperative cannot overlook or forego the claim to a solution of the refugee problem. Under these circumstances, Israel's readiness, with UN assistance, to absorb and rehabilitate a reasonable number of refugees would force a serious breach in the wall of hatred surrounding her, render it more difficult to stir up animosity against her, and give encouragement to the forces of peace in the Arab world. Such initiative, while not weakening, would actually increase the validity of Israel's demand that the majority of the refugees be rehabilitated in the Arabs countries. It would lead to added pressure by the refugees themselves in that direction.

Obviously a comprehensive and complete solution of the refugee problem is conditional, primarily, on a peace settlement between Israel and the Arab states and especially with Jordan, in which most of the refugees are concentrated.

From several points of view, particular importance attaches to the relations between Israel and Jordan. This is not because of any prospects for a separate peace with Jordan; the urge for unity among the Arab peoples is too powerful, their apprehensions about Israel too great to permit of any such way out. It is so because the distinguishing fact about Jordan is that—more than any other of the Arab states—she needs peace to safeguard her very existence and future.

The principal Arab states—Egypt, Syria, Iraq and Saudi Arabia—do not as yet have any vital stake in peace with Israel. To some extent, they actually benefit from the anti-Israel boycott (which prevents Israel's commerce and industry from competing in Middle East markets has caused oil pipelines, aerial and maritime lines of communication to be transferred out of Israeli territory to neighboring countries, etc.). Jordan's situation is different.

The area of Palestine lying east of the Jordan River, named Transjordan, was separated administratively from the rest of Palestine and handed over in the year 1921 to Emir Abdullah of the Hashemite line; it did not constitute a self-sufficient national, political or economic framework.

The annexation of the so-called "Arab Triangle" of western Palestine to Abdullah's realm did not alter the situation fundamentally. Jordan's Palestinian inhabitants, who today constitute the great majority of the kingdom's population (900,000 out of a total of 1,400,000), gave it added impetus in its struggle to abrogate the treaty with Great Britain. They did not provide any basis for its independent economic existence.

The Palestinian Arabs at first displayed opposition and demanded separation on the grounds of the suppression and discrimination to which they were being subjected by the Jordan authorities.

With the passage of years, this situation has changed. The Arab states no longer demand the establishment of a Palestine Arab state (although they do continue to demand implementation of the 1947 Partition Resolution of the UN General Assembly). The Palestine Arabs in Jordan have gradually achieved a status of civil and political equality. Latterly, they have become a hegemonic majority economically, culturally and politically, and have desisted from raising the slogan of separation.

The fact is that Jordan has become the successor state to the Palestine Arab state (exclusive of the Gaza Strip) which was to have arisen as provided by the UN Resolution of 1947.

This fact could serve as the basis for a complete solution to the problem—if the politically determining factors in Jordan were to acquiesce in the existence of Israel and to follow the recommendations of the UN, which indicated the necessity of economic union between the two states. Were this the case, it would not be difficult to arrive at an agreement on the joint exploitation of water supplies, electricity and natural resources. This, in turn, would make possible a complete solution of the refugee problem.

Such, however, has not been the approach of the political circles in Jordan, especially amongst the Palestinians. The latter, even after having reconciled themselves to their new political framework, within which they became a determining factor, have been pressing primarily for the affiliation of Jordan with a federative organization of other Arab states, mainly with Egypt and Syria.

This approach has tended to overlook the fundamental fact that Jordan's economic future and her capacity to solve the problems of her inhabitants, including hundreds of thousands of destitute refugees, are conditional upon economic collaboration with Israel. Even should Jordan join any Egyptian-Syrian union, she would be unable to get water from the Nile or electricity from the Aswan Dam. Her main source for water and development projects would remain the Jordan River, her chief industrial prospect—the Dead Sea, her natural outlets—Haifa and Eilat-Akaba. Exploitation of these readily available resources is the *sine qua non* of Jordan's economic existence and rehabilitation of the refugees.

The fact that there is no political force in Jordan orienting itself on peace and economic collaboration with Israel is due in large measure to the fact that nothing has been done to encourage such an orientation. Israel's failure to reveal any initiative toward a solution of the refugee problem, the clamorous campaigns conducted for "reintegrating the country" through military conquest, the continued maintenance of the military administration in the Arab areas of Israel, where it constitutes a regime of discrimination—all these things have not helped the hundreds of thousands of Palestine Arabs, today a majority of Jordan's population, to forget the impact of the calamity of 1948. They have not served to implant in their hearts the desire to fashion anew their relations with the Jewish people and with Israel on the basis of unity and partnership.

Israeli policy must draw to the full all conclusions from these facts. A constructive approach to the refugee problem, extension of the scope of the Family Reunion Arrangement, a special colonization program for Arab DP's within Israel, abolition of the military administration and the extension of full equal civil and national rights to the Arabs of Israel, cessation of all propaganda for military conquests, and a positive approach to a program of economic union with Jordan—all these can evoke and encourage within Jordan forces amenable to conciliation and able to work for this solution to the problem. Their apprehension as to the danger of Israeli "domination" could be offset by pointing out that such a solution in no way conflicts with the idea of Arab union and could be part of a broader federative project.

The foregoing analysis has ignored the background of Great Power rivalry in the area which has recently, in particular, reached new levels of asperity and tension. Obviously, intensification of the Cold War, with all its concomittant phenomena, has turned the area into an erupting volcano that threatens to set off a world conflagration. Extrication from the clutches of Great Power rivalry and the Cold War is necessary for the peaceful existence and cooperation of peoples in the Middle East. Jewish-Arab peace is the first step in this direction.

3. Israel Between Europe and Asia

BY DAVID SHLOMI

THERE HAS BEEN a great deal of discussion recently about two separate trends in Israel foreign policy. The first of these is the *Asian,* which emphasizes the need for Israel to find its place among the nations of the region and among the states of Asia which have achieved independence since the Second World War. The second trend is the *European,* which argues that closer political, economic and cultural relations with the countries of Europe will best serve the vital interests of Israel. In reality, however, these two tendencies do not conflict.

The aim of Zionism was not only the establishment of a Jewish state or the creation of a new society according to Herzl's vision, but also cooperation with the Arab peoples awakening to a new spirit of activity after the destruction of the Ottoman Empire.

Unfortunately, however, the leaders of the Arab national movement saw in the Jews not allies in their struggle for political independence, but invaders and enemies. After the establishment of the state of Israel, and particularly after the signing of the armistice agreements, it seemed at times that the Arabs had begun to grasp the meaning of the Jews' return to their homeland and to accept their intense desire to rebuild the desolation and to live in peace with their neighbors.

A short time before the establishment of the state, it had seemed possible that King Abdullah, a practical and intelligent

Reprinted from *New Outlook,* Vol. 1, No. 3 (Tel Aviv, 1957), pp. 22–26; by permission of the editor.

ruler, would find some path to agreement with the Jews in Palestine. Even before the establishment of the state, and again immediately after the War of Liberation, the Jews had established contact with Abdullah. These discussions might have borne fruit were it not for the intransigence of the other Arab states, which branded as treason every hint of contact, to say nothing of negotiations.

For a time, too, Israel had placed some hopes in the leaders of the Wafd, many of whom had come to recognize the strength of Israel and its constructive role. But these hopes, too, were disappointed. The Wafd failed in this, as it failed to wipe out corruption in its own land, or to establish a truly democratic regime for the benefit of the masses of the people.

Neguib's rise to power, in turn, awakened new hopes, and Ben Gurion's dramatic appeal to General Neguib to work for Egyptian-Israeli agreement, since there were no conflicts between the two which could not be solved by negotiations, is still remembered.

All these hopes were frustrated because the Arab leaders had not learned to understand the new reality of the Middle East after the Second World War, and were beset by the dream of destroying Israel and driving its people into the sea.

The cornerstone of Israeli policy has been, with scarcely any divergence of opinion between the various parties, the desire for close cooperation with the neighboring Arab states for the benefit of all the peoples of the region. To those who stood at the helm of the Jewish state, it was clear that its development depended to a great measure on her relations with the Arab states in the fields of politics, security, economics and culture.

The political sphere: The international situation which developed after the Second World War reduced the importance of small and isolated states and enhanced the importance of *blocs,* not only of the two world powers but also of the regional groupings whose influence has grown in the United Nations and for whose favor the world powers compete. Israel would be interested in becoming a member, equal in rights as in duties, of the bloc of Middle East nations.

Security: Peace between the Arab states and Israel would have meant for the latter the possibility of diverting large sums to development and the absorption of immigration. The arms flowing to the Arab states are aimed today only at Israel. The funds invested in these arms could have found much better use

even in the richest of the Arab lands. Further, it is clear beyond
doubt today, that were it not for the arms deal with Czechoslovakia, Nasser would have received American funds to build
the high dam at Aswan.

Economics: Before the War of Liberation, the Jewish sector of
Palestine provided an excellent market for the agricultural
produce of the Arab states. Israel would undoubtedly have continued to import this produce in exchange for industrial exports.
One of the reasons for the backwardness of the neighboring
countries, apart from the absence of capital for large investments, is the lack of technical experts. Israel could have been of
great aid in filling this need.

Culture: Close cultural relations between Israel and her
neighbors would have served as a stimulus to the development
of the cultural forces of both peoples. Such cultural cooperation
is possible, and even necessary, in the fields of education, science, literature, art and sport.

But it was not only the Arab states which refused to recognize
the presence of Israel in the Middle East; the newly liberated
states of Asia failed to understand the difference between Jewish
immigration to Israel and English colonization in Rhodesia or
Kenya, or French settlement in Tunis and Algeria. Fearful for
their new independent status, they saw in every newcomer an
enemy and invader, threatening the sovereignty and autonomy
of the peoples of Asia and Africa.

Mighty India, which won the respect of the world for its
struggle against the Cold War and the division of the world into
two blocs, has persistently refused to establish diplomatic relations with Israel, although she has long since "recognized" her
in theory. The Asian nations which met in the famous Bandung
Conference agreed under Arab pressure to exclude Israel from
the Conference and then adopted resolutions against her without allowing her to plead her case.

Under the influence of this mistrust, the members of the
Afro-Asian bloc on many occasions yielded to Arab pressure and
voted resolutions against Israel.

The case of Europe was different. Though many Jews had
been compelled to leave Europe because of the attitude of the
population and the regimes, which had seen in them a "foreign
element," the European governments recognized Israel and welcomed her establishment. And this was not the case of Western
Europe alone, where, although in various periods the Jews had

suffered at the hands of anti-Semitic groups, they had for the most part enjoyed freedom and equality, or of Scandinavia, where the Jews had always been equal citizens under the law and in practice, and where both the governments and the population had done so much to save Jews from the Germans. Soviet Russia, too, and the other countries of Eastern Europe, welcomed the establishment of Israel.

The countries of Western and Northern Europe saw in the birth of Israel the hand of Providence, and a fitting recompense for the hundreds of years of suffering and tribulation in exile. This was also the view of wide circles in West Germany, of all parties and classes, who were conscious of guilt and shame for the actions of their own people during the Nazi regime. The countries of Eastern Europe regarded the emergence of Israel as the natural development of the national idea, guaranteeing to every people the right to self-determination and national autonomy. The Soviet Union was one of the first nations to recognize Israel. At that time both Gromyko, today the Soviet Foreign Minister, and Charapkin, both then Soviet delegates to the United Nations, enthusiastically justified the right of the Jewish refugees in Europe to join their brothers in Palestine and to found an independent state. In later years, however, Soviet policy has changed, and the dependence of the popular democracies on Moscow finds its expression in their branding of Israel as an aggressor and the tool of imperialism. But as soon as one of the Communist states frees itself to some degree from the Soviet embrace, its attitude toward Israel changes and becomes more positive. This has been demonstrated in the case of the Poland of Gomulka and even in Hungary after the fall of Rakosi. Were it not for Soviet pressure, friendly relations with Israel would be the rule in Eastern Europe. Political and economic relations between the European countries and the state of Israel have been good, although there has been some restraint on their part due to the desire not to become entangled in the Israeli-Arab quarrel.

The repercussions of the Sinai campaign brought the fact home to the countries of Europe that the Israeli-Arab dispute was not a merely local affair, but part of the global conflict. This revelation was the chief factor in bringing about a European reevaluation of Israel's position.

New developments have recently become manifest in Western Europe. The generations-old dream of European unity has

come closer to realization. The first steps have taken place in
the economic sphere, with the proposed establishment of the
Common Market and the Free Trade Area, including Holland,
Belgium, Luxemburg, West Germany, France, Italy and, in
some measure, Great Britain. Since 60 per cent of all Israeli
exports, and 80 per cent of her citrus exports, go to the countries of the Common Market, there is a growing conviction in
Israel of the need to find ways of joining these new groups,
which are intended in the future to embrace the countries of
North Africa as well.

The Sinai operation created some tension in the relations
between Israel and the Asian countries. For many of them, still
savoring the first tastes of independence and embroiled in quarrels with their neighbors, (e.g. India-Pakistan), the operation
represented an Israeli conspiracy with France and Great Britain
designed to solve certain differences by force. Even a friendly
nation like Burma found it necessary to vote against Israel in the
UN Assembly.

After the abatement of the storm, however, and following the
Israeli retreat from the occupied territories, some of the Asian
countries began to see the situation a little differently. Here,
too, as in Europe and in America, public opinion often leads the
way. Part of the Asian press, some labor leaders and scientists,
have begun to look to Israel as an example of the development
of modern agricultural and irrigation schemes and the building
of large housing projects and industries. They are attracted by
the vitality and dynamic character of Israel's society, which has
succeeded in building its state in spite of the numerous political,
military, economic and social difficulties. Slowly but surely the
governments of Asia are following the direction of public opinion.

The state of Israel must gain sympathy in Africa, too. Were it
not for the Egyptian atrocity propaganda, we could establish
normal relations with Ethiopia and even with Libya, Tunisia
and Morocco. Only the desire to maintain at least a semblance
of solidarity with the Arab world restrains Prime Minister Bourguiba of Morocco from openly adopting a more positive stand
toward Israel. Despite the hermetically sealed Arab boycott of
Israel and Israelis, delegates from Israel were welcome guests at
the Conference of the International Confederation of Free
Trade Unions in Tunis last June. Israel has succeeded in establishing close relations with Ghana, the youngest independent

state in Africa, and there are signs of future cooperation in many fields.

The Prime Minister of India, who at one time supported Nasser unreservedly, spoke out at the meeting of the British Commonwealth in support of Israel's right to free passage through the Suez Canal. To this may be added the recent statement by the Prime Minister of Pakistan, in which, with all its reservations, he said that the Arabs must accept Israel as an irreversible, if undesirable, fact, and suggested himself as mediator.

We are witness also to a number of changes within the Arab world itself. As a result of the Sinai campaign, Nasser's star has paled, and the bloc he built up has fallen apart. The separation of Jordan, Saudi Arabia and Lebanon from Cairo will promote, if not immediate peace and an Arab-Israeli agreement, then at least quiet on the borders, and that may help pave the way to peace. The United States, which has gained a large measure of influence in the region as a result of the acceptance of the Eisenhower Doctrine by many of the Middle East countries, must take upon itself the responsibility for finding ways and means for the settlement of the Arab refugees in the underpopulated Arab countries.

Israel sees its future tied to the development of the region as a whole and to coopearation with the peoples of Asia and Africa. She hopes that with the passage of time all enmity will disappear and be replaced by a period of cooperation and mutual aid. But at the same time, Israel must continue to establish closer relations with the countries in Europe. It is our fervent hope that Israel will some day form a bridge between Europe, from which so many of her inhabitants and builders originate, and the peoples of the Middle-East, of which she is a part.

4. China and Israel

BY MORDEHAI NAHUMI

DURING THE PAST two and a half years, the Chinese People's Republic has been revealing an increasing interest in the Middle East. This interest has been reflected, for instance, in her growing support for Arab hatred of Israel, a support which has led Peking during the last year to adopt the Palestine Liberation Organization headed by Ahmed Shukairy.

On the 15th of May of this year, Palestine Day was celebrated in Peking, and on this occasion the *People's Daily* wrote that: "The Chinese people strongly supports the struggle of the Arab peoples against American imperialism and against its aggressive tool—Israel, and the struggle of the Palestinian Arab people for the liberation of its homeland."

The official Chinese paper does not, however, stop with supporting the Arabs' anti-Israeli struggle and with attacking imperialism and its tool in Israel, but also strongly criticizes the partnership between "Soviet revisionists and the Israeli Zionists." The paper criticizes the Moscow weekly, *New Times,* which "openly argued for expanding the application of the 'spirit of Tashkent' to the Israeli-Arab dispute" instead of attacking Israel as a "tool of imperialism" that was created for aggression and which should be removed from the world by the methods of armed war of liberation. The Chinese paper defines this argument by the Soviet Russian weekly as a "plot of the Soviet revisionists in cooperation with the American imperi-

Reprinted from *New Outlook*, Vol. 9, No. 6 (Tel Aviv, 1966), pp. 40–48; by permission of the editor.

alists, to betray the interests of the Palestinian people and the Arab peoples in their anti-imperialist struggle."

This extreme anti-Israeli attitude is the product of the developments of the past two and a half years since Chinese Prime Minister Chou En-lai's tour, in December of 1963 and January-February of 1964, of ten of the fifteen African countries which maintained or were about to establish diplomatic relations with China. Five of these ten—Egypt, Tunisia, Algeria, Morocco and Sudan—were members of the Arab League, while a sixth—Muslim Somalia—was officially sympathetic to the Arab countries. The four other countries—Mali, Ghana, Guinea and Ethiopia—belonged to the group of Negro states which maintained normal diplomatic ties with Israel. Chou En-lai's proposed visit to three countries of East Africa—Tanganyika, Uganda and Kenya—which also maintain ties with Israel, was cancelled because of military revolts in January 1964.

Egypt had been the first Arab state to recognize Popular China, in May 1956, as a demonstration against the Western refusal to finance the Aswan Dam, and as a result of the tension over Suez and the closer ties between Egypt and the USSR at that time. Peking established relations with the government-in-exile of the Algerian FLN and the government of Morocco at the end of 1958. Diplomatic relations with Sudan, Iraq and Yemen were established in 1959. Except, however, for her political and material support to the FLN, China did not show any special active interest in the Middle East and North Africa in the years 1956–62, and Peking therefore had no particular reason to demonstrate any anti-Israeli position. Though the Chinese delegation headed by Chou En-lai had met Arab representatives, including Nasser, and the African liberation movements as early as the Bandung Conference of 1955, its attitude was careful and restrained, in keeping with the principles of coexistence that Chinese foreign policy supported at that time. China's main interest at that period was in the developments in her own immediate neighborhood in Asia, where she demonstrated her sympathy for all the new countries established on the ruins of the empires and her desire to maintain friendly relations with all of them (including India).

China's interests and aims were completely different when Chou En-lai left for his tour of Africa. Peking had already developed to its fullest extreme its concept of the "revolutionary anti-imperialist potential" of the three continents (Asia, Africa and South America) against the bulwarks of imperialism in North America and Europe (without, however, giving up hopes for "interimperialistic" conflicts that would end Western Europe's subordination to America. The tour took place on the eve of the establishment of diplomatic relations between Peking and Paris, to Washington's displeasure). The USSR under Khruschev had meanwhile changed from the "great friend and the leader of the revolutionary world" to the source of "revisionistic-treasonable" concepts of "coexistence in peace with imperialism" and an opponent in the struggle for the leadership of the international Communist movement.

FIRST STEPS IN THE MIDDLE EAST

Chou En-lai's Arab and African tour of the winter of 1963–64 was therefore intended to pave independent Chinese roads to Africa. In accordance with Mao's thesis of the two stages in the complete revolution (anti-imperialistic and anti-feudal national liberation and socialist revolution), all the countries that Chou En-lai intended to visit were in some part of the first stage. China's solidarity with the liberation struggles and the defense of national independence against the plots of imperialism and colonialism, both old and new, was the main theme in Chou's appearances.

In addition to this, however, Chou En-lai's tour was intended to discover how China could tender financial and technical aid to the new countries of Africa. The tour undoubtedly also had a third aim: to improve China's "image" among the Africans, after the "falsifications" by "colonialism and imperialism," as well as by the Soviet Union, which had already won important positions in the Arab world and in "Black" Africa. In all three fields, however, Chou had to tread his way carefully because of the problems and difficulties of the countries he visited, and to feel out what he could do and how far he could go.

In the Negro countries, the Chinese Minister concentrated on the sore spots of completing the liberation of the continent, the war against white racialism, etc. In Egypt, the Maghreb and the Sudan, the Chinese guest learned to play on special Arab strings. He was careful not to attack the USSR directly, or to criticize the policy of nonalignment and neutralism. He even avoided attacking Tito, knowing the latter's popularity in Egypt, the Maghreb and in the new African states. At most, he worked indirectly, helping to prepare the ground for a second Bandung, without setting it up as competition or opposition to the "second Belgrade" (the conference of nonaligned countries that met in the fall of the same year, 1964, in Cairo).

It is on the background of these first Chinese independent moves in Africa and the Maghreb that we can understand the development of the attitude toward Israel. In the countries of Black Africa, the Middle East, Palestine and Israel were not mentioned at all. In Egypt, North Africa and the Sudan, China's tones were moderate at first, and only later more strident. The reason can be found in the fact that during Chou's tour, the First Arab Summit Conference met in Alexandria (in January 1964). That meeting centered about the "struggle against the robbery of the Jordan waters by Israel" and the plan to divert the sources of the Jordan River.

Joint statements published after the visits by Chou En-lai and Chinese Foreign Minister Chen Yi in Cairo, Algiers, Rabbat and Tunis, therefore mentioned only "unreserved support for the return of the legitimate rights of the Palestinian Arabs" (or of the "Palestinian people" or of the "Palestinian Arab people"—the version changed from one capital to another).

In Khartoum, however, where the joint Chinese-Sudanese statement was issued on January 30, 1964, it already mentioned support for the resolutions of the First Arab Summit Conference, and the clause on Palestine was more extensive:

> The two Sides condemn the present situation in Palestine. The Chinese Side expresses its support for the Arab people of Palestine in its strivings to win back its rights. The Chinese Side believes that the Arab Summit Conference contributed toward furthering the cause of the Arab countries in maintaining their unity against imperialism, and the Chinese Side supports the resolutions of the Conference. It supports the Arab and African peoples in their struggle against imperialism, old and new colonialism, and for national independence. It supports them in pursuing a policy of peace, neutralism and nonalignment. It supports them in their efforts to achieve unity and solidarity in the manner of their own device.

In China, too, the organ of the Communist Party, the *People's Daily*, also sharpened its tone. On January 27, 1964, it attacked

a speech made a few days before by Assistant Secretary of State
Alexis Johnson: "Johnson's speech was directed against the Arab
Summit, against its right to discuss its common problems in general and the problem of the diversion of the Jordan by Israel in
particular." And it went on:

> With the help and encouragement of American imperialism
> Israel is carrying out her plan to divert the waters of the
> Jordan, without considering the opposition of the Arab
> peoples. Israel ignores the rights of the Arab countries
> which use the water. This is also a serious step towards
> realizing the *Zionist* policy [the emphasis is mine; this was
> apparently the first time that the Chinese used the word
> "Zionism."—M. N.] of expansion and of serving the forces
> of imperialism and colonialism in order to create tension in
> the Middle East.

TONES BECOME HARSHER

From this point on, Peking's anti-Israeli tones become harsh-
er, following closely on every step and declaration made by the
Arab rulers. At a mass meeting held on March 24 in Peking,
organized by the "Chinese Committee for Afro-Asian Solidarity," the Committee's vice-president, the writer Mao Tung,
declared that:

> The United States has incited Israel to numerous acts of
> provocation, like the diversion of the Jordan's waters,
> which is a severe threat against Palestine and the Arab
> countries . . . The Chinese people denounce American
> imperialism for giving encouragement to Israel's provoca-
> tive acts; it gives its full support to the just demands of the
> Palestine people and the Arab countries. Together with
> them, the Chinese people will wage an energetic struggle
> against the common enemy—American imperialism.

In 1964, Peking was visited by a number of African statesmen,
but it was only with the visit of the president of Sudan, General
Abboud, that "imperialism and Israel" were mentioned together
once more. The joint statement published on May 19, 1964, declared that:

The two Parties severely condemn the criminal activities carried out by the imperialists in collusion with Israel, which encroach on or threaten the interests of the Arab peoples, and express firm support for the struggle of the Arab people of Palestine to restore their legitimate rights and to demand to return to their homeland.

After the Second Arab Summit and the establishment of the Palestine Liberation Organization, Peking became even more extreme, in a transparent effort to ride the horse of enmity toward Israel in order to win popularity among the most extreme elements in the Arab camp. An article in *People's Daily* of September 14, 1964, presents Israel as "the tool of American imperialism for aggression against the Arabs." As the paper writes:

The demands of the Palestine Arabs for the restoration of their legitimate rights and their return to their homeland, were given close attention at the Summit Conference. This is because recently United States imperialism has further aggravated the problem of Palestine by brazenly championing Israel, its tool for aggression, in all possible ways. Assistant Secretary of State Alexis Johnson, the President and their ilk have tried to bolster up Israel by repeatedly announcing their intention to ensure Israel's "security and integrity" . . . This year, along with big sums of US dollars in "aid," US imperialism has supplied Israel with Hawk missiles, large numbers of tanks, aircraft and other weapons, and helped it with nuclear research for military purposes . . . Since the meeting of the Palestine National Congress last May, the struggle of the Palestine Arabs has been advancing to new heights. The Second Summit has welcomed the establishment of the Palestine Liberation Organization, as a vanguard in the joint Arab action for the liberation of Palestine. It supported the creation of a Palestine army.

In Chou En-lai's report to the session of the National People's Congress (the Chinese parliament), on January 1, 1965, he promised China's support (alongside support to Indonesia against Malasia) "to the people of the Arab countries in its struggle against imperialism, headed by the United States, and against Israel, the tool of aggression; support for the Palestinian Arab people in its war for its right to return to its homeland."

A new peak was reached after the revelation of West German military aid to Israel and the establishment of diplomatic relations between 'Bonn and Jerusalem. The new general line was that American imperialism, West German militarism and Israel (or Zionism) had joined forces for aggression against the Arabs.

Commenting, on March 12, 1965, on Harriman's visit to Israel, the *Peking Review* wrote that:

> Harriman's visit to Israel at a time when the US Government was rapped on the knucles for its part in West Germany's arms deals with Israel, is an open challenge to the Arab people . . . Coupled with the Beirut visit by US Assistant Secretary of State Philip Talbot, to monkey with the Arab plan to divert the Jordan River waters, Harriman's journey into occupied Palestine pointed to increasing US machinations in the Middle East . . . By arming the fanatics of Zionism against the Arab nations, while itself trying to hide behind West Germany, the US has stirred up strong feelings in the Middle East.

A delegation of the Palestine Liberation Organization visited Peking in March 1965 and was welcomed with a mass meeting. A joint statement was published stating that:

> The essence of the Palestine problem is the undiluted aggression of Zionism and imperialism, headed by the United States on one side, and the struggle of the Palestinian Arab people and of all the other Arab peoples on the other . . . The Chinese people support the great struggle of of the Arab people against imperialism, colonialism old and new, and Zionism.

On that occasion it was also decided to establish a permanent delegation of the Liberation Organization in Peking. All later developments are only a direct continuation of the decision to accord full Chinese support to Shukairy's organization.

Peking's attitude to the Israeli-Arab problem combines the three elements of Chinese strategy: to promote "anti-imperialistic national liberation movements," to exploit anything that can intensify hatred for the United States, "the spearhead of imperialism," to carry on the conflict with the USSR over its "revisionistic leadership."

China does not share those inhibitions and limitations which the USSR must have as part of her general policies, her positions in the Middle East and . . . her share in the establishment of Israel. There is no doubt that the Soviet Union's influence in the region is much greater than China's, both because of her strength and because of her ability to supply aid. To some extent, this also explains China's extremism in attempting to exploit the most fanatically anti-Israeli elements in the Arab camp.

WHAT MIGHT HAVE BEEN

In encouraging the most barren and fanatic anti-Israeli extremism and opposing the application of the principle of negotiations and peaceful settlement to the Arab-Israeli dispute, the Chinese are not contributing to the maintenance of peace in the Middle East. Its dangers should not be overlooked even if they are not very actual at present. China is the largest of the world's nations, and her international importance will continue to grow.

This analysis of the motives behind Chinese policies today should not free us of the obligation to bring up some "ancient history": the opportunities that Israel wasted to establish relations with China to their mutual benefit; the policies that Israel adopted in the distant and not-so-distant past, policies which showed her as cooperating in depriving China of her elementary rights to represent the Chinese people in the United Nations and to share in the solution of problems in which she has a direct interest.

Israel recognized Popular China in January 1950, that is, only a few months after the declaration of the People's Republic in October 1949. This was during the period when nonalignment was still the official policy of the Israeli government; when Washington still deliberated between accepting the victory of the revolution in China and trying to overthrow it. London, too, had taken the initiative in recognizing the new regime. However, when the Korean War broke out in the summer of 1950, the Israeli government abandoned the policy of nonalignment and supported American actions carried out under the banner of the UN.

In 1953 the Korean War concluded as it did, and Israel once more found the way open to move from formal recognition to real political and commercial ties. Israel was then making her first steps in Southeast Asia. The *Burma Diary* by Israel's first ambassador to Rangoon, David Hacohen, gives us instructive details of the potentialities that appeared at that time, in 1954–55, to establish diplomatic and commercial relations with the Chinese People's Republic. About a half year after his first contacts with the Chinese ambassador in Rangoon, David Hacohen met with Chou En-lai, while the latter was passing through Rangoon. Chou revealed interest in the planned visit of an Israeli delegation to China. The visit took place in February 1955, only two months before the Bandung Conference. It lasted three weeks and encouraged Israel's ambassador to urge the Israeli government to exchange ambassadors with Peking. Mr. Hacohen points out that at the end of 1954, in discussing China's foreign relations before Parliament, Chou En-lai mentioned that steps would be taken to exchange diplomatic representatives with Afghanistan and Israel; this was after Chou had met Hacohen in Rangoon and talked to him.

The Israeli Ambassador repeatedly urged Jerusalem to expedite the establishment of diplomatic relations, but, as he says, "All the letters and cables were to no avail."

The end of April 1955 saw the meeting of the Bandung Conference, where the first contacts between the Chinese and the Arab delegates were made. As we know, the Conference adopted an anti-Israeli resolution. The Chinese delegation, like delegations from many other countries, including some which maintained normal and even friendly relations with Israel, voted for the resolution, which demanded the return of the refugees and criticized Israeli policies. However, as David Hacohen points out in his dairy, though he supported the refugees in his speech, Chou En-lai did not attack Israel as a state. The Chinese ambassador to Rangoon told Mr. Hacohen after Bandung that China was still interested in friendly relations with Israel.

David Hacohen goes on to tell about the "friendly" pressure exerted upon him by American representatives in Rangoon, especially after his return from China. During John Foster Dulles' visit to Rangoon, some of Dulles' aides attempted to convince Hacohen that "it wasn't worthwhile" for Israel to establish ties with a regime that was "about to fall." If that was the situation in Rangoon, we can imagine the pressure on the Israeli government in Jerusalem. Perhaps here we can find the reason for the silence in reply to David Hacohen's urgings.

After Bandung, in the years 1955–58, Peking began to be very active in paving some way to the Arab capitals. Cairo and

Damascus were the first to establish diplomatic relations with China (breaking with Formosa). They were followed in 1959 by Yemen, Iraq and Sudan. In improving their relations with China, the Arab countries undoubtedly worked against Israel. The Israeli government, however, contributed its own share to make the Arabs' work easier. Israel's cooperation with France and Great Britain in the Suez War naturally made her the object of a strong Chinese "anti-imperialist" attack. Israel's behavior in the UN every time the question of China's representation came up, however, also contributed to the animosity. Peking saw Israel as one of the countries opposing her representation in the United Nations, in accordance with the American line, no matter what "legal" garb Israel's position was given.

As a matter of fact, when the number of countries in favor of China grew larger, Israel took a position which was even more openly negative. In the 1965 Assembly the votes were tied, with 47 for and 47 against, with 20 abstaining and three absent. Israel, which had previously often abstained, added her vote to those against. The arguments presented in defense of this vote (the resolution mentioned the Conference of Nonaligned Nations in Cairo in 1964, which had adopted anti-Israeli resolutions; China had taken an anti-Israeli position and supported Shukairy, etc.) were not very convincing. Both India and Yugoslavia voted for China despite China's attitude towards them. Belgrade and New Delhi looked further ahead, and knew that denying China's right to take her place in the United Nations and to help in solving the great international problems could only aggravate the world situation and drive China to greater extremism.

PROSPECTS FOR THE FUTURE

Do we think that if there had been diplomatic, commercial and other relations between Israel and China, the latter would now be less pro-Arab and less anti-Israel? We won't try to give an unequivocal answer. We do think, however, that if the opportunities of 1954–55 had not been wasted, and if mutual ties had helped both sides learn more about each other, China would now face some restraints and limits in adopting such an extremely anti-Israeli position.

What about the future? The practical conclusion we wanted to draw was that there was no room for despair or for the feeling that "anyway everything was lost," and since there was nothing to lose, Israel could act according to any immediate interests in matters in which China was directly or indirectly involved.

We don't know whether the mistakes of the past can easily be rectified. It is much easier to add even more hurdles on the way to an improvement in relationships in the more distant future.

Of course, in the light of Peking's present aim of appearing as the "friend of the Arabs against Israel," the prospects of improvement do not depend upon Israel alone. Israel's actions can be an auxiliary factor if and when other factors lead Peking to act otherwise in the Middle East. These are factors deriving from China's own interests and experiences, the attitude toward her of the other world powers (and especially the United States and the USSR), as well as from the general policies adopted by the Chinese leadership in foreign and domestic affairs.

Recent news from China, including things said and written by official Chinese leaders and organs, gives the clear impression that there are certain "oppositionary" trends within the ranks of the party and the intelligentsia and even certain parts of the leadership itself. We, of course, only hear the attacks of the orthodox leadership against these trends. We don't know from firsthand what these "heretical" views are, how clear they have become, how they are expressed and what their ideological and political bases are. We can assume, however, that these oppositionary trends derive from a more sober view of China's potentialities on the international field, and from fear of a second "big leap" which is liable to repeat the mistakes and exaggerations that caused the Chinese people so much suffering in the first "big leap" of 1958–61.

China's activities on the international field under the inspiration of her extreme revolutionary concepts have recently suffered defeats in various countries in Asia and Africa. Even in the Middle East, China has not had too much success in comparison with her most important rivals—the United States and the USSR.

China's future policies will depend, of course, not only on the outcome of her internal conflicts, but also on her relationships with the outside world. This depends mainly on the United States, which by trying to restrain communism by military force, only intensified the fears of the revolutionary regime that America hadn't given up the hope of destroying it and was even liable to make war upon it directly if other means failed.

It is not by "restraining" China and certainly not by preparing for war against her that China's "revolutionary extremism" can be modified. The only hopes for any modification lie in serious and persistent efforts to have her share in solving the problems which affect her own interests and security.

It is to Israel's own interest to avoid any suspicion of belonging to the "isolaters" and "restrainers," and to support every step toward involving China in international agreements. That will give her the hope that when the time comes for China to change her international policies, these changes will affect her attitude to Israel as well.

5. The Arab League in Perspective

BY CECIL A. HOURANI

I

In its relation to recent Arab history, the Arab League is neither a beginning nor an end. It is neither a new idea which burst into being during the recent war, indicating some vital change in the course of Arab affairs, nor the culminating point of a long process beyond which there can be no further development or progress. The Arab League is rather a stage in a series of developments which is by no means ended. In relation to particular historical events, it may be regarded as the first important step in the dual process of Arab unification and liberation since the Arab Revolt of 1915. It is to some extent, indeed, a continuation of that unfulfilled revolution.

The Arab movement, or the Arab awakening, as it has sometimes been called, may be defined as an effort to recreate and to reintegrate the Arab community; to bring this community once more into the larger community of active and creative societies; and thus to re-form a culture which is at once universal and Arab, modern and yet linked to the past. It is essentially a movement of synthesis; while on the one hand it seeks the liberation of Arab territories and states from foreign external domination, on the other it seeks no less unification on all levels within the Arab domain. The struggle for unity among the Arabs cannot be disassociated from their struggle for independence.

Throughout the four hundred years in which they formed part of the Ottoman Empire, the Arabs, although no longer sovereign in their own home, nevertheless preserved the sense of a community. They had a common past in which all Arabs shared and took pride. They had a common religion which was identified with the greatest period in Arab history and which had shaped

Reprinted from *The Middle East Journal*, Vol. 1, No. 2 (Washington, D.C., 1947), pp. 125–37; by permission of the editor.

the main outlines of Arab society and Arab character. They had a common language with a vast and splendid literature which could feed men's minds and keep them alive. They had a common framework of society and law, and a common way of life. These factors preserved the identity of the Arabs, and gave them both distinctness and the power of resistance to external pressure and disintegration.

At the beginning of the nineteenth century, when the forces of nationalism in the world came into their own, the Arabs had retained sufficient identity and self-consciousness to create their own movement for national independence. The different phases of its evolution have often been told; all that is necessary to point out is that the Arab League is only the latest in a chain of developments, the links of which include the creation of modern Egypt by Mohamed Ali; the rise of Wahhabism in central Arabia; the literary activities of the Syrians and Lebanese; the movement of Islamic modernism associated with the name of Muhammad Abdu; the Pan-Arab Conference of 1913 in Paris; the Arab Revolt of 1915 and its partial collapse in 1920; the Iraq Revolt of 1920; the Syrian Revolt of 1925–26; the Palestine Revolt of 1936; the Pan-Arab Conference of 1937; the Interparliamentary Conference in Cairo in 1938; and the 1939 Palestine Conference in London in which all the Arab governments participated.

The ease with which the outside world was able, at the end of World War I, to cut up the Arab countries into a number of different states was a symptom of Arab weakness, and this political division in turn created further weaknesses. The Ottoman regime, with all its defects, had preserved many of the externals of unity. If the Arab lands were dominated from without, it was from one center; and the compensation of inclusion in a large empire did something to offset the fragmentation of Arab society. The postwar political division of the Arab world had none of these compensations. It cut the Arabs off from each other physically, administratively and economically. The existence of differing educational systems tended to produce different types of thinking. Arab youth was subjected to a variety of outside influences. To many Arab nationalists, it appeared that the independence of a number of small and weak Arab states was bought at too heavy a price if it precluded permanently the possibility of their ultimate unification.

But while the post-1918 settlement split up the Arab world,

all the forces of history, both internal and external, were working in the opposite direction. The revolution in transportation and communication brought about by the automobile, railway and airplane drew every part of the Arab domain closer together. The old ties of blood and kinship, trade and grazing, were suddenly strengthened. The communication of ideas led to the growth of common interests. The printing presses of Cairo and Beirut supplied reading matter to the whole Arab world and fostered common ways of thinking and writing. The radio went one step further and had a tremendous effect not only upon the communication of ideas and knowledge, but even on the language of daily life. The growing Arab film industry in Egypt is producing the same result. The telephone, telegraph and airplane brought every corner of the Arab domain within easy reach of one administrative center; today there is no important city of the Arab world which cannot be reached from any other in a single day.

At the same time, the nations of the outside world were being aligned in powerful groups, and the fate of small nations seemed precarious. Together, the Arab lands constituted a significant bloc; individually, they counted for scarcely anything. The creation of an Arab League was thus a natural expression of trends which were already present and which could not be denied eventual fruition.

II

The immediate impetus for the formation of the Arab League may be found in the initiative taken by Prime Minister Nuri Pasha al-Said of Iraq, which led eventually to the signature of the Pact of the Arab League in Cairo in March 1945. At the end of 1942, Nuri al-Said compiled what has come to be known as the "Blue Book," which was printed in Baghdad in 1943 but never published. The "Blue Book" consisted of a covering letter to Mr. Casey, then British Minister of State in Cairo, a "Note on Arab independence and unity with particular reference to Palestine," and a number of pertinent documents.

There were two principal ideas behind the proposals Nuri al-Said set forth. The one was that the formation of a Greater Syria, and its union with Iraq in a league, would help to solve the problem of Palestine by reducing the fears of the Arabs of Palestine that they might one day become a minority, and by increasing their ability to resist Zionism through incorporation in a larger political entity. The other was that Arab unity should be based upon a union of those countries which were closest in their general political and social conditions, i.e. the countries of the Fertile Crescent; and that such a union would be strongest if it began by being small and cohesive. In order to achieve such an Arab union, he emphasized that "sacrifices of sovereignty and vested interests may have to be made."

The Arab league envisaged by Nuri al-Said did not, however, come into existence. To many Arab nationalists there appeared a number of defects and dangers in his proposals. Although he argued that by inclusion in a wider unit the dangers of Zionism in Palestine would be diminished, it was also arguable that the contrary might be true: that the Zionist movement, so far from being checked, might be given the opportunity to expand. In a Greater Syria it would be impossible to discriminate between Arab and Jewish citizens, and the Jewish population could not be prevented from extending its economic roots over a much wider area than previously. Moreover, the proposal that the Maronites of Mount Lebanon might revert to their pre-1914 status, although it might have allayed the fears of some Christians that they would be "swallowed up" in an Arab Muslim state, nevertheless revived all the disadvantages of the old regime—the limitation of opportunity which had forced so many of the inhabitants of the Mountain to emigrate in the past, the feeling of separation and distinction which a special regime inevitably gave them, and the encouragement of outside loyalties—without providing any new or positive advantages. Finally, many Arab nationalists believed that it would be unwise and impracticable to distinguish between different Arab countries on the grounds of their "similarity" or "nearness" to each other, and in particular that it would be unwise to found a league of which Egypt should not be a member at the beginning. It might then be difficult to induce Egypt to join later; moreover, in the eyes of these nationalists Egypt would give an international status and strength to a league which the countries of the Fertile Crescent alone could not.

In the outcome the Arab League was formed, not as Nuri al-Said had at first envisaged it, but on a more general and looser pattern, and with Egypt taking the lead. This was due on the one hand to the prevalence of the views enumerated above, and on the other hand, to the fact that during World War II

Cairo had become the most accessible and the most internationally important of the Arab capitals. This latter fact was the natural result of Cairo's location on vital routes of communication and its role in the military strategy of the democratic powers. The passage of leadership to Cairo was facilitated by the temporary overshadowing of Iraq's sovereignty after the Rashid Ali revolt of 1941, and the then still undefined and only partially independent status of Syria and Lebanon.

Accordingly the next step in the creation of the Arab League was taken by Mustafa Nahhas Pasha, then prime minister of Egypt, who was urged by Nuri al-Said and other Arab nationalists to invite the various Arab governments to send representatives to Cairo to discuss the possibility and desirability of calling a general Arab conference. Nahhas Pasha discussed the matter with Nuri al-Said in July and August 1943; with Tawfiq Abd al-Huda, Prime Minister of Transjordan, in August and September; with Yusuf Yassin, personal representative of Ibn Saud, in October; with Saadullah Jabri, Prime Minister of Syria, in October and November; with Riad al-Sulh, Prime Minister of Lebanon, in January, 1944; and with Sayyid Husayn Kibsi, representative of the Imam of Yemen, in February.

There was sufficient unanimity of opinion among all those who took part in the Cairo conversations to induce Nahhas Pasha to call a general Arab conference, which met at the Antoniades Palace in Alexandria from September 25 to October 8, 1944. In addition to representatives of the governments of Egypt, Iraq, Syria, Lebanon, Transjordan, Saudi Arabia and Yemen, a representative of the Arabs of Palestine, Musa al-Alami, took part in the conference on a footing of complete equality with other members.

The Alexandria Conference formulated what has come to be known as the "Alexandria Protocol," which delineated the outlines of an Arab League.[1] The Protocol characterized the participants in the conference as "desirous of ascertaining the close relations and the numerous bonds which unite all the Arab peoples; anxious to strengthen these bonds and to direct them toward the well-being of them all to improve their situation, to insure their future and realize their aspirations; and answering the appeal of public opinion through the Arab world." The proposed Arab League was to be composed of those independent Arab states which wished to join it. It was to have a Council which would meet periodically to execute agreements reached by the states among themselves, to coordinate their political programs, and "generally to watch over the affairs and interests of the Arab peoples." The decisions of this Council were to be binding upon those states which accepted them, except in cases where conflict had arisen between two member states, which would then have to accept the Council's decisions. The use of force to settle disputes between member states was to be forbidden.

As for the relations of members of the League with the external world, the Protocol laid down that a member state would have the right to make agreements with other states in or out of the League so long as such agreements were not contrary to the text or the spirit of the League's constitution. It went on to make the very important proviso that "in no case would a state be permitted to pursue a foreign policy which could be detrimental to the policy of the League or to any of its member states."

The Protocol provided for close cooperation between member states on economic, cultural and social problems, and recommended the setting up of commissions of experts in each field to elaborate programs of joint action. The Protocol then went on to envisage still closer ties between the Arab states in the future.

Two special annexes of the Protocol dealt with Lebanon and Palestine. The first reaffirmed the respect of the Arab states for the independence and sovereignty of Lebanon within its present borders. The second declared that the rights of the Arabs of Palestine could not be touched without affecting the peace and stability of the Arab world as a whole. Promises made by Great Britain to end Jewish immigration, to safeguard Arab land, and to lead Palestine toward independence constituted a recognition of Arab rights, and the Protocol pressed for their execution; in other words, it accepted the principles although not the details of the 1939 White Paper. The Arab nations pledged their full support to the cause of the Arabs of Palestine.

It is probable that in spite of its supersession later by the actual Pact of the Arab League, the Alexandria Protocol will continue to play an important role in the movement for Arab unity, and tend to be looked back to and appealed to by Arab nationalists in the future. Its importance may be summarized under a number of headings:

It was a strongly *popular* document, appealing constantly to "public opinion throughout the Arab world," "the Arab peoples," and "the Arab nation." It was thus infused with the spirit of popular Pan-Arabism.

It recognized that the proposed League was only a first step toward a still closer union which should keep pace with the trend of events in the world in general. It thus did not envisage that the League would cease to evolve, but that it would develop in accordance with the internal situation in the Arab world and general progress toward unity, and the tendency in the outside world toward the formation of larger regional groupings.

It envisaged a common orientation of the Arab countries toward the outside world. They were to face in one direction only, and not maintain divergent foreign policies or fall within different spheres of influence. The immediate significance of this concept was to preclude the possibility of Syria's and Lebanon's concluding treaties with France which would give it a special position unless all the Arab countries were to do likewise. It was this aspect of the Protocol which more than any other, perhaps, aroused the suspicion of the French and fostered the belief among them that the League was a British "trick" to get them out of the Levant.

By recognizing the independence and sovereignty of Lebanon within its present borders, the Protocol attempted to show to certain sections of the Lebanese that Lebanon was accepted as an equal member of the Arab comity of states, and that the League was in no way directed against Lebanese independence. The secular and nonreligious nature of Arab nationalism was thus indirectly affirmed by the Protocol.

Finally, the Protocol made the problem of Palestine once and for all the responsibility of the whole Arab world, and thus incorporated into more permanent form the precedent set by the St. James Conference of 1939.

Between the publication of the Alexandria Protocol and the creation of the Arab League in Cairo in March 1945, governmental and constitutional changes took place in Egypt, Syria, Lebanon and Transjordan. Partly as a result of these changes, partly as a result of hesitation on the part of some Arab governments, the Pact of the League, although following in general the lines laid down by the Protocol, was in some respects a less strong document, and safeguarded more carefully and more specifically the sovereignty of the member states.[2] Whereas the Protocol had envisaged a progressively increasing surrender of sovereignty, the Pact lays emphasis on its retention. For example, the prologue, after the statement "desirous of strengthening the close relations and numerous ties which link the Arab states and anxious to support and strengthen these ties," adds the phrase "upon a basis of respect for the independence and sovereignty of these states." The Pact omits the clause of the Protocol which stated that "In no case will a state be permitted to pursue a foreign policy which could be detrimental to the policy of the League or to any of its member states." It also omits Article 3 of the Protocol looking toward a further degree of unity in the future, but specifies that states will cooperate "with due regard to the organization and circumstances of each state." Finally, the Pact specifically binds each member state not to interfere in the systems of government of the others, whereas the Protocol had no such clause.

A further important respect in which the Pact differs from the Protocol is the omission of the guarantee of Lebanon's independence in view of the fact that the Pact already contained sufficient guarantees of the sovereignty of all the member states. The Pact, however, contains a special annex recognizing Palestine as *de jure* independent, and allowing it to participate in the work of the Council. This stand was in conformity with public opinion in the Arab world, which would not have regarded the League as complete without the inclusion of Palestine. Another annex provides for the participation of nonindependent Arab countries in the work of the committees of the League, and pledges the League to work for the interests of these countries "with all the political means at its disposal." The reference clearly is to the countries of North Africa under foreign rule.

III

How does the Arab League stand in relation to the Arab nationalist movement? There is general agreement among Arab nationalists that a league is necessary, but there is not complete agreement as to whether the present Arab League constitutes the best method of achieving the desired goal.

There are three main schools of thought concerning the present form of the Arab League. One holds that by preserving intact the sovereignty of the member states, the League tends to preserve special interests and to crystallize into permanent form the present political divisions; and that by providing at least the skeleton of union, it may tend to satisfy many Arabs that the goal has been reached. This school of thought would have preferred the immediate establishment of a federation of Arab states or even a unitary state.

Another group argues that a closer union than the League provides should have been formed, and that if it could not have been formed of all the Arab states, it should have been formed by the union of those states which were willing to give up their sovereignty. It is generally agreed that the only two states which might have taken such a step are Syria and Iraq.

A third, and perhaps the largest school of thought argues that the inclusion of all the independent Arab states in the League, and its consequent *international* status, more than compensates for any other disadvantages. This group believes that since the League has been formed in its present shape, there can be no radical change, but that its existing possibilities should be exploited to the full.

The League, as it stands, represents a victory for moderate Arab nationalism; that is, for the view that at the present time it is impossible to establish a single Arab state, and that union can only come as a result of evolution and a gradual surrender of sovereignty. It also represents a victory for secular liberalism in Arab thought. The League is sometimes accused by ill-wishers of being reactionary, xenophobic, Pan-Islamic. An examination both of the actions of the League and of the personalities who created it is a sufficient refutation of these charges. The framers of the League were men brought up in the tradition of nineteenth-century liberalism, not in the tradition of the Pan-Islamic movement, which has long ceased to be an effective force in Arab politics, if indeed it ever was, nor in the tradition of twentieth-century totalitarian movements. The ideas of Mazzini express perhaps better than any others the dominant concepts of the Arab nationalist spirit incorporated into the League.

However, the Arab League, while it is not reactionary, xenophobic or extreme, is inevitably Pan-Arab. Professor H.A.R. Gibb has made a distinction between what he calls moderate Arab nationalism and Pan-Arabism. "Pan-Arabism," he says, "is an ignorant, intolerant, explosive force." [3] But this distinction is not a valid one. In every movement there are people and sections which are "ignorant, intolerant, explosive." But the very nature of any Arab nationalism is such that it cannot help embracing within its scope the whole Arab world. There is no good reason why an Arab nationalist should be interested in the freedom and unification of part of the Arab world and not of the whole, or draw the frontiers of the Arab world at Libya. And thus inevitably the League, both by its own constitution and by the forces which move it, must interest itself in the liberation of the entire Arab world. There may be differences among Arab nationalists about the order of importance of certain Arab questions, but there is no disagreement about fundamental aims, which cannot stop short of the entire Arab world from the Atlantic to the Persian Gulf, and which embrace all levels of Arab society—the social, economic and intellectual no less than the political.

But in saying that Arab nationalism as embodied in the Arab League is Pan-Arabism, it should not be understood that there is any comparison with or resemblance to such movements as Pan-Germanism or Pan-Slavism. There is a radical difference between Arab and European political ideology. In Europe nationalism has been built on two concepts: that of the state inherited from the traditions of Roman law and society; and that of a homogeneous racial group. Arab nationalism is based on neither. On the one hand, Arab society was not based on the Greco-Roman political tradition, and has never had a concept of a strong sovereign state. On the other, Arab society has never been exclusively racial, but has consisted of racially and religiously heterogeneous groups bound together by a common Arabic culture and world of thought. It is thus dangerous to compare conditions in Arab countries with conditions in Western societies.

The failure to grasp the heterogeneous character of Arab society is responsible for the underestimation made by many Western "experts" of the strength of Arab unity. Even Robert Montagne can say that "Iraq is only a conglomeration of ethnic, religious and linguistic minorities." [4] There is a general tendency for Western political theorists to regard all Arab society in this way and to disbelieve in the possibility of any real union among the Arabs. A deeper study and understanding of the roots of Arab society is thus increasingly urgent if we are to understand the relationship of such political structures such as the Arab League to the general movement of ideas and social development in the Arab countries, or to appreciate correctly how deeply rooted the idea of the Arab League is in the minds of the Arab people.

6. The Problem of Arab Unity

BY EDMOND RABBATH

THE ARAB "NATION" is no longer the myth that some were content to include, a quarter of a century ago, in the catalog of foreign importations. It is a condition rooted deeply in the feelings of the folk, through which their political aspirations are constantly channeled. There is little point in denying its compelling force; in our time it represents a sociological fact molded into a form appropriate to the Arabic-speaking peoples. Behind the appearance of this unique phenomenon is a combination of factors:

A spiritual heritage, the roots of which go back not only to the great Arab conquest but to the very beginnings of Semitic civilization.

A literary language, unaltered by regional dialects, becoming today a means of expression used by all Arab countries from the Persian Gulf to the Atlantic to establish among themselves a real community of ideas and attitudes.

Islam, above all a specifically Arab Islam, slowly detaching itself from the backdrop of universal Islam, the Islam which has shaped Arab mentality and directed Arab customs so as to render all Arabs, in spite of their geographical diversity, latitudinally identical from east to west. Islam is another fact, as powerful as Arabism, which was integrated with and acted catalytically upon the development of Arabism, and is still eminently active. Its impulsive force can only decrease as an inverse function of the movement which leads human societies—once they have

Excerpts reprinted from *Middle East Forum*, Vol. XXXI, No. 4 (Beirut, 1956), pp. 9-11, 32; by permission of the editor.

arrived at a certain point in their evolution—to secularize themselves and continually to reduce the areas of social life in which
religious influence remains predominant.

In this Arab unity, which derives from these conditions, the
Arabic-speaking peoples today recognize a common denominator by which they, more or less confusedly, expect to resolve the
economic and social conflicts still separating them.

A characteristic phenomenon, fundamental in Western nations, is beginning to appear in Arab countries and particularly
in the Arab East. No one will deny that the formation of large
national enterprises in Europe and America has brought about a
parallel class differentiation within each nation, indicated everywhere by an emerging bourgeoisie, intent upon the domination
of the affairs of the world.

The same pattern is being woven at this moment into the
structure of Arab societies. The last war brought about a movement from which there emerged a class of big businessmen,
financiers, industrialists and brokers. Their network is strengthening and extends across the frontiers of Arab states. Their
growth is based upon the common ground of a spirit of enterprise and possession of capital, appealing vaguely to youthful
energies that turn up almost everywhere—in Syria, Iraq, Lebanon, Saudi Arabia, even Egypt. To this new breed, it is becoming more and more evident that only their\ bounding energies
unite them—or must unite them—in a common effort. That is
why governmental administrations appear troublesome and transitory to them, obstacles thrown in their paths, and subordinate
to their goals.

By the multiplication of points of contact between their businessmen, by the interweaving of their interests, by their common need of markets for the employment of their idle populations, by the exploitation of their undeveloped resources, the
Arab states will inevitably be faced with the necessity of finding
solutions to their internal economic and social problems in the
wider context of Arabism.

But the soul of the Arab movement is in the thinking elite.
The public mind, which dominates the Arab scene, is their
product. Personal ties are multiplying between the intellectuals,
crossing political and religious barriers. Lebanese, Syrians, Egyptians, Moroccans, Tunisians and Iraqis are intermingling, corresponding with each other, meeting in conferences and symposia.
The result is the creation of a common political psychology,

which is itself a reflex encouraging any emergence of political cooperation.

But this psychology is supported by an intense literary renaissance in which all Arab countries participate. Egypt plays the leading role here. Writers from every star in the Arab constellation make effective contributions to the renaissance. Literary productions also cross frontiers and infiltrate more and more the depths of the Arab consciousness, awakening there an echo and creating there a community of thought that permeates hitherto resistant layers.

The renaissance has not yet, however, gone beyond the literary stage. The scientific attitude is still lacking in most Arab minds. And yet the Arab spirit will never blossom into a national **consciousness** without the immense brotherhood of science, which can really integrate it with contemporary civilization.

It is, in fact, as a result of this detachment from universal culture that a number of Arab weaknesses in the comprehension of concrete necessities arise, for instance, in the area of Arab security.

The creation of the state of Israel in the heart of Arab lands has opened Arab eyes to reality. For centuries during the stagnation of Islam, when Arab character wasted away, the West was known to the Arabs only through its merchants, missionaries or occasional conquerors. But whether the West appeared seductive or threatening, the Arabs never despaired of winning over it, if not by arms, at least by the numbers and the inertia that the centuries had taught them to use against it.

But then the Zionist Jews came, a category of unscrupulous pioneers who had assimilated the very essence of Western technology and methodology. The awakening of the Arabs was brutal. The meeting with reality, concrete, tough, immediate, like a mortal disease in their entrails, seemed an atrocity to them—a million of them are still shivering in flimsy shelters just outside prosperous cities. They have not forgotten, however, that without Western aid—in which they ironically see the origin of their sufferings—the tragedy would have even more disastrous results.

Because of the nature of their enemy, they fear even more encroachments. That is why they now feel an imperious necessity to unite their defensive forces in a cohesive system of military security. They can naturally sense only the danger of Israel. No one doubts that their scattered armies would be powerless before the science and the organization of the enemy force, which continually absorbs all kinds of support which the West, with a kind of criminal innocence, continues to provide.

Joined in this race for life, the Arabs could have no choice. They allied themselves necessarily—like Churchill in 1941—with the devil. But the same race for life forces them to unite—at least in the preparations for a common defense against their common enemy. It is appropriate to recall Arndt's words: **"The Moors promoted, in spite of themselves, the unity of Spain; the English, in the Hundred Years' War, that of France. It is Napoleon who will unify Germany."**

And Israel will insure Arab unity. If this does not happen, there will be no more Arabs.

This is a necessity upon which life and death depend. Does it seem chimerical? Undoubtedly, there are a number of obstacles strewn in its path.

The inequality of social evolution is the greatest barrier. What is there in common, a superficial observer might ask, between a Lebanese and a Saudi Arabian, or even between an Egyptian and an Iraqi, except language and religion? Does not everything else separate them? Political tendencies, economic rivalries, and above all the differences in their ideas and their habits of life, their intellectual development, and their degrees of acceptance of Western ways?

These differences are obvious, of course; the inequalities in the peoples making up the Arab nation are actually shocking. But it would be a mistake to think that such disparities are capable of arresting the convergence upon unity. Other peoples whose national and united character are fully recognized exhibit even greater divergences in their collective structure.

It is nevertheless true that this situation is at the root of whatever holds back the full expression of an effectively national Arab consciousness. Still colored by religion, it often mistakes itself for a community instinct which, however respectable it may be, is nonetheless far removed from a clearly considered national awareness reflecting a corresponding reality. But it is upon such points of conjunction that the efforts of men of action can concentrate, in order to accelerate the movement and bring it to maturity.

On this problem there is also grafted the feeling of religious partisanship, which in the Arab states of the Mediterranean periphery, Egypt, Syria [and] especially Lebanon, openly blocks the unitary movement. In its political aspect, it hides the fear which continues to torment Christians, even in the city where Christianity was founded—would they in the last analysis enjoy the right to absolute equality with their Muslim fellowcitizens on social and psychological levels? The total equality of citizens is an essential condition of national homogeneity, without which the body, improperly called a nation, would be merely a grouping of communities eventually dominated by the strongest. And equality is impossible, intangible, without an interpenetration —I could say, a digestion—of all the elements of the collectivity. But does not such a development presuppose the principle of a secular civil code that would freely govern the assortment of communities? This problem of personal status will sooner or later arise in the formation of a national Arab state. It was the motive for the creation of the state of Lebanon as separate from Syria, although beyond that motive was a history of five thousand years.

To these divisive forces there is added the dynastic quarrels between reigning families, distrusts and hatreds nourished by government leaders against leaders of other governments, and prestige rivalries stemming from the memories of ancient empires competing for the hegemony of the Orient. The drive toward unity, however, would be stronger than these shadows if the unfortunate policies of certain great powers did not obstruct it—as if, in certain chancelleries, the spirit of the Crusades or the route to the Indies still survives, forcing them to oppose, as in the nineteenth century, the formation of any state sufficiently large and powerful to replace the "sick man" that was the Ottoman Empire.

But it would be folly for the Arabs—and perhaps a tragic mistake—to expect help from an Occident whose international policy is still wrenched by various anachronic imperialist tendencies on the economic, strategic, and even spiritual levels.

Arab unity will be formed—or not at all—by the firm, tenacious will of the Arabs. If it does not appear, there will result instead a blind, total disunity leading to a final catastrophe.

This is a tragic dilemma, one for which the Congress of Arab Graduates has tried to provide the solution by planning for a federal Arab state. To such a union, each Arab state could freely adhere, in full cognizance of its responsibilities and consenting to a partial abandonment of sovereignty in the cause of unity. Such a project, uniting logic with the naural tendency of related peoples to grow steadily toward a concentration of political power, could lead the Arabs towards a unified state modeled on the great European nations.

It is undeniable that with such a scope, and in view of so many points of conflict, any such attempt would be at present not only impracticable but dangerous, because of the apprehensions it would create everywhere. But for the Arabs, the science of constitutional law supported by the examples of the great American republic and of Switerzland, both the results of a long evolution not devoid of either difficulties or diversities, offers an adequate formula. Such a system would permit the Arab countries to realize their need for unity in the crucible of common interest while maintaining their regional personalities.

7. Draft Constitution for the Arab Union

(OCTOBER 1956)

THE ARAB STATES, *convinced that their Arabic-speaking peoples participate in one nationality, i.e., the Arab nationality, and therefore constituting one nation, i.e., the Arab nation, and aspiring to realize the unity of the Arab countries in one federated state, have agreed on the following pact which shall form the Constitution of the federated state hereby created.*

CHAPTER I. BASIC RULES

ARTICLE 1. The Arab states signatory to this pact constitute one federated state called "The Arab Union."

Every other Arab state has the right to join the Union by submitting a request to the Federal Congress which decides on its acceptance by a two-thirds majority vote.

ARTICLE 2. Each member state shall exercise its own authority in all areas that are not defined in this Constitution.

ARTICLE 3: The Arab Union has chosen as its capital the city of ____ located in ____. The city, the boundaries of which are drawn by the Federal Congress, shall be administered directly by the Federal Congress.

ARTICLE 4: The flag of the Arab Union shall consist of three vertical stripes, from right to left, green, white and black. Stars equal in number to the member states will be placed in the center of the white stripe.

Reprinted from "Plan to Unite Arab States," Brijen K. Gupta, in *Peace News* (London, Oct. 12, 1956), pp. 1–4. The Draft Constitution is the work of the Constitution Drafting Committee appointed by the Arab Graduates Association (Beirut).

ARTICLE 5: The Federal State insures the organization, autonomy, constitution and frontiers of each member state.

ARTICLE 6: The Federal State guarantees to all citizens of the member states, regardless of race or creed, the human rights and the fundamental freedoms asserted in the Universal Declaration of Human Rights.

ARTICLE 7. The Federal State guarantees to all religions and sects in the member states their respective traditions and their particular systems as molded by the personal character of their followers insofar as they do not conflict with the national unity and the welfare of the Federal State.

ARTICLE 8: Treaties or agreements of any kind between two or more of the member states do not become final until they are confirmed by the Federal Congress by a two-thirds vote.

ARTICLE 9: Disputes between two or more member states shall be referred to the Federal Congress for arbitration. The Congress passes its decision by a two-thirds vote.

The member states are in all respects subject to and bound by the decision of the Federal Congress.

ARTICLE 10: If because of the acts of one or more of the member states, or any other cause, internal peace and security are endangered, the Federal Congress shall have the right to order the Federal Army to take the necessary military measures to restore order.

The above decision must be reached by an absolute majority in the Federal Congress.

The Congress may be called upon to take the above action by the Federal Government, by a member state, or by a congressman.

ARTICLE 11: Citizens of the Federal State must serve the Arab flag, which service shall be regarded as a holy obligation that cannot be waived either by the legislative or by the executive authorities.

Subject to military-service laws, military service shall be compulsory for everyone who has completed the age of twenty.

CHAPTER 2. POWERS OF THE FEDERAL STATE

ARTICLE 12: The Federal State shall administer all affairs deemed vital to its welfare. Problems relating to foreign affairs, national defense, economy and education shall fall exclusively under its control.

ARTICLE 13: The following functions shall be specifically administered by the Federal State:

1. The representation of the Arab Union in foreign affairs, including the conclusion of treaties, international agreements and their ratification.

2. All questions of war and peace.

3. The acceptance of other Arab states into the Arab Union as members of the Federal State.

4. The execution of the injunctions of this Constitution; the supervision of the execution of the constitutions of the respective member states. The Federal State shall have the right to take the necessary measures to enforce the proper execution of these constitutions.

5. The approval of boundary changes among the member states.

6. The organization of national defense in the Arab Union and on its frontiers and the commanding of all the armed forces in the territories of the member states.

7. Internal and external peace.

8. Customs and laws appertaining thereto.

9. Commerce and industry and laws appertaining thereto.

10. Public-development plans the execution of which involves two or more of the member states.

11. Land, sea and air communications.

12. Oil and questions appertaining thereto.

13. The issuance and regulation of the Arab Union currency.

14. Banking insofar as it affects the welfare of the national economy and public funds.

15. The coordination of taxation systems among the member states.

16. The basic legal principles pertaining to labor.

17. Laws pertaining to nationality of the citizens of the Arab states.

18. The basic principles of national education including the drafting of broad educational curricula in the member states.

19. The administration of the statistical affairs of the Federal State and of its citizens.

20. The right to perform functions that fall specifically or generally within its authority. It imposes and collects direct and indirect taxes in ways and means prescribed by federal laws.

ARTICLE 14: The member states shall continue to exercise authority in all areas that are not consigned by virtue of this Constitution, either explicitly or implicitly, to the Federal State.

CHAPTER 3. FEDERAL AUTHORITY

I—Legislative Authority Article 15: The Federal Congress shall constitute the legislative authority in the Federal State; it shall exercise all the legislative functions consigned by this Constitution to the Arab Union.

The Federal Congress alone has the right to approve the budget of the Federal State. At the beginning of each year, the budget is submitted by the executive to the Congress; the latter shall have the power of increasing or cutting the budgetary allotments.

Article 16: The Federal Congress shall consist of two supplementary houses: A. The House of Representatives; and B. The Senate.

The House of Representatives represents the people of the Federal State. The election of its members is made on the basis of the number of citizens (men and women) in each member state. All citizens who have completed the age of twenty can vote, provided they were not deprived through a court order of their civil and political rights.

The Senate represents the member states equally on the basis of seven senators from each.

A. HOUSE OF REPRESENTATIVES

Articles 17 and 18: The House of Representatives consists of members elected on the basis of one (or more) deputies to each electoral district whose population is _____.

Each member state shall be considered a large electoral district and shall supervise its own elections.

The election of the Federal House of Representatives, for the first time, shall follow the electoral laws of the respective member states. The first Congress shall prepare an electoral law governing the election of the members of the House of Representatives.

The duration of the House of Representatives is four years beginning with the date of the decree of the Federal Government issuing the election.

Article 19: The representative cannot be at the same time a member of the Senate. The representative who becomes a member of the Senate must choose, no later than ten days after his nomination, between the one or the other and must consequently resign his previous post.

ARTICLE 20: The House of Representatives elects in the beginning of each year its president and his assistants, i.e., two vice-presidents and two secretaries who supervise the sessions of the House.

ARTICLE 21: The members of the House of Representatives receive emoluments determined by the Federal Congress every three years.

B. THE SENATE

ARTICLE 22: The Senate is composed of representatives from the member states. Their appointment or their election is subject to the decision of each state in accordance with its laws and constitution.

ARTICLE 23: The term of the senator is seven years, beginning from the date of the decree, issued by the government of the member state, delegating him to the Senate.

ARTICLE 24: The Senate elects in the beginning of each year from among its members, its president and his assistants, i.e., two vice-presidents and two secretaries who supervise the sessions of the Senate.

ARTICLE 25: The members of the Senate receive emoluments determined by the Federal Congress every three years.

C. THE SESSIONS OF THE TWO HOUSES AND THE CONGRESS

ARTICLE 26: Each house meets separately unless they disagree on the budget or the passing of a bill, and unless a majority of the House of Representatives requests a joint session to debate certain specified questions.

ARTICLE 27: The Congress meets jointly in the following instances:

1. War and peace.
2. Treaties and international agreements.
3. The appointment of the members of the Federal Government.
4. The amendment of the Constitution.
5. The trial of a member of the House of Representatives in the manner described in the Constitution.

ARTICLE 28: When the Congress meets in joint session the

meeting is presided over by the President of the Senate or by one of his vice-presidents; then the office of the House of Representatives (i.e., the vice-president of the House of Representatives and its secretaries) performs the secretarial functions of the Congress.

2—**Executive Authority** ARTICLE 29: The executive authority of the Union is exercised by a council called the "Council of the Union" which consists of five members equal in rank and authority.

ARTICLE 30: The Federal Congress elects the members of the Council of the Union in a joint session by a two-thirds majority. The Council shall hold office for a period of four years beginning from the date of its election.

ARTICLE 31: The Federal Congress may renew the term of the members of the Council.

ARTICLE 32: The members of the Council of the Union must be from outside the House of Representatives and of the Senate.

ARTICLE 33: The members of the Council of the Union may not occupy any other office or undertake any kind of business during their term of office.

ARTICLE 34: If because of death, resignation or any other reason, a vacancy occurs in the Council of the Union, the Federal Congress must, not later than one month after its official notification of the vacancy, elect a new member to fill the vacant position. The new member shall serve to the end of the term of the Council of the Union.

The vacancy need not be filled if it concerns one position only and if it happens in a period not exceeding six months before the expiration of the current term of the Council of the Union.

ARTICLE 35: The Council of the Union is responsible to the people of the Federal State only. If a conflict arises between the Council of the Union and the Federal Congress and is not resolved by political means, each of the parties has the right to refer the conflict to the Supreme Court for decision in accordance with the provisions of this Constitution and in light of the public interest.

ARTICLE 36: The Council of the Union elects, in the beginning of each year and for a period of one year only, a president from among its members who will be the president of the Arab Union. At the same time a vice-President is elected to carry over the office of the presidency if, due to unforeseeable courses, the president cannot discharge the functions of his office.

The president of the Union cannot be reelected more than once during a period of four years.

ARTICLE 37: The Council of the Union shall in the person of its president or vice-president represent the Arab Union in internal and external affairs. As the executive authority it shall exercise the functions of government, in the Federal State and in all fields consigned to its jurisdiction.

It should perform in particular the following functions:

1. The administration of the affairs of the Federal State in accordance with the provisions of this Constitution and of the federal laws.

2. The execution of the Constitution and federal laws; the right to take all necessary measures, administrative or military, to guarantee their proper execution.

3. The preparation of bills, laws and of the budget within the jurisdiction of the Union and their submission to the Federal Congress.

4. The negotiation and conclusion of treaties and agreements with foreign countries provided they are submitted to the Federal Congress for approval before they are put into effect.

5. The proposal of internal and foreign policies within the jurisdiction of the Federal Congress.

6. The appointment of ambassadors, ministers, plenipotentiaries and consuls and all the paraphernalia of officers connected with the embassies, legations and consulates.

7. The receiving of ambassadors, ministers and consuls of foreign countries accredited to the Arab Union.

8. The defense of the Union against foreign attack and the supervision of internal peace and security in the Union.

9. The commanding of the armed forces of the Union and the appointment of its generals and officers.

10. The organization of the internal administration of the Federal State and the supervision of its operation, either directly through the creation of special agencies in each of the organs of internal government, or indirectly through the local administrations that are subject to the member states.

11. The execution of the federal budget, the administration of the federal treasury and the collection of federal taxes and duties.

12. The submission to the Federal Congress at the opening

of its yearly session (i.e., the beginning of each year) a report on the state of the Union covering the political, social and economic developments. It must also submit to the Congress at its request special reports on specific questions.

ARTICLE 38: The administration of the Federal State shall be entrusted to the Council of the Union. It shall supervise the various departments of the government which operate under secretariats general; each department being under one secretary general who is subject to and responsible before the Council of the Union.

3—The Federal Supreme Court ARTICLE 39: The Federal Supreme Court deals with conflicts arising from the following: First, as a court of first instance as well as a final tribunal and in accordance with the Federal Constitution.

1. The constitutional validity of laws passed by the Federal Congress.
2. The constitutional validity of laws passed by the legislative bodies of the respective member states.
3. The constitutional validity of the acts of the governments of the member states.
4. The constitutional validity of conflicts between the legislative and the executive authorities in the Union.

Second, it annuls or confirms the following in accordance with the Federal Constitution:

1. The constitutional validity of each judgment or decision issued in a final form by the courts of the respective member states.
2. The constitutional validity of each governmental or administrative act passed by the governmental or administrative bodies of the respective member states.

Third, in its capacity as the supreme criminal court, it deals as a court of first instance as well as a final tribunal and in accordance with constitution and the federal laws with the following:

1. The trials of the members of the Council of the Union.

2. The trials of the members of the Federal Congress in acts committed in violation of this Constitution.

Each act violating the Constitution shall be regarded as a criminal act.

Upon the confirmation of the criminal act the Federal Supreme Court shall pronounce its punishment in accordance with the penal law of the member state to which the criminal belongs.

If this particular penal law does not provide for a punishment for such a crime, the Federal Supereme Court shall then choose the pertinent penal provision from the laws of any of the respective member states.

ARTICLE 40: Cases shall be referred to the Federal Supreme Court either in the form of an independent case or as an emergency case during the consideration of a case which is subjudice in the ordinary courts of member states. In the latter event the emergency case shall not be accepted by the Supreme Court except with the final judgment or decision given in such a case.

ARTICLE 41: Every citizen and every government of the member states may avail himself or itself of the above procedure, provided it is conducted in conformity with the special law of adjudication before the Federal Supreme Court. This law shall be passed by the Federal Congress.

ARTICLE 42: The Federal Supreme Court shall consist of seven members, from among whom the Federal Congress elects by a two-thirds majority the president of the Court and his vice-president and the advisory members.

The Federal Congress shall not have the power to dismiss any member of the Court unless he proves to be deficient or commits acts in violation of his office.

ARTICLE 43: The president, vice-president and members of the Supreme Court shall receive emoluments commensurate with their positions. The emoluments shall be determined by the Federal Congress every four years. During this time the salary cannot be changed except when the change seeks to increase it, subject to the economic standing of the country.

Chapter 4. The Amendment of the Constitution   ARTICLE 44: Debate purporting the amendment of the present Constitution is not allowed except after five years from its adoption. After this period the motion of amendment can be initiated by any of the following:

First, the third of the members of one of the houses of the Federal Congress.

Second, the federal government in unanimous approval of its members.

Third, a government of a member state.

The adoption of the amendment is subject, however, to the approval of the two-thirds majority of the members of the Federal Congress in a joint session.

8. The Breakup of the United Arab Republic BY PATRICK SEALE

THE TECHNIQUE of the *coup d'état* has in Syria achieved a high degree of perfection. A standard drill exists for seizing power which all putschists since 1949 have followed: A tank column is sent on the capital shortly before dawn from Qatana, a camp twenty miles away; small detachments of two or three vehicles filter through the sleeping city, arresting half a dozen key men and occupying the radio station, the central telephone exchange, the headquarters of the army, police and *gendarmerie,* the airport, and the prison at Mezze. The populace hears the news at breakfast time.

On September 28, 1961, the United Arab Republic was destroyed by an army coup in Damascus. It is too early either to write a balanced obituary of the Union or to predict with any confidence the consequences of the rupture. Too many questions remain unanswered for its proper appraisal. A more pressing consideration for the immediate future is the caliber and political ambitions of the group of Syrian officers who led the breakaway. The Syrian army, from its first intervention in politics in 1949 to the Union with Egypt in 1958, was for a decade the most important single force in domestic affairs. Sometimes its chiefs assumed direct power; more often they left the front of the stage to civilians. This is what the officers in Damascus have now done. But no one should be deceived. Short of a total change of heart, the Syrian army remains the final arbiter of the situation.

The army chiefs precipitated the Union three and a half years

This article originally appeared in the November 1961 issue of *The World Today* (pp. 471–479), the monthly journal published by the Royal Institute of International Affairs, London. It is reprinted here by permission of the author and editor.

ago, and it is they who have now dissolved it. The whole byplay of civilian politics—the tentative pre-electoral regrouping of former political parties, the maneuvers and tactical alliances of old stalwarts of pre-Union days, the pressure for restitution by sectional interests hard hit by the Union—cannot obscure the fact that the army is the main repository of power.

The question is not whether the army will now go back to its barracks. Its disappearance from the scene in the present uncertain interregnum is almost unthinkable, in spite of the address to the troops on October 9 [1] of Major General Abd al-Karim Zahr al-Din, the Commander-in-Chief. "We have all returned to our barracks and duties," he declared. "After rescuing the ship, we handed it over to the people for them to pilot it. Politics are not our profession or our ambition. Our profession is the defense of our homeland against the aggressors, plotters, and subversive saboteurs." But the very next day, the Supreme Arab Revolutionary Command, in its role as a military Cabinet behind the scenes, put its name, side by side with that of the Council of Ministers, to an appeal for a decentralized union of Arab states. The return to the barracks is evidently not complete. Indeed, the army's role as the vigilant guardian of the nation's welfare is likely to assume even greater significance as the internal security forces—the police and intelligence apparatus—have been unsettled and dislocated by Egyptian-Syrian rivalry, by Colonel Saraj's eclipse, and by the new government's purges.

In each Syrian *coup d'état*, the army has acted in temporary alliance with a number of politicians. Finance and broad policy directives have sometimes come from outside the country. But the army must not be thought of as a pliant tool in the hands of civilian and foreign interests. It has had its own distinct motives for action without which, as the September secessionist revolt well illustrates, the bankers, industrialists, merchants, landowners and out-of-work politicians, however disgruntled and victimized, would have been powerless. President Nasser's error, in crude terms, was to give the Syrian officers cause for revolt. What, in fact, were their reasons?

One of the first public statements by the Syrian Revolutionary Command, broadcast on October 2,[2] outlines the army's grievances. "From the very first day," the statement says, "we wanted unity to be represented by an exchange of officers from both regions. Our youths went, full of vitality and Arabism, to the south. What was sent us from Egypt? All the evils and sins committed under the name of unity started from this point. They sent us officers who took up positions in the intelligence machinery before any other machinery. They came to us with the mentality of intelligence officers and not with the nationalist spirit with which we faced them, nor with the Arab brotherliness which inspires sincerity and confidence. These people began spreading like octopuses into the various machineries, poking their noses into the various affairs and imposing themselves on all occasions. . . ."

Another major grievance was that the Egyptian officers showed little respect for the chain of command, but bypassed their senior officers if these were Syrian, and made contact between themselves. Soon, "they dominated all the sensitive positions in the First Army Command and the unit commands, while our officers sent to Egypt were just filling wooden chairs without authority or power." When the Syrians complained, they were accused of the crime of "regionalism," of failing to take the broad view. It soon became apparent that the Egyptians had a plan for "an organized collective liquidation" of Syrian officers: "The number of those transferred from the army increased daily. Various means of transfer were used, such as transfer to the Foreign Ministry or the other ministries, or pensioning them off and thus burdening the budget with retired pay. . . . What occurred in the army, occurred on a large and subversive scale in the rest of the machinery of state." These specifically military grievances must be placed first in any inquiry into the demise of the UAR—even though President Nasser's authoritarian rule in Damascus and his unpopular economic policies may be judged contributory causes.

The army's own distinct motives for revolt have been emphasized here in order to place the events in Syria within the context of the current debate on the role of the army in politics. In Syria, whatever may be the case in Pakistan, Egypt, Turkey, the Sudan, or in the half-dozen other countries where the army has seized power, the officers are neither radical soldier-reformers nor the docile instruments of sectional interests. If the first title gives them too much credit, the second does them too little justice. They cannot claim to have any considered solutions for the nation's ills, but neither are they the paid hirelings of capitalist reaction. What, in effect, spurred them to action was that their jobs and commands were in danger, and in any power game that is what counts.

The test of the coming months will be whether the army can find unity around a single chief who understands the limits of its role and is prepared to give the politicians a clear run; or whether, as in pre-Union years, ambitious young officers split into rival factions, each with its supporters among the civilian politicians. It was this sort of pattern in 1957–58, resulting in the paralysis of the Syrian army and the virtual breakdown of civilian government, which caused the young army chiefs, sobered by the threat of civil strife, to appeal to President Nasser. Has the lesson now been learned, and can this suicidal fragmentation be avoided in the continued absence of any dominant figure or group on the Syrian political scene?

These pre-election months will see the re-emergence of many a familiar figure. The sterile years of the Union have no doubt drawn the venom from some old quarrels, but it is unlikely that men who in 1958 were locked in mortal combat should now work harmoniously together. Politicians such as Akram al-Hawrani, Khalid al-Azm, Sabri al-Asali, and the People's Party leaders, Rushdi al-Kikhia and Nazim al-Qudsi, cannot be expected to maintain the truce which their forced retirement and common opposition to the Union imposed on them in the last two years. The Communists can do nothing on their own, although their persecution under the Union and their record in opposing Nasser may have won them some popular sympathy. Their hopes, today as in pre-Union years, must lie in tactical alliances with the Ba'th and with "independents" such as Khalid al-Azm. The People's Party, still widely respected in the north, may once again be the rallying center for the urban business class; but its leaders have seemed, in the past, to lack political courage, and the future may lie with the party's younger men, preaching enlightened and prosperous free enterprise in an independent Syria. Akram al-Hawrani, matured by his clash with Nasser in the first year of the Union, but still enjoying peasant support, may have a second chance to show his worth as a national leader, while the more intellectual wing of the Ba'th leadership, represented by Michel Aflaq and Salah al-Din al-Bitar, will no doubt resume its indoctrination of the young. To all these men the dissolution of the Union must seem like a reprieve and a real test of their statesmanship. It is the delicate task of Dr. Ma'mum al-Kuzbari's interim administration to ensure elections at least as free as those which followed the fall of General Adib al-Shishakli in 1954. Dr. Kuzbari, one of Shishakli's leading civilian associates, had a ringside view of that last great upheaval in Syria's political life.

Time may show that President Nasser's rule gave Syria a salutary three-year breathing space from the turbulance of domestic politics. Problems of economic development were put into the hands of technicians. Land reform was carried through without the vindictiveness and bloodshed which might otherwise have accompanied it had the Hama peasant leader Akram al-Hawrani had his way unchecked. The Union coincided neatly with the end of a decade of rapid, and even spectacular, development in agriculture, due almost entirely to merchant enterprise in opening up to the tractor virgin lands in the northeast. Further expansion depended on state intervention to promote large-scale irrigation works, fertilizer production, and improved communications. Under the Union, detailed plans were drawn up and foreign credits assured for a vast dam on the Euphrates which will irrigate an estimated 800,000 hectares and for a railway which will carry Syria's grain and cotton from the Jezira to the Mediterranean port of Latakia. At Homs in central Syria, an important industrial complex, including a 110,000-ton fertilizer plant, is springing up astride the Iraq Petroleum Company's pipeline. The Union's critics say that none of these plans are new, but the fact remains that the last three years have seen Syria's long-term development tackled with greater seriousness and purposefulness than ever before. Were it not for the drought which plagued the Union from its first year and to which many of the unpopular economic measures may be attributed (if not the last wave of drastic nationalization last July), Syria's prosperity might well have been the envy of her neighbours.

President Nasser's failure in Syria was in the political sphere, that of statecraft. He failed to devise a formula for government which would both satisfy the Syrians and encourage other Arab states to join the UAR. From first to last, his rule in Syria bore the marks of improvisation and uncertainty. No durable institutions were created, and the Syrians were given no clear feeling of participation in the running of their own affairs. One of the first acts of Dr. Kuzbari's secessionist Cabinet was to abolish the National Union, the government-sponsored organization designed to channel popular grievances to the top of the pyramid and pass down directives. It died unregretted. To the sophisticated Syrian public, it was never an effective substitute for their dissolved political parties.

In 1958, Nasser inherited a country which had been for the twelve years of its independence the target of the rival ambitions of its neighbors. Syria had been at once the prize and the battleground in the inter-Arab feuds which opposed Iraq, Jordan, Egypt and Saudi Arabia in pre-Union years. These outside pressures were reflected in the fragmentation of Syria's internal political structure. Too few Syrians believed in the durability and territorial integrity of their country; most politicians were committed to one or another of Syria's neighbors and saw political salvation in terms of an alliance or union with one or another camp. Nasser, authoritarian by temperament and perhaps insufficiently informed about the detail of the Syrian political scene, felt that under these conditions he could safely rely on none of the pre-Union political groups. Indeed, his policy appears to have been to destroy any center of authority in Syria which might have rivaled his own. The result was that he was left to run a country in which all indigenous political leadership had been eliminated.

His solution was empirical, unimaginative, extremely cautious, but in the short run, safe. Government was conceived in terms of keeping order rather than as a constructive experiment in harnessing Syrian talents and enthusiasm in the cause of the Union. Nasser, in effect if not in intention, instituted a police state under the direction of Colonel Abdel Hamid al-Saraj, a taciturn, reclusive young Syrian of undoubted loyalty to himself and great organizational ability who, as chief of military intelligence since 1955, had been primarily responsible for thwarting the numerous plots to unseat the Syrian government in 1956–57. Saraj was good at catching the regime's enemies, but not at encouraging its friends. A police chief cannot easily turn statesman overnight. In time, Nasser himself is thought to have seen that Saraj was an obstacle to broadening the base of the regime. But by then he had become indispensable as the one man who could control the Union's many opponents. At least half a dozen times in the last two years there have been persistent rumors that the President was considering amending the constitutional framework of the Union in order to attract new men and new member states. He was said to be thinking in terms of a looser federal structure which would allow each state a large measure of internal autonomy and an opportunity to develop its own "personality." Regrettably, he never took the plunge. His fault seems to have been an excess of political realism: he was reluctant to sacrifice the relative security of Syria under Saraj for a more nebulous formula of obvious danger and unpredictable political benefits.

President Nasser sought to temper Saraj's rule in Syria by investing Field Marshal Abdel Hakim Amer with special responsibility for Syrian affairs. Amer was sent on extended missions to Syria both to keep Saraj on his toes and to provide disgruntled Syrians with an outlet for their grievances. He earned some local popularity in this latter role. But his grasp of Syrian affairs was never firm enough to enable him either to curb Saraj or to govern effectively himself. His open conflict with Saraj last September, ending in the Syrian's resignation, took the lid off the pressure vessel and gave the rebellious officers their chance.

For advice on Syria, President Nasser has relied on one other Egyptian who must bear some respnsibility for the final breakdown. Mahmoud Riyad, the President's special adviser on foreign affairs, knows the Syrian scene better than any other Egyptian leader. His skillful work as Ambassador in Damascus from 1955 onwards, explaining the nature and aims of the Free Officers' revolution to a Syrian public wearied of military regimes, did much to prepare the ground for the Union.

It is perhaps worth recalling how little the Egyptian officers knew of the world outside the Nile Valley in the first years of their revolution. From 1952–54 they were too busy destroying their local opponents and consolidating their regime to give much thought to Arab affairs. But the continuing problem of Israel, as well as the threat of the Baghdad Pact to Egypt's status in the Arab world, caused Nasser to adopt a dynamic policy aiming at Arab solidarity under Egyptian leadership. If the Egyptian leaders knew little of Arab Asia, how much more ignorant and indifferent was Egyptian public opinion. In his campaign to make Egyptians feel at one with Arabs everywhere, President Nasser has had to fight a hard core of isolationism in Egyptian opinion. This tendency has now been strengthened by the sight of his Arab policy in ruins, in much the same way as it was stimulated after the Palestine war by the conviction that Egypt had been betrayed by her Arab allies. "Egypt First," a slogan used by some Free Officers after their 1952 revolution, is likely to be heard once more. Cairo radio[3] recognized this danger in the first week of the Syrian coup by accusing imperialism of trying to isolate the Arab people of Egypt by "pushing them towards disbelief in Arabism and hate for all that is connected with the idea of Arab nationalism."

No one has been quicker than Nasser himself at sensing and combatting these developments:

> Brethren [he cried on the morrow of the coup] there is no more important a time which calls us to adhere to our Arabism than now. I know that there is bitterness and pain here . . . Voices say that while we were fighting in Palestine in 1948 . . . the army was stabbed from the back; at this time King Abdallah was negotiating with the Jews. However, this was not the first treachery and not the last . . . After the nationalization of the Suez Canal, what was Nuri al-Sa'id doing? Nuri al-Sa'id was telling Eden that it was essential to seize this opportunity to get rid of the revolution in Egypt. But have Nuri's steps affected us? Have King Abdallah's steps affected us? Never. These steps have made us adhere even more to our Arabism and our nationalism.[4]

But despite these brave words, there seems little doubt that the idea of Arab unity has received a setback in Egypt itself and that a popular revulsion against Nasser's Arab policy is to be expected. Nasser will find himself "contained" on the Nile as much by the secessionists in Damascus as by the mood of his own people.

Within hours of the Syrian coup on September 28, Nasser was facing its implications squarely in a live broadcast from Cairo: [5]

> . . . What has happened today is an act which affects the targets which we have all demanded. It is an act which affects our long struggle for our Arabism and for our Arab nation. It affects the call for Arab nationalism for which our fathers and grandfathers were martyred. It is an act which affects all the slogans we have issued. It affects our present and our future lives.

The loss of Syria means far more to Nasser than that of a distant and factious province. In Damascus, that "throbbing heart of Arabism," he was acclaimed as the worthy successor of both Saladin and Faisal. It was from the foundation of the UAR, which linked Arab Asia to Arab Africa, that he could proudly write to King Hussein last March that "our people . . . have been chosen by destiny to be both the vanguard and the base of the Arab struggle." [6] It was in the UAR that he hoped to build his model "cooperative, democratic, and socialist" society. Nasser's hold on Syria was his prime title to Arab leadership. It was also his title to world stature. His operations as far afield as the Congo must be seen as a function of his power in the Arab world; his rule in Syria, by shielding that country from inter-Arab politics, "froze" the whole region and thereby allowed him free play on a wider international stage.

In that same letter to Hussein of March 13, 1961—perhaps his most memorable statement of faith—Nasser wrote that "We believe in Arab nationalism, a real and profound current leading to an integral Arab union of which the constitutional form is to us of less importance than the will of the Arab peoples." The admission is significant, as it was precisely on the poverty of its constitutional structure that the UAR foundered. Few theorists of Arab nationalism have bothered to give the aspiration for unity a precise constitutional definition. It was felt to be a secondary problem which would solve itself once the people had declared in favor of Nasser. So powerful was Nasser's appeal to Arab nationalists everywhere that his supporters were led to overlook the importance of robust institutions and constitutional safeguards if union was to work. The Syrian experiment has, in consequence, been highly instructive, if painful. To Arabs everywhere it has been a lesson in the dangers of unfettered personal rule; it has brought home the profound differences between the various regions of the Arab world; it has split the Arab national movement into those who believed that Nasser should be given blind allegiance and those, like the Ba'th, his first and closest associates in the Union, who came to see his policies in Syria as damaging to the Arab cause. The issue was not confined to Syria alone, but was debated in Iraq, Jordan, the Lebanon, indeed in all Arab nationalist circles. The Ba'th, forcibly dissolved by Nasser, faced with the demolition of their early work in Syria, have in the last year pinned their hopes on an independent Algeria to check Nasser's dreams of hegemony and to provide an alternative focus for the Arab national movement.

Following Syria's secession, the immediate future is in fact likely to see a phase of what Arab theorists call "polycentrism"—i.e. the existence of a number of rival nationalist centers, indeed almost as many as there are Arab capitals. "I am confident," Nasser said in his great speech on October 5,[7] "as confident as in my belief in God, that this first experiment in Arab unity will not be the last, but that it was a forerunner operation, from which we have benefitted a lot, and what we learnt from the experiment will be useful for the Arab future . . ."

PART 4

Squaring the Circle: Israel and the Arabs

It is written: "They saw not one man his brother, neither rose any from his place." He who will not look at his brother will soon come to this: He will cleave to his place and not be able to move from it.

"The Darkness of the Soul," *Ten Rungs: Hasidic Sayings.* Collected and edited by Martin Buber (New York, 1947)

1. Palestine's Role in the Solution of the Jewish Problem BY CHAIM WEIZMANN

ALMOST HALF the Jews in the world find themselves today under the Nazi heel. It is impossible to determine the rate at which their physical destruction is proceeding. Nor is it possible to visualize the condition in which the Jewish masses of Poland, Rumania, occupied Russia and even Hungary will be found when the pall of darkness is finally lifted from Nazi-occupied Europe. Tragic as is the position of the Polish peasant, he is rooted in his native soil—at least where he has not been dragged away from it and made to slave in an armament factory. The Jew in his ghetto, on the other hand, finds himself despoiled of everything. Deprived of his meager possessions, driven from his home, torn from his family, he has become the most abject of all the abject victims of the terror. In the reconstruction of a new and—let us hope—a better world, the reintegration of the Jew will thus present a peculiarly difficult problem, and one which is likely to tax both the energies and the good will of the countries of Eastern and Central Europe.

The experience of the past twenty years, and the vexed problem of "minorities" which has caused so much trouble in Europe, hardly give much ground for hope of a satisfactory solution on the spot. No doubt many Jews will return and readapt themselves to the new conditions; but there will be vast masses which will have to emigrate. It would probably be unduly op-

Reprinted by special permission from *Foreign Affairs*, Vol. 20, No. 2 (1942), pp. 324–338. Copyright is held by the Council of Foreign Relations, Inc., New York.

timistic to assume that countries like the United States, Canada,
and some of the South American republics will radically change
their immigration policy after this war—particularly in the
strained economic conditions then to be expected. The hunted
and disinherited will once more be faced with the eternal question: "Whither?" And little promise can be held out for them
unless decisive steps are taken towards a radical solution of their
problem.

It is a complex problem, which means that it will have to be
faced with courage, imagination and sympathy. After the ago-
nizing experiences through which European Jewry has passed in
the last eight years, no makeshift or temporary expedients can
suffice, and indeed such would be unworthy of the spirit of the
Atlantic Charter and the principles so often enunciated by the
leaders of the democracies. Responsibility for the solution will
rest with those charged with the task of reconstruction, and also
with the Jewish communities which have escaped the fate of
their European brethren. Of the latter, it is estimated that the
Jews in the western hemisphere number about five millions; in
the British Empire about half a million; in Palestine about half a
million; and there are smaller communities in Turkey, Egypt,
Syria, Iraq, India and French North Africa, totaling perhaps a
further half-million (though some of them can hardly be ranked
as "free" communities).

The Nazi attack on the Jews came at first as a rude shock to
the outside world. But its effects soon wore off. Many European
statesmen and politicians found it convenient to treat the whole
business as a purely internal German affair; they felt it more
"politic" not to consider its darker implications. Persecution of
the Jews, as practiced by the Nazis, has served many useful
purposes of the persecutors. They have succeeded in ridding
themselves of a group which, by reason of its long-standing liberal democratic traditions, could never have made real peace
with the new regime. They have enriched themselves considerably from the wealth of their victims, and have thus been able to
increase the "wages of sin" available for payment to their
friends and adherents. They have flooded neighboring countries
with tens of thousands of refugees who, though generously received and befriended, were almost bound—once the first emotional wave of pity and indignation had subsided—to cause
difficulties and create problems and friction, contributing thereby to the bedevilment of relations between Jew and gentile

even in tolerant and free countries like England or pre-war France or Switzerland. This part of the Nazi scheme has not fully succeeded. It has, however, made the West "Jew-conscious"—aware of one more complexity in a life already overcrowded with urgent problems.

As the numbers of refugees swelled, it became obvious that their problems required a fresh approach and coordinated effort on the part of the Powers. The President of the United States, animated by humanitarian considerations and generous impulses, initiated two conferences. The intention was that representatives of Europe and America should devise ways and means of assisting the wanderers, of enabling them to begin a new life without becoming a burden on the communities which had offered them temporary shelter.

The Evian Conference achieved something, but on the whole, the measures there adopted were mere palliatives. Attempts naturally were made to find a radical solution—e.g. the delimitation of a territory somewhere on the earth's surface to which the stream of immigration could be diverted, a territory vast enough to allow the refugee to begin a new life without having to insinuate himself into the pores of an already mature organism. Many countries were mentioned, and even seriously considered. The Polish government sent a Commission of Experts to Madagascar; the British government sent one to British Guiana; Alaska was named as a possible "territory"; so was Santo Domingo, as also a remote part of southern California bordering on Mexico. There is no reason why these geographical exercises should not be continued indefinitely. But the countries under discussion had all to be admitted to be either too hot or too cold; none could be discovered in the temperate zone.

Curiously enough, a *mot d'ordre* seemed to have gone out to pass over in silence the possibilities of Palestine. This was the more remarkable in view of the contribution which Palestine was even then making to the solution of the refugee problem. Refugees had flocked to this small country in tens of thousands, and had been absorbed with great advantage to themselves and to the country. New settlements had sprung up, old settlements had been expanded, new industries had arisen. Up to the beginning of the war, about 100,000 refugees from Greater Germany had found homes in Palestine. The reason for this studied silence was no doubt the British government's desire not to emphasize Palestine in the role of a country of mass immigration, since to do so might, in their view, complicate the already rather disturbed internal conditions prevailing there. But apart from this, there was always the opinion (shared by many participants in the Evian Conference) that Palestine was too small to meet the pressing need. This view was fostered by the advocates of the various utopias who gathered on the fringe of the Conference, and in particular by certain Jewish philanthropic (and perhaps anti-Zionist) groups, who were prepared to send their fellow-Jews to almost any country in the world, provided only that it was not Palestine. Even now one has still to contend with the recurrent argument that Palestine lacks sufficient size. Admittedly the argument is one which has to be answered—and answered it can be.

Two great colonizing experiments have been made by Jews in the past fifty or sixty years, one in the Argentine and the other in Palestine. Colonization in the Argentine was begun under the best possible auspices. Practically unlimited areas of fertile soil were at the disposal of the settlers; a benevolent government placed no obstacles in their way. The price of land was moderate, and the committee conducting the operations had great resources at its disposal (something like £10,000,000 in gold, which fifty years ago represented a vast sum of money). The Jewish Colonization Association was a body of most competent men, commanding great authority in the Jewish world, and devoted to their work. They acquired some 1,500,000 acres of land for agricultural settlement. But after fifty years of colonization, no more than 30,000 people have been settled there. Moreover, the younger generation of the settlers shows little disposition to remain on the land.

The first modern settlers to arrive in Palestine, on the other hand, were mostly poor young students who had abandoned Russian universities in search of a free, independent and simple life. This they intended to make for themselves on the soil of Palestine. They entered upon their task without experience, without funds, unaided and untutored. The leaders of the Jewish communities looked askance at this quixotic undertaking, and prophesied its early and dismal failure. Moreover, the Turkish government placed every imaginable difficulty in the way of the first pioneers. It was an upstream passage for them. But the men who set out on it were inspired by a sacred faith in a future. They were the men of destiny, called upon to blaze the trail—however narrow and steep—on which later generations were to tread. Their awareness of a great mission sustained them and gave them the endurance and spirit of sacrifice which laid the foundations of the first Jewish settlements—chiefly in the coastal plain. Small in their beginnings, these villages have grown gradually and continually. They have a place—and a very honorable place—in the development of Jewish life in Palestine, and with them will always be associated the name of their founder—Baron Edmond de Rothschild—a man whose heart and power of vision were as great as his wealth. At first it was a mere trickle of new settlers which came to join them, rising after 1905, and in full tide since 1919.

Today there are in Palestine some 250 Jewish rural settlements, with a population of more than 140,000. Towns have been built up and industries established. The country has been awakened from its age-long neglect. The ancient Hebrew tongue has been revived and is heard today in the fields and orchards of Palestine, in the streets and workshops, as well as in the schools and the University. The total acreage of land in Jewish hands—acquired by slow degrees by purchase in the open market—is now approximately 400,000 acres. On this land a close-knit, well-organized, modern Jewish community of over half a million souls has arisen. It is normal in every way—in its structure, its occupational distribution—and the whole edifice, moral, social and intellectual, has been built up in a comparatively short space of time by the efforts of the Jews themselves on the neglected land of Palestine. Jewish labor, highly organized and creative, has played a leading part in this performance.

It should be realized that the labor movement in Palestine is not just a copy of the labor or trade-union movements in other countries. Its object is to create a Jewish working class by fostering Jewish immigration and the absorption of the immigrants into the expanding economy of the country. Its field of activity and the structure of its organization are shaped accordingly. Apart from purely trade-union activities, it comprises agricultural settlements, building guilds, industrial cooperatives, transport cooperatives, cultural institutions, and so on. It unites all workers in town and country who live by labor without exploiting the labor of others, i.e. hired laborers, members of guilds and cooperatives, independent smallholders, and collective settlement groups. Sir Arthur Wauchope, for seven years British High Commissioner for Palestine, speaks of the last-named in the following terms:

These 30,000 Jewish settlers have not only in theory, but in actual practice, solved the problem of the equal distribution of wealth, by the simple, if drastic, method of having none. . . . During the last twenty or thirty years the Jewish immigrants have proved most successful farmers. The villagers generally prefer mixed farming. They own many herds of dairy cattle, the number of their sheep and poultry increases every year. . . . In over eighty well established settlements the land is held in common, and not only the land, but also the produce, the means of production and transport, are all owned by the community as a whole.[1]

There is, of course, no compulsion about these communal settlements, nor any state control (as in Russia). The farms are run by mutual agreement among their members, and communal organization of the settlement's economic life does not interfere with the freedom of the individual or of the family.

The passing of Palestine from Turkish to British rule, and the policy of the Balfour Declaration and the Mandate (grudgingly and halfheartedly though they were applied), have provided the indispensable background for this development. But the decisive factor has been the character of the immigrant and his consciousness of returning to his homeland. The Balfour Declaration was a call to Jewish honor and dignity, and it was answered with all the sacred zeal latent in an oppressed people.

From the last twenty years of trial and error, certain conclusions can be drawn about the possibilities of Palestine in connection with future mass immigration. Two salient facts emerge.

A Jewish family can live on five acres (twenty dunams) of irrigated land—in some cases on even less—provided the scientific principles of modern mixed farming are applied. Many such settlements have been established in recent years, where people live by the labor of their hands, employ no hired labor, and lead lives of modest toil. They have acquired a sense of security; modern social institutions provide them with many amenities of life; they can give their children a sound education and pay back the investment in easy installments over a period of thirty years or so. The repayments go to the Jewish Agency, which employs the funds for further colonization. Most of the settlers also find themselves in a position to put by something for a rainy day. In the case of nonirrigable land, some fifteen acres (sixty dunams) are needed for a family.

It is not easy to establish with precision the area of land available. Much of the land which figures in surveys as "uncultivable" is so described by the government because account has been taken only of the standards and methods of the average Arab cultivator, and not of modern methods of cultivation. Adding together the large uncultivated area south of the Gaza-Beersheba line, the irrigable free stretches in the Jordan and other valleys, and the Maritime Plain, and allowing for some intensification of agriculture in the hills, it is hardly over-optimistic to say that at least 100,000 more Jewish families can be settled on the land. Experience shows, further, that for every family which settles on the land, three others are absorbed in urban pursuits—industry and commerce. Room can therefore be created for something like 400,000 families, or nearly two million souls. This is likely to be approximately the number of people whom Palestine will in fact have to take care of very rapidly after the war in order to relieve to some extent the terrible misery in the distressed areas of Europe.

But is an appreciable industrial development to be reckoned on in a country with very limited natural resources? Compare Palestine with Switzerland. This is another small country, also poor in natural resources; yet the Swiss people have built up a firmly founded and varied industry, including engineering, electrical, chemical and textile industries, food products, manufacture of watches and other instruments of precision, which enjoys an excellent reputation in the world market for quality products. The country is prosperous; the standard of life high; all in all, it is one of the most orderly and stable of European democracies. Two causes have contributed to this result. First, the character of the Swiss people, molded by their hard struggle with nature. In carrying their civilization up to the snow line, they have had to contend for every inch of ground and extract out of it the maximum of subsistence. A sturdy and disciplined race has grown up, with a deep belief in and respect for moral and intellectual values. The second element in Switzerland's success is her central geographical position, which affords her easy access to the great European markets.

Roughly similar conditions obtain in Palestine. There, too, the population has to face a hard struggle with a soil neglected for centuries, denuded of vegetation, and so eroded that its reconstruction involves great expenditure of energy. But Jews have been trained in the school of adversity and are patient and persevering. Besides, they have no choice: they must succeed or go under. The Jews also have a long tradition of intellectual training and are learning rapidly to apply it to the problems of their new life. Palestine's geographical position is even more favorable than that of Switzerland, lying as it does on the sea and at the crossroads of the great trade routes of the Old World—a bridge between East and West. There are already in Palestine considerable industrial achievements. There are the great electric works on the Jordan; the Dead Sea works near Jericho, which produce potash, bromine, etc., and are capable of further expansion into an important basic heavy-chemical industry; oil and soap works, a modern cement factory and an iron foundry in Haifa; a textile industry (cotton and silk); a clothing industry; canned fruit, jam, furniture, drug and shoe factories; various small engineering works with modern workshops in which repairs are now being effectively carried out for the British Army; and a number of minor industries. In all, Palestinian Jewish industry employs today some 35,000 persons and has an annual output valued at some £13,000,000. In the first year of the war, it supplied the army with goods to the value of £1,000,000, and with as much again in the first five months of the second year. This industrial war effort is due entirely to the initiative of the Jews themselves; it could be greatly intensified if afforded reasonable encouragement and opportunity. Just as Palestine could now do much more for the war effort, so after the war it can make—given suitable economic and political conditions—a much greater contribution than so far it has been allowed to make.

The financial responsibility of the Jewish people in connection with the absorption of some millions of new settlers in Palestine will be heavy. Jewish money sunk in Palestine so far amounts to roughly $500,000,000, of which public funds account for some 15 per cent, while the rest is private investment. This represents an investment of about $1,000 per settler. The immigration and settlement of each 100,000 persons would accordingly require $100,000,000. Only a fraction of this sum could be expected from voluntary contributions. The financing of such a large-scale operation over a period of years would necessitate the raising of state loans. These would have to be repaid from the revenue of the country. But this would demand a radical modification of the Palestinian fiscal system. The very conspicuous increase in its state income has been due almost entirely to the rapid development initiated by the Jews; but financial control has been vested in the government of Palestine, and the Jewish Agency has had to rely entirely on private contributions. Today the impoverishment of the Jewish masses of Europe is so complete that one can no longer count on any substantial contributions from European Jewry.

In 1937 a Royal Commission under the late Lord Peel came to the conclusion that the present form of administration in Palestine had outlived its usefulness.[2] It recommended the partition of the country into two states—a Jewish state in the west and north, embracing the Maritime Plain and Galilee, and an Arab state to the east and south. Without entering here into the question of how far such a second limitation of the area of the Jewish National Home (already truncated in 1922 by the severance of Transjordan) could be justified, I merely record the fact that the Jews, dissatisfied as they were with the area actually allotted to the Jewish state, were nevertheless prepared to try and negotiate a settlement on the basis of the principles laid down in the Peel Report. But the plan, though at first accepted by the British government, was subsequently abandoned under Arab pressure. Arab states like Iraq and Egypt, which had no *locus standi* in Palestinian affairs, were first allowed, and later encouraged, to exercise a powerful influence, and the Arabs were lined up in a united front against the Jewish national home. The government held a conference in London with the Arabs and the Jews; and, after much maneuvering, it laid down its own policy in the White Paper of May 1939. The principal features of this policy were: complete stoppage of Jewish immigration after another five years (during which period the total Jewish immigration was not to exceed 75,000); Jewish acquisition of land to be restricted to certain diminutive areas (the first modern case of discrimination against the Jews under the British flag); and the establishment of a "Palestinian" state in which the Arabs, artificially secured of a two-to-one majority, would naturally have administrative control of the country. This policy was opposed by Labor and Liberal leaders in the House of Commons, and by leading Conservatives, foremost Mr. Churchill, who severely criticized it in his famous speech of May 23, 1939. It was condemned by the Mandates Commission as incompatible with the spirit and letter of the Mandate. In fact, its sole purpose was to appease the Arabs. But events in Egypt, Iraq and elsewhere, and the attitude of many Arabs even in Palestine and Syria during the present war, have sufficiently illustrated the failure also of this dose of appeasement.

The Palestine administration applied itself to the enforcement of the White Paper of 1939 with an energy and promptitude which contrasted strangely with its hesitations and vacillations in putting the policy of the Mandate into effect during the past twenty years. The Jews have refused, and continue to refuse, to accept the White Paper, since it is contrary to their historic rights and to the spirit of the Balfour Declaration, and is a breach of a solemn agreement concluded by the British government, sanctioned by British public opinion, by the League of Nations, and by the United States of America.

This attempt to degrade the promise of a National Home for the Jewish people to minority status in an Arab Palestine is mainly due to the peculiar relationship between the British and the Arabs on the one side, and the British and the Jews on the other. The British in Palestine have never clearly explained to the Arab population the real meaning and implications of the Balfour Declaration; at best they have been rather apologetic about the policy they were appointed to carry out; at worst, some of them have been openly hostile to it. Among British administrators and politicians in the Near and Middle East, there is a school of thought which is all too ready to ascribe every difficulty encountered by British policy in Egypt, India or elsewhere to the Jewish National Home in Palestine. The Arabs have been quick to seize on this evidence of weakness, and with the help of the Axis powers, have succeeded in whipping up an agitation which at times has assumed threatening dimensions. The Arabs had to be pacified at any price, and the Jews had to foot the bill. To the Palestinian administrator the Arab presents no problems: He is a "native," and the methods which have proved their efficacy in various backward British dependencies can be applied to him with their usual success. The Jew does not fall into the same category. He has come to Palestine to construct there a modern civilization, and has brought with him a number of new, complex and baffling problems. He is "difficult," critical, always anxious to be trying something new, and he does not fit into the time-honored framework of administrative routine which has proved serviceable in Nigeria or Iraq.

This is reflected in the attitude of the British government and of the Palestine administration towards the Jewish war effort today. At the outbreak of the war, all the available Jewish manpower of Palestine offered itself for war service. Many were men with some training and a thorough knowledge of the country. Technical and industrial assistance could also be made available, and these, too, were offered. But the zeal of the Jews was somewhat blunted by the cold politeness which greeted their readiness to serve. They were allowed, it is true, to enlist in limited numbers in the British Forces, but—so far as fighting units were concerned—only *pari passu* with Arab volunteers, who showed little disposition to come forward. The "parity" principle was eventually dropped, under pressure of circumstances, a short while ago, and about 10,000 Jews now form part of the Nile army, as combatants or in auxiliary services. They have given a good account of themselves in Libya, Crete, Greece and Syria, but even now they are not allowed to fight under their own name and flag; and their presence with the British forces is camouflaged under the description "Palestinian." One wonders why, shipping difficulties being what they are, the British authorities should find it necessary to bring men and material from Australia and New Zealand instead of utilizing what is available on the spot.

This peculiar and—to the Jews—disheartening attitude is presumably designed to demonstrate to the Arab world that the Jews have no particular status or stake in Palestine. Even after the bitter experiences of the present war, this idea seems to be a fixation, ineradicable from certain minds. The vain effort to obliterate the very name of a highly active community in Palestine is a tragic anomaly, due to a total lack, in quarters responsible for Middle Eastern policy, of a real sense of the values involved in the present life and death struggle.

In any settlement of Middle Eastern problems, account must be taken of the Arab nationalist movement, inspired by Pan-Arab ideas on the one side, and by exaggerated local chauvinism on the other. These two aspects are, curiously enough, not mutually exclusive; they coexist in a state of unstable equilibrium. So far, with the exception of Saudi Arabia, Arab nationalist energies have not been directed into constructive channels; they are devoted to wielding the Sword of Islam rather than the spade or the plowshare. The movement is emotional, turbulent, made heady by the unexpected political gains which have vicariously accrued to it since the last war. It is fashioning itself on the totalitarian pattern; young Arabs stand in awe before the achievements of Germany and Italy, and still believe in their

coming victory. Groups of Arab students from Iraq, Syria and
Palestine were encouraged before the war to make pilgrimages
to Berlin, Nuremberg and Rome, and there worship at the Nazi
and Fascist shrines. There they were indoctrinated with "modern" ideas, which they have now transplanted into their respective countries. The Rashid Ali revolt (accompanied by a regular
pogrom in the best Berlin-Bucharest manner) testifies to the
success of Nazi-Fascist teaching, and no doubt rejoices the
hearts of the tutors. The Baghdad pogrom (120 killed, 850
wounded) was perpetrated on an ancient native Jewish community resident there for centuries. These happenings, inciden-
tally, belie the idea, so assiduously spread by Arab propagandists, that their people have always lived in harmony with their
native Jewish populations, and that their animosity is directed
only against incoming "foreign" Jewish immigrants. Of these
there are none in Baghdad.

It is to be hoped that this state of mind among the Arabs will
prove transitory. A great opportunity awaits the Arab
peoples—to rebuild their countries, to bring happiness and prosperity to the oppressed fellaheen. This will be the acid test of
Arab nationalism. Pride in a glorious past is of value only if it
serves as a spur to the hard task of rebuilding a happier future.

In the early stages of our work in Palestine, there were distinct possibilities of reaching a reasonable *modus vivendi* with
the Arabs. In 1918, at the suggestion of His Majesty's government, and with the approval and encouragement of General Allenby, I went to Transjordan on a visit to the Emir Feisal, then
commander-in-chief of the Arab forces. We had a frank discussion in which I clearly stated the aims and aspirations of the
Jews. He expressed himself prepared to give them his full consent, after consultation with his father, then Sherif of Mecca. A
year later, in London, a treaty of friendship was concluded between us, embodying the main points of this conversation in the
desert. Lawrence of Arabia—often erroneously quoted as an
anti-Zionist—helped in the drafting and negotiation of this treaty
and acted as interpreter. Articles III and IV read as follows:

In the establishment of the Constitution and Administration of Palestine all such measures shall be adopted as will
afford the fullest guarantees for carrying into effect the
British Government's Declaration of November 2nd, 1917.
All necessary measures shall be taken to encourage and

stimulate immigration of Jews into Palestine on a large scale and as quickly as possible to settle Jewish immigrants upon the land through closer settlement and intensive cultivation of the soil. In taking such measures the Arab peasant and tenant farmers shall be protected in their rights and shall be assisted in forwarding their economic development.

Developments in Syria prevented the implementation of the Treaty, and after Feisal's death things in Iraq went from bad to worse. With him an important link between the Jews and the Arab world was broken. Nevertheless, even in Palestine, where relations between Arabs and Jews were of late rather acute, there remained among the Arabs some who were ready to discuss terms of cooperation. After all, though our work in Palestine has for its object primarily the welfare of the Jews, the benefits derived from it by the Arabs are incontestable. The Arab population of Palestine has increased—by natural growth and through immigration—far more rapidly than in Transjordan, or even than in wealthy Egypt. The increase has been greatest in precisely those parts of Palestine where Jewish activity has been most intense. Arab wages are higher in Palestine than in any Arab country, and this accounts for a very considerable Arab influx.

But the Mufti of Jerusalem assumed the leadership of the extreme nationalist party. He is an implacable enemy of both the Jews and the British. Supported by powerful outside influences (and sometimes even favored by the British administration), he has gained a great ascendancy over the Palestine Arabs, and by terrorizing the moderates, has succeeded in frustrating all attempts at reconciliation. Even so, the Mufti has never represented the whole of the Palestine Arabs, and there is some ground for thinking that, had the government made a determined attempt to implement the Royal Commission's proposals, many Arabs would have acquiesced in them, and a Jewish state in a part of Palestine might today have been a going concern. I believe I am not too bold in adding that in that case the military situation on this front might have been more favorable than it is.

For Palestine's strategic importance cannot be forgotten. The countries which stretch from the Euphrates to the Nile constitute a vast and greatly underpopulated region. In ancient times they were great centers of civilization. But though they

fell on evil days, their geographical importance remains
unchanged—in fact it is, if anything, greater than ever. These
countries are a bridge between the three continents of the Old
World. The Suez Canal is the gateway to the Far East and India, and thus, in a sense, one of the approaches to the Pacific; its
fate may even affect the interests of the western hemisphere.
Small wonder, then, that the predatory countries have long
sought, and still seek, to obtain a foothold in this part of the
world. They will continue to regard it with covetous eyes so
long as it remains weak, undeveloped, unstable, and a prey to
political intrigue. Once these countries have been rebuilt and
raised to a higher level of culture and administration, this undesirable situation will show a rapid change for the better. Their
reconstruction, however, cannot be brought about by capitalist
exploitation, but only through the energies and efforts of their
own inhabitants. On the first stages along this road they will
certainly need to be guided by nations like England or America;
in return, I believe that a Jewish Palestine will be able to contribute much to their progress and prosperity. But if Palestine
plays such a role, there is a countervailing obligation on the
Arabs to acknowledge Jewish rights there.

Whatever the Arabs gained—and it was a great deal—as a
result of the last war; whatever they may gain—and they have
already gained something, and will gain more—as a result of this
war, they owe, and will owe, entirely to the democracies. It is
therefore for the democracies to proclaim the justice of the Jewish claim to their own commonwealth in Palestine. There is
nothing new in this principle. It was implicit in the Balfour
Declaration; it was reaffirmed by the Peel Commission. And we
have now acquired the invaluable experience of the last twenty
years, which has proved beyond doubt that when the Jew is reunited with the soil of Palestine, energies are released in him
which have been stored up and suppressed for thousands of
years—energies which, given an outlet, can create values which
may be of service even to richer and more fortunate countries.

To sum up. The Arabs will greatly profit from a British victory by obtaining independence in Syria and Libya, and as large
a measure of national unity as they themselves are capable of
achieving. On the other hand, it is essential to obtain such a settlement in Palestine as will help to solve the Jewish
problem—one of the most disturbing problems in the world. The
Arabs must, therefore, be clearly told that the Jews will be

encouraged to settle in Palestine, and will control their own immigration; that here Jews who so desire will be able to achieve their freedom and self-government by establishing a state of their own, and ceasing to be a minority dependent on the will and pleasure of other nations.

In that state there will be complete civil and political equality of rights for all citizens, without distinction of race or religion, and in addition, the Arabs will enjoy full autonomy in their own internal affairs. But if any Arabs do not wish to remain in a Jewish state, every facility will be given to them to transfer to one of the many and vast Arab countries. Considering the strategic and economic importance of Palestine, the inclusion of the Jewish state within the British Commonwealth of Nations would be to the interest of both. But we should also be ready, if necessary, to consider joining, under proper safeguards, in federation with Arab states.

A Jewish state in Palestine would be more than merely the necessary means of securing further Jewish immigration and development. It is a moral need and postulate, and it would be a decisive step toward normality and true emancipation. I believe that after the war Jews everywhere can gain in status and security only through the rise of a Jewish state, and this would be especially the case if that state is a part of the British Commonwealth. Anti-Semites, determined to reduce the Jews to slavery or drive them into exile, have not waited for the excuse of the establishment of a Jewish state in order to proceed against them. The latest manifestation of Nazi ingenuity is the decree by which every Jew under Nazi rule must bear on his breast a so-called "badge of shame"—the Shield of David. We wear it with pride. The Shield of David is too ancient and too sacred a symbol to be susceptible of degradation under the pagan swastika. Hallowed by uncounted ages of suffering, of martyrdom patiently and unrevengefully borne, it will yet shine untarnished over Zion's gates, long after the horrors of our present night are forgotten in the light of the new day that is to come.

2. A Solution Through Force?

BY JUDAH L. MAGNES

EVERYBODY who considers the Palestine question has to ask himself two things. First, what does he really want? Second, how does he expect to get that? Those who have answered the question to themselves and have said, we really want a Jewish state or the Jewish Commonwealth, have very good reasons for that, and I don't have to go into those reasons.

The tragedy that has happend to the Jewish people, its virtual homelessness, the lack of a voice in the United Nations organization or anywhere else, those are negative reasons on the one hand, very powerful. There are positive reasons also for a Jewish state, namely, that the Jewish people ought to be given the opportunity, as every people is given, to set up governments, to try its hand at that very difficult exercise of power which one calls sovereignty, government. That would be a great challenge to the Jewish people. Instead of giving advice from the sidelines, it would be in the midst of the struggle itself, which every people ought to have the privilege of confronting.

A Jewish state would give all of that presumably, at least in theory, and more besides.

As I said, it is not necessary for me to tell you, who have been in favor of that, what the arguments for a Jewish state are.

Reprinted from *Towards Union in Palestine: Essays on Zionism and Jewish-Arab Cooperation*. *This is the stenographic record of an address given by Dr. Magnes in New York, on July 17, 1946, before an important Zionist organization which had invited him to discuss the political situation. The discussion which followed has been published in the Jan.–Feb. 1947 number of Ba'ayoth, the Hebrew Monthly of Ihud*. M. Buber, J. L. Magnes and E. Simon, eds. (Jerusalem, 1947), pp. 14–21.

It is an entirely different question as to how you are going to get it. You have to try to make up your mind on that with as much clarity, insofar as it is possible, as you make up your minds on the question of the Jewish state itself.

I don't know if those who advocate a Jewish state have given sufficient thought, systematic, orderly, responsible thought, to that second problem. How are you going to get it? I should like to express the opinion, which is not my personal opinion alone, that a Jewish state can be gotten, if at all, only through war, war in the literal sense of the term, fighting with arms insofar as the arms are available; insofar as they are not available, they are to be secured.

Those who have been for a Jewish state and who have been trying to build up Jewish armed groups are not only logical, but they are also realistic, because they know that if they want a Jewish state and want it hard enough, the only way to get it—you may perhaps succeed in getting it—is through the use of arms, through warfare. If you teach the Jewish youth, as so many of us are teaching them—mistakenly it seems to me—that the only hope for the Jewish people is a Jewish state, that the Jewish people is doomed everywhere, in America as elsewhere, and that betimes a Jewish state has to be established; if you teach the Jewish youth that—that Judaism, the Jewish spirit, the Jewish religion, Jewish culture are all in danger of deterioration, if not extinction, if there be no Jewish state—then of course, with an idealistic Jewish youth such as we have in Palestine, in America and elsewhere, this idealistic Jewish youth will draw the conclusion which I have tried to draw for you, even though you yourselves don't draw it, that the way to get that is through force.

You see that the Jewish youth is ready to go out on that battleground. When British soldiers are killed in their beds within what is presumbably the hospitable city of Tel Aviv, when officers are kidnapped, when bridges are blown up, when all of these things take place that have been taking place, that is the logical and the natural and the inevitable consequence of the theory which our youth is being taught, that without a Jewish state we are lost. If not today, then tomorrow.

Those, therefore, who have advocated a Jewish state and who condemn what is being done are, I think, taking an illogical ground. The youth who go out at night with their bombs and their other weapons are ready to sacrifice their own lives there, and not just talk about it here. They are drawing the natural and inevitable conclusion, the only conclusion that can be drawn from the premise that a Jewish state is absolutely necessary.

I do not regard it as my function today to argue with you. I am just trying to put the problem to you. I should like to put another side of the problem to you. Before I do that, let me say why I am sure that a Jewish state cannot be achieved, if it can be achieved at all, except through violence and warfare.

You can talk to an Arab on everything in the world; You cannot talk to him about the Jewish state. You cannot talk to him about a Jewish state because a Jewish state means, in the definition of it, the rule by Jews of others, of others who live in that Jewish state. You may try to persuade him that Jewish rule is going to be just and generous, and we may all believe that; we certainly all hope for that. But that is prophesy, and one cannot be guided by that.

If you talk to an Englishman, and he is another factor in the situation, you will find that there are differences of view. There have been some Englishmen who have thought that a Jewish Palestine could be a bastion to the British Empire at this very sensitive center of communications. I know that some of the earliest Zionist reading that I had done, years and years ago, by Mr. Sidebotham and by other Englishmen, was based just upon this premise.

These Englishmen believed that it was necessary to have a loyal Jewish Palestine in order to safeguard what they then foresaw would, actually even more than they could then foresee, become a crucial center of communications. You don't find as many Englishmen saying that today as you did then or as you did a year ago. The conception of a loyal Jewish Palestine has disappeared. Both Englishmen and Jews have to realize that a people is loyal or a state is loyal when it is to their interests to be loyal, and we see today that situations may arise which may prompt us to think, correctly or mistakenly, that our interests do not lie with England, and we are therefore endeavoring to show England that she need not count upon our loyalty.

In general, the conception of loyalty on the part of the Jews has long since disappeared out of the British vocabulary. I think you ought to know that. I am not trying to assess the blame for it.

You have, therefore, these two main factors: the Arabs, not only of Palestine, but the whole Arab world, and beyond that, the world of Islam. Then you have the British factor, which you are not going to eliminate, however hard you try, because Palestine is too important for the British scheme of things.

You would find that to get a Jewish state from either of them, or with either of them against the other, would mean the application of force, warfare. That also is something that those who are engaged upon this terror understand. They say, the only way we can get it from Britain is through force, because Britain has shown in Ireland or in India that when sufficient force is applied concessions are made. I don't want to go into what to me are fundamental differences between Palestine and the Jews on the one hand and Ireland and India on the other hand. I think they are radically different and the analogy is a basically false analogy.[1] But it is correct when they say, if you want the state, the only way you can get it is through force.

Jabotinsky knew that long years ago. He was the prophet of the Jewish state. Jabotinsky was ostracized and condemned and excommunicated, and we see now that almost the whole Zionist movement has adopted his point of view. There is not sufficient credit given to Jabotinsky and the Revisionists for their foresight and for their loyalty to this idea, which all these years was exceedingly unpopular, at least on the surface. He saw that the only way to get a state was through force.

He said in his early writings: "Has it ever been known that a people would willingly give up its soil? No more would the Palestine Arabs yield their sovereignty without force." He endeavored to get the British to understand that, and he found a large following among the Poles, those Poles who are now carrying on these pogroms. They wanted to get rid of the Jews in Poland and therefore accepted his plan of evacuation.

All these things were in his mind and were recorded by him more or less in a prophetic way. These things are being adopted now by those who excommunicated him and who pilloried him and who made his life a great burden. I tell you that in order to indicate that sometimes ideas have a way of marching and of accomplishing themselves long after they have been subjected to derision and opposition, and not Jabotinsky's ideas alone.

I would like then to put before you another side of the problem. There are those who say they want a binational state, and they have tried to put to themselves the question how they are going to get it. They want a binational state because they think that, in the first place, that is a worthy ideal, a high ideal, an ideal to which the Jewish youth can be educated to give their best mind, their best spirit. They have this in mind also because of the practical situation. We find the Arabs there, a fact which, of course, cannot be overlooked, although it has been overlooked over and over again.

I met with a group not so long ago and they asked me to say something on this problem, a group of leaders in the community here, a couple of hundred of them. At the end of that meeting one man came up to me and said, "Well, you know perfectly well that whenever we want to come to an agreement with the Arabs we can; it is the British." So I said to him, "Why don't you come to this agreement with the Arabs, if you think it is so simple?"

I have heard that said by many people on many occasions: "Of course when we choose to come to an agreement with the Arabs we can." Well, there was a time when that might have been possible. That time is long since past. The Arabs have grown in political maturity, and the Arabs are more and more afraid of us. So the initiative is out of our hands. When that man said, "We can come to an agreement with the Arabs whenever we want," he meant that the political initiative was still in the hands of the Jews. It is not; it has passed out of the hands of the Jews.

The question therefore is—I am not trying to go into the question so much as to why we want a binational state; I have indicated that in a few words—the question that I want to ask and try to answer is, how do we expect to get it? We have worked out a program for that, which was presented in writing to the Anglo-American Committee; and was supplemented by oral testimony, which is also available in print. I don't expect in the brief remarks that I make to go into the same detail that you can find in these documents.[2]

We want to get the binational state through, as far as possible, argument, persuasion, not through the use of force; certainly not through the use of Jewish force; not through warfare. And we think we can get that.

The reason we think we can get it is because we know of Arab circles in Palestine who are in favor of it. We know there are Arab circles outside of Palestine who favor it. I have had two conversations in New York with important representatives of the Arab world and they favor it.

So that the question that I ask and the question that I answer is just this: What do we want? We want a binational state, because we think the Jewish genius for government can be given full play through the binational state. How do we expect to get it? Through argument, persuasion, and finally through life itself. And this is an important point which I should like to make with you as one of the details we have tried to work out.

We were greatly disappointed that the Anglo-American Committee did not go further in the report. They adopted a great deal of what we said, sometimes in the very words of our statements. But they overlooked a primary consideration, namely, that the process of self-government be begun at once, expedited.

Why do we think that that is so important? Because in that way Jews and Arabs would come together in one of the most important concerns of life, government. We therefore contended, and we still contend, that there should have been a concurrent declaration on the part of the Anglo-American Committee, proclaiming a binational state on the one hand and the beginnings of self-government on the other. The Arabs want, above all things, self-government. The Jews, for the most part, want above all things, immigration. We have tried to make these balance one another. Our formula is: political parity and numerical parity for the two nationalities.

Our proposal is that immigration be permitted up to parity, equality. That would give the Jews the chance of five to six hundred thousand additional immigrants until parity was reached. It would not mean the discontinuance of immigration when parity was reached, because the Arab birth rate is higher than the Jewish, twice as high. So that the additional Jewish immigration would be at least that much, in order to make up the disparity between the birth rates.

Moreover, it is our contention that if there be some political peace, as there might be, in connection with a binational state, the Jews and the Arabs could work out together some further arrangement as to additional Jewish immigration, after parity was reached and after the disparity of the birth rates had been covered.

In our program we have worked out a series of steps. We proposed three stages for this self-government; now, before the Mandate ends; tomorrow, when trusteeship takes over Palestine; and in the third stage when Palestine becomes an independent autonomous unit within a larger federation in that part of the world.

We think that these things are practical. We certainly know that they cannot be introduced through warfare. We think we can find a common language, a language of understanding and of peace with the Arabs, as we have found with many individuals. We think if the binational state with self-government were made the policy of the British and of the American governments and of other governments, and this policy were adhered to, and if both the Jews and the Arabs understood that that was the policy for Palestine which had the approval of the United Nations, we think that the Jews and the Arabs in the course of a not very long period would be finding one another increasingly, year by year. You find that today. You find it in the government itself. There are Jews and Arabs who participate in government, but in the lower positions. There was this government strike. The Jews and the Arabs carried it on together. The Jews were in the minority, the Arabs were in the majority. But the Jews and the Arabs stuck together because the interests of their life required it. It wasn't an abstract formula that was presented to them.[3]

Jews and Arabs work together in the country districts. The kibbutzim and the fellahin are on good terms. They are not on such good terms today as they were a year ago, and they probably will not be on such good terms tomorrow as they are today, if all of this goes on. But they have laid the basis of understanding and cooperation between them. Not on the basis of a Jewish state but on the basis of life, of what one can give to the other, of what one can receive from the other.

There are Arab workers' organizations now, particularly the left-wing workers' organizations, which have as a plank in their platform the cooperation between Jews and Arabs, although on other matters they are almost as chauvinistic as some of the Effendi Arabs themselves. But it is an indication that points the way.

We cannot afford to lose much time. The sands are running out. The war that is taking place now—and it *is* warfare—the beginnings of warfare were inevitable, they were not to be avoided as long as the Jewish state was the official policy of the Zionist movement. It has not been the official policy of the Zionist Congresses as yet; for that reason those of us who are opponents of the Jewish state still feel that we have the right to be members of the Zionist organization, to buy the shekel as we do. I am hoping that with the developments of the next six months, before the Zionist Congress takes place, there will be a greater measure of calm and of understanding. But if we simply keep reaffirming what the Biltmore Program began, and simply shake our fists and say to Great Britain, "You are our enemy," and say to the Arabs, "You are our enemy"—that is what we are saying to them at the present time—with this war on two fronts, which every book of strategic warfare warns against—why then, of course, the situation will go from bad to worse.

I have to add one point. The Ihud group is not the only group advocating the idea which I put forward to you today. The Hashomer Hatzair advocates these ideas, with certain differences, but the general tendency is the same, and they are an important group. I should like to say that in the Mapai there are also persons who are not unimportant and who at least flirt with the idea of the binational state. And in the Aliyah Hadasha I think there is a majority now who are for a binational state. I would like to say that some of the Zionist executive, who do not say this publicly, nevertheless say it privately, "Oh, if you could get what you are after, how happy we should be."

There are some in the Zionist executive who talk about the Jewish state and who also would be very glad if there could be partition. We oppose partition. We oppose partition not only for all the reasons that are usually given, but because partition is going to mean the intensification of chauvinism on both sides.

When you draw these borders, when you draw these frontiers and have the Jewish schools on the one side of the line and the Arab schools on the other side of the line, have you any idea what is going to be taught in them? Well, I have. There is going to be the hatred by the Jews of the Arabs and the hatred of the Jews by the Arabs. That is being taught today. But it is not being taught in the same way, because, after all, we meet, we see one another. If there be this partition and there be those watertight compartments, there is going to be a hatred engendered in comparison with which this present-day hatred is just a plaything. Moreover, those of you who are thinking of the Jewish state and who are ready for this warfare, which will be inevitable, which will be much more serious than it is today, may think that we Jews have these great caches of arms, which we have—this Yagour is only one, as you probably know. You may think that we are better armed than the Arabs, and we are, much, much better armed, and we are better trained than the Arabs. Well, all of our sons and all of our daughters go out for training, and we are going to get at least 12,000 trained men and women from the Jewish Brigade, and we are going to get among the 50,000 young men and women who are coming in among these hundred thousand refugees I don't know how many who have been or are being trained.

The day we lick the Arabs, that is the day, I think, when we shall be sowing the seed of an eternal hatred of such dimensions that Jews will not be able to live in that part of the world for centuries to come. That is something that you had better try to avoid.

I have great confidence in some of these leaders who are to be in Paris for a meeting soon, confidence even in some of the most violent of them, that they may be ready now to make these admissions that this is not the way. *Lo zeh ha-derech*,[4] this is not the way.

I can only repeat to you that this is the inevitable way on the basis of the Jewish state. I do hope the idea of the binational state is going to be taken seriously, taken up seriously in Paris; if not in Paris, it certainly will be in the coming Zionist Congress. By that time I am hoping that the movement of the 100,000 will have begun in good earnest, and that many who are engaging upon all of this simply out of understandable despair, will say, "It is time to lay down our arms"; and this would be the beginning, this is what we want.

We cannot maintain a Jewish state or a binational state or a Yishuv in Palestine if the whole surrounding world be our enemies. We may be doing this and we may be doing that, but the existence of that Yishuv or that state, or whatever one calls it, will be precarious, and that is not what we want nor what the Jewish people require.

3. Why the Arab States Entered Palestine

ARAB HIGHER COMMITTEE DELEGATION FOR PALESTINE

THE FACTS OF THE PALESTINE CASE

Palestine is an Arab country and has been so for the last thirteen centuries. It is an integral part of the Arab world.

In 1914, Palestine, together with Lebanon, Syria, Transjordan, Iraq and Saudi Arabi, was part of the Ottoman Empire.

In 1915, in pursuance of their struggle for secession and complete independence, Arabs fought against the Turks on the side of the Allies.

In 1918, the British army, with the help and cooperation of Arabs outside and inside Palestine, occupied the territory now known as Palestine.

In 1919, in accordance with Article 22 of the Covenant of the League of Nations, a special regime was devised which provided that certain countries were to be placed under a mandatory system. A special paragraph was inserted in that Article to cover the position of the peoples living in Syria, Lebanon, Palestine and Iraq. The paragraph runs as follows:

> Certain communities formerly belonging to the Turkish Empire have reached a stage of development where their existence as independent nations can be provisionally recognized subject to the rendering of administrative advice and assistance by a mandatory until such time as they are able to stand alone.

Excerpt from the *Memorandum* by the same name, submitted by the Arab Higher Committee Delegation for Palestine to the United Nations, (New York, 1948), pp. 1–7.

The population of Palestine in 1919 was composed of 93 per cent Arabs and 7 per cent Jews.

In 1920, Great Britain was appointed as the mandatory power over Palestine in order to lead the country to complete independence.

In 1922, the draft of the Palestine Mandate was prepared by Anglo-Zionist authorities in a way inconsistent with the aforesaid principle of mandates. They inserted in it the Balfour Declaration, whereby Great Britain announced that its government viewed with favor the establishment of a national home for the Jews in Palestine without prejudice to the civil and religious rights of the inhabitants of that country.

For thirty years, Britain administered Palestine as a Crown colony, deprived of any trace of self-government. Instead of leading Palestine to independence, Great Britain put the country under political, administrative and economic conditions favorable to the creation of a Jewish national home. Consequently the Jewish population in Palestine increased from 52,000 in 1917 to 700,000 in 1947.

Britain suppressed the Arab national movement, exiled Arab leaders, put in concentration camps thousands of Arabs, enacted coercive laws and adopted severe measures to crush Arab resistance to Jewish immigration and to the Zionist policy adopted in Palestine.

While keeping the Arabs in Palestine defenseless and unarmed, Great Britain armed the Jews and acquiesced in their smuggling and acquiring of arms and ammunition. With Great Britain's tacit knowledge, Jews put up military fortifications in their towns and villages. While banning any form of Arab military training, Great Britain allowed Hagana units to be formed and shut its eyes to the vast military training and preparations made by Jews.

Since 1945, the Jews openly challenged the authority of the Mandatory Power by invading Palestine with thousands of illegal immigrants. When Great Britain started to exercise control over the flow of Jewish immigration, Jews revolted against the Mandatory. Jewish gangs, financed by funds raised in the United States and aided by the whole Jewish community in Palestine, committed the most outrageous crimes against both the Arabs and the British.

In 1947, Britain threw the question of Palestine into the lap of the United Nations for a final peaceful settlement.

On November 29, 1947, the General Assembly under very strong pressure by the United States, recommended in a resolution the partition of Palestine into an Arab state and a Jewish state, with economic union.

The said resolution was not a decision of the United Nations; it was a recommendation under Article 10 of the Charter. It was addressed to the Mandatory Power, to the Security Council, and to the people of Palestine.

On November 30 (one day after adoption of the partition resolution), the Arabs of Palestine rose in self-defense against partition which deprived them of the greater and better part of their country. The Jews, on the other hand, committed the most atrocious crimes. They bombed and destroyed Arab dwellings, murdered innocent and defenseless old men, women and children, as in Deir Yasin, committed acts of sacrilege against churches and mosques, as attested to by all Christian religious authorities. These perpetrations caused 300,000 Arabs to leave their homes and belongings and take refuge in adjacent Arab countries.

The overwhelming majority of the people of Palestine—namely the 1,300,000 Arabs—refused to accept the recommendation to partition Palestine. The Mandatory Power, too, refused to take any part in the implementation of the partition scheme. The Security Council, after debating the implementation of the said scheme, refused to accept it on the ground that its implementation could not be effected peacefully. The Security Council has no legal authority under the Charter to implement the partition resolution by force. Consequently the Security Council pursued the course of a peaceful settlement by endeavoring to effect first a truce, then a peaceful and just settlement.

The Security Council, after several consultations with Jews and Arabs, started to study a Colombian proposal for a truce in Palestine, which was adopted with modifications on April 19. The Arabs accepted this truce and the Zionists rejected it.

On May 1, 1948, and after the adoption of this ceasefire resolution, the Jews attacked the Katamon Arab quarter in Jerusalem.

In the meantime, the Truce Commission was negotiating with the Arabs and Jews for an effective truce in Jerusalem. The British Higher Commissioner for Palestine also took an active part in these negotiations. On May 5, an Arab delegation headed by the Secretary General of the Arab League met with the Truce

Commission. On May 8, the said Arab delegation met with the former British High Commissioner of Palestine in Jericho. **The Arab delegation agreed with the British High Commissioner and the Truce Commission to have a ceasefire in Jerusalem, and consequently the Arabs ceased fire on May 9. On May 12, the High Commissioner communicated to the Arabs the truce conditions concerning Jerusalem, which the Arabs accepted unconditionally. On May 14, the Jews broke the truce and attacked the Old City of Jerusalem and engaged the Arabs in fierce fighting, exposing the Holy Places to immeasurable danger. The Jews started also to occupy most of the Arab quarters in the New City of Jerusalem and have looted most of the Arab houses and shops.**

While the General Assembly was meeting in a special session, several proposals were submitted with a view to finding a peaceful and just settlement. Preliminary and temporary measures were taken to meet the urgent situation. A municipal commissioner was appointed for Jerusalem. And although the truce proposals were not seriously pursued in committees, a final resolution was drafted for the appointment of a mediator to use his good offices. Among other things, he was instructed to promote a peaceful adjustment of the future situation in Palestine. With that resolution, the Palestine Commission which was appointed by the General Assembly on November 29, 1947, was discharged.

On May 14, the rebellious Jewish minority declared a Jewish state in a part of Palestine, ignoring the natural rights of the Arabs, the resolution of the General Assembly and the democratic procedure which must be followed to make the creation of a state and the form of government it should assume contingent on the desires of the majority of the country's population. **In the area alleged to be the Jewish state, there are 509,780 Arabs and 499,020 Jews.** Not only are the Arabs the majority in the alleged Jewish state, but they are the majority in all but one of the districts covered by the Jewish declaration. The distribution of population in these subdistricts is as follows:

SUBDISTRICTS	ARABS	JEWS
Safad	87%	13%
Tiberias	67%	33%
Beisan	70%	30%
Haifa	53%	47%

Tulkarm (partly)	83%	17%
Jaffa	29%	71%
Beersheeba	99%	1%

In a spectacular and dramatic way, on May 14, the government of the United States of America recognized the Jewish state one minute after its declaration, contrary to international law and practice and the traditional policy of the United States in such matters.

The declaration of a Jewish state by a Jewish minority, defying the will of the Arab majority and assisted by the international Jewish Agency and the World Zionist Council, is an act of great treason. And in view of the armed insurrection of the Jewish minority and of the most savage crimes committed against the defenseless Arab population, the Arab Higher Committee for Palestine, representing the Arabs of Palestine, asked the League of Arab States to send them all military help possible in order to put down the Jewish rebellion and maintain law and order in Palestine.

By the Pact of the League of Arab States, signed in Cairo in 1945, its state members recognized Palestine as an independent country, and accordingly the Arab Higher Committee was admitted to the League as a permanent member. On the strength of that pact, it is the duty of these Arab states to come to the help of the Arabs of Palestine engaged in self-defense in view of the armed aggression of the Zionists.

Relying on all these facts, and at the invitation of the Arabs of Palestine, the Arab states sent their armies into Palestine for the sole purpose of maintaining law and order, and for the establishment of civil democratic government representing the will of all its citizens, irrespective of race, color or creed.

On the entry of the Arab armies into Palestine, His Majesty King Abdullah of Transjordan and the Secretary General of the League of Arab States, sent cablegrams to the President of the Security Council explaining the reasons for the action of the Arab states.

On May 17, the United States delegation submitted a draft resolution asking that the Security Council determine that: "The situation in Palestine constitutes a threat to the peace and a breach of the peace within the meaning of Article 39 of the Charter."

On May 18, the Security Council decided that in order to

elucidate the facts, certain questions should be addressed to the Arab states, the Arab Higher Committee for Palestine and the Jewish Agency.

On May 20, the representative of the Arab Higher Committee for Palestine made a statement clarifying the position of the Arabs of Palestine.

On May 22, the Security Council rejected the United States resolution to treat the matter of Palestine as falling under Chapter 7 of the Charter and adopted instead a resolution calling upon all parties to "cease fire."

Between May 24–26, the Arab states sent their replies to the Security Council explaining the position of the Arab League and expressing the willingness of the Arab states to study any suggestion which the Security Council may make along the line of a solution of the Palestine problem.

On May 27, the Soviet Union delegation submitted a resolution calling upon the Security Council to decide "that the events in Palestine constitute a threat to peace and security within the meaning of Article 39 of the Charter." This proposal was rejected by the Security Council.

On the same day, the United Kingdom delegation submitted a resolution calling on the United Nations' mediator "to make contact with both parties as soon as the ceasefire is in force with a view to making recommendations to the Security Council about an eventual settlement for Palestine." This resolution was adopted.

The Security Council instructed Count Bernadotte as mediator to make contact with all parties as soon as the ceasefire is enforced, with a view to carrying out his functions as determined by the General Assembly, i.e. to make recommendations for the "peaceful adjustment of the future situation in Palestine."

On May 29, 1948, the states of the Arab League sent a cable to the Secretary General of the United Nations accepting the four-week truce.

THE LEGAL POSITION

Basis of the Arab Claim: The Arab case rests on the following legal and natural grounds:

(1) By Article 22 of the Covenant of the League of Nations of 1919, the people of Palestine were recognized as a provisionally independent nation. The exercise of their inherent and legal

sovereignty was suspended during the twenty-seven years of the Mandate. The Mandate having ended on May 14, 1948, the people of Palestine are entitled to exercise that right of independence and sovereignty.

(2) The Arabs of Palestine, by their inalienable right to self-determination and their natural right to independence in their own country, are entitled to preserve the natural integrity of their territory and live in freedom under a democractic constitution.

(3) The natural rights of the native Arabs are also sustained by the principles enunciated in the Atlantic Charter and the United Nations Charter. On August 14, 1941, a joint declaration was made by the United States of America and the United Kingdom in which it was solemnly declared that "they desire to see **no territorial changes that do not accord with the freely expressed wishes of the peoples concerned,**" and that "after the destruction of the Nazi tyranny they hope to see established a peace which will afford to all nations the means of **dwelling in safety within their own boundaries.**" The said declaration, known as the Atlantic Charter, was formally adopted by other members of the United Nations on January 1, 1942.

The very basis of the United Nations Charter is the respect for the integrity of countries and the right to self-determination. Therefore no regime could be established in Palestine, and no territorial changes could be made therein, without the expressed wishes of its citizens.

Basis of the Jewish Claim: On the other hand, an armed Jewish minority, aided by international Jewry, carried out an armed insurrection, unilaterally declaring independence in an area where the native Arabs are the overwhelming majority.

What was called a declaration of independence was issued by the Jewish Agency and the General Zionist Council. Their claim was alleged to be based on the natural and historical right of the Jewish people and the recommendation of the General Assembly of the United Nations.

Against this alleged natural and historical right, there exists the natural right of the Arabs established by actual continuous occupation and possession of all of Palestine for more than 1,300 years. In all of Palestine now there are only 258,000 Palestinian Jews against 1,300,000 Palestinian Arabs. The rest of the Jews who are residing in Palestine still retain their foreign nationalities. Neither they, the international Jewish Agency, nor the General World Zionist Council, have natural or legal rights in Palestine. The Jewish minority at present existing in Palestine is an immigrant minority mainly from Eastern Europe, who have come to Palestine during the last thirty years.

In basing their claim on the resolution of the General Assembly, the Zionists were also basing themselves on nothing more than a recommendation. The United Nations cannot pass any judgment or decision to mutilate a country. The resolution of November 29 was a recommendation, not a *diktat*. This view has been widely expressed by many authorities on international law. Dr. Clyde Eagleton, Professor of International Law at New York University, wrote:

> It is clear to any student of the Charter that a resolution of the General Assembly, such as that for the partition of Palestine, is no more than a recommendation, and that it can have no legally binding effect upon any state whatsoever.[1]

This recommendation was not accepted by the Mandatory Power. It was rejected by the overwhelming majority of the citizens of Palestine. The Security Council refused to implement it on the proper ground that it has no legal powers to do so, and the General Assembly, in dismissing the Palestine Commission on May 14, 1948, indicated that it has no wish to implement the recommendations. Furthermore, the plan of partition as recommended by the General Assembly is conditioned by the acceptance of the people of Palestine, because it envisages the establishment of two independent states with economic union. No such regime could be established by a unilateral declaration of an armed minority supported by international Jewish bodies as long as the 1,300,000 Arabs, whose land it is, do not agree.

Recognition of Jewish State Equally Illegal: Illegal as was the declaration of a Jewish state in a part of Palestine, the immediate recognition thereof after one minute of its revolutionary declaration by the United States is equally illegal. It is neither in conformity with the policy of the United States nor with its established practice in international affairs, nor in accordance with international law.

On March 12, 1947, President Truman, referring to the question of the right of the Greek people to self-determination, declared before the Congress of the United States: "I believe that it must be the policy of the United States to support free people who are resisting attempted subjugation by **armed minorities or outside pressure.**"

On May 15, 1948, the United States government did just the opposite in recognizing the "armed minorities and outside pressure" now claimed to be the "Jewish state."

Mr. B. L. Penrose, prominent American who spent many years in the Near East and was recently appointed president of the American University of Beirut, described the recognition of the Jewish state as "a unilateral pronouncement" that

> took no account of the United Nations, undercut the United States delegation to the United Nations, bypassed the advice of the National Security Council, of the area experts in the Department, the military establishment and the Central Intelligence Agency, to say nothing of the Congress. Such a decision so hastily and secretly taken, on a subject fretted with such import for world peace and security that the United Nations has spent months on it without reaching a decision, is not only dictatorial, but dangerous in its many implications.

Mr. Penrose added that this action "has in effect made a mockery of United States participation in the United Nations, has given our blessing to the intensification of divisive nationalism rather than to the principles of friendship among nations and conciliation of international differences, has aligned this country in opposition to the sovereign Arab nations and to the entire Muslim world of 300,000,000." [2]

According to international law, before any state can be recognized, **an organized state system must have been created which is able to assert its power regularly and effectively within the territory** and thus carry out the **normal functions of a state.** The new state cannot be considered to have come into existence before **the fight against its opponents has practically come to an end, so that there is no longer any appreciable probability that the insurrection may be put down.**

The practice of the United States in recognizing foreign governments was stated in a letter dated April 2, 1936, by Secretary of State Hull:

The rule of the United States is to defer recognition of an executive until it shall appear that it is in **possession of the machinery of the state, administer government with the assent of the people thereof and without substantial resistance to its authority and that it is in a position to fulfill all the international obligations and responsibilities incumbent upon a sovereign state** under treaties and international law.[3]

These same requirements were set forth thirty-five years ago in a memorandum of March 27, 1913, prepared by the then Assistant Secretary of State Mr. Adee, for the Secretary of State, in which it is stated:

> Ever since the American Revolution, entrance upon diplomatic intercourse with foreign states has been de facto, depending upon the existence of three conditions of fact: **The control of the administrative machinery of state; the general acquiescence of its people; and the ability and willingness of their government to discharge international and conventional** obligations.[4]

It seems that Zionist pressure of today has led the United States government to contravene its own policy and the centuries-developed practice of international law.

LEGAL BASIS FOR ARAB ARMIES' ENTRY INTO PALESTINE

(a) The Arab armies entered Palestine on the invitation of the native Arabs of Palestine who are "resisting attempted subjugation by the armed (Jewish) minority and outside (Jewish) pressure." In the same way, the British forces went into Greece at the invitation of the Greek people who were resisting subjugation by the armed Communist minority and outside pressure. Furthermore, the Arab states are part of the Arab League, established in order to safeguard the independence and sovereignty of the Arab states. Palestine is an integral part of the Arab world. It was recognized by the Charter of the Arab League as an independent country and was allowed the right of participation in the work of the Council of the League.

(b) The principle underlying the Charter of the Arab League in safeguarding the territorial integrity and sovereignty of the Arab countries is similar to that upon which rests the Monroe

Doctrine for America. In a message to Congress on December 2, 1823, President James Monroe declared:

> As a principle in which the rights and interests of the United States are involved, that the American continents, by the free and independent conditions which they have assumed and maintain, are **henceforth not to be considered as subjects for future colonization by any European powers.**

The message runs:

> We declare that we should consider any attempt on their part to extend their **system to any portion of this hemisphere as dangerous to our peace and safety.**
> It is impossible that the allied **powers should extend their political system to any portion of either continent without endangering our peace and happiness; nor can anyone believe that our Southern Brothers, (i.e. Latin Americans) if left by themselves, would adopt it of their own accord. It is equally impossible, therefore, that we should behold such interposition, in any form, with indifference.**

If the United States could not see the subjugation of their South American brothers with equanimity by the European powers, how could the Arab States see the subjugation of their Arab brothers by an armed rebellious Jewish minority and international Jewry?

(c) The action of the Arab States is pursuant also to their obligations and responsibility under the United Nations Charter. Article 52 of the Charter states:

> 1. Nothing in the present Charter precludes the existence of regional arrangements or agencies for dealing with such matters relating to the maintenance of international peace and security as are appropriate for regional action, provided that such arrangements or agencies and their activities are consistent with the purposes and principles of the United Nations.
> 2. The members of the United Nations entering into such arrangements or constituting such agencies shall make every effort to achieve pacific settlement of local disputes through such regional arrangements or by such regional agencies before referring them to the Security Council.
> 3. The Security Council shall encourage the development

of pacific settlement of local disputes through such regional arrangements or by such regional agencies either on the initiative of the states concerned or by reference from the Security Council.

4. This Article in no way impairs the application of Articles 34 and 35.

The League of Arab States is a regional arrangement within the meaning of Chapter VIII of the Charter. It was in such capacity that it was introduced in the San Francisco Conference, and its Charter filed there.

The States of the Arab League are not only honorbound, but they are also dutybound to help in maintaining law and order in Palestine.

Zionist propagandists and some interested Zionist-controlled politicians have tried to label the Arab intervention as an aggression. These accusations are nothing but deceitful propaganda which have no legal foundation and have been turned down by the Security Council.

The Security Council has jurisdiction to decide whether there is aggression or not, but before it can do so, it must refer the matter of Palestine to the International Court of Justice for a legal opinion, under Article 96 of the Charter, on all the complicated and complex points of law involved. These points include: (a) the status of Palestine after the termination of the Mandate; (b) whether the minority of the Palestine Jewish citizens, who are no more than 18 per cent of the citizens of Palestine, can proclaim a state in an Arab country; (c) whether the entry of Arab armies in Palestine, on the invitation of the overwhelming majority of the citizens of that country, is a violation of the Charter.

4. The Lesson of Palestine

BY MUSA ALAMI

THE ARABS were faced by a challenge, the first since their liberation from foreign rule; and they did not meet it. A great national disaster has been inflicted upon them, exposing them in turn to further blows and disasters. The challenge and disaster are those of Palestine.

The disaster was not inevitable. During the course of the struggle, we had an opportunity to finish with Zionism and its dangers altogether, but we did not take it.

We were greatly shaken and began to question ourselves, asking, how did the disaster happen? Why did matters take this turn? What were our mistakes? Where were the sources of weakness in us, and the gaps through which the enemy entered? How can we repel the great and imminent danger and recover the beloved and violated fatherland?

This is what we shall now try to analyze.

The prime causers of the disaster were the British. It was they who gave the Jews the Balfour Declaration in 1917 with its "national home," and then opened the doors to them. British protection and patronage enabled the Jews to make Palestine their home and to multiply. Under the protection of British arms, Jewish colonies were founded and extended, and Jewish immigration flourished. Under the wings of the British Mandate, Jewish terrorism hatched and grew and was trained by British hands until it became an organized military force. During all

Excerpt reprinted from *The Middle East Journal*, Vol. 3, No. 4 (Washington, D.C., 1949), pp. 373–76, 385–90, 394–405; by permission of the editor.

this the British prevented us from arming, and shut our eyes to the arming of the Jews, until the time came when they were strong enough to stand on their own feet. Then the British withdrew and announced their neutrality.

Thus the British were the prime causers of the disaster, and on them lies its responsibility. They were assisted by the Americans and the Russians. So much is clear. At all events, we found ourselves face to face with the Jews, and entered into battle with them to decide the future; and in spite of what the British, the Americans, and the Russians had done, it was still within our power to win the fight.

There were two phases to the battle of Palestine. In the first phase the burden of defense was thrown on the shoulders of the Palestinians; in the second, it was taken up by the Arab armies. The Arabs failed to defend Palestine in either phase.

In the first phase, the fundamental source of our weakness was that we were unprepared, even though not taken by surprise, while the Jews were fully prepared; that we proceeded along the lines of previous revolutions, while the Jews proceeded along the lines of total war; that we worked on a local basis, without unity, without totality, without a general command, our defense disjointed and our affairs disordered, every town fighting on its own and only those in areas adjacent to the Jews entering the battle at all, while the Jews conducted the war with a unified organization, a unified command, and total conscription. Our arms were poor and deficient; the arms of the Jews were excellent and powerful. It was obvious that our aims in the battle were diverse; the aim of the Jews was solely to win it.

These same weaknesses were the source of weakness in our defense in the second phase, that of the Arab armies: disunity, lack of a unified command, improvisation, diversity of plans, and on top of all, a slackness and lack of seriousness in winning the war.

Just as we failed in the military sphere, so we failed in the political. Our actions were improvised, our conduct of affairs a chain of enormous mistakes; we had no clear objective and no fixed policy. The natural result of all this was disaster and the loss of Palestine.

These weaknesses were a reflection of the state of the Arab nation and of the existing regimes: A disjointed political order based on dismemberment was reflected in its ranks in battle, as was its slackness. Further, its affairs were in the hands of inefficient governments, and the nation itself was still weak in consciousness and maturity.

The loss of Palestine was a great disaster with far-reaching results for the very existence of the Arab nation. If the Arabs hasten to face the danger before it overwhelms them, there is still time and opportunity. But if they do not, these beginnings will lead to their inevitable conclusions.

The first remedy lies in unity, so that we may become again a strong, cohesive body politic. Fortunately this unity has been the principal aim of our national movement from its inception, just as historically it was the beginning and basis of our existence. Nevertheless, there are obstacles in the way of complete unity at the present time. The field must be narrowed so that it may be nearer actual realization. Here the Fertile Crescent presents great possibilities. Let us then be convinced of regional unity which will bring together the countries of this Crescent, and can be a pattern for general unity, while the door remains open for those other Arab countries that may wish to enter.

But unity is not enough. The inefficiency of the present regimes is also responsible for the disaster. Thus along with unity must go a modernization of government, assuring reforms in organization and progress in aims, and embracing both internal and external policies.

But even all this is not enough without solicitude for the people, for their revival and endowment with the primary elements of power, so that their strength may be transferred to the state. The people must participate in the direction and supervision of their own affairs; they must be given all their rights, just as duties are demanded of them. The first and most sacred of their rights is freedom in all its forms. Then come real equality, security of work and social security, and the spread of social services. The people's first duty is to know their rights, to believe in them, and to act by them.

There must be a strong universal system of education with the object of creating a new, powerful, conscious generation capable of defending the Arab homeland and of recovering its self-respect. There must also be a complete program for the exploitation of Arab sources of wealth, so that a powerful defensive system may be created to preserve the country, to raise its standard of living, and to revive its people.

These are the matters of the hour in these difficult circumstances. The future history of the Arabs will be determined for a long time by the way we deal with them and the results we achieve. . . .

MAIN CAUSES

How did matters take this turn? There are three aspects to the answer: lack of unity and dissension among the Arabs; the existing regimes in the Arab countries; and the state of the Arab peoples. The disunity at the front was a reflection of the disunity within; the weakness of the military and political preparations was the result of a general governmental weakness of preparation; the shortcomings and lethargy of the governments was the result of the weakness of popular control over them; and the weakness of this popular control was the result of a general weakness in the Arab peoples.

In the face of the enemy the Arabs were not a state, but petty states; groups, not a nation; each fearing and anxiously watching the other and intriguing against it. What concerned them most and guided their policy was not to win the war and save Palestine from the enemy, but what would happen after the struggle, who would be predominant in Palestine, or annex it to themselves, and how they could achieve their own ambitions. Their announced aim was the salvation of Palestine, and they said that afterward its destiny should be left to its people. This was said with the tongue only. In their hearts all wished it for themselves; and most of them were hurrying to prevent their neighbors from being predominant, even though nothing remained except the offal and bones.

The structure of the Arab governments was old-fashioned and sterile. The regimes did not even understand the situation, or the importance and danger of the hour, or the course of events. They did nothing positive in accordance with the exigencies of the situation, neither politically, legally, administratively nor socially. Their political and military inefficiency has already been noted. As for their administrative inefficiency, the Arab states occupied part of Palestine where there was an administrative vacuum after the evacuation of the British. However, the elements of administration were still there—officials, offices and records. It was the first duty of the Arab governments to continue to administer and not to hold up common interests. All this was quite easy, and of great value for the course of the war. Nevertheless, offices and services were suspended, an indication of incompetence and lack of understanding of the value of local administration.

In the social sphere, the incompetence of the Arab governments has revealed itself in the matter of the refugees. The matter is most urgent. In the eyes of the outside world it is a test of the value and the preparedness of the Arabs. The essence of the matter is not charity, but organization and assistance and the opening up of new opportunities. It is shameful that the Arab governments should prevent the Arab refugees from working in their countries and shut the doors in their faces and imprison them in camps. The matter needs adequate effort, a will to work, sincerity and good organization.

So the blow came through the lethargy and rivalry of the Arab states, the incompetence of their governments, and the unawareness of their peoples. These are our faults, the weaknesses in our ranks, the loophole through which the enemy entered and brought on us shame and loss. So long as these weaknesses remain, the Arabs will remain groups and states ruled by inefficient governments through antiquated regimes; the people will remain feeble, careless, and far from attaining control over their own affairs; and Palestine will not be the last or the most serious disaster to afflict them.

Nevertheless, Palestine and the self-respect of the Arabs must be recovered. Without Palestine there is no life for them. This our ancestors understood truly as of old. Their understanding was better than ours, when Europe attacked and took Palestine from them. They were willing to die for it and continued to struggle until they recovered it. Thus it is today. This is the first phase of a long war. But so long as the conditions of weakness persist, the recovery of Palestine will be a futile hope.

THE JEWISH DANGER (SUMMARY)

With the establishment of a Jewish foothold and base, the Arabs are faced with a new danger. The ambitions of the Jews are not limited to Palestine alone but embrace other parts of the Arab world. In a message to his people last year, Mr. Ben-Gurion said: "Prepare to achieve our final goal in the construction of the Jewish state, the gathering-in of the Jews of the world, and the fulfillment of scriptural promises." The Zionist program dates back to the days of Herzl, and it is based on the colonization of Palestine and the revival of the Jewish kingdom as it was in its golden age. Palestine will then become the base for exploiting all the East and for extending the economic interests of the Jews. In their definition, Palestine includes present-day Palestine, Transjordan, and large portions of Syria, Lebanon and Egypt. They dream of "a greater Jewish state between the Nile and the Euphrates."

This program they are implementing step by step. The next step will be an attempt to take all of Palestine, and then they will proceed according to circumstances—circumstances which they themselves will attempt to create. To this they will bring all their power, influence, wealth and abilities.

This is the danger which faces the Arabs, and which obliges them to change their way of life in order to be able to meet the new situation.

THE LESSON (SUMMARY)

Although the Arabs have seen and heard something of the disaster which has befallen their brothers in Palestine, its full extent goes far beyond anything they have seen or heard or imagined.

Hundreds of thousands of the Arabs of Palestine have left their houses and homes, suffered the trials and terrors of flight, died by the wayside, lived in misery and destitution, naked, unprotected, children separated from their parents, robbed, raped and reduced to the most miserable straits.

Had the Palestinians been able to foresee their fate, they would have willingly given up all they possessed in order to preserve their country and to avoid their exodus and dispersal. Today Arabs as a whole have been given the opportunity to look into the future and to profit from this lesson. If they learn this lesson, they must from now organize themselves and prepare to defend their homes and their country. Force can only be repelled by force. But the Arabs will not be strong until they are united and take the road by which nations become powerful. Time does not wait for us; we must hurry.

The Arabs are still stronger than the Jews if they unite and cooperate. Palestine slipped from their hands very cheaply; it was not defended as one should defend one's home. The Arabs need cohesion, organization, training, so that their potential strength may become real.

The first essential is to end our quarrels about Palestine, and to recover our unity of plan and action. The greatest danger is that we should remain divided and backward, while the enemy grows stronger.

ARAB UNITY

The Arab nation has a deep desire to revive, to lift itself up, to recover its place in history, to be counted as a great nation with a glorious past. But it is dismembered, as the disaster in Palestine revealed in particular. This dismemberment constitutes the principal obstacle in the way of our national resurgence. Unless we realize unity and do away with fragmentation and all its accompanying features of backwardness and disruption, we cannot take the road to revival.

From its beginning the Arab national movement has had two principal aims: the freedom of the Arab countries from foreign domination, and their unification in one great state. The motto of the movement consisted of two words: "Independence and Unity." These two aims have remained basic throughout the period of the struggle for independence, until they have become complementary to each other—freedom means unity, and unity means freedom and independence.

Thus Arab unity has been in the forefront of our national aims ever since we were dismembered. Imperialism came between us and it; we resisted both imperialism and partition and considered them complementary to each other. We used to say that partition was the work of the imperialists, a method of weakening us and dividing our country and of securing their own position in it.

Now that the imperialists have gone and we have realized one of our major goals, shall we abandon the other and preserve the fragmentation they left behind? Surely not. No Arab country has any special interest in fragmentation. The interest of all lies in unity; only the enemy and the foreigner benefit from it. No one can dispute this, although in every country there are individuals who cling to dismemberment and derive private benefit from it.

Even these regional governments which are based on partition talk of unity. As a matter of fact, their chief figures were, for the most part, those of the national movement for independence, and unity was one of their first principles. But each government now seeks from unity its own predominance and sovereignty, power for its own personalities, and influence for its own sphere.

What of the League of Arab States? It is true that we attempted to achieve a kind of cooperation and grouping together by forming this League as a step toward Arab unity. But the attempt failed; the evils of partition remained, and the Arabs continued to meet and to disagree. More than that, they split into two rival camps, and the League was unable to remove the causes of rivalry—it was, indeed, itself one of the causes. This was because its Charter was based on the preservation of the status quo, which is based on partition and on the strengthening of the little states. The League itself has no kind of sovereignty and no operative executive power.

So we must return to unity. What is this unity, and how can we achieve i.? Can it be by the development and evolution of the League of Arab States? If that is possible to achieve, this is what we want. But unity necessitates that each state of the League give up some or even all of its independence and sovereignty, in order to form out of the total a joint, unified state endowed with sovereignty. And we have seen that the states of the League, or some of them at least, are watchful to preserve all of their independence and sovereignty, and to surrender nothing for the sake of unity. Thus it is impossible to reach real unity along the path of evolution in this League, and so it is with every similar plan that aims at the unity of all the Arab countries.

The achievement of unity in a partitioned fatherland can come in two ways: through consent and agreement, each state conceding some of its independence and joining together voluntarily to form one independent state from the sum; or through compulsion—by one of the parts dominating the others and joining them to it willy-nilly, playing the role of Prussia in the unification of Germany. For a long while Arab thinkers have been hoping that an Arab Prussia would arise and unify us, but so far it has not come about. The force necessary to impose and establish unity and to compel all to accept it does not now exist. Thus only the way of persuasion and agreement is open to us.

Some of the Arab states are jealous of their independence and little, if at all, really anxious for true unity. If we look at the Arab peoples, we find that some are not enthusiastic about unity or are unable to direct their governments toward it; others are more enthusiastic and anxious to realize it, and are at the same time more conscious of the Jewish danger, because of its proximity. These latter peoples find themselves faced with a choice: either to remain inactive in face of the danger until it overwhelms them one by one, and to suffer the fate of Palestine, or to wake up and unite so that they may ward it off. The instinct of self-preservation impels these peoples powerfully toward unity. . . .

MODERNIZATION

Unity alone is not enough. There must also be complete modernization in every aspect of Arab life and thought, including its external and domestic policies. The realization of unity is one aspect of this modernization which we are demanding. But even if we achieved unity, and the governmental setup remained the same, matters would be no different, and the same mistakes would be repeated. Now especially, when the Jews have obtained a foothold in the heart of our country and their danger has become concrete, the present level of government cannot remain as it is, for it cannot endow us with the power which we need: What lacks power cannot give it.

We do not mean by modernization of government a change in form, but one in its very essence and ends. Should the government be republican or monarchical? This is not important. There are in the world some republics and monarchies which are successful, some which are backward. What is important is the foundation: its effectiveness and the excellence of its ends.

The basic elements which must be present in a sound regime are (a) that it should be constitutional, not merely in name and form, but truly so; (b) that its organization and administration should be based on really scientific foundations; (c) that it should recruit its best resources; (d) that it should be progressive in its spirit and aims, living in its own age and marching in the caravan of progress; and (e) that it should be for the benefit of the whole people, not of a special class or specific element.

In the sphere of Arab foreign policy, the principal determining elements are usually three: Firstly, the stupidity about "the traditional friendship" between the Arabs and the British. This is in reality a continuation of the effects of foreign rule and the lack of self-respect which it produced. Great Britain does not base its relations with us on something called "traditional friendship," but exclusively on its interests, as every great nation does. Secondly, emotion. A specific policy may be adopted merely out of opposition to the British, or a line of action rejected simply because people are carried away by emotion. This also is a bitter and painful legacy of foreign rule. Thirdly, the influence and attraction of great world movements. The time has come to place our foreign policy on a basis of national interest alone.

Among the topics of the hour regarding our foreign policy is that of alliances. Some people believe that we should avert the Jewish danger by means of an alliance with a strong foreign power; but the lesson of Palestine can teach us something in this regard. Who was it who created the Jewish danger, brought it up in its lap, lent it wings, nourished and protected it until it grew strong? Who opened the doors of Palestine to the Jews? He who did all this may repeat it tomorrow and conspire against another part of our fatherland. Nor are the Americans and the Russians preferable in this respect to the British; we have seen the influence of the Jews with the former, and the support they have received from the latter. We cannot rely for protection on the foreigner, for the foreigner demands a prey. We must rely primarily on ourselves for the repulsion of the danger.

I do not mean a reliance on isolation, however. We live in an interconnected world of give and take, where we occupy a central position from which we cannot abdicate. We need a friend on whom we can count, and we must arrange to gain one through give and take. This does not mean that circumstances are favorable for an alliance. There was a time, before the disaster, when they were, but we lost the opportunity and must now wait. Our prestige has fallen since the fiasco in Palestine, and an alliance between the strong and the weak would be exploited by one side. It is unity today which is the need of the hour and the basis of success.

THE PEOPLE: THEIR RIGHTS AND DUTIES

This Arab people of good stock is the source of the strength we need. Unity and modernization of government are not enough unless they are based on care for the people and their endowment with the main elements of power, so that their power will be reflected in the state.

To determine the rights of the people is a vital matter for any nation, because this knowledge determines the kind of political and social regime which the nation wishes to realize. The political and social regime is nothing but the organization which enables the people to exercise its rights, and every political and social regime bears within it at least an implicit understanding of these rights.

Just as the political and social regime is based on a specific understanding of the rights of the people, so the rights of the people are based on a specific understanding of the nature of man and his end in life, and the nature of society and its relation to the individual. Is man free? Are men equal? Do material needs affect human dignity and prevent the exercise of freedom? Does the moral principle which applies to the individual also apply to society? Is it the duty of the individual to merge himself in the group and to sacrifice his personality and opinions in its interest? Or is it the duty of society to preserve the individual's freedom of opinion and to strengthen his independence? These are some of the questions on the answers to which depends our determination of the rights of the people.

The rights of the people are also related to the existence and survival of the nation. The connection becomes clear in times of crisis and danger. A people that does not know its own rights is a people incompetent to struggle for its existence. For example, the right of the people to care for its health and the health of its stock has a direct material bearing on its ability to make war. There is also the right of the people to education: How can people struggle for their nation when most of them do not know the meaning of the word? Are not the stories of heroes and martyrs among the strongest incentives to their zeal? The virtues on which the urge to struggle depends, such as duty, freedom and sacrifice, are all taken in through education and instruction. How can he who has not learned them in school or seen them exemplified in living people believe in them truly and deeply? The people are in great need of a "myth" to fill their consciousness and imagination, a myth of which they dream in times of peace and in times of trouble, because it gives their life meaning and gives them self-respect and freedom. If Arab nationalism has failed until now to spread to all classes of the Arab people and has remained a belief of only the educated class, it is because in its present state it is hard to understand except through advanced education: It is still formal.

This is a critical moment for us. There are before us today three logical possibilities. First, to be stricken with the disaster and to lose a part of our fatherland until we finally become homeless and our existence as a nation comes to an end—if we continue to exist at all—and we become backward human creatures, without honor or right, treated like the negroes of South Africa or America. Second, to abandon our Arab nationalism and our political freedom, to mingle our existence and personality in a wider and more general one, and to become a ghost without real existence; a republic or republics in a large communist state. Or third, to wake ourselves up and be ready to die for our freedom and independence; in other words to be ready to die for the sake of building our own world based on our ideas and dreams, on our history and sufferings. Every step we take bears within it our choice between these three possibilities. As Arab nationalists, we do not want our people to dissolve, to become a spectre without real existence. We believe in the people and that they should live their own life, not that of others, and build their own world. It is therefore essential that we know this world and work for its realization.

What are the rights of the people?

Freedom. The first and most sacred right is freedom in its widest sense: freedom from outside and internal oppression; freedom in its simple forms, such as freedom of belief, of speech and writing; in its political forms, such as the freedom to form political groups and to hold elections; in its material forms, such as freedom from poverty and want. Every situation and regime which conflicts with any of these freedoms must be removed.

To secure freedom from external imperialism, empty bluff and violent words are not enough. First of all, the cooperation of all classes of the nation must be secured—a cooperation unto death. Second, the utilization of all material and moral force, and the creation of an efficient working organization to accomplish this. To encourage the people to sacrifice and battle without providing a real organization or the necessary material means for battle creates bitterness and undermines popular morale.

As for the internal field, the freedoms of the people are necessary to preserve their morale and self-respect. No one must be imprisoned without cause, or other than legally. Censorship of the press must be abolished, and a stop put to the persecution of those holding free opinions and working for the truth. There must also end the era of government intervention in political freedom. It must not be that the survival of political parties is dependent upon the desires and whims of the governors. The government must not prevent a group from forming the political organization it wants, nor persecute a group for its political opinions, so long as it abides by the constitution of the country and does not harm public security.

Equality.   Equality, like freedom, has the most intimate connection with the people's dignity. Whoever does not feel freedom or equality between himself and others loses dignity. A people, the greater part of whom have lost the deep feeling of dignity and the confidence which extends from it, are a weak and incohesive people. Thus it is necessary to change formal equality before the law into real equality, not before law only, but in every aspect of life. People must feel social equality, equality in respect and treatment, and equality in opportunity for work and learning.

Work.   It is the right of every individual in society to work, and it is one of the duties of the government to find him suitable work. If he be a peasant, the government must provide a piece of land sufficient for him and his family and help him exploit it; and if he be an industrial worker, the government must find him suitable industrial employment.

Social Security.   If the government cannot find work for an individual, it must guarantee him an income sufficient for him and his family until he finds employment. As for the circumstances which prevent a person from working, either illness or disability or old age, the government must organize a fund to which the workers and owners of factories and the government contribute, and which shall be responsible for securing the life of such persons and their dependents.

Social Services.   The first and most important of the services which the government should provide is education, because of its bearing on every aspect, material and moral, of human life. It is up to the government to guarantee education to every member of the people, men and women, and to make it compulsory. As for secondary, vocational and university education, they should be free and open to all children equally. It is the right of the people also to have adequate health care and to have access to all means of medical prevention and cure from birth to death.

Rights of Women. In all these rights and duties, the woman must be equal to the man, so that she may share in the formation of this new Arab society.

Is it possible to postpone the demand for these rights? Perhaps someone may say that talk of the rights of the people at this moment is unrealistic; the crisis demands a strong government, and strong government is inconsistent with the wide freedoms which we are demanding. Social services require heavy expenditures which a government weak and loaded with duties of national defense cannot secure. In this there is some truth, but it conceals one big danger. If the people give up something of this freedom for the sake of a greater freedom, or some of their rights for the sake of a higher right, or some of their material needs for the sake of larger aims, and accept hardships today for the sake of security in the future—this is one thing. But the denial of their rights by force, or the failure to acknowledge those rights, is something else.

It is true that we need a strong government. Our situation is that of every nation that passes through a great crisis, no matter what stage of development or progress it has reached and no matter how great its democratic heritage. But the government which can be really strong is the government which is deeply rooted in the people, which recognizes their dignity and works for their security, believes in all their rights, and works with sincerity to achieve them in (their) full. To such a government the people give their confidence.

It is true that social services require much expenditure and that they are second in order of importance to the duty of national defense, but the people want a guarantee that these rights will be secured and respected. When they are satisfied of that, they will agree to their realization by stages, according to the country's circumstances and the needs of defense.

Therefore it is necessary that it be clearly stated in the constitution that the guarantee of these rights is one of the primary duties—and the most sacred—of the state. If popular rights are recognized in the constitution in this way, and there is mutual confidence between the government and the people, then the first step toward achieving these rights will have been realized.

Duties of the People. By placing the discussion of the duties of the people after the discussion of their rights, it is not meant that the latter are the more important. Both right and duty impose themselves on everyone without distinction: He who has rights has duty, and he upon whom there is no duty has no rights. The first duty of the people is to know that they have rights, to believe in them, and to act with determination to realize them. Then it is the duty of the people to love their fatherland with a real love, and to be ready to exert every effort for it.

NATIONAL EDUCATION

Experiments performed by a number of modern states have shown that any political regime which aims at the realization of speedy and total reforms and the creation of a new life, demands an educational system to spread its principles and beliefs among the people. Such an educational system cannot be realized in one institution such as the school, but must be implemented through the various institutions of the state. More than that, it must employ all the apparatus of the state. The army, youth organizations, parties, societies, clubs, unions; the family, the press, broadcasting are all means for the spread of the principles it proclaims.

Each one of the educational systems adopted by such modern states has been derived from a complete political and social philosophy. It is up to our thinkers at this moment to propound such a national philosophy on which an educational program may be built.

THE ECONOMIC SYSTEM

It is generally agreed that the Fertile Crescent is a country rich in natural resources; but in spite of this wealth, its production is small, and the standard of living of its inhabitants, who are few in number in proportion to its wealth, is extremely low. A complete program must be developed for the exploitation of its wealth, for otherwise the Arab people will be unable to establish a strong defense system, raise their standard of living, and perform the social services necessary to the uplifting of the people.

To execute this program, the following must be provided: (a) a well-established administrative body; (b) technical experts; and (c) sufficient funds.

Administrative Body. Large-scale construction projects must have one central, stable administrative body which does not change with the government and whose members are known for their ability and honesty and their remoteness from party and political matters. This body, or council, must derive its authority from special legislation passed for that purpose. It will be up to it to propound constructive plans, to organize them according to importance, and to implement them. The special advantage of this setup is that it can supervise operations over a long period of time and implement a coordinated line of action, whereas if the matter were left to governments, which are liable to change, each would make a new plan, or the government would be changed before anything constructive could be realized.

Technical Experts. We do not yet have in our country the class of technical experts needed to exploit its sources of wealth and raise its economic standards. Yet we cannot implement any constructive scheme without such experts. So we must act to create this class from among our youth. Until this is done, we shall have to appoint technical experts from abroad and use their services in implementing our projects. But to be sure that these experts are not instruments of any political aim, we must choose them from several nations, not from one nation, and preferably from nonimperialistic nations.

Funds. There is no doubt that constructive schemes need much money. This we can raise from (a) an increase in taxes; (b) internal loans; (c) increased governmental participation in the exploitation of resources; and (d) foreign loans.

(1) An increase in taxes will not be worthwhile unless a modern financial system is created, with graduated taxation. There are in particular two taxes that can increase the state's income without affecting its economy or standard of living; these are the income tax and the inheritance tax. As for the first, it exists in most of the Arab countries but produces far less than it could. The taxes demanded are small in comparison to the incomes from which they are deducted. By improving the system of collection and increasing the rate, it would be possible to increase the state's income significantly. As for the inheritance tax, it is nonexistent as yet, although it is applied in all advanced coun-

tries. There is no doubt that the introduction of an effective inheritance tax would increase the income of the state and help to create social stability.

(2) The government should encourage saving in all kinds of ways and should find the means of directing these savings into constructive projects. The best method is through internal loans. To encourage internal saving, imports must be severely limited, and the import of luxuries prohibited for a long time. A central government bank, a national currency, and the putting of the whole monetary system under the auspices of the government would simplify the process of national savings and internal loans considerably.

(3) An increase of the government's share in the resources exploited by foreigners, the most important of which is oil, and the allocation of this increase for constructive projects, is another means of acquiring funds and directing them to the proper ends.

(4) Foreign loans are a refuge which should be sought only with extreme caution. They should not be assumed except for productive schemes, so that they can be repaid in the future, and the absence of any political interests behind them should be assured. If these two conditions are not fulfilled, foreign loans will be a great danger to the country's existence.

In addition to constructive projects, the state, if it wishes to realize all its social aims, needs to direct its economy toward the following matters:

(a) Small farms should be created and their independence secured.

(b) As many industries as possible should be introduced into the country.

(c) The wealth of the country must be placed in the hands of the people as far as possible.

(d) In the event of the participation of foreign capital in the exploitation of the country's resources, attention must be paid to two basic conditions: that the proportion of national capital in any scheme be not less than 51 per cent of the total capital, and that the introduction of foreign capital not be permitted except after ascertaining the absence of political motives behind it. In cases where foreign concessions have been previously granted, the old agreements should be altered to conform to these two conditions.

The above principles in the spheres of defense, economy, education, instruction, health and social security, and all that they involve, must not remain mere theoretical principles, but work must immediately be begun to implement them. This implementation will no doubt proceed by stages, and the matters to be implemented in each stage must be determined precisely and in detail; the period necessary for their accomplishment must be estimated, and all this announced to the people as a constructive program to be carried out in that fixed time. And then all the physical and moral strength of the people must be brought to bear for the success of the program.

OPPOSITION

The call to Arab unity and modernization will meet opposition, open or hidden, from two sides: from the Jews and from the British.

As for the Jews, they have ambitions at our expense. They fear us, and they want to preserve the opportunity to implement the remaining parts of their program. It is important to them that no Arab force capable of recovering Palestine or of constituting a danger to their state be created in neighboring territories. They are afraid that this force will be created through unity and modernization. So we should pay attention to their intrigues and to their fifth column among us.

As for the British, it was they who partitioned us. They are satisfied with this and with the fact that we should be distracted from true unity by the weak and ineffective Arab League. Partition and backwardness and rivalry further their interests and aims. But they are a practical people, and mature in their politics. Their method is to accept the *fait accompli*. If we achieve unity, they will recognize it and cooperate with it.

Those who plunged us into the disaster will try to delay our progress toward unity and modernization, to strengthen the existing regimes, with their regionalism and partition and bad government, and to distract us from thinking about their crimes against us by waving in front of us loans and welfare projects. It is up to us to keep our eyes on the goal and our feet in its direction, allowing nothing to prevent us from reaching it.

CONCLUSION

In every great endeavor, and at every development in its course, there are three stages: the stage of faith, when the goal is believed in and dreamt of; the stage of thought, when the belief becomes an idea and a creed, and the idea becomes operative and demands realization; and the stage of work, when the idea emerges to the level of action. The major objectives of unity and modernization which we have been discussing have passed the first stage. This message is part of the second stage of thought. We are now at the threshold of the third stage, that of work and implementation.

After the disaster of Palestine, the Arabs stand at the crossroads. Change and development are inevitable. It is the duty of every thinker and worker to strive to prevent this development from taking the wrong direction and to guide it to the right one. If the Arabs have vitality and will, and men of maturity and wisdom and drive, they must act swiftly, without hesitation, before time runs out. If they do nothing and remain dreaming, it will be a sign of the fact that they have reached a stage of stagnation and disintegration which will not enable them to march with the times. This I do not believe is the case: I have a deep-rooted belief in the Arab nation and its great capacities.

The disaster has shaken us profoundly, and wounded us deeply, and opened the door to a great danger. If the shock wakes us up, brings us together, and impels us to a new life from which we can derive strength, the wound will heal, the danger will be averted, and Palestine will be recovered. And the misfortunes will be a blessing.

But if not, woe to the outcome.

5. The Arab-Israeli War: How it Began

BY CHARLES W. YOST

I

THE RECENT Six Day War in the Middle East grew out of the sterile confrontation to which the peoples of the region had committed themselves over the past twenty years. Both parties had frequently proclaimed their intention to go to war under certain circumstances. It seems unlikely, however, that any of them plotted and planned war for 1967. It seems more likely that they blundered into it.

Both sides might on many occasions have moved to end their confrontation by compromise, but this neither side showed the slightest willingness to do. The Israelis, feeling themselves beleaguered by fifty million hostile neighbors, acutely conscious of the recent fate of six million Jews in Europe, believed any significant concession would merely whet insatiable Arab appetites and start Israel down the slippery slope to extinction. The Arabs, looking upon the establishment of Israel as the latest in a series of imperialist occupations of their homeland, of which the presence of a million Palestine refugees was a constant reminder, found it emotionally and politically impossible to accept Israel as a permanent fact of life or to forego harassing it and conspiring against it.

This common intolerance and mutual harassment had brought on war in 1956. It is pertinent to note that, in his *Diary of the*

Reprinted by special permission from *Foreign Affairs*, Vol. 46, No. 2 (1968), pp. 304–320. Copyright is held by the Council on Foreign Relations, Inc., New York. This article was written when Ambassador Yost was Senior Research Fellow at the Council on Foreign Relations, before he returned to public service as the United States representative to the United Nations. It is an expression of his personal views.

Sinai Campaign published in 1966, General Dayan wrote that the three major objects of that campaign from the Israeli point of view were "freedom of shipping for Israeli vessels in the Gulf of Aqaba; an end to the Feydayen terrorism; and a neutralization of the threat of attack on Israel by the joint Egypt-Syria-Jordan military command." With slight variations, these were the issues that brought on war again eleven years later.

II

Through the latter part of 1966, so-called "El Fatah" incursions into Israel, sometimes carried out by Palestinian refugees, sometimes moving through Jordan or Lebanon, but for the most part mounted in Syria, grew in numbers and intensity. In October two particularly serious incidents in which several Israelis were killed caused Israel to appeal, as it often had before, to the UN Security Council. However, a relatively mild resolution proposed by six of its members, calling on Syria to take stronger measures to prevent such incidents, was, as on previous occasions, vetoed by the Soviet Union in the supposed interests of its Arab friends.

A new and more radical Syrian government had come to power by *coup d'état* earlier that year. It enthusiastically supported the claims and machinations of the so-called Palestine Liberation Army which mobilized and inflamed the refugees and carried out some of the raids. The Syrian Prime Minister declared in a press conference in October: "We are not sentinels over Israel's security and are not the leash that restrains the revolution of the displaced and persecuted Palestinian people." Early in November, moreover, a "defense agreement" was concluded between Syria and the United Arab Republic, involving a joint military command and other measures of "coordination and integration" between the two countries.

It had long been Israel's practice, whenever it judged that Arab raids had reached an intolerable level, to retaliate massively. It did so on November 13 against Es Samu in Jordan where, according to UN observers, eighteen Jordanian soldiers and civilians were killed and fifty-four wounded. The fact that moderate Jordan rather than extremist Syria was the target of retaliation seemed ill-judged to most of the world, but was excused by Israel on grounds that there had recently been thir-

teen acts of sabotage committed on Israeli territory from Jordanian bases. Be that as it may, the consequences, in and out of
the region, of this disproportionate and misplaced retaliation
were considerable.

The UN Security Council, by a vote of fourteen to one ab-
stention (New Zealand), censured Israel "for this large-scale military action in violation of the UN Charter and of the General
Armistice Agreement between Israel and Jordan," and emphasized to Israel "that actions of military reprisal cannot be tolerated and that if they are repeated, the Security Council will
have to consider further and more effective steps as envisaged in
the Charter to ensure against the repetition of such acts."

Perhaps more important in its effect on subsequent events,
the Jordanian Prime Minister in a press conference charged the
UAR and Syria, which had been denouncing King Hussein's
government, with failing to bear their share of the confrontation
against Israel. He accused the UAR of failing to supply promised
air cover and urged that Egyptian troops be withdrawn from
Yemen and sent to Sinai on Israel's southern flank. The UAR
Commander-in-Chief of the Arab Command replied publicly
with similar recriminations, but the charges must have struck
home to a regime so peculiarly sensitive to face and prestige.

From January to April 1967, the Syrian-Israeli frontier was
agitated by an ascending series of clashes ranging from potshots
at tractors plowing to exchanges of fire between tanks, artillery
and aircraft. These clashes were primarily caused by the refusal
of both sides, at different times, to permit the UN Mixed Armistice Commission even to mark the armistice line at disputed
points and the insistence of both parties on farming and patrol-
ling disputed areas.

On April 7, 1967, one of these clashes escalated into what in
retrospect appears to have been the curtain-raiser to the Six
Day War. An exchange of fire between tanks gave rise to intervention first by Israeli and then by Syrian aircraft. This led by
the end of the day to the appearance of Israeli planes over the
outskirts of Damascus and to the shooting down of six Syrian
planes.

The most serious aspect of this affair was that for the second
time in six months Arab forces suffered a very bloody nose at
the hands of Israel without the "unified Arab Command" in
Cairo lifting a finger. President Nasser, who aspired to be leader
of the Arab world and who had formally established a military

apparatus at least for the containment of Israel, had sat quietly by while first his rival and then his ally had been conspicuously and roundly chastised. Neither the rival nor the ally hesitated publicly and privately to point out this dereliction. Nasser could of course reply, and perhaps did, that the El Fatah raids were excessive and untimely, that the Arabs must not be provoked into fighting before they were ready, and that the UN Emergency Force standing between his army and Israel blocked its coming to the rescue of his Arab allies. These excuses, however genuine and well-founded they may have been, were quite clearly wearing thin in the eyes of the Arabs after the April 7 affair. Those knowing President Nasser's temperament could hardly have felt any assurance that he would hold aloof a third time.

III

Yet the respite was brief. A month later, on May 11, the UN Secretary General declared at a press luncheon:

> I must say that, in the last few days, the El Fatah type of incidents have increased, unfortunately. Those incidents have occurred in the vicinity of the Lebanese and Syrian lines and are very deplorable, especially because, by their nature, they seem to indicate that the individuals who committed them have had more specialized training than has usually been evidenced in El Fatah incidents in the past. That type of activity is insidious, is contrary to the letter and spirit of the Armistice Agreements and menaces the peace of the area.

On the same day, May 11, Israeli Prime Minister Eshkol was saying in a public speech in Tel Aviv that his government regarded this wave of sabotage and infiltration gravely. "In view of the fourteen incidents of the past month alone," he said, "we may have to adopt measures no less drastic than those of April 7." In a radio interview two days later, he declared: "It is quite clear to the Israeli government that the focal point of the terrorists is in Syria, but we have laid down the principle that we shall choose the time, the place and the means to counter the aggressor." Eshkol went on to say that he intended to make Israeli defense forces powerful enough to deter aggression, to repel it, and to strike a decisive blow within enemy territory.

It would appear that a senior Israeli military officer also made a public comment on or about May 12, the exact text of which it has not been possible to find, but which, whether or not correctly understood, significantly contributed to Arab apprehensions. President Nasser referred to it in a speech on May 23, saying, "On May 12 a very important statement was made. . . . The statement said that the Israeli commanders have announced they would carry out military operations against Syria in order to occupy Damascus and overthrow the Syrian government."

These Israeli exercises in verbal escalation provoked far more serious repercussions than they were no doubt intended to do and, far from sobering the exuberant Syrians and their allies, raised probably genuine fears in Damascus, Cairo and Moscow to a level which brought about the fatal decisions and events of the following week. Indeed the Secretary General, disturbed that his statement of May 11 on the El Fatah raids might stimulate Israeli military action, announced on May 13 that that statement "cannot be interpreted as condoning resort to force by any party."

On the same day, the Syrian Foreign Ministry summoned ambassadors from countries which were members of the Security Council and told them that a plot against Syria was being concocted by "imperialist and Zionist quarters." The Ministry described "the prearranged aggressive role Israel is preparing to play within the framework of this plot" which, it declared, "began with the abortive April 7 aggression" and was revealed by "statements of Zionist Chief of Staff Rabin."

Another component in the accumulating mass of explosive elements was mentioned by President Nasser in the famous speech of June 9 in which he offered to resign. He declared at that time:

> We all know how the crisis began in the first half of last May. There was a plan by the enemy to invade Syria, and the statements by his politicians and his military commanders declared that frankly. The evidence was ample. The sources of our Syrian brothers and our own reliable information were categorical on this. Even our friends in the Soviet Union told the parliamentary delegation which was visiting Moscow last month that there was a calculated intention.

There seems little doubt that the Soviets did transmit warnings along these lines to the Syrian and Egyptian governments. Eastern European sources have justified these warnings on the grounds that the Israeli government itself advised Soviet representatives that, if the El Fatah raids continued, it would take drastic punitive action against Syria. This was, of course, no more than they were saying publicly, but the Israelis may have hoped that direct notice to the Soviets might induce them to persuade their Syrian friends to stop the raids.

Indeed there is evidence that Israeli officials were at this time disseminating their warnings rather widely. *The New York Times* correspondent in Tel Aviv, James Feron, reported on May 12:

> Some Israeli leaders have decided that the use of force against Syria may be the only way to curtail increasing terrorism. Any such Israeli reaction to continued infiltration would be of considerable strength but of short duration and limited in area. This has become apparent in talks with highly qualified and informed Israelis who have spoken in recent days against a background of mounting border violence.

However, these private warnings, coupled with the provocative pronouncements by Eshkol and others, would seem to have backfired by convincing the Soviets, Syrians and Egyptians that a major retaliatory strike against Syria was fixed and imminent. In a speech to the United Nations on June 19, Premier Kosygin declared: "In those days, the Soviet government, and I believe others too, began receiving information to the effect that the Israeli government had timed for the end of May a swift strike at Syria in order to crush it and then carry the fighting over into the territory of the United Arab Republic."

On the other hand, the Israelis state that on May 12 the Director General of the Israeli Foreign Ministry, on May 19 the Foreign Minister, and on May 29 the Prime Minister, each invited Soviet Ambassador Chuvakhin, who had accused Israel of massing forces on the Syrian border, to visit the area and see for himself, but that in each case he refused to do so. Furthermore, in his report to the Security Council on May 19, Secretary General Thant had referred to allegations about troop movements and concentrations on the Israeli side of the Syrian border, but concluded: "Reports from UNTSO observers have confirmed the absence of troop concentrations and significant troop movements on both sides of the line." US representatives in Israel at the time also saw no evidence of the alleged troop concentrations. Moreover, on May 15, the Israeli government, observing that Egyptian forces were crossing the Suez Canal into Sinai in considerable strength, instructed its representative at the UN, Ambassador Rafael, to request the Secretary General to assure Cairo on its behalf that it had no intention of initiating any military action. The Secretary General immediately complied with the request.

Nevertheless, it should also be noted that in the May 19 report referred to above the Secretary General remarked:

> Intemperate and bellicose utterances . . . are unfortunately more or less routine on both sides of the lines in the Near East. In recent weeks, however, reports emanating from Israel have attributed to some high officials in that state statements so threatening as to be particularly inflammatory in the sense that they could only heighten emotions and thereby increase tensions on the other side of the lines.

Press accounts of these statements also seemed so inflammatory to US State Department officials that they expressed concern to Israeli authorities.

The situation in mid-May was therefore the following: The aggravation of the El Fatah raids originating in Syria would seem to have brought the Israeli government to the decision, announced publicly in general terms by responsible officials and confided in more specific terms to journalists and perhaps to foreign diplomats including the Soviets, to retaliate sharply and substantially if the raids continued. There is no solid evidence, however, that they intended anything so massive as a drive on Damascus. Nevertheless, this prospect had in both Moscow and Cairo an impact which the Israelis probably did not fully anticipate or correctly assess.

The Soviets had particular reason for not wishing to see the Syrian government humiliated, defeated and perhaps overthrown. The increasingly radical Syrian governments which had assumed power during the previous eighteen months, though they were far from being communist (the Communist Party was and still is banned), had come to rely more and more on Soviet military and economic aid, to permit increasing numbers of Soviet advisers to be stationed in the country, and all in all to offer the most promising field for Soviet penetration and influence to be found anywhere in the Middle East. The particular Soviet concern for Syria was dramatically shown at the end of the Six Day War when the prospect that Israeli forces might then drive to Damascus caused the Soviets suddenly to join in a demand, which they had up to that point stubbornly opposed, that UN observers police the ceasefire. It may well have been that by mid-May they genuinely feared massive Israeli retaliation which might topple the Syrian government, and that they therefore spurred the Egyptians on to vigorous counteraction, the full repercussions of which they did not foresee. In fear of "losing" Syria, they overreached themselves and urged the Arabs to take action which resulted in much more disastrous losses for their side.

Nasser, for his part, saddled with responsibility for the unified Arab Command which was supposed to protect all the Arab states from Israel, jealous of his already damaged position as would-be leader of the Arab world, having been ridiculed by his allies and rivals for his failure to stir at the time of the Es Samu and April 7 affairs, categorically assured by Syrians and Soviets that Israel was about to attack Syria, for which public statements by Israeli leaders seemed to give warrant, may well have felt that he could no longer stand aside without fatal loss to his prestige and authority.

Israeli public statements between May 11 and 13, therefore, regardless of how they may have been intended, may well have been the spark that ignited the long-accumulating tinder. On May 14, the Egyptian Chief of Staff flew to Damascus and, according to the Syrian official spokesman, discussed with Syrian officials "important matters concerning joint defense against Israel." On May 16, the Cairo radio announced that the United Arab Republic had declared a state of emergency for its armed forces because of "the tense situation on the Syrian-Israeli armistice lines, Israel's large military concentrations, its threats and its open demands for an attack on Damascus." On that same day, according to the Cairo radio, Foreign Minister Riad received the Soviet, Syrian and Iraqi Ambassadors in separate audiences, and Minister of War Badran received the Soviet Ambassador accompanied by his military attaché. The fourth act of the tragedy was about to begin.

At 2200 hours local time that evening, May 16, General Rikhye, Commander of the UN Emergency Force in Sinai, was handed the following letter from General Fawzi, Chief of Staff of the Egyptian armed forces:

> To your information, I gave my instructions to all UAR Armed Forces to be ready for action against Israel the moment it might carry out an aggressive action against any Arab country. Due to these instructions, our troops are already concentrated in Sinai on our eastern borders. For the sake of complete security of all UN troops which install OP's along our border, I request that you issue your orders to withdraw all these troops immediately. I have given my instructions to our commander of the eastern zone concerning this subject. Inform back the fulfillment of this request.

Secretary General Thant received General Rikhye's report at 1730 hours New York time that same evening, and an hour and a quarter later (at 1845 hours), at his urgent request, received the UAR representative to the UN, Ambassador El Kony, to whom he presented the following views:

> (1) General Rikhye could not take orders from anyone but the Secretary General.
> (2) If General Fawzi was asking for a temporary withdrawal of UNEF from the line this was unacceptable, because UNEF "cannot be asked to stand aside in order to enable the two sides to resume fighting".
> (3) If General Fawzi was asking for a general withdrawal of UNEF from Gaza and Sinai, the request should have been addressed by the UAR government to the Secretary General.
> (4) The UAR government had the right "to withdraw the consent which it gave in 1956 for the stationing of UNEF on the territory of the UAR".
> (5) If the UAR government addressed such a request to the Secretary General, he "would order the withdrawal of all UNEF troops from Gaza and Sinai, simultaneously informing the General Assembly of what he was doing and why".
> (6) A UAR request for a temporary withdrawal of UNEF from the line would be considered by the Secretary General

"as tantamount to a request for the complete withdrawal of
UNEF from Gaza and Sinai, since this would reduce UNEF
to ineffectiveness."

Early the next morning, May 17, Egyptian troops began to
move into and beyond some UNEF positions along the armistice
line. At noon GMT that day, General Fawzi conveyed to General Rikhye a request that the Yugoslav detachments of UNEF
(which occupied the main portion of the Sinai armistice line) be
withdrawn within twenty-four hours, adding, however, that
UNEF Commander might take "twenty-four hours or so" to
withdraw the UNEF detachment from Sharm el Sheikh (which
commands the Straits of Tiran but is far distant from the armistice line).

Space permits only the briefest summary of the events which
followed in rapid succession. On the afternoon of May 17 in
New York, the Secretary General consulted with representatives
of countries providing contingents to UNEF (Brazil, Canada,
Denmark, India, Yugoslavia, Norway and Sweden). According to
his subsequent report to the General Assembly, two of them
expressed serious doubts about complying with "a peremptory
request" for withdrawal and suggested reference to the Assembly, whereas two others maintained the United Arab Republic
had the right to request withdrawal at any time, and that request would have to be respected regardless of what the Assembly
might say. Later that afternoon the Secretary General presented
to the UAR Representative an aide-memoire reiterating the
points he had made the previous evening and concluding that, if
Egyptian troop movements up to the line were maintained, he
would "have no choice but to order the withdrawal of UNEF
from Gaza and Sinai as expeditiously as possible."

The next morning, May 18, Foreign Minister Riad informed
representatives in Cairo of nations with troops in UNEF that
"UNEF had terminated its tasks in the UAR and in the Gaza
Strip and must depart from the above territory forthwith." At
noon New York time, the Secretary General received a formal
request from the Egyptian Foreign Minister to the same effect.
That afternoon he met with the UNEF Advisory Committee,
where he encountered the same divergence of views as at the
meeting the previous day, but where the members finally acquiesced in his belief that, in the absence of any proposal to
convene the Assembly, he "had no alternative other than to
comply with the UAR's demand." He did so that same evening

by a message to Foreign Minister Riad and by instructions to the UNEF Commander.

The immediate reaction of Israel also deserves mention. On the morning of May 18, the Secretary General received the Israeli Representative, who presented his government's view "that the UNEF withdrawal should not be achieved by a unilateral UAR request alone and asserting Israel's right to a voice in the matter." When, however, the Secretary General raised the possibility of stationing UNEF on the Israeli side of the line, the Representative replied that this would be "entirely unacceptable to his government," thus reaffirming the position in regard to UNEF which Israel had taken ever since the establishment of the Force in 1956.

The intent and rationale of the decisions taken in Cairo during those critical days in mid-May are still shrouded in obscurity, while those taken in response in New York are still bedeviled by controversy. What seems reasonably clear is that, as so often in the prelude to war, the control of events slipped from everyone's hands, and limited decisions hastily taken had sweeping consequences no one desired.

No doubt the Egyptian government decided sometime between May 13 and 16 that, in view of its assessment of the threat to Syria, it must move some of its armed forces up to the Sinai armistice line in order either to deter Israel or to come to Syria's assistance if deterrence failed. Reliable Arab sources maintain that:

> (1) The UAR government had as late as May 16 no intention to request the withdrawal of UNEF; (2) it desired merely the removal of several UNEF posts along the Sinai line which would inhibit the contemplated redeployment of Egyptian forces; (3) it saw no incompatibility between this redeployment and the continuance of UNEF in its other positions *including* Sharm el Sheikh; (4) the implementation of the redeployment was left to the military leaders who failed to consult the civilian authorities, including the President, about either the scope of the redeployment they intended to carry out or the demand addressed to General Rikhye on May 16; (5) when the Secretary General confronted the UAR government with the naked choice between reversing the redeployment, to which its military leaders had publicly committed it, and requesting the with-

drawal of UNEF, it felt obliged to choose the latter; (6) furthermore, when it unexpectedly found its forces once more in possession of Sharm el Sheikh, it felt it could not fail to exercise, as it had from 1954 to 1956, its "belligerent right" to forbid the passage of Israeli vessels and "war material" through the Strait.

As to the decisions taken in New York, the UN authorities have maintained that:

(1) The indicated redeployment of UAR forces *was* incompatible with the continuance of UNEF, since it deprived UNEF of its essential function as a buffer between Egyptian and Israeli forces; (2) UNEF had hitherto been able to function effectively only because of an informal UAR agreement that its forces would be held 2000 meters back from the armistice line in Sinai (Israeli forces patrolled right up to the line); (3) once confrontation between the two forces was reestablished, conflict between them was, in the existing state of tension, very probable, and UNEF units scattered among them would be wholly unable to prevent it; (4) two of the troop-contributing states, India and Yugoslavia, had made clear their intention to withdraw their contingents whatever the Secretary General decided, and others were likely to follow suit, with the probable result that UNEF would disintegrate in a disordered and ignominious fashion; (5) the UAR government had the legal right both to move its troops where it wished in its own territory and to insist on the withdrawal of UNEF at any time, just as Israel had the right to refuse it admittance; (6) if the UN contested that right, peacekeeping would become "occupation" and other governments would not in the future admit UN peacekeeping forces to their territories; (7) a reference of the Egyptian request to the Security Council or the Assembly would merely have produced, as subsequent events proved, a prolonged debate during which UNEF would have either disintegrated or been helplessly involved in war.

No conclusive judgment can be pronounced on these two lines of argument. What does seem apparent is that both the UAR and the UN, like Israel a few days before, acted precipitately and with little resort to diplomacy. If the Egyptian account is accurate, temporization on the part of the UN might conceivably have led to some modification in UAR military dispositions which had not been authorized by its own government. It seems very doubtful, however, that in the prevailing state of emotion, dispositions once taken, even without full authorization, could have been reversed. By May 17 the crisis had already acquired a momentum which seemed inexorably to sweep all parties toward and over the brink.

Nevertheless, we can hardly fail to note parenthetically the serious shortcomings of a peacekeeping procedure whereby, as in this case, a UN force can be ordered out of a critical area at the very moment when the danger of war, which it is stationed there to prevent, becomes most acute. The fault, however, lies not with the UN but with the great powers whose rivalries ever since 1945 have blocked the application of the enforcement procedures provided by Chapter VII of the Charter, under which a UN military force could be, for example, interposed between two prospective combatants regardless of the objections of either or both. In the absence of great-power willingness to permit the Security Council to apply compulsion of that type, the UN has been obliged for many years to rely on a much more fragile form of peacekeeping where under a UN force, whatever may have been the arrangements under which it entered the territory of a state, can in practice remain there only so long as its government consents. Such was the situation in Sinai before May 16.

V

To return to the concluding events of that month: President Nasser on May 22 announced his intention to reinstitute the blockade against Israel in the Strait of Tiran. This was the final fatal step. Whether, in whatever advance planning did take place, it was contemplated that Sharm el Sheikh would be reoccupied and the blockade reimposed, or whether the military exceeded their orders and one step led to another in dizzy and unpremeditated succession, is not certain. There can hardly have been any doubt at any time, however, about the grave risks involved in restoring the blockade. It seems probable that the Russians were consulted about the redeployment of Egyptian forces and perhaps the subsequent request for the withdrawal of UNEF. Reliable Soviet sources have claimed, however, that they were not informed in advance of the reimposition of the blockade, implying that they would have objected had they known.

In any case, the reaction in Israel and elsewhere was immediate. On May 23 Prime Minister Eshkol declared in Parliament: "The Knesset knows that any interference with freedom of shipping in the Gulf and in the Straits constitutes a flagrant violation of international law. . . . It constitutes an act of aggression against Israel." On the same day, President Johnson declared in Washington: "The United States considers the Gulf to be an international waterway and feels that a blockade of Israeli shipping is illegal and potentially disastrous to the cause of peace. The right of free, innocent passage of the international waterway is a vital interest of the international community."

Unavailing efforts were made to persuade President Nasser to revoke, suspend or moderate the blockade but, the action once taken, he did not feel politically free to reverse it, even had he so desired. Equally unavailing were efforts made to forestall a unilateral Israeli response by organizing a group of maritime powers to issue a declaration reaffirming the right of free passage through the Strait and presumably, if passage continued to be denied, to take effective multilateral action to reopen it. Very few maritime powers showed any interest in participating in a confrontation with Nasser and the Arab world, nor did members of the US Congress who were consulted manifest any enthusiasm for risking another conflict in addition to Viet Nam. The exploratory dialogue between the US and the UAR, however, continued up until the outbreak of war; as late as June 4, an agreement was announced that UAR Vice President Mohieddin would visit Washington within the next few days, and Vice President Humphrey would later return the visit.

In the meantime, however, the crisis had assumed proportions far beyond an argument over maritime rights. The advance of the Egyptian forces to the armistice line, the ouster of UNEF, and the reimposition of the blockade were received with enormous enthusiasm throughout the Arab world. All the pent-up emotions which had been accumulating for twenty years, and which were continually refreshed by armed clashes, inflammatory propaganda and the presence of a million refugees, erupted in paeans of triumph from Baghdad to Marrakesh.

Nasser's prestige, which had been falling for some time, rebounded overnight. Expressions of solidarity poured in. Iraq, Algeria, Kuwait and Sudan promised troops. In a startling rever-

sal of long-standing hostility, King Hussein of Jordan appeared
in Cairo on May 30 and concluded a mutual defense pact with
the UAR which a few days later was extended to Iraq. The
armed forces of Egypt, Jordan and Syria were more and more
concentrated around Israel's frontiers, and there seemed every
likelihood they would soon be reinforced by other Arab states.

This Arab euphoria, moreover, led also to verbal exaltation
which could not have been without its effect on Israel. For instance, the Syrian Chief of State, Dr. Al-Atasi, said in a speech
on May 22:

> Arab Palestinians who were expelled from their homeland
> now realize that armed struggle is the only way to regain
> their homeland. . . . The state of gangs [Israel] will not
> benefit by blaming others for inciting fedayeen activities.
> The cause of these activities is the aggressive Zionist exis-
> tence itself. Let Israel know that the Palestinian fedayeen
> activities will continue until they liberate their homeland.

In a speech addressed on June 1 to troops departing for the
"frontlines" in Jordan, President Arif of Iraq declared: "It was
treason and politics that brought about the creation of Israel.
Brethren and sons, this is the day of the battle to revenge your
martyred brethren who fell in 1948. It is the day to wash away
the stigma. We shall, God willing, meet in Tel Aviv and Haifa."

Yet even at this late date, despite all these verbal pyrotech-
nics and concentrations of force, there does not seem to have
been any intention in Cairo to initiate a war. In reply to a question by British MP Christopher Mayhew interviewing Nasser on
June 2, "And if they do not attack, will you let them alone?" the
President said, "Yes, we will leave them alone. We have no intention of attacking Israel." Similar assurances were repeatedly
given the United States by the highest Egyptian authorities.

There seems little reason to doubt them. Nasser had up to
that point achieved a spectacular victory. Arab unity seemed
closer to reality than it had ever been. Israel had suffered a serious setback in prestige, power and security. The mood in Cairo
was an odd mixture of exaltation and fatalism, exaltation over
what had been achieved, fatalism before the inescapable realization that Israel might prefer war to a political defeat of this
magnitude. There was a clear understanding that Israel might
attack at any time, no overweening confidence as to the out-

come, but a determination to defend, whatever the costs, the intoxicating gains which had been won. Whether this determination might have been overcome by negotiation over a period of time, for example by the visits of the Vice Presidents between Cairo and Washington, cannot be known for certain. In view of the support which the Soviet Union was providing its Arab friends, this seems unlikely.

In any case, the Israeli government obviously decided that it could not wait. All the factors which had induced it to go to war in 1956—a multiplication of raids into its territory, a substantial buildup of Egyptian and other hostile forces on its borders, the blockade of the Strait—had reappeared in even more aggravated form. Efforts of the UN and the US to relieve them by international action seemed unavailing. On May 30, Foreign Minister Eban said in a press conference in Jerusalem:

> Less than two weeks ago a change took place in the security balance in this region. The two most spectacular signs of this change were the illegal attempt to blockade the international passageway at the Strait of Tiran and the Gulf of Aqaba and the abnormal buildup of Egyptian troops on the Israeli frontier. The government and people of Israel intend to insure that these two changes are rescinded, and in the shortest possible time.

Six days later Israel struck with this end in view; twelve days later it had achieved its objective, and much more beside.

VI

It is not difficult in retrospect to identify the ventures and responses on both sides which over preceding months and weeks, compounding the hatreds which had been allowed to fester for twenty years, led almost inevitably to war.

First were the El Fatah raids, organized from Syria, involving the "Palestine Liberation Army," subjecting peaceful Israeli villages to recurrent jeopardy and terror, building up through the months from October to May, unpunished and, because of the Soviet veto, even uncensured by the UN Security Council. Remembering the history of the previous twelve years, it is difficult to see how any Arab or Soviet leader could have failed to realize that this murderous campaign would eventually bring forth a murderous response.

Second were the Israeli "massive retaliations" at Es Samu in November and in the air over Syria and Jordan in April, designed to punish and deter, but disproportionate in size, visibility and political impact, causing also the death of innocent people, condemned by the Security Council in the strongest terms in November, as similar disproportionate retaliations had been repeatedly condemned in the past. It is difficult to see how any Israeli leader could have failed to foresee that such repeated massive reprisals must eventually place the leader of the Arab coalition in a position where he would have to respond.

Third were the public and private statements by high Israeli authorities in mid-May which indicated the probability of even more drastic retaliation against Syria in the near future if the El Fatah raids continued. These statements, even though no doubt designed to deter the raids, almost certainly convinced the Syrian and UAR governments that such retaliation was definitely projected, and may well have persuaded them and the Soviets that the Syrian regime itself was in jeopardy.

Fourth was the decision by the UAR government, presumably encouraged by Soviets and Syrians, to move its armed forces up to the Sinai armistice line, thus reestablishing at a moment of acute tension the direct Egyptian-Israeli military confrontation which had been the major immediate cause of the 1956 war. This redeployment of Egyptian forces was under the circumstances critical whether or not it was originally intended to be accompanied by a demand that UNEF be withdrawn.

Fifth and finally was the decision of the UAR government, finding itself whether by intent or accident once more in command of the Strait of Tiran, to exercise its "belligerent rights" by reimposing the blockade, thus reproducing the third of the elements which had brought on the 1956 war. The likely consequences of this step were indeed foreseen but, in the climate of fear, passion and "national honor" which by then prevailed, were faced with fatalism and desperation.

It remains, however, the thesis of this article that no government plotted or intended to start a war in the Middle East in the spring of 1967. Syria mounted raids against Israel as it had been doing for years, but more intensively and effectively; Israel retaliated disproportionately as it often had before, but in more rapid succession and in a way that seemed to threaten the existence of the Arab government; Nasser felt his responsibilities and ambitions in the Arab world did not permit him again to stand aside in such a contingency and took hasty and ill-calculated measures which made major conflict, already probable, practically certain. All concerned overreacted outrageously. Yet there is no evidence—quite the contrary—that either Nasser or the Israeli government or even the Syrian government wanted and sought a major war at this juncture.

Of course the fault of all of them, and indeed of the great powers and the United Nations, lay not so much in their actions or omissions in May and June 1967 as in their failure, indeed their common blunt refusal, to face the facts of life in the Middle East during the twenty years before that date.

There will be no peace there, no security for its inhabitants or for the great powers involved there, until the Arabs recognize that Israel, however unjust its creation appears to them, is a fact of life, that it has as much right to exist as they have, that to threaten and harrass it, to arouse among their people false hopes about its dissolution, is actually as much a threat to Arab as to Israeli security, that the two equally have more to gain than lose by peaceful coexistence. On the other hand, there will also be no peace in the Middle East until the Israelis recognize that the condition of their long-term survival as a nation is reconciliation with their much more numerous Arab neighbors, that survival cannot indefinitely be preserved by military force or territorial expansion, that displays of inflexibility and arrogance are not effective modes of international intercourse, and that in particular there will be no security for Israel until, whatever the political and financial cost, the million or more Palestine refugees have been compensated, resettled and restored to dignity.

6. The Moment of Truth:
Toward a Middle East Dialogue

BY CECIL A. HOURANI

THIS ESSAY *is addressed to the educated classes in the Arab countries: to those who still participate actively in the political, social and intellectual life of their countries, and to those who have been excluded forcibly or by their own free will. To all, I trust, it will have a message of hope. Destructive as much of my argument is, my aim is positive and constructive. On the understanding of our errors in the past may be built the new society of the future. I have no recrimination against states or individuals. Time and history will provide their own judgment. The moment is one for solidarity and mutual tolerance, and above all for a free discussion among ourselves. In a climate of honest self-criticism and free expression, those truths may emerge which can lead us from our present disarray to a new vision of ourselves and the world we would like to build.*

At this moment when the destiny of the Arab nation is being decided, it is the duty of every Arab thinker to witness to the truth as he sees it, without fear and without dissimulation. For too long has the field of publicity and expression been left in the hands of professional demagogues, blackmailers and semi-educated fanatics. Our silence on the one hand, their vociferation on the other, have led the Arab nation not merely to disaster, but to the brink of disintegration.

The primary condition of a redressment of this situation is to

Reprinted from *Encounter*, Vol. XXIX, No. 5 (London, 1967), pp. 3–14; by permission of the editor. This article was originally published in Arabic, in the Beirut daily, *an-Nahar*.

see things as they are, in all their brutal clarity; then to take action to change them in the light of the ideals and objectives we set ourselves. A victory over ourselves is more important than a physical defeat on the battlefield. Governments, states, regimes, frontiers, are all transient things, subject to fluctuations and fortune. What is important is that a people should survive, not as a mere agglomeration of individuals, but as a living, creative force in history. We can only survive by acting positively ourselves, not by reacting negatively to what others may do, or seek to do, to us.

History has given to the Arab nation in the twentieth century a unique chance to return to the community of living creative forces in the world: a conjunction of international affairs which made possible the independence of all our territories; and the discovery of enormous wealth which with almost no effort on our part gives us the means to accomplish all we need to refashion our society and to raise it to prosperity and progress.

This unique chance we are now in danger of losing. Our sovereign and political liberty gives us the means to bring about our own destruction more easily than we can construct our future. Our very freedom implies dangers greater than existed when we were dependent. No one will now save us from the consequences of our own mistakes and follies, except ourselves. The fact that we inhabit certain territories in this world of strategic importance or material wealth is not a sufficient guarantee of our safety or survival. We can be driven from these territories or lose control of these riches. We can commit suicide as a nation. And history will then judge us as a people who did not know how to use the chances which had been offered them, and condemn us to the fate we shall have deserved.

The most dramatic, but not the only, example of our weakness, and of our failure to recognize both our weakness and our strength, lies in our relationship with the Zionist movement and with the state of Israel. We have been able neither to come to terms with them, nor to destroy them, nor even to contain them.

As a result of our failure to decide what position to adopt, or to take the necessary measures of self-defense, we have allowed Israel to usurp the whole of Palestine and to occupy the most important strategic positions in the Near East.

While it is true that the Zionist movement did not develop wholly in relationship to the Arab world but also in an international climate outside our control, nevertheless, since the establishment of Israel in 1948, against our will, our struggle against that state has taken place within the framework of the international community and largely within the United Nations Organization. The frontiers established in 1948 as a result of the ceasefire were not wholly advantageous to Israel, because they set a territorial limit to Zionism.

The Arab objective, therefore, if we had thought clearly and calmly, should have been the *containment of Israel* within its boundaries as limited by *de facto* arrangements arrived at after two wars we had lost, rather than its conquest and destruction.

That we were unable to distinguish clearly between containment and conquest was due primarily to a psychological weakness in us: *that which we do not like we pretend does not exist.* Because we refused to recognize a situation which was distasteful to us, we were unable to define our own relationship to that situation, or to distinguish between what we would have liked ideally and what we were capable of achieving in practice.

As a policy of containment, the moves of the UAR until June 5, 1967, could have been successful. But it had implicit dangers, the greatest of which was that in the minds of those who were practicing it, it could be at any moment transformed successfully into a policy of conquest. By this confusion in their own minds about their aims, and by their misjudgment of their own strength, the Arab governments brought about the disaster of June 5. They also lost the battle of public opinion. By foolish and irresponsible statements, they allowed themselves to appear as the aggressor instead of the victims. While they talked of war and conquest, Israel prepared it.

For years Israel had cultivated the image of herself as a small defenseless state surrounded by heavily armed neighbors bent on destroying her. While in fact we were trying to contain her, some of our spokesmen, for home consumption, were exaggerating our military capacities and promising our people conquests. This gave Israel a pretext for arming to the teeth. The balance of power which Israel was trying to maintain was not one between Israel and Egypt, but between Israel and all her neighbors combined. The higher technical skills of the Israelis, and the integration of her armed forces into her civilian population, combined with supplies of arms qualitatively at least equal to those of the Arabs, in fact gave her an advantage which we should have foreseen.

The greatest defeat, however, was not that on the battlefield or in propaganda and public opinion, but that which our governments inflicted on their own people: countless lives lost uselessly; a great new exodus of refugees from their homes; economic losses and misery not yet calculable; a new despair and a new humiliation.

What greater proof of our capacities for self-deception and moral cowardice than that Ahmed Shouqairi still sits with our responsible leaders, or the claims of one Arab Head of State that we were not defeated because we did not use our full strength? Does not all this make one suspect that the "final victory" of which some talk would be nothing less than a *coup de grâce* delivered to the Arabs?

This is indeed our moment of truth: but some of our leaders cannot make up their minds whether they want to be *torero* or bull!

Another consequence of our unwillingness to accept as real what we do not like is that *when reality catches up with us, it is always too late.* At every debacle we regret that we did not accept a situation which no longer exists. In 1948 we regretted that we had not accepted the 1947 UN plea for partition. In May 1967 we were trying to go back to pre-Suez. Today we would be happy—and are actually demanding the UN—to go back to things as they were before June 5. From every defeat we reap a new regret and a new nostalgia, but never seem to learn a new lesson.

Yet every human situation—except annihilation—contains within it the seeds of its final reversal. Take for example the creation of Israel in 1948. It is true that in relation to our right to the total possession of Palestine this represented an Arab loss; but there were also gains to us in what happened in 1948. We won independence for part of Palestine in place of total dependence on the Mandatory Power before. Under the Mandatory Regime, Jewish immigration and the expansion of Zionism could have continued in the whole of Palestine: After 1948 Zionism was confined to a tiny territory which was strategically weak and scarcely viable economically. Had we consolidated the independence we had gained, we could have contained Israel, and with it world Zionism, for fifty years, after which Israel itself would have ceased to be a threat to us, and become just another Levantine state, part Jewish, part Arab, but overwhelmingly Oriental.

388   *The Middle East Reader*

Instead of which, twenty years later, we have not only lost
what remained of Arab Palestine; we have also helped Zionism
to leap forward yet another stage in its dynamic progress toward
full Jewish nationalism. The enormous material and moral
support which the state of Israel received from Jewish citizens
of other countries in the recent crisis shows that what extremist
Zionists have always hoped, and moderate Jews always feared, is
happening: namely the polarization of Jewish nationalism
around the state of Israel, and the progressive alienation of Jews
from the societies in which they have been assimilated or at
least accepted. The potential population of Israel is thus not the
unborn generations in that country alone, but Jews from everywhere in the world.

Shall we in one, or ten, or twenty years, seek another "victory" like the one we have just gained, and lose the other side of
the Jordan, the fertile plains of Jaulan and Hauran in Syria, and
the Litani and Hasbani Rivers in Lebanon? And shall we still
have Ahmed Shouqairi with us to consecrate the final victory of
stupidity over intelligence, of fanaticism over common sense, of
dishonesty over truth?

The answer lies with us. What we do in reaction to the events
of the last few weeks will determine the future of our people
not for ten or twenty years, but for centuries. This time there
can be no second chance. Either we continue on the same road
that has led us to our present state, defeats, retreats, debacles,
and the rapid transformation of our settled urban and peasant
populations in the Near East into a new nomadism; or we take
positive measures to stop the process of disintegration, to limit
the collapse, and to transform our military defeat into a political
and a psychological victory.

What are these positive measures, and what are the psychological victories we may hope to gain?

We must first of all ask ourselves the question, what does victory mean in terms of our actual situation and our real strength?
Does it mean victory over others—Israel, or the Anglo-
Americans, or Western imperialism or international indifference, or all together? Does it mean we can impose our
terms on others, draw frontiers as we want, dictate the conditions on which we agree to live with the rest of the world, and
make others see us as we would like to see ourselves?

Our first effort must surely be to win a victory over ourselves:
over defeatism on the one hand, extremism on the other. These

two dangers are in fact intimately linked together. The real defeatists are not those who look facts in the face, accept them, and try to remedy the situation which brought them about, but those who refuse to do this, who deny facts, and who are thus preparing for new defeats.

The extremists are those who argue that our concepts were correct, but that we did not implement them seriously, and that therefore we should continue along the same path, but use more violent methods.

If, however, our concepts were wrong, the use of the same methods even in a more violent form can only lead us to another defeat. It is therefore essential to re-think our basic ideas in terms of *reality,* rather than of wishes. What could we realistically hope to achieve?

OURSELVES AND ISRAEL

I have pointed out the disastrous effects of not having formulated clearly in our minds the distinction between the containment and the conquest of Israel. The principal reason why we did not make this distinction, and imagined that we could at any moment switch from one to the other, was our failure to appreciate our own strength and weakness relative to Israel and the rest of the world. We must therefore examine this question honestly and fearlessly.

(1) The first basic truth we must face is that the Arabs as a whole do not yet have the scientific and technological skills, nor the general level of education among the masses, which make possible the waging of large-scale modern warfare. This is not merely a deduction from recent events; it is a statistically demonstrable fact. We do not have the educational facilities or standards at home, nor enough students abroad, to provide the General Staff, the officers and the men capable of using modern weapons and modern methods. Nor do we have civilian populations sufficiently disciplined and educated to collaborate with the armed forces and the civil authorities to the degree which modern warfare demands.

By not recognizing this fact, our military leaders tried to fight the wrong kind of war. It is a classical accusation made against General Staffs that they use methods appropriate to the previous war. Our military thinkers and planners were trying to fight the next one. As a result, our soldiers were not only unable to use the modern weapons that were placed in their hands; they were actually handicapped by them. Trapped in the tanks they could not maneuver, relying on the air support that never came, they fell easy victims to their enemies. And the material they had to abandon will be incorporated into the army of Israel, so that in fact we have helped to arm our opponents.

(2) The second truth is that the rate of technological and scientific advance is so rapid in the modern world that even if in twenty years we can catch up with the military standards of today, we shall still be outdistanced by the Israelis, whose technological and scientific skills are the product not only of their own schools and research institutes, but of Jewish—and non-Jewish—talent throughout the world.

(3) The third truth is that even if we had been able to defeat Israel militarily, we would have been deprived of the fruit of that victory by some of the Great Powers, who would have intervened to save Israel's political existence.

(4) The fourth truth is that in twenty years, or even less, even if we succeed in bringing our scientific and technological skills to a point where we could wage a modern war, warfare itself will have taken on quite another aspect. The possession of nuclear weapons by smaller powers—including the Arab states and Israel—will offer a choice either of mutual annihilation or of international control; and in neither case shall we be able to get our own way on our own terms.

It is evident, therefore, that if we think primarily in terms of military power we shall be making a fundamental error. This does not mean that we should disarm. It does mean that we must reappraise our own strength and find a new relationship between military power on the one hand, and our political, economic and geopolitical assets on the other.

What are the conclusions we should draw from these facts about our relationship to Israel? We must first of all realize that the immediate consequence of the present war has been to modify the strategic situation in favor of Israel, which has now reached more natural frontiers than she had before, both for defense and attack. If, therefore, we try to rectify this situation by military force, we shall be in an even weaker position than we were in 1948, in 1956, or before June 5, 1967. And not only are we in a weaker position to attack; we are also less able to defend ourselves.

The conclusions to be drawn are two: In the first place, the resort to military force as a basic element in Arab policy toward Israel is an error. In the second place, our best chance of containing Israel lies in international pressures either within or outside the United Nations. These international pressures, of whatever nature, have, however, a price. What is the price we are prepared to pay, is a question I leave to later on.

If the balance of military power has now been seriously upset in favor of Israel, there are other aspects of the balance of power which remain in our favor. Some of these have always existed, though we have not used them properly; others spring from the defeat of June 5 itself, for in all situations lie the seeds of their reversal. In the first place, Israel's military victory was a limited one—limited by those territorial, geopolitical factors which make the physical conquest of the Arab world impossible. Military occupation is one thing, permanent conquest and domination quite another. In the second place, Israel's military victory was not a political one: It has not led her any nearer to that peace on her terms which she would like, or any nearer to the negotiating table with the Arabs. It has, on the contrary, brought against her a coalition of international pressures which never existed before, and liquidated the fruit of twenty years' work to win friends in Africa and Asia.

If military force is not the Arabs' best card, neither is it Israel's. By a military action far out of proportion to the immediate situation it had to face, Israel has brought into play other factors which in the long run may modify the situation within Israel in ways which their present leaders had never envisaged.

Firstly, let us suppose that international pressures do not succeed in forcing Israel to withdraw to her pre-June 5 frontiers. By incorporating the Gaza Strip and the West Bank into her territory, the proportion of Arabs to Jews in Israel will be radically changed. The higher birth rate of the Arabs will give them equality in numbers, then a majority, in a few years. And as the proportion of "Arab" Jews to European Jews is also changing, the total population of Palestine will eventually, and before long, take on an Oriental character. As we acquire some of their virtues and they acquire some of our defects, the gap between Arab and Jew will narrow, and in fifty years could almost disappear.

Secondly, it is clear that the Zionist movement as a whole, and the Israeli leaders in particular, must now face a dramatic dilemma as a result of their blitzkrieg of June 5. This dilemma is the following: If the Israeli government accepts the Arabs within the territories she controls as full Israeli citizens, with equal civil and political rights, the concept of Israel which has hitherto been incorporated into her laws will have to be changed. Israel will no longer be a Jewish state, in which, as it does now, full citizenship requires not only membership of the Jewish religion, but Jewish ancestry. It will become a Jewish-Arab state in which nationality will be a function of residence or citizenship. Israel, in other words, as she has been since 1948, will no longer exist, and Palestine, with Arabs and Jews living together, will have been restored.

If, on the other hand, the Israeli authorities refuse to accept the Arabs as full citizens with equal civil and political rights, she will have on her hands a large population which she will be unable to liquidate or to govern.

It is the perception of this dilemma which is now leading some of the Israeli leaders to force the hands of the others and to try to have it both ways: to keep the territories they have conquered, and try to reduce the Arab population in numbers by encouraging their exodus across the Jordan. It is not difficult to foresee that the next step will be to encourage a new wave of Jewish immigration into Israel, to replace as many Arabs as possible in as short a period as possible.

If the extremists within Israel succeed in forcing the hand of the more reasonable, and getting the world Zionist movement to follow, then they will in fact make forever impossible their dream of an Arab-Jewish *rapprochement*. For the way in which the Arabs are ultimately going to judge the advantages of peace or war in their relations with Israel will depend on the way Israel treats the Arabs within its borders. If there is a genuine attempt to live together with the Arabs on terms of complete equality and within the same juro-political framework, the way to an eventual conciliation between Israel, or Palestine, and the rest of the Arab world will have been opened. But if the Arabs are excluded from full citizenship and reduced to the status of a colonized, dependent population, no peace will ever be possible, either inside or outside Palestine.

It is not difficult to draw logical conclusions about what Arab policy should be in the light of this situation, and of this dilemma which faces Israel. If the goals of Arab policy should be, as I have suggested, (1) the containment of Israel within whatever boundaries we can get international pressure to agree to and to stablize, (2) the gradual transformation of Israel from a European-dominated "exclusive" Jewish state into a predominantly Oriental Arab-Jewish state, then the problem of whether or not to make a formal "peace" becomes a secondary one. It will no longer be a question of principle on which no Arab leader can compromise; it becomes a question of expediency and efficacy. But there is no reason why we should accept the Israeli argument that peace can only be obtained by direct negotiations with them. Since the United Nations, or some other international group, will have to be a party to any attempt to stabilize frontiers, all our efforts to obtain a settlement can be canalized through that organization. What we cannot afford is to have no policy at all: to be unable to support the conditions of war, and incapable of profiting from the advantages of peace.

The formulation of a consistent Arab policy toward Israel within the framework of the international community is thus perfectly possible and not difficult if we define both our aims and our methods. I have stated what these aims could be. As for the methods, a few are obvious, although others may also be found, and the way these methods are used will be up to the Arab negotiators to determine.

(1) We should do all we can to secure the return to the frontiers as they were before June 5, 1967, not indeed as a final settlement, but as a first step toward an arrangement in which the questions of frontiers, the rights of the refugees to return, and compensation will find a solution. The means we adopt to bring pressure on other powers to accept our point of view should be realistic, however; that is to say they should be capable of success, and they should not do us more harm than they can bring us benefits.

It is unlikely that we shall be able to achieve our objective without making some concessions. What these concessions might be, it is up to those governments who would have to make them to decide. But we should hope and insist that these governments would not act unilaterally and thereby prejudice the outcome of any compromise they may accept.

(2) In the event of our being unable to accept the terms on which a withdrawal from occupied territories is offered us, our second line of policy should be based on the principle that the forcible occupation of a territory involves a responsibility toward the inhabitants of that territory. We should not only bring the maximum international pressure to prevent Israel from ex-

pelling Arabs and expropriating their possessions in favor of new Jewish immigrants; we should bring the same international pressure on Israel to accord full political and civil rights to her Arab population, as well as the right of the Arab refugees to return. If all Palestine is reunited, there is no reason why any Palestinian should be prevented from returning to his country. Not only the refugee masses now living in camps (old and new) should return; in addition all those Palestinians who have been able to find work and prosperity in the Arab countries should go back and help to rebuild the Palestine Arab community, and play their proper role in reestablishing the rights of the Arabs in their own country. The returning Arabs will not be a fifth column; one cannot be a fifth column in one's own country. The relations which the Palestinian Arabs within Palestine are then able or willing to establish with the Jews will be their own responsibility. The other Arab countries must help them by all means in their struggle to restore their rights and their human dignity; but the primary responsibility for their future will lie with the Palestinians themselves.

There remains one more question perhaps more important than any I have yet discussed, because in the long run it will determine our relations with the Jews and their relations with us. *The fate and the peace of the Near East should not be left to the initiative of Israel alone.* Even if Israel opts for the closed, exclusive type of society, and rejects the Arabs as fellow citizens, *we should not do the same.* If there is no room in Israeli society for the Arabs, we should show that there is room in Arab society for the Jews. This has always been the pattern of our society, and the greatest victory of militant Zionism would be to get us to abandon it and to adopt their concept of the state. For in their hearts they know that a closed, exclusive, fanatic Israel can never coexist with an open, liberal and tolerant Arab society. There are Jews, however, in Israel and throughout the world who also reject the narrow vision and fanatical aims of some of their leaders, and who can be our allies in combating the introduction of racial nationalism into the Near East. Our greatest victory will be the day when the Jews in Palestine will prefer to live in an Arab society rather than in an Israeli one. It is up to us to make that possible.

OURSELVES AND THE WORLD

I have suggested that we formulate and try to implement a

consistent Arab policy toward Israel within the framework of the international community, which means in effect the United Nations. But it is not only in the problem of Israel that the international community can be of service to us. In many of our foreign relations, our numbers and our potential strength make the UN a suitable instrument of action. This implies, however, a correct appraisal of our strength and our weakness in the world.

Our greatest mistake in the past has been to overestimate our actual and to underestimate our potential strength. From this combination of misjudgments spring almost all the errors of our international behavior. We have formulated and pursued policies we could not implement; we have neglected to practice policies which might have succeeded.

Nothing illustrates this truth better than the international policies we have adopted toward Israel. All our attempts to find military solutions have ended in failure, and led to subsequent political and diplomatic failures. On the other hand, our diplomatic, political and economic efforts have often met with success until we lost our advantages by pushing them too far, or not realizing what these advantages were.

For example, the St. James's Conference in London in 1939 between the British government and some of the Arab governments led to the White Paper, which was in our favor, but which we rejected. In 1948 we secured the evacuation of British civil and military authorities from Palestine, but we did not take the necessary steps to take their place. In 1948 again, after our first unsuccessful war, we could have turned our military defeat into a limited political victory and confined Israel to an insignificant territory. Instead, we preferred our theoretical rights and principles to our real advantages. By 1967—and this was the basic cause of Israel's aggression on June 5—we had succeeded in building up an economic situation in Jordan and most of the other Arab countries to a point where foreign investors were beginning to have serious doubts about putting money in Israel if that meant exclusion from Arab markets. We had also isolated Israel diplomatically in wide areas of international life. We lost all these advantages by failing to analyze the situation correctly. We did not perceive that the disparity between Israel's growing economic and diplomatic difficulties and her military strength would inevitably tempt her to restore the balance by a generalized rather than a localized military action. Instead of removing all possible pretexts for such an action, we provided the pretexts they had difficulty in inventing themselves.

It is not only in relation to Israel that we have shown no understanding of our real strength and real weakness in international life. Our relations with the Great Powers and with the international community as a whole show the same pattern of unrealism. Our governments have behaved as if international goodwill and friendship are taps to be turned on and off as we please, and as if the definition of satisfactory relationships with other powers is a one-sided operation for us to undertake. We make agreements and break them because we have changed our minds. We make threats we do not intend or cannot carry out. We take actions when they can no longer be effective.

I shall limit myself to one example, though I could give many. Arab oil, and the very considerable cash holdings which it generates for governments and private individuals, gives us the potential ability not only to solve most of our internal problems of poverty and underdevelopment; it could also play an important role in giving us influence in the economic and financial life of Europe, with a consequent political influence. In order to be effective, however, there are two necessary conditions to be fulfilled. We must define our long-term and short-term aims in terms of the possible; and we must coordinate the policies of the oil-producing countries, as well as the relations between them and the non-oil-producing countries.

The present crisis is an example of our failure to fulfill either of these two conditions. Before war broke out, we took no effective steps to use our bargaining power on the diplomatic and political scene to prevent a war. When it did break out, we took only half-hearted measures which could not succeed because they harm us more than they harm Israel, and do not constitute an effective means of pressure on any of the Great Powers. And not only has our action in this field been a failure; *it may also bring about a new situation in which our future ability to use our present potential strength will be seriously limited, if not abolished altogether.*

This danger can already be detected. Western Europe is now taking measures to reduce its dependence on Arab oil. Though it may not succeed in achieving complete independence for many years, it can certainly prevent a sudden paralysis of its industrial and civil life; and it can increase its ability to resist a long privation to a point where it will do more harm to the Arab economies than it does to its own.

The ineffectiveness and partial paralysis of Arab policy in this one field can be matched by similar failures in others. The prestige and the image of the Arabs in the world have suffered collectively and individually, and much of what we say or do is not taken seriously. The first step to remedying this situation must therefore be to take *ourselves* seriously: to introduce common sense, consistency and honesty into our relations with one another, and our relations with the outside world.

In the long run, there are certain fundamental facts about international life which we must not ignore. Whatever natural advantages and potential assets we may possess in terms of numbers, territory, natural resources, our actual position and influence are a function of our ability to exploit them. We cannot expect to exert more influence than we have real power. Policies based on bluff or on self-deceit must sooner or later collapse. The facts of life count more than the illusions of power.

There are two kinds of international relationships to which we must pay special attention: our relations with the United Nations Organization and with the Great Powers.

Ever since 1947, we have been unable to make up our minds about what our attitude to the UN should be. We resist its recommendations when they do not please us; we invoke them when it suits our purpose. We try to act on our own when we think we are winning; we come to the UN when we fear we are losing. One result of this is that in our minds the international organization is associated with failures and setbacks, and rarely with successes.

Of course we are not alone in this vacillating attitude: Israel and other governments act in exactly the same way. The question we must ask ourselves, however, is how far do we *need* the organization, or any form of international system or support.

In answering this question, there are two facts to be noted and reflected on. All the Great Powers—except China—feel the need to belong to the UN even though they could exist quite well outside it. The second fact is that within the United Nations the Arab states could enjoy considerable influence and power, both because of their numbers and because of their membership [in] both the Asian and the African group of states.

From these two facts an important deduction can be made: If we need the protection and support which the international organization can provide, we must be prepared to compromise, for every human community involves that. It is therefore important to understand what compromise really is. It is not, as some think, the sacrifice of the unessential in order to retain the essential; this is merely tactics. True compromise lies in giving up something which you may regard as your natural right in exchange for some greater advantage, not necessarily to you, but to the community to which you belong. If states renounce force as an instrument of national policy, this may favor the weak at the expense of the strong; but the strong may have a greater interest in world peace than in national aggrandizement. To accept compromise is thus not a disgraceful sign of weakness; there is no absolute strength or power. The only disgrace is to try to reject by force what we are later obliged to accept because of weakness.

If, then, we wish to remain within the international organization because we need it, we should logically do everything we can to strengthen it and turn it into an effective instrument. We cannot expect to use it uniquely as an instrument of our national policies and our particular interests. We may sometimes have to accept decisions which we do not like. But the long-term benefits from strengthening the organization may be greater than the short-term advantages of weakening it.

Our attitude to the UN, therefore, both on a matter of general policy, and on particular issues, should be based not always on what appear to be our own immediate interests, but on the degree to which we may hope to benefit, in the short and long term, from our membership of it, and on the need we find to use its collective strength on any particular issue. This does not preclude us, however, from working within the international organization to secure for ourselves the maximum influence and strength which, when we need it, we shall then be able to exert.

The realism we should cultivate in our relations with the international organization we should also cultivate in our relations with the Great Powers. Here again, we have been in the past neither realistic nor consistent. We try to play them off against each other, but we get angry when they do not support us. We try to switch from one side to another in the hope of getting the best terms from them all, but we risk permanently alienating one side and thus becoming dependent on the other. We proclaim neutrality but do not practice it. We talk of our freedom of maneuver, but limit its effectiveness to a point where it may disappear. We would like some or all of the Great Powers to adopt our policies and see things from our own perspective, and forget that we are small and they are great. Our interests are often on one side, our sentiments on another, and thus we vacillate schizophrenically from one policy to another, and succeed in none. As a result, our relations with the individual Great Powers are ones either of unfriendliness or of dependence. And we are always at the mercy of their coming to terms with one another at our expense.

To establish our relations with the Great Powers on sound and positive bases which will give us the maximum advantage both from their quarrels and their agreements should be a major objective of our foreign policies. This implies an ability to grasp the realities of international life and to adopt common policies consistently and honestly, which we have not hitherto possessed.

THE ARAB LEAGUE

Our most urgent need is therefore to put our own house in order if we are to play an effective role in the world. There are two levels at which this must be done: The relationships between the Arab states must be put on sounder and more realistic bases, and each of them must make more serious efforts to solve their own particular problems.

The League of Arab States was established in 1944 with the principal aim of bringing into existence a joint foreign policy which would enable them to deal with the problem of Palestine as it existed at that time. By failing to prevent the establishment of Israel in 1948, the authority and effectiveness of the League suffered a serious setback. As in every crisis ever since, after a temporary solidarity in the face of war, the relations between the Arab states deteriorated as the responsibility for failure was thrown from one capital to another. By crystalizing their disagreements and by providing a forum in which they could attack each other, the League gradually became not the instrument of a common foreign policy nor of a genuine *rapprochement* between its members, but quite the contrary.

With the decay and discredit of the Arab League, further attempts to unify and coordinate foreign policy have been made in summit meetings of heads of states and occasional meetings of foreign ministers, but none of these have succeeded where the League failed; on the contrary, these failures have been even more spectacular than those of the League, insofar as they have crystallized and made public not merely divergencies of views, but also divergencies of personality and temperament between Arab leaders. The depersonalization of Arab foreign policy is thus a pressing need.

The basic condition for a realistic Arab foreign policy is the recognition that not all Arab states have the same geographic and economic conditions, or the same interests. Before they can agree on what are their *common* interests, they must decide where they diverge. If there is no recognition of each one's legitimate interests, then at every crisis there is the risk that there will be no real coordination of effort, and that mutual recriminations will follow the inevitable failure of whatever joint policy they may attempt to apply. In fact, the Arab states have based their relations not on a realistic appraisal of the interests and the capacities of each one, but on an emotional solidarity which disappears once the immediate occasion is over.

If, however, there is to be a new attempt to establish a serious Arab foreign policy—and the problem of Palestine makes this now more urgent than ever—the Arab League could provide a better instrument than either summit meetings or meetings of foreign ministers. There is now a real political justification for reviving the League as the framework within which collective decisions can be made and which could help to restore the relationships of the Arab States with the outside world. For while individual Arab leaders have always been anxious to obtain the credit for success, none of them are anxious to acquire the discredit of failure. The League would be a much more acceptable target of criticism, but it would have also to be endowed with the real ability to take decisons, for responsibility implies power, just as power imposes responsibility. The depersonalization of inter-Arab relations, the reestablishment of a collective responsibility, and effective direction in the office and the personality of a dynamic secretary general could do much to restore the image and revive the influence of the Arab states in the world.

But this image and this influence can never be better or greater than their real as opposed to their imaginary or their merely potential strength. To revive the Arab League merely as an instrument of publicity and propaganda would be a waste of energy and of money. The important—the urgent—need is now to create the conditions—*through concrete institutions, not resolutions or recommendations*—through which effective power and strength may be generated.

The greatest weakness of the Arab League ever since its establishment has been the failure of its members to agree among themselves except at the lowest common denominator. This has its roots in their inability or their unwillingness to recognize different priorities and different degrees of involvement in particular problems. They have either set their aims too high or too low. To do everything or to do nothing is not a practical choice in politics or any other sphere of life. What is important is to begin to take those steps which will in the end enable you to reach your final objective. The Arab League, faced with the difficulties of achieving its final goal—the political unification of the Arab world—never did anything seriously at all.

The first stage, therefore, in setting the Arab League into motion again is for it to call a meeting similar to the Alexandria Conference of 1944 to reconsider its methods and to modify its Constitution. High on the agenda of this meeting would be the question of *responsibilities*. Since not all Arab states are in a position to take effective action on all matters of common interest, a practical division of responsibilities should be made. The special circumstances of each country and of each region should be taken into account. Effectiveness rather than gestures of solidarity should be the only criterion.

From this point another and more important matter must be taken up: namely, the question of modifying existing political structures within the Arab world. When the United Arab Republic was formed, the Arab League was pushed into the background because it seemed to be unnecessary: If the United Arab Republic offered the focal point of a united Arab world, of what use was the League?

Circumstances have now changed, not only because of recent events, but also because for some time it has been evident that the UAR itself has not been anxious to undertake the political and administrative obligations of an expanding union. There is no reason why the entire responsibility and onus of political modifications in the relations of other Arab states to each other should rest upon the UAR, nor is it probable that the government of the UAR would now place obstacles in the way of any new arrangment which, by strengthening the Arab capacity to resist Israeli expansion in the east, would thereby also strengthen Egypt's position in the south.

If the territories occupied by Israel in the recent war are not recovered, it is obvious that some new Arab political structure east of the River Jordan will have to be created. If a vacuum of power is allowed to exist, the rest of Jordan will be overrun in a few years. To prevent this, steps will have to be taken to create a new political framework within which King Hussein may continue to fulfill the role which destiny has given him.

What that new political framework could be I do not intend to discuss now. What we must hope for is that the Arab regimes will be able to transcend their suspicions and jealousies of each other, to end their meaningless quarrels, and to take positive steps to halt the rapid degeneration which now threatens the very foundations of our national existence.

THE ARAB REGIMES

The greatest source of weakness in the last twenty years has been the introduction into Arab political life of methods of government and of ideological slogans which are unsuitable and irrelevant to the actual conditions of the Arab countries. These methods and slogans have not only poisoned the relations between different Arab countries; they have also blinded some of their regimes to their real problems and their real interests.

The military regimes, for example, which have installed themselves in certain Arab countries since 1949 had their only justification in terms of the necessity of meeting external dangers. They have now given a public demonstration of their incompetence in war. What reason do we have to suppose that they are likely to be more successful in economic planning and development, in education, foreign affairs, finance or culture?

Among the most harmful consequences of military regimes to the political, economic and social structure of the countries they have tried to govern is the exclusion from public life which they have deliberately or indirectly effected of vast numbers of educated and skilled citizens, who now languish idle either in their own countries, or in exile in others. This fact represents an enormous loss in terms of an investment in human resources going back at least forty years. The resulting poverty of technicians is felt not only in civilian affairs, but even in the armies themselves, so that it can reasonably be argued that the military regimes, instead of strengthening their armed forces, have in reality weakened them.

The introduction of ideological slogans and political and economic doctrines which derive from contents radically different from those of the Arab countries has done even more harm to these countries both in their relations with each other and in their internal affairs. They have divided the Arab world into camps on issues which are not really relevant or along lines which do not make sense.

First of all, that between the so-called "progressive" or "revolutionary" and the "reactionary" or "conservative" regimes. It is interesting and significant that all those regimes which call themselves "progressive" are, in fact, military. What has led some of our leaders to adopt the language and imitate the style of movements and regimes with which they really have nothing in common? There are two basic reasons: the desire to find foreign allies and friends, and the need to seek popular support. Since most of the Arab countries have only recently emerged from Western domination or colonization, it was natural for leaders seeking an easy popularity among the masses to align themselves with the enemies of the West in foreign policy, and to promise them economic and social welfare through "land reforms," "nationalization," and other elements of the program of certain socialist countries.

Except in Egypt, however, the "progressive" military regimes have not only failed to implement socialist programs; they have actually lowered gross national products and seriously damaged the economic welfare of some sections of the population without improving that of others. Nor have they been able, or willing, to take those social and juridical measures which would have given a progressive character to their regimes, at least on paper. Not one of the "progressive" regimes, for example, has abolished polygamy. On the contrary, some of them have been trying to reintroduce a conservative interpretation of Islam into public life. And certain of the regimes which have been classified as "conservative" or "reactionary" have done much for their populations in terms of economic progress and social legislation.

Secondly, the attempt to identify Arab nationalism with the "progressive" as opposed to the "reactionary" regimes has led to a senseless and dangerous conflict between some of the Arab governments, just as it has inflamed and divided public opinion all over the Arab world. We must reject and resist the claim that any one regime or party or leader has a monopoly on Arab nationalism, and refuse to accept that differences of opinion or of interests provide an adequate basis for classifying regimes or individuals as genuine nationalists or traitors. The poisonous campaigns waged by the radio stations and the press in certain

countries should be condemned, ignored or ridiculed, and every
pressure should be brought on those governments which utilize
or permit them to put an end to this scandal of the Arab world.

THE REAL PROBLEM

The introduction into Arab life of political and social doctrines which are not relevant to it at its present stage not only
weakens the Arab countries by dividing them on irrelevant
issues; it also diverts their attention from their real problems.
The only valid distinction at this time between the Arab countries lies in the degree of their economic and social development, and in the resources they possess to promote their progress. The real difference is between the less and the more
underdeveloped, and between the rich and the poor. There is no
reason why we should anticipate the problems of more highly
developed societies before we have reached the stage where
these problems become real and demand solutions. There is no
reason why we should adopt the language and the political
forms of social and economic conflicts which are not relevant to
our societies.

The most immediate and urgent problems which face nearly
all the Arab countries are those involved in establishing the minimum conditions on which a modern society may eventually be
built. While the nature of that society, and the social and economic content of the measures to be taken to bring it into existence must certainly be studied and discussed, and will certainly
provide eventually the grounds for divergent opinions and political movements, we have not yet reached that stage. There is a
wide area for action where interests are common and basic
enough for us to ignore or at least to postpone questions which
may divide us at a moment when we need to be united.

For some of the underdeveloped countries of the world, the
necessity of finding an outside source for the capital investments
and the technical skills they lack forces them to an involvement
in the ideological conflict and divisions of the more developed
world. No such necessity exists for the Arab world, which has all
the material and many of the human resources that it needs.
There is sufficient capital and liquidity to make us independent
of outside financial help, and to promote our own economic and
social progress, provided we use our resources intelligently and
take a broad view of both the existing and the future needs of

the Arab world as a whole. We have vast territories, enormous natural resources, and vital strategic positions. What we need is to exploit them in terms of today's and tomorrow's needs. Countries which are rich today may not be always; others which are poor today possess potentialities which may one day make them rich. The total human and natural resources of the Arab world must be studied and then exploited in the light of a general plan, a moving idea.

It is this great responsibility which now faces the educated classes in the Arab countries. They have a unique chance which is not given to many of the educated classes of more developed countries and societies, weighed down as they often are by traditions and already established patterns of life which do not give much scope to originality or to individual initiative. It is our good fortune to be born at a time when not only great tasks await us, but when the possibility of action is also present.

Instead of the sterile and irrelevant discussions, the bitter divisions and mutual suspicions which dominate our political and intellectual life, we should try to establish among ourselves an understanding, an agreement on principles, a mutual confidence which will make possible the action which must now be undertaken if the Arab world is to be saved from a rapid decline.

7. A Soldier Reflects on Peace Hopes

BY MOSHE DAYAN

AT THIS COURSE, people learn how to make war. But on this occasion, if I may, I should like to discuss the other side of the picture—the question of peace between us and the Arabs, or more precisely, the problematics of peace. In a brief address, obviously, it is impossible to treat the subject exhaustively, and I, at all events, am not capable of doing so. I shall therefore merely try to cast some light on the subject.

I have chosen Dr. Arthur Ruppin as one personality who casts light on the subject. He came to Israel for the first time in 1907, was expelled "forever" by the Turkish Governor Jemal Pasha, and came back to the country after the English conquest, this time really forever.

Two unique elements are involved if we wish to present the problem through the eyes of Dr. Ruppin. The first is the period in which he lived. From 1920 to 1942, Dr. Ruppin was one of the architects of the Zionist venture, the "father of Zionist settlement." This was the interwar era, a concentrated period of twenty successive years, whose distance from us lends itself to evaluation and review. At the same time, the period is not quite so distant that its links with the present day are severed. From this standpoint of distance on the one hand, and links on the other, it might perhaps be proper to pinpoint 1936 as the focal year of the period. This was the year of the riots, which raged thirty years before the Six Day War.

Reprinted from the *Jerusalem Post Weekly*, Monday, Sept. 30, 1968 (Jerusalem 1968), by permission of the author. The address was delivered to a graduating class at the Army's Staff and Command College in the summer of 1968. It has since been incorporated with other writings by Moshe Dayan in a book entitled, *A New Map–New Relationships* (Hebrew), published by Maariv, Tel Aviv 1969.

Not only was the period unique, but perhaps the man himself more so. Not the man as a typical representative of the period, but Dr. Ruppin with his special qualities, which permitted him to see things with greater clarity, depth and honesty than many other men of his day.

Dr. Ruppin was a humanist by nature, a man of conscience, and when he encountered the "Arab question," he wanted to be persuaded that Zionism could be fulfilled without detriment to the Arabs of Palestine. In his education and schooling alike, he was a scientist, and he studied things not only through their concrete expression, but also through the forecast of their future development and transformation. Above all, Ruppin was a man of action: "For the Jews of Europe," he wrote in his diary, "Zionism is a religion, but for me, it means action." And in the Arab question, he did not look for appropriate formulas but for practical solutions. Moreover, since his life was utterly dedicated to Jewish settlement in Israel, he inevitably saw the "Arab question" as it was reflected through settlement. The ground he had his feet on was Zionist fulfillment, and he was only prepared to turn his gaze toward what was capable of achievement, without quitting this basic posture.

I cannot conclude my remarks about Ruppin the man without including a paragraph from Berl Katznelson's eulogy of him.

> From generation to generation we see the thirty-six righteous men, whom we depict in the form of drawers of water, foresters or peasants. It would never occur to us to seek one of these thirty-six righteous men on some congress platform, in an office, in a university chair, or among public figures. I would not have used this figure of speech had I considered it an exaggeration. Ruppin embodied unique characteristics which we associate solely with the thirty-six righteous men. He was modest without being self-effacing. He was not infected by the taint of power. Even the great publicity which he enjoyed from time to time in the course of his functions left him unspoiled.

I do not think it would be too outrageous of me to assume that most of the people here have not read the three volumes of Dr. Arthur Ruppin's autobiography. I shall therefore permit myself, in the following, to quote relevant extracts from this diary of his.

Ruppin was put in charge of Zionist settlement in Israel in

1920, after the First World War. He obviously anticipated that with the collapse of the Ottoman Empire, the wave of national liberation would also reach the Arab countries, and the Palestine Arabs as well. In the first days of his work, he may perhaps have not realized the implications of this development for Zionism. But in 1923, three years after taking over his functions, not only did the "Arab question" reveal itself to him, but he also discovered that his predecessors had overlooked it.

At this period, in 1923, Ruppin underwent the first phase in his approach to the "Arab question." He not only recognized the existence of the problem, but even diagnosed a solution, namely the merging and integration of the Jews among the peoples of the Middle East. Although he was already nearing his fifties, his criticism of others and his confidence in himself are steeped in the spirit of youth. In 1923 he wrote in his diary:

> Herzl's conception was naive, and can be explained by the fact that he failed utterly to understand the conditions among the peoples of the Orient, and create, along with our brethren of the same race—the Arabs (and the Armenians)—a new Near East cultural community. More than ever before, it appears to me, Zionism can only find its justification in the racial association of the Jews with the peoples of the Near East. I am currently gathering material for a book about the Jews, whose basic premise will be the racial issue. I propose to include pictures of the ancient Oriental peoples, and of the modern populations, and to portray types which were to be found in the past, as well as in the present, among the group of nations of Syria and Asia Minor. I intend to show that those very same types are still to be found among present-day Jewry.

Ruppin understood that this approach implied a fundamental change in the Zionist concept, but he was not deterred by this fact. "Zionism will last" he wrote, "only if it is given a radically different scientific basis." The scientific foundation, the aspiration to find in Zionism some justification vis-à-vis the Palestine Arabs, and the need to lay down realistic answers based on a knowledge of local conditions—these principles are an integral part of Ruppin's nature. He clung to them, later too, even when he discovered that the question was more complicated than it appeared at first and required other solutions.

Ruppin did not hold on for very long to this idea of integration among the Arab peoples. As soon as he got to know realities better, he sensed that the common racial origins of Israelis and Arabs and the resemblance between the Jewish nose and the Armenian nose did not constitute an adequate basis on which to construct a "new Near East cultural community." In 1925, Ruppin arrived at the second phase of the "Arab question"—the binational phase.

During his binational-state phase, which coincided with his adherence to the Brit Shalom Movement, which he founded in 1926, and left after differences with his fellow members in 1929, Ruppin believed that Eretz Israel ought to be a common state for two nations. The Jews and the Arabs, in other words, should continue their existence as different and separate peoples, and not merge into a "new cultural community"—but at the same time they should maintain one single state, a binational state.

At this point, two things should be stressed. Firstly, as Ruppin grew more and more immersed in his Zionist work and increased in stature, his awareness of the need to ensure the Jewish people became stronger and more profound. He believed that this could be attained if the aims of Zionism were realized. "World history knows no laws, not even the laws of reasonableness. There is therefore no sense in predicting the future. This is also the answer to those who claim to 'prove' that Zionism has no future," [1932]. The second thing is that he saw the essence of Zionism as persistent and expanding immigration and settlement. He regarded these as "essential conditions," and did not diverge from them even when he feared there might be a contradiction between Zionism and the "Arab question."

As early as 1928, in fact, inner doubts of this sort troubled him.

> In that conversation it became clear how difficult it is to realize Zionism and still bring it continually into line with the demands of general ethics. I was well and truly depressed. Will Zionism indeed deteriorate into a pointless chauvinism? Is there in fact no way of assigning, in Israel, a sphere of activity to a growing number of Jews, without oppressing the Arabs? I see a special difficulty in the restricted land area. Surely the day is not far off when no more unoccupied land will be available and the settlement of a Jew will automatically lead to the disposession of an Arab fellah? What will happen then?

The idea of the binational state was supposed to reply to three problems. The first problem was that of nationality. Each people would preserve its own nationality. The second problem was to prevent the Jews dominating the Arabs, and vice versa. "Under the aegis of the League of Nations, Eretz Israel must become a state in which Jews and Arabs live side by side, as two nations with equal rights. Neither shall be dominant, and neither shall be enslaved." On the third problem, that of Jewish immigration and the dispossession of the Arabs, Ruppin wrote: "Just as it is the right of the Arabs to remain in the country, so is it the right of the Jews to immigrate thereto," [1929].

This phase, like its predecessor, was a revolutionary one. Here again, as before, Ruppin believed that points of difference could be ironed out objectively speaking, but in order to achieve this, other mistakes must not be repeated. "We want to extricate ourselves from the error which was prevalent in Europe for one hundred years, and which caused the World War—namely that only one nation can rule in one state."

As regards the abstract formulation, the binational state may have provided the answer for Ruppin to the question of how Arabs and Jews would live in common. But as he came to know realities better, he discovered more and more difficulties, and Ruppin, with his intellectual integrity, did not allow generalizations to obscure factual truth.

> I am therefore convinced that a number of serious conflicts of interest exist between the Jews and the Arabs. For the time being I do not see how these conflicts can be resolved in such a way as to allow the Jews the possibility of free immigration, and free cultural and economic development—things which are essential conditons for Zionism and in such a way that the interests of the Arabs should not be impaired, on the other hand [1928].

Ruppin knew, moreover, that the idea of the binational state was merely an ideological point of departure, an indication of a framework within whose bounds he hoped it would be possible to solve the problem.

> In the course of debates within the Brit Shalom Movement, we formulated the concept that the solution must necessarily lie within a binational state. . . . even the binational

state, obviously, gave a general reply to the problem, and it was my intention to make use of the Brit Shalom further, as a means of clarifying decisive questions, which would emerge from this general answer [1936].

And the questions, in fact still remain: "The 'conflicts of interest' were of a substantive nature." There was the question of land. "On every site where we purchase land and where we settle people, the present cultivators will inevitably be dispossessed." Thus he wrote about immigration: "Since our immigrants, for the vast majority, are people without means, the possibility should not be ruled out that these immigrants would take away the livelihood of the Arabs." Then there was the different standard of living and other factors.

But the main difficulty stemmed from the fact that the Arabs simply did not want the Jews to come to Eretz Israel. Every solution—including the establishment of a binational state—faced the alternative of either making allowances for the views and desires of the Arabs and putting an end to Zionism, or carrying on with immigration, land purchase and settlement, while denying the right of the Arabs of Palestine to determine the future of the country. Any solution or arrangement which would be contingent on the agreement of the Arabs, or on the introduction of a democractic constitution whereby decisions on questions at issue would be taken by a majority (an Arab majority naturally)—this implied the cessation of immigration and of Jewish economic development.

Ruppin understood this, and in his letter to Hans John (May 30, 1928), he wrote:

During our last conversation, you pointed out quite rightly that all the Arabs of Eretz Israel oppose the Zionist movement, and until we are capable of suggesting a satisfactory solution to the conflict of interests they will carry on being our antagonists. If, under these circumstances, a constitution worthy of the name were granted, it would stand to reason that the Arabs would make use of all the rights assured them by the constitution, to prevent, as a majority, all economic progress on the part of the Jewish minority. The meaning of this would be, quite simply, the end of the Zionist movement.

The crux of the problem, therefore, lies in the impossibility of arriving at agreement and cooperation with the Arabs. But at this stage, Ruppin still believed that it was possible to find the "redeeming formula" which would serve as a bridge for understanding between Arabs and Jews. And so he founded the Brit Shalom Movement.

As time went on, the "Arab question" did not become any less grave, but in fact worsened. In 1936, Ruppin needed to find a solution for it, no less than he did in 1923, and in fact more. He saw this as a vital necessity, not just to resolve the conflict with the Arabs, but also in order to put relations with himself and with his conscience into proper order. But was there a way of squaring the circle? Did the magic formula exist, to reach agreement with the Arabs "without thereby ceding the fundamentals of Zionism?"

> I was at odds with the other members of the Brit Shalom, in my appraisal of the prospects of reaching an agreement with the Arabs. In this respect, the Brit members displayed great optimism. They thought that economic advantages, and certain political guarantees, would in themselves be calculated to persuade the Arabs to accept the Jewish national home. There was nothing new in this concept. It was, in fact, just a continuation of the false approach toward the Arabs, which had prevailed in the Zionist movement from its beginning. Nobody ever imagined, beforehand, that those very same Arabs who during the days of Turkish oppression were prepared with equanimity to accept year by year a few hundred meek Jews who lived on *halluka* charity, would struggle by force against tens or hundreds of thousands of strong, straight-backed Zionists at a time when the country was under a free British administration. The "peaceful infiltration" which they hoped for so much, proved in reality to be a deceptive illusion. If we could learn any lesson from the history of the world in recent decades, this lesson would be that the political posture of nations is not dependent on considerations of good sense, but on instincts. All the economic advantages and all the logical considerations will not move the Arabs to give up the control of Eretz Israel in favor of the Jews, after they consider it was handed to them, or to share this control with the Jews, as long as the Arabs constitute the decisive

majority in Eretz Israel. I gave expression to these ideas in a letter to Dr. Jacobson, December 3, 1931, when I wrote: "What we can get today from the Arabs—we don't need. What we need—we can't get."

The year 1936 brought Ruppin to the third phase of his approach to the "Arab question." He ceased believing in the possibility of persuading the Arabs to agree to cooperate. No "legal formula," no "political guarantees," no "economic advantages," and no "negotiations" would bring the Arabs to consent to the Jews' return to Zion. This was undoubtedly due not only to the cumulative failures of attempts at dialogues with the Arab leaders, but also to the fact that the Arabs' anti-Zionist political stand grew a great deal more outspoken, and found expression in bloody outbreaks of violence, especially during the 1936 riots.

What next? What are the conclusions? After sixteen years of trial and inner doubts, Ruppin demolished his own entire ideological structure. He had long since abandoned the Brit Shalom Movement. He was perhaps disappointed, he was certainly wiser, but he did not despair, on any account.

> Nowadays, I personally am in a mood of calm and dispassion. I have formulated the following theory for myself: It is only natural and inevitable, that Arab opposition to Jewish immigration should find an outlet from time to time in outbreaks of this sort. It is our destiny to be in a state of continual warfare with the Arabs, and there is no other alternative but that lives should be lost. This situation may well be undesirable, but such is the reality. If we want to continue our work in Eretz Israel, against the desires of the Arabs—then we shall be compelled to take such loss of life into consideration!

As regards his own conscience, and as regards his self-recounting, Ruppin was calm and dispassionate. He had formulated a theory for himself, and it satisfied him. But what of the practical aspect?

> And what ought to be done in order to reduce or remove tensions between the two peoples, since after all, this tension cannot continue interminably? To my mind, no negotiations with the Arabs today can help us move forward,

since the Arabs still hope to be able to get rid of us, over
our heads . . . Not negotiations, but the development of
Eretz Israel, as we increase our ratio of the population, and
strengthen our economic power, can lead to a lessening of
tension. When the time comes, and the Arabs realize that
it is not a question of negotiations, in which they are asked
to grant us something which we do not yet have, but of
conceding the existence of a reality, then the weight of
facts will lead to a lessening of tension.

To create the facts: immigration, settlement, economic development and so forth. In these activities, Ruppin sees not only
the fulfillment of Jewish longings; once translated into facts,
they will also convince the Arabs to stop fighting against us. "We
must increase our strength and our numbers, until we reach parity with the Arabs. The life or death of the Zionist movement
will depend on this. . . . Perhaps a bitter truth, but it is the
truth with a capital T," [1936]. "The weight of facts"—the increase of our strength and numbers will lead to a lessening of
tension with the Arabs. When will we reach that stage? "Within
five to ten years," [1936]. In this timetable, things like the policy
of Hitler, the World War and the end of the Mandate were not
taken into account.

Ruppin's heart-searching over the path to agreement with the
Arabs had thus come full circle. The fulfillment of Zionism
embodied the solution to the "Arab question." Does this mean
that Ruppin realized he was wrong, while his colleagues in the
leadership, whom he called "naive" and "ignorant of the Arab
problem," were correct? Not at all. The prevalent point of view
held that the "Arab question" should be left alone, and it would
find its own solution thanks to the prosperity, the development,
the progress and the culture which the Jews would bring to the
Arabs of the country. Ruppin, on the other hand, stopped dealing with the "Arab question," because he realized that the Arabs would not agree to Zionism, *in spite* of all these things.

In the years that followed, developments were determined as
a result of factors unconnected with the pattern of relationships
between the "Arab question" and Zionist fulfillment. Nevertheless, I should like to quote Ruppin's point of view on two more
issues: the Peel Commission's partition proposal, and the White
Paper. They are of interest for the subject of this lecture—if not
directly, then indirectly.

Apart from Ruppin, the British Empire, too, was in a quandary in those years over the question of Arabs and Jews in Eretz Israel. The solution it proposed (the Peel Commission, 1939) was partition—not integration, not a binational state, and not cooperation. This means the establishment of separate states for Jews and Arabs. The Jewish state was assigned an area of some 5,000 square kilometers. To give some idea of the proportion, the state of Israel, today, has an area of 20,250 square kilometers, in other words four times as large, while the area within the present ceasefire lines is 88,000 square kilometers, eighteen times larger than the area of the "Jewish state" in the Peel Commission's proposals.

On August 1, 1937, Ruppin wrote:

> After studying the partition proposal, I have come to the conclusion that we shall not be able to absorb the 300,000 Arabs in it. Since it will be impossible to get them to leave of their own accord, it is essential that the Jewish state should have other boundaries, inside of which not 300,000 but at the most 100,000 Arabs, would remain. I have put my "personal" plan for the new Jewish state in writing. According to this plan, the area will be reduced from 5 million to 1.5 million dunams.

(It should be recalled that in those days there were 363,000 Jews in Eretz Israel, and the 100,000 Arabs whom Ruppin was ready to absorb in the Jewish state would have been equivalent to 750,000 Arabs absorbed by the Jewish state we have today).

During the Zionist Congress in Zurich, Ruppin brought to the Zionist executive his proposal to give up two-thirds of the area proposed by the Royal Commission, and to establish a midget Jewish state on an area of 1.5 million dunams. After the executive meeting he wrote in his diary: "I explained my ideas to him [Weizmann]. I did not feel they made a great impression . . ." [1937]. We may disagree with Ruppin's conclusion, but we cannot accuse him of not having learnt the bitter lesson of life side by side with the Arabs.

And finally—the White Paper.

> The White Paper was eventually published yesterday. It contains no surprise . . . I do not know why, but this document irritates me far less than it irritates all the other Jews. Is it because I have grown old, and my senses are dulled?

Or perhaps it is because I no longer believe in policies on paper? This White Paper is a direct function of a specific political setup (a united Arab front, England's fear of the Arabs) and it will be just as short-lived as this political setup [1939].

Chief of Staff, officers and guests: I trust you will forgive me for having spoken at length. In other circumstances, I would have been able to end at this point. But in the present forum and in these days, in surveying the development of Ruppin's ideas on the "Arab question," I do not want to avoid making a number of concrete observations.

Firstly, about what Ruppin called "political setup." When he said that the White Paper was the product of a political setup, and that this would leave nothing of the White Paper when it vanished, he was perfectly correct. Ruppin understood this, not because old age had dulled his senses, but because he had amassed wisdom during his years of work. His view of the White Paper was the result of his understanding, and not of dull senses.

Between then and now, the political setup has in fact changed entirely. A Jewish state has been established, with close on three million inhabitants. We have been victorious in three wars. We have an army whose strength should not be underestimated, and a people standing behind it, investing huge sums of money to aid our economy. Secondly, the dimensions have changed. When Ruppin thought in terms of Arabs, he meant the Palestine Arabs. When we talk about Arabs nowadays, we mean the Arab states. Not only that, but these states are also supported by the world's second-greatest power—the Soviet Union.

Dimensions have changed in the "demographic question" in terms of the size of our own population as well as that of the Palestine Arabs. Geographically, too, there have been changes in the areas settled by us, as well as the areas occupied by our forces today.

Thirdly, the facts are no longer the same. Ruppin was wrong to hope that by creating facts, tensions between us and the Arabs would be lessened. What greater "creation of facts" could there be than the establishment of the state, the concentration of 2.5 million Jews there, and the victories in three wars? But despite this, do the Arabs today agree to sign a peace agreement with us? The facts have been created, but the tension is no less than it was before.

Here I shall permit myself to add one observation. We see the facts which we ourselves create, but everybody who believes that facts are decisive in this issue must remember that the Arabs, too, could well point to facts—their large and steadily increasing numbers, their influence in the world, the oil resources at their disposal, and so forth. In other words, everybody who adheres to the formula whereby the facts we create will bring the other side to accept us, can just as well point to significant facts on the Arab side the moment he steps into the Arabs' shoes.

At any rate, if we return to Ruppin's forecasts, the facts he hoped for, as regards the increase in strength and numbers, did come to pass. But I fear that they have not yet convinced the Arabs to accept us, or our political existence, to regard us as an acceptable neighbor state with equal rights. Perhaps Ruppin's error on this point stemmed from the fact that he thought in rational categories, whereas Arab opposition stems from emotions.

Fourthly, there is his letter to Jacobson of April 12, 1931, about the prospects of an agreement with the Arabs, in which he said: "What we can get today from the Arabs—we don't need. What we need—we can't get." This definition sounds to me very up to date, when I sometimes read that today the Arabs are offering us the 1947 partition plans.

And finally, today too, unfortunately, a year after the war, and despite the fact that we are standing on the Suez Canal and on the River Jordan, in Gaza and in Nablus; despite all our efforts—including a willingness for far-reaching concessions—to bring the Arabs to the peace table, the things which Ruppin said thirty-two years ago still seem sound. It was during the 1936 riots that he wrote: "The Arabs do not agree to our venture. If we want to continue our work in Eretz Israel against their desires, there is no alternative but that lives should be lost. It is our destiny to be in a state of continual warfare with the Arabs. This situation may well be undesirable, but such is the reality."

8. Arab-Israel Parley: Steps Toward a Political Settlement

WHAT FOLLOWS IS the transcript of the third session of conversations held between five prominent Palestinians and Israelis, in Jerusalem, in August of 1968. The first two sessions dealt with the general questions of war or peace, in the Arab-Israeli context, and with what might have happened if, "instead of Israeli troops today sitting in Nablus, Ramallah, Hebron, Jericho, Arab troops—Egyptian, Syrian, Jordanian and Iraqi as well as Palestinian—were not sitting in Tel Aviv, Haifa, Beersheba, Eilat." The fourth conversation centered on the question of terrorism and neutrality.

In the present parley, an Israeli moderator, five Israeli guests, and four of the five Palestinians participating in the round-table, took part. They are: Amnon Cohen, assistant at the Hebrew University Institute for Asian-African Studies; Hazem Khaldi, formerly a Lieutenant colonel in the British army, later a brigadier with the Syrian forces, currently a businessman (described by himself as out of business); Perez Merhav, member of Kibbutz Beit Zera and Secretary of the International Department of the Mapam Party; Anwar Nusseiba, lawyer, former Jordanian Defense Minister and Ambassador to London; Aziz Shehadeh, Palestinian lawyer and civic leader from Ramallah; Moshe Sneh, head of the Israeli Communist Party and editor of the Hebrew daily, *Kol Haam;* Shmuel Tamir, Israeli lawyer and member of the Knesset; Moshe Shamir, Hebrew novelist, former

Reprinted from Arab-Israel Parley, transcript 3, pp. 48–63, *Israel Magazine,* Vol. 1, No. 8 (1968), editor Maurice Carr; by permission of Spotlight Publications, Ltd., 88 Hahashmonaim St., Tel Aviv.

captain of Palmach; Mahmud Abu-Zuluf, Jaffa-born editor and journalist of Arabic daily in Jordanian Jerusalem prior to the 1967 war, and now editor of Arabic language newspaper, *al-Quds,* published in Jerusalem.

MODERATOR: Gentlemen, we've looked back at the past long enough. Let's get on with the present and the future. We have heard—not unexpectedly that peace is preferable to war. Not unexpectedly, also, we have heard that war may all the same break out again if we don't achieve a political settlement. The question therefore is: How do we proceed toward a political settlement? In stages, beginning with a peace pact between Israel and the Palestinians alone, or between Israel and the Palestinians plus Jordan? Do you consider such a piecemeal arrangement desirable, practicable? Or are you of the opinion that peace is to be had only through an all-embracing settlement right off between the whole Arab world and Israel?

AMNON COHEN: As I see it, if we wait for an all-embracing peace treaty with all the Arab countries, including the most important one, Egypt, we may have to wait until doomsday. So our problem boils down to this: Do we come to terms with the Palestinian Arabs alone, assuming this is possible? Or do we aim at a settlement also with Jordan in consideration of the links between Palestinians and Jordanians?

The experience of the last twelve months and more has shown that a peace treaty with Jordan is as remote as with Egypt and the rest of the Arab world. In practice, therefore, what we have to examine is the possibility of peace between Israel and the Palestinian Arabs, to serve as the basis of a wider peace that will emerge some time in the future. While an arrangement with the Palestinians alone is by no means ideal, it seems to me the most fruitful solution here and now.

I don't subscribe to the view, which I have heard expressed here on the Israeli side, that Arab nationalism is a miscellany of separate, even conflicting movements. Despite differences between one Arab country and another, I agree with those Arab friends who speak of an overall Arab nationalist movement. The Palestinian Arabs form part of this general movement. In the past, they've not made their influence felt, which is a pity. It's high time they asserted themselves and took their due place.

My wish and hope is that the Palestinians will come to an agreement with Israel, which can be done without betrayal of

the Arab cause and without quislings. As to precise terms, these
need to be worked out.

King Hussein is unlikely to give his blessing to an arrangement between Palestinians and Israel. It is, therefore, up to the
Palestinians to take their fate into their own hands and get a
settlement which, king or no king, is fully compatible with Arab
ideals.

AZIZ SHEHADEH: I have always maintained that the Palestinian
Arabs should live up to their role of the party most directly
concerned in the dispute with Israel. So far, the Palestinian case
has been handled by the Arab states which have tried
unsuccessfully over the past twenty years to set up a state for
the Palestinians. Within what boundaries is another matter, we
won't discuss that now. A Palestinian Arab state, of course, was
envisaged in the United Nations decision to partition Palestine.

In all these years we've got nowhere because the Palestinians
weren't invited to speak up on their own behalf. We never will
get anywhere if we look to an agreement between all the Arab
states and Israel as the answer to our problem. Remember, each
Arab state has its own approach. A common Arab policy may be
unattainable. Other difficulties which have frustrated past attempts to achieve a solution may crop up again. I believe we
should for a start confine ourselves to the specific question of the
Palestinians. If we settle this, then we plant the seed of peace
which will grow and grow until there is peace all round.

How about Jordan? In the 1948 war, the Palestinians in this
West Bank area were annexed to Jordan and became Jordanian
citizens. But the comity of nations never accorded legal recognition to Jerusalem as belonging to Jordan—Jerusalem was marked
out to be an international city. There was nothing final about
the boundaries between Israel and Jordan—they were armistice
lines. In principle, the partition scheme is still valid. Which
means that two states should coexist in this region.

Now if the Palestinians are accorded—by agreement—the right
of self-determination, this does away with the main cause of
trouble between Israel and the neighboring Arab states. There
will still remain the problem of territories taken away from the
Arab states by Israel in the Six Day War. I don't feel that in
advocating first and foremost a settlement of the Palestinian
question, I am isolating myself and my fellow-Palestinians from
the Arab world in general or from Jordan in particular. The next

stage may well be our entering into a federation with Jordan, which federation can later be extended to other neighboring countries. Such unity, I am convinced, will come after the Palestinians have achieved an honorable settlement with Israel.

So, if you Israelis first settle your dispute with the party most directly concerned, that is, with us Palestinians, you are well on your way to all-round peace. But if you insist on peace with all the Arab countries right off, I don't think you'll get it. And even if you do, it won't last unless you satisfy the Palestinians' rights. The Palestinians will not be denied their independence, their own state, which may one day become part of a broad federation of Arab states, if such a federation materializes.

DR. MOSHE SNEH: Of course the best solution would be an all-embracing settlement with all the Arab states. But for the present, no Arab government sees eye to eye with any other Arab government, except that they one and all declare they won't enter into negotiations with Israel and won't conclude a peace treaty. This two fold refusal obstructs Dr. Jarring's mission, and obstructs the United Nations resolution of November 22, 1967.

The diplomatic ruse of the Egyptians in demanding a timetable for the implementation of the resolution is altogether too flagrant. Suppose you fix a date—say, December 17—for implementation of the clause calling for a just solution of the refugee problem. How do you work out a just solution without negotiations? Mr. Nasser is joking when he says: "All right, we accept the resolution, Mr. Jarring, and now you go ahead and set a timetable for its step-by-step execution, but without negotiations and without a final peace treaty."

To be practical, I think we should first have negotiations between the Israeli government on the one hand, and a representative body of the Palestinian Arabs on the other. How this body is elected or otherwise established, it is not for us Israelis to say; that's an internal matter for the Palestinian Arabs themselves. What is wanted on the part of our government is readiness to recognize such a body if and when it is set up, and to enter into negotiations with it on a basis of full equality, not as between victor and vanquished.

I have one remark to make about frontiers. Until now Israel has had no definitive frontiers. The United Nations partition scheme was destroyed by Arab invasion on the very first day of

the proclamation of the State of Israel. Not for a moment did
frontiers exist. In the 1949 Armistice agreements, no frontiers
were mentioned either by the Arab States or Israel—only demar-
cation lines. Now we have ceasefire lines, which I regard as
temporary military lines to be replaced by agreed frontiers. In
the end these will have to be agreed between Israel and all the
Arab states, but to begin with, inside Palestine we can have
agreed frontiers as between Israel and the Palestinian Arabs.

I lay the stress on self-determination for the Palestinian Arabs.
I deliberately avoid any kind of stipulation about a federation
with Israel. What sort of self-determination will you have, if we
make it conditional on federation with Israel? If you want to
join us, that's up to you. Make the request and we'll consider it.
But if, after we have achieved peace with Jordan and not before, you are inclined to enter into a union with Jordan, we shall
not mind. Quite the contrary, we are ready to have the most
friendly relations with a Jordanian-Palestinian Union, or whatever you may call it. Choose your own name. What we must
have are peaceful frontiers. You and I can't be good neighbors
so long as you don't know what is mine, and I don't know what
is yours. What belongs to each of us, to Israel and to the Palestinian Arabs, is something we can decide between ourselves—
without interference from other Arab states.

Maybe some of our Arab friends here present, at any rate one
of them, would regard such an arrangement as separation of the
Palestinian Arabs from the overall Arab nationalist movement.
That is not so. It would simply hasten a settlement between Israel and the Arab states. After which you would be free to join
them, if you wish. You know we Israelis might also be willing to
join them—in a vast federation of national-states covering the
Middle East.

Don't forget, however, that the Middle East, while being predominantly Arab, is not wholly Arab. You have Iranians and
Kurds, for example. We Jews are not the only non-Arab people
here.

You may well prefer a strictly Arab union, with the exlusion
of non-Arab units. That's up to you. We have nothing against
Arab unity. The only thing we object to is the sad fact that the
only common denominator of Arab unity, so far, has been antagonism to Israel. If and when you have positive factors and aims
as your common denominator, we shall be happy to see Arab
unity. Why not? Just because colonial powers in the past

divided the Arab world, does that mean that you have to stay divided forever?

If you wish to link up with all the peoples of the region on a territorial basis, by all means! If you prefer an exclusive Arab union, go ahead! What we reject, categorically, is the concept—which I heard here a little while ago over lunch—that Israel must be eliminated because it is a roadblock to Arab unity. Why a roadblock? Why not an open bridge? Given peace, we shan't obstruct communications between African Arab states and Asian Arab states. We will open the existing railways between Egypt and Lebanon, and open roads through the Negev from Egypt to Jordan and on to Iraq. Just as we want freedom of passage through the Suez Canal, so you are fully entitled to free passage through Israeli territory between the Arab countries. If you have a vision of peace, then you stop thinking in terms of roadblocks. I don't conceive of the frontiers which are to be determined between us as closed frontiers. After you have your state and we have ours, I want to be at liberty to visit Nablus whenever the fancy takes me and for you to come to Tel Aviv any day of the week. Why not? We have consular agreements with Switzerland and Austria and France exempting Israelis from entry visas. Why should two-way traffic between Palestine and Israel be in any way restricted? Each nation will enjoy sovereignty on its own territory and yet be accessible to neighboring people. How else?

There was talk of pleasant surprises. I'll surprise you by not recalling unpleasant recent history. Instead, I'll go back to the time when Sallah A'din conquered Jerusalem, or liberated it from the Crusaders. The Jews then said: "The Ishmaelites have conquered the Holy City, so that the Israelites may dwell therein." For it was you Muslims who opened the gates to Jerusalem to the Jews. Do you know that? And do you know that Maimonides wrote his principal work in Arabic? But that was spiritual fraternization in Spain, and I am concerned with political cooperation, as exemplified by Jews and Muslims against the Crusaders from the West. In Judeo-Arab history we certainly have chapters of cooperation and friendship. Maybe the recent strife is a transitional period which will lead to a new chapter of cooperation between the two great Semitic peoples.

HAZEM KHALDI: You don't repair a wrong by committing another wrong. The Six Day War wouldn't have happened if beforehand you had found a just solution for the Palestinians.

Yes, the Palestinians, who are most directly concerned, could be the intermediaries between Israel and the Arab countries. The moment you restore their rights to the Palestinians, there are no more problems. For a start, you must withdraw from the territories you now occupy.

You have to realize that all the surrounding Arab nations consider Israel an alien body. Everybody, every child, believes that Israel's purpose is to annex Arab lands and expand more and more, and kick out more and more Arabs. If you prove the contrary, that will be perfect. So far you've done nothing, not a single blessed thing, to indicate that your professions of good will are genuine. You won't convince us until you suit your actions to your words.

I think the Palestinians are the means to diluting the problem between Israel and the Arab countries. When the Palestinian question has been fully diluted, there'll be no more trouble. But as Nasser has pointed out, it won't do if Israel merely withdraws from the occupied territories. You have to restore the Palestinians' rights. The proper course for you, I think, is to do the right thing by the Palestinians—now, without waiting. If you don't, then more wrongs will be committed and the gulf between us will be enlarged, not filled in. That's how I see things.

MOSHE SHAMIR: Everyone wants to be served on a golden platter.

There are different kinds of peace. One is on the human level, and that already prevails in Israel between Jews and Arabs. It isn't a heavenly kind of peace, it's down to earth, it's the peace that people on this planet have enjoyed all through history when they've not been otherwise engaged in killing each other.

The other kind of peace is on the political level as between states and within the state—peace which is an absence of war between countries and an absence of civil war inside a country. This peace, in the wake of war, has to be reached by negotiated agreement. I don't believe we can get such agreement with just one among the many Arab states. Political peace, with mutual recognition and mutual respect, is to be had with the entire Arab world around us or not at all. Or at any rate, with three or four or five countries simultaneously, somewhat after the fashion of the 1949 Rhodes agreements.

I'll try for a moment to put myself into the shoes of an Arab and look at the situation as an Arab does. Do I want peace? Do

I need peace? I'm not sure. I, the Arab, don't believe the Israelis mean peace. So let's get ready for war, let's prepare the next onslaught. This time we'll win. What's the use of peace, if it won't bring us the things we want? I don't want to sign a treaty with a state that I'd sooner see wiped off the face of the earth. But then I have a second thought. I, the Arab, realize that I'm going to lose the next war even as I lost the last one. I take stock of all that I've already lost by waging unsuccessful war. I've lost territory, I've lost face, and I've wasted the opportunity to tackle my domestic problems, to build up my social, economic, educational system. In fact, I'm throwing away my future—unless I change my ways. So, hard though it may be, I adjust myself to the realities, I strive for self-betterment.

Speaking now as an Israeli, I am convinced the day will come when the Arab elite, the young intellectuals, the professionals, the progressives, the nonconformists who use their brains and at the same time listen to the promptings of their heart, will say: "Enough of this witch hunt against Israel! Let's get busy putting our own house in order." They will aspire to live in a democratic, liberal, progressive society. They will want to take care of their own country. What they need is a genuine revolution. They will throw out their totalitarian dictatorships. They will secure freedom of speech and thought, set up more and better schools and universities, factories, research centers. At that point, they will decide to stop throwing away their substance on war with Israel. They will overthrow their present mock-socialist regimes. And then, only then, will the way be open to political peace in the Middle East.

Meanwhile, the best that Israel can do is to make life between Jews and Arabs in this country as happy as possible, and to leave no doubt in anyone's mind in the world at large that the moment the Arab countries consent to live in peace, Israel will be ready for peace. Honestly, I don't think Israel can get peace by crawling on its hands and knees and making concessions which, in sacrificing our security, will tempt the Arabs to try yet another onslaught on us. I may sound disillusioned, but what illusions I had were shattered in the crisis of the Six Day War. I'm sorry to say so, but we'll not have peace with Arab military dictatorships. Only when the Arab countries develop real democracy will they desire peace, and only then will Israel be able to trust their pledged word.

Peace is to us as the air we breathe. But we've been pushed

to the point where some of our best people think: "Hell, why should we keep shouting for peace? It doesn't do any good. Let's declare we don't want peace. Maybe the Arabs will then start suing for peace. Egypt doesn't recognize Israel. Okay, we don't recognize Egypt. You think we don't have the right to exist. We think you don't have the right to exist." Maybe we're going sour, but we've lost all confidence in regimes that, well, gang up with the Soviets.

MAHMUD ABU-ZULUF: Much as I'd like to see peace between the Arab world and Israel, I don't think there's any Arab country willing to make peace. Perhaps a transitional period is necessary, during which time Israel restores the Palestinians' rights in this country. Discussion is possible if you guarantee our rights. But frankly, I don't foresee a peaceable solution to our problems, because they're insoluble.

SHMUEL TAMIR: The consensus is that peace with all the Arab states is much to be desired, but is not on the cards so long as the present regimes in Egypt, Syria and Jordan last. They'll not sign a peace treaty with us. But without a peace treaty, Israel won't withdraw from the existing ceasefire lines, which with every passing day are becoming more and more like permanent borders. The people of Israel will never allow its government to retreat one step without a peace treaty. There is complete unanimity on this, all the way from Dr. Sneh to myself. Were we to withdraw without peace, we'd simply be moving toward another war.

Mr. Khaldi told us that the Arabs lost territory but not their souls. I don't understand. Suppose on June 4, 1967, a day before the outbreak of hostilities, Gamal Abdel Nasser had condescended to make peace with Israel—Israel within its old territorial confines. Virtually all Israelis, beginning with Eshkol and not excluding myself, would have gladly accepted such a peace settlement, lopsided though our borders would have been. And twenty thousand good men, mostly Arabs, who are now dead, would still be alive. Half a million Arabs, Egyptians, Syrians, people of this country, who are today fugitives, would be living in their own homes. Arab prestige would not be at its present low ebb. We would not be witnesses to the sordid spectacle of Nasser blaming Amer for having lost the war and Amer committing suicide, or getting murdered—I don't know which—and Shams Badran being sentenced to life imprisonment, and other

Egyptian heroes treacherously calling each other traitor. If this, Mr. Khaldi, is your idea of the Arabs having saved their soul, I'm perplexed. I would say that Arab dignity and Arab virtues have been sacrificed to the vain ambition of a dictator who, growing more and more ruthless, has allied himself to the darkest forces of the century.

[*Cries of protest*]

SHMUEL TAMIR: I correct myself. The darkest forces since Hitler. So much for the Arab soul! Soul-searching, that should be the order of the day.

I was taken to task by a colleague here for my earlier statement that the Arabs might push us into imposing a peace settlement. I stand by it. I repeat it. If Jordan, with Egyptian backing, persists in its campaign of terrorism through El Fatah and the Arab Legion, if Israeli blood continues to be shed, day in, day out, more and more, then we may end up with a war on our hands, a war which this time we'll take a full month to finish off—properly, with an imposed peace. Heaven knows we don't want it. So let there be soul-searching in the Arab capitals. Let's have observance of the ceasefire, coexistence, and finally peace.

HAZEM KHALDI: Does Mr. Brezhnev speak any differently to the Czechoslovaks?

SHMUEL TAMIR: He certainly does! He orders their lives for them, politically, militarily, economically. All we ask of the Arab nations is to leave us in peace, to cease plotting our destruction. We are a nation who have lost a third of our men, women and children. Now we want to live at peace. Leave us alone, that's all! Brezhnev doesn't say that to the Czechs or anyone else.

We say there is one spot on earth, a bit of territory, where we wish to be at home, independent, in the majority. It's a minimal request which, I believe, Israel and the Jews are entitled to make to the world in general and to their neighbors in particular. But you, Mr. Khaldi, equate this with Nazism. You seem to forget you are talking to Jews who equate Nazism with Auschwitz. We Jews know what Nazism and Auschwitz mean. How can you speak to us in that fashion, when you see for yourself that the Israel army in Nablus, in Hebron, is conducting the most liberal military occupation the world has ever witnessed? Or don't you see, are you blinded by your passions?

Concerning the Arabs in Eretz Israel, I have heard Mr. Shehadeh and Dr. Sneh suggest that the Arab community be
granted autonomy. Well, they didn't use the term autonomy.
They spoke of self-determination. But, as you know, there is talk
of setting up a Palestine Arab National Home under Israeli tute-
lage. I don't myself think that in this twentieth century a National Home keeps for very long. It soon turns into a state, as
our Jewish National Home did. So let's get this straight.
Self-determination means an independent Palestinian Arab state.

Now, independence is independence and no nonsense. It will
entail withdrawal of the Israel army from the Palestinian Arab
soil. It will entitle the new Arab state to federate—and this is
what Mr. Shehadeh dreams of—with Jordan or eventually with
Syria or even Egypt. What guarantee can you offer that this will
not be a federation of belligerents against Israel? No firm guarantee is possible!

The artificial frontiers which existed up to June 5 and which
we would then have accepted as permanent in a peace settlement, vanished in the Six Day War. Because they were utterly
artificial, they cannot be put together again, any more than you
can change an omelet back into separate eggs. Now we have
one country, an indivisible country, all of whose provinces belong together, just as East and West Jerusalem make an integral
unit. An Israeli government that tries to break up Jerusalem
again and relinquish the Old City won't survive a day. A split
Jerusalem is a sick Jerusalem. A country where Jerusalem is
under one sovereignty and Bethlehem under another is a sick
country. Sick situations don't endure.

Mr. Shamir imagined himself, for argument's sake, to be an
Arab. I don't know that this is fair. But to be realistic, I would
urge the Arabs—looking at things from their point of view—to
seize the chance of their acquiring full citizenship rights in
sovereign Israel. I heard Dr. Khaldi say—I don't know if he was
being rhetorical or earnest—but I hear him say he might now
become an Israeli. I want you, Dr. Khaldi, to become an Israeli,
an Israeli in every sense of the word. I want you to sit next to
me in the Knesset. I want you to represent this country in the
United Nations side by side with Abba Eban and Yosef Tekoa.
Here is a great opportunity. I did say that this was the one
place on earth where Jews want to be in the majority. But we
also want this undivided country to be fully democratic.

ANWAR NUSSEIBA: I don't understand you. If we take you at

your word, you'll not have a Jewish state for very long. You'll be submerged.

SHMUEL TAMIR: I'm willing to take the chance. I say that this must be an undivided and fully democratic country. In Israel within its present boundaries, you Arabs are one and a quarter million, and we Jews are two and a half million. You are entitled to have the Deputy Premiership, to have Ministers serving in the government, to have a third of the seats in the Knesset, to be fully represented in the municipalities and in our embassies. I want to see a new citizenship law which makes you absolute equals of the rest of the population.

ANWAR NUSSEIBA: Are the Arabs who've been living in Israel since 1948 first-class citizens?

SHMUEL TAMIR: Yes. Maybe not quite, maybe here and there injustice has been done. I know of cases. As a lawyer I took them up and fought for redress. The government, especially the Eshkol government—and I speak as a member of the opposition—took great strides toward meeting the Arabs, even before June 5.

What should we do now? Number one, the unification of Jerusalem should be made total, and therefore we should take immediate care of the property that the Arabs of East Jerusalem lost when the city was divided. Where possible, this property should be handed back. Where restitution is impracticable, compensation should be paid, at once, fully, generously.

What I advocate for Jerusalem applies, *mutatis mutandis*, to the whole country. We have to have a new citizenship law granting equal rights to all inhabitants. The law of Israel has to cover the whole territory.

Then there is an issue which, morally and psychologically, takes precedence perhaps over all else—the Arab refugees. This is our problem, and we have to tackle it with courage and morality. We who were refugees, we who were carried on the waves of world sympathy into this country to build it up, we can and must do everything in our power to help the Arab refugees. And we have it in our power to do a lot. Jewish funds from all over the world, which have been streaming so abundantly to Israel, must in conjunction with international funds help rehabilitate the Arab refugees.

The Arab states don't mind about the Arab refugees rotting in

Gaza. Nasser had them there for twenty years, and he didn't give a damn. For all he cares, they could stay in those camps, men, women and children, another fifty years, to serve as his political pawn, as a propaganda weapon that he can cynically wield against Israel.

How do we go about their rehabilitation? Those who want to stay in this country should be resettled, drawn into the normal life of our society. Those who prefer to go elsewhere should be amply compensated. And we shouldn't wait. We should start today. We should have got going yesterday. What is morally right is also politically right.

As to the process of Jewish-Arab integration in Israel, you and we should launch it in all spheres, political, economic, social. Cousins, like brothers, can be the worst enemies. But they can become the best friends. You Arabs, and we too, have blundered in the past. We won't put things right by false sweetness. Let's be open, look each other in the eye, say yes when we want a thing and no when we don't. Take it from me, your best chance is with people who talk to you straight out, who bear you no animosity, who make it clear that they are here to stay, come what may, and who want to stay together with you in an integrated country called Israel. Thank you.

Aziz Shehadeh: Mr. Tamir, you have said you want a state where the Jews will constitute the majority. You want your own traditions, your own culture, your own way of life. Don't you see that we Palestinian Arabs have similar aspirations for ourselves? We too want to be independent, with our own culture, our own life. So integration is out of the question. You believe in the wholeness of Israel. We believe in the wholeness of Palestine.

How can we have an independent Palestine if you incorporate us into a Greater Israel? You mentioned Jerusalem. You don't want it to be divided. I assure you I don't like to see it divided, either. But a Palestine state without Jerusalem is unthinkable.

You are worried about the security of Israel if a Palestine state is set up on the West Bank. With all due respect, I can't see your security guaranteed by the mere fact that your border lies on the river Jordan. You will be better off with a Palestine state on your doorstep, a Palestine state that is friendly and doesn't want to fight you.

I believe the question of security can be solved not by your annexing the whole of Palestine, but by your having international guarantees from the Great Powers and from the United Nations. On top of this, there can be a transitional period during which a federation is formed between the Palestine state and a nonbelligerent Jordan of the East Bank. And if we sit and reason together, we may well set up a federation of three states—Israel, Palestine, Jordan—with Jerusalem as the capital of the federation. And in this way, instead of having two hostile armies facing each other across the river Jordan, we'll have them jointly defending our wider boundaries. And with peace between us, our armies will be of lesser importance, anyway. We'll struggle for social, economical, cultural advancement.

Take the case of Japan. Japan was occupied by the United States, and when the American army left after ten years——

DR. MOSHE SNEH: They're still there.

AZIZ SHEHADEH: Oh, they're still there. But they're not fighting. On the contrary, Americans and Japanese are cooperating. Why? Because it's in their reciprocal interest.

Mr. Tamir, I don't believe that by annexing Palestine——

SHMUEL TAMIR: Integrating, not annexing.

AZIZ SHEHADEH: Call it what you like, it's not going to bring peace. Neither with the Arab states nor with the Palestinians themselves. But take the alternative I offer. Reach an agreement with the Palestinians, give them satisfaction, and they will be the bridge of peace between Israel and the Arab states, a good bridge of permanent peace, not an artificial one that is doomed to collapse.

How do you satisfy the Palestinians? By giving them independence. There's no other way. It's no good your coming to us and saying: "We're going to rule you, but here's a piece of chocolate to keep you happy."

SHMUEL TAMIR: In a democratic regime, you'll fully participate in ruling the country.

AZIZ SHEHADEH: Participation can come by way of a federation, but not by our being integrated into Israel against our will. Both the Palestinians and the Arab states will reject integration. What we want is a solution acceptable alike to the Palestinians and the Arab states. If we make peace with you—believe me, we have our links with Amman, with Damascus, we Palestinians are scattered all over the Arab world—a wider peace will follow. Give the Palestinians a square deal, and instead of their agitating you and crying out for another round against you, they will be your advocates for peace.

You won't guarantee peace by having your borders on the Jordan. Your best prospect is to reach an Arab solution with the Palestinians who will hold out one hand of peace to you and the other hand to the rest of the Arab world.

Anwar Nusseiba: We have had such a good lunch, that I personally feel rather somnolent—and a little bit depressed. Depressed by the tone that this discussion has taken. Everybody seems to think that the prospects of peace with the neighboring Arab world are minimal. Now either I am differently informed, or I am not informed at all. Only today, I believe, Dr. Jarring has again come to Jerusalem. I know you laugh, I know that he is making very slow progress, but as long as he represents the United Nations, as long as he continues his mission, I don't think it would be correct on our part to give him up and to say he has failed.

What depresses me even more, really, is that within the Israeli ranks I find no unified approach to the problem of peace. We all want peace, but peace with whom? Peace with the Israelis. But now the Israelis are not in accord with each other as to the kind of peace they want.

Dr. Moshe Sneh: Put us to the test.

Anwar Nusseiba: All right, what has the Israel government said. They have said they will accept peace on the basis of the Security Council resolution. All right, this is a formula which we also accept. When I say we, I mean we Palestinians, we Jordanians, we Egyptians, the United Arab Republic, the whole Arab world, accepts this resolution.

Amnon Cohen: Not Syria and Algeria.

Anwar Nusseiba: Syria and Algeria will follow. The details are perhaps even now under discussion between Dr. Jarring and the parties concerned, in search of a consensus; or failing a consensus, some sort of approach whereby his good offices will bring about an ultimate understanding. I therefore don't agree in the least that his mission is to be written off, and we must seek alternative ways to peace.

Dʀ. Mᴏꜱʜᴇ Sɴᴇʜ: One word, please. We are all agreed that the most desirable solution is an all-embracing peace with the Arab states. We differ in our appraisal of the nearness or remoteness of overall peace. Those of us who call for immediate negotiations with the Palestinian Arabs do so as a means to hastening the much-desired all-embracing peace. This is not in contradiction to the mission of Dr. Jarring.

Aɴᴡᴀʀ Nᴜꜱꜱᴇɪʙᴀ: Thank you, Dr. Sneh, for enlightening me. But certain statements you have made arouse in me a doubt as to your willingness to conclude peace with the Arab states. I will give you an example. You read an article by Muhammed Hassanain Haikal in which he said we cannot have victory without progress, and we cannot achieve progress without peace. You then went on to say that this was a useful lesson. I gather you drew the conclusion that it is necessary to deny the Arabs peace, because by denying them peace you retard their progress, and by retarding their progress you deny them victory. Am I wrong on that?

Dʀ. Mᴏꜱʜᴇ Sɴᴇʜ: I specified that in order to have progress, you must have peace with Israel, and peace is what we want.

Aɴᴡᴀʀ Nᴜꜱꜱᴇɪʙᴀ: All right. Another thing that disturbed me was a remark by my friend Mr. Shamir. He said there cannot be peace with authoritarian Arab regimes. I think you said that. Correct me if I am wrong.

Mᴏꜱʜᴇ Sʜᴀᴍɪʀ: I would sign a peace treaty with the devil, but I don't believe these regimes will sign one with me.

Aɴᴡᴀʀ Nᴜꜱꜱᴇɪʙᴀ: In other words, you as an Israeli are not psychologically conditioned even to contemplating peace with the existing Arab states.

Mᴏꜱʜᴇ Sʜᴀᴍɪʀ: Pardon me, Mr. Nusseiba, but you may have heard on the radio a speech by Mr. Nasser—only a fortnight ago, with Dr. Jarring on his mission—a speech in which Nasser proclaimed there will be no peace, there must be a military victory. Well, we listen and we say, realistically, it seems the other party does not want to sit down at the conference table. Then you come and tell me I'm not in the psychological mood for peace. Is that not going too far?

ANWAR NUSSEIBA: Nonetheless, I am right in assuming, Mr. Shamir, that you meant what you said about the impossibility of achieving peace with the present Arab regimes? Correct? All right. So unless you change your psychological outlook, there is going to be an impediment in the way of peace. Now if we go along with you and say you are right, what happens? We will have to cooperate with you in subverting neighboring Arab regimes in order to reach a situation where peace will become possible. Is this what you want us to do? Would it be reasonable to expect this either of the Palestinians living here or of the Israelis who wish to live in peace with their neighbors? I think it would be unreasonable. I think, therefore, that apart from what you hear on the radio, apart from all other considerations, you should show readiness to go along with Arab governments which accept United Nations resolutions, and which are ready to implement in its entirety as a package deal, not in part, not according to a timetable, but in its entirety, the Security Council resolution of November 22, 1967. I am of the opinion that peace—if you like, you can call me naive—peace, like justice and freedom, is indivisible. I do not honestly believe that you can have peace within this area of Palestine while you remain at war with the encompassing Arab world. Therefore, if we want to tackle peace, we must face the problem squarely and not try to nibble at it. Peace should be attempted not piecemeal, not with only the Arabs of Palestine, though mind you the Arabs of Palestine are very, very important, but with the whole Arab world.

How to achieve it? Mr. Tamir gave us the binational concept—a country belonging to two nations, governed by two nations and sharing a common political entity, joint institutions and so on. I think this ultimately will emerge—in the distant future. Personally I think it will be very difficult. Therefore we should try to reach this unity—if we want to reach it, and I am all for it—we should try to reach it in stages. And the first stage could be that suggested by Dr. Sneh, namely, recognition of the Palestinian Arabs' rights within this country to a national existence of their own. By the same token, we expect the Palestinian Arabs to recognize the rights of the Israelis to a national existence of their own within this country. And then perhaps we can sit down and, not on emotional grounds, but mainly on economic grounds, on practical grounds, try to seek a formula giving proper expression to this dual ownership of the country. Having done this, you have no quarrel any more with the

United Arab Republic, you have no quarrel with the Syrians, you have no quarrel with the Jordanians. And this is what I think President Nasser meant when he said that elimination of the consequences of aggression will not in itself solve the Palestine problem. Therefore we have a dual task, the task of not retaining the territories of other countries which are recognized by the United Nations and the task of resolving our Palestinian problem among ourselves. I think this can be achieved.

PEREZ MERHAV: It would be too audacious of me to say I am optimistic about peace, but let's say at least that I am not as pessimistic as some of the participants in this colloquium.

I must, most regretfully, point out that some of the theses presented by Mr. Shamir and Mr. Tamir are complementary to those of Mr. Khaldi. Mr. Khaldi asked, "Peace with what kind of Israel?" Now we hear the question, "Peace with what kind of Arab states, with what regimes?" I think peace, coexistence, must be sought irrespective of regimes. If we declare peace is possible only with such and such a regime, which is to our liking, then there'll never be peace anywhere on earth.

SHMUEL TAMIR: You have to differentiate between an ideological attitude and an appraisal of facts. Mr. Shamir said he is willing to make peace with any regime, even with the devil. But his—and my own—analysis of the situation is that certain retrogressive regimes, by their very nature, will not make peace with Israel.

PEREZ MERHAV: It comes to the same thing. You rule out peace with certain regimes. I say that even the worst regime may find itself under compulsion to seek peace. Take Jordania. Jordania is in a bad way when shorn of part of Jerusalem, but it can't exist at all as a state without the West Bank. When the Jordanians become convinced that they can't get the vital West Bank back without peace, then I believe they'll make peace, in spite of all the obstacles placed in their way by Nasser, the Great Powers and others.

Next, Mr. Tamir, I don't think you're being helpful to the cause of peace—on the contrary, you're strengthening the tendencies against peace—when you invite our Palestinian Arab friends to join the state of Israel as a minority, with a chance of their eventually becoming a majority. The problem, as I see it, is not to effect a merger, but to achieve coexistence, a *modus vivendi*, between two independent nations.

Now, I disagree with some of my Arab friends here about the role the Palestinians can play in bringing about peace between Israel and the Arab states. Certainly representatives of the Palestinians, whether elected delegates or notables, should be present and involved in any future peace negotiations between ourselves and the Arab states. But I don't think we can solve our problem through self-determination of the population in the occupied territories here and now.

There are two imperative arguments against such immediate self-determination. The first is that we are—let's face it—still at war with the Arab states, including Jordania and Egypt, or to be more precise, they're at war with us. So we can't give the occupied territories the right of self-determination at this juncture, unless they are definitely, resolutely for peace with Israel.

The second consideration is that, while we should hold the idea of a Palestinian state in reserve as a last resort, we should remember that our encouragement of Palestinian separatism in any form or fashion will play into the hands of the worst extremists in the Arab countries. They will scream their heads off that we're playing the game of divide and rule. As far as the Jordanians are concerned, it's all the same to them if we annex the West Bank or grant independence to the West Bank. Jordania without the West Bank will be in a mess and will be raging against Israel and there'll be no peace.

Therefore, I submit, we should do this: We should speak to the Palestinians, we should hammer out with them a draft peace treaty, which they will then present to the Arab states. They, the Palestinians, are very directly concerned, and moreover they travel back and forth, in particular between Tel Aviv and Amman. And it is there, in Amman, that we have our best chances of getting an agreement. As I have said, Jordania cannot do without the West Bank, and is therefore the first candidate for peace.

AZIZ SHEHADEH: I have a question to put to you. Suppose these Palestinian emissaries who, like Jarring, commute back and forth, fail to persuade any single Arab state to negotiate, let alone sign a treaty, what then? How do we break the ice?

Do we just sit back and wait for centuries? Or do we do something, do we find an alternative?

PEREZ MERHAV: I appreciate your point. What I say now holds

good for the present. Maybe in a few months' time or in a year, we shall have to change our minds. I don't know. But already at this stage to give up hope of our coming to terms with the Arab states would be a big mistake. At this juncture, a separate settlement between Israel and the Palestinians would just add another obstacle to a general peace. It would anger the Arab states which are at war with us, and it would irritate the Great Powers—both those which back the Arabs and the others which occasionally support us—and we would just be complicating matters.

No, when you are at war, you try to come to terms with your enemy. Just as you can't choose your enemy, so you can't choose your partner for peacemaking.

Let me divulge a little-known fact. After the Six Day War, my party, Mapam, which is composed of Arabs as well as Jews, asked our Arab members to sound out the West Bank Arabs. Their almost unanimous finding was that the West Bank Arabs consider Jordania—the Jordania of both East and West Banks—as the Palestine state of 1968. They probably didn't think that way in 1948, but twenty years have passed, all sorts of things have happened, and that's the way they feel now. If we come to an arrangement today with the population of the West Bank alone, because they happen to be within our reach through occupation, then this won't be peace, it'll be only a semblance of peace.

Let's not yet give up hope of a settlement with the Arab states through the good offices of the vitally interested Palestinians. The one and only final solution is all-round peace.

I speak as one who formerly championed the cause of a binational Palestine State. After several wars, I no longer see binationalism as an intermingling of Arab and Jewish communities, but as a confederation of a sovereign Israel with a sovereign Jordanian-Palestinian state lying to our east. One advantage of a confederation is that it will help us cut through the Jerusalem tangle, but that is a subject in itself.

HAZEM KHALDI: A central question which we dealt with previously and which I feel every Israeli here present would like to know more about, is: Do we Arabs recognize the Israeli state? Well, I'd put it this way: inwardly, I think, most of us—I wouldn't say all Arabs, but the majority—recognize the Israeli state as a fact. How they came to recognize the fact varies with the individual, of course. I can't speak for any other Arab except myself.

Personally, I have come to recognize in my heart the Israeli state through the history of the Israeli people. For two thousand years they endured what they endured, all for the sake of practicing their religion and maintaining their nationality. That is something I respect. Equally I respect them for their soul-searching, for their hesitations—even the originators of the Jewish state were in two minds as to where this state should be situated, in Israel or in some other part of the globe. There were those who argued that the location didn't matter; what counted, they said, was the spirit of the thing, not the physical or historical associations. But that's by the way.

We come to the present day. I think the problem of the Jews—and now I underline the word Jews, because I see this as a problem not only of Israelis or of Zionists, but of all Jews everywhere in the world—is a problem of regaining racial and spiritual equilibrium. The Jew has now proved that he is a good soldier, as he previously proved that he is a good scientist, a good musician, a good academician and also, in many cases, a very good human being.

We come to the problem which everyone has been trying to tackle, namely, the attempt of the modern Jew—whether he be in Israel or outside Israel—to achieve reconciliation with our part of the world, the Middle East, and ultimately with the whole world.

Up to the Six Day War, I saw the problem as largely one between Arabs and Israelis. But since the Six Day War, I see it as a problem between Moslem and Jew and, because of twentieth-century communications media and human interrrelations, as a global problem.

We are up against a conflict of concepts, but to keep a sense of proportion we should remember that it's far from being the only conflict of concepts. Most religions have clashed down the ages, though in time most of them have come to some understanding and, above all, have come to respect one another's feelings and frontiers. Today there is a great ideological conflict in the world. In some countries one may be sentenced to death for being a communist. Elsewhere, a person known to have, or suspected of having, communist sympathies, will be barred from the economic and social life of the country. In other lands, he may not be so utterly shunned, but will still be working under a handicap. Now all this doesn't mean that communism is wrong, or that capitalism is right. It doesn't follow that one

economic policy is heavenly, and another is diabolical. Internationalism isn't necessarily good, and nationalism bad, or vice versa.

I think my good friend Mr. Nusseiba was very practical in
throwing a possible solution into the ring. It's open to discussion, but at least it's a solution proposed by the United Nations,
the world body on whose authority the sovereignty of Israel was
founded as an inheritance from the late League of Nations,
where the identification or association of the Jewish people with
their ancestral home was, shall we say, very thoroughly debated.
Now all this contributes to peace.

From the day of the caveman onward to the atomic age, man
has satisfied his material needs by practical expedients, but only
partially so. The needs of his soul have been met by the proph-
ets, but again only partially so. In the contemporary world
the struggle goes on to provide him not only with bread, but
with a code of behavior toward his neighbor, who may hold
different views on the other side of a frontier.

My grandmother died without the Arab concept; hers was the
Islamic concept. I don't know what my sons' concepts are going
to be. I brought up my children with the understanding that we
don't discuss politics until they start earning their own
livelihood—and they haven't started yet.

[*Interruption*] Does the understanding work?

HAZEM KHALDI: Yes, because it takes two parties to have a
discussion. [*Laughter*].

[*Interruption*]: So you've imposed peace?

HAZEM KHALDI: Not imposed. Shall we say that civilized rights
give me preeminence until my children reach a certain age.
Economic rights, too, give me preeminence. When women are
dependent, it is not, shall we say, realistic to talk of their having
equal rights.

To get back to the business on hand, I find myself in partial
agreement with some of you, but not wholly in agreement with
any of you. I have myself been casting around for solutions to
our problems. Straight after the Six Day War I began very enthusiastically to study the possibility of a binational state. Now I
have given that up, not because of any particular event which
refuted this concept, but out of respect for the Israelis and the
Jews, whom I have since got to know more intimately. I withdrew from the binational concept on human grounds—I learned

there was a very genuine motive in the heart of every Jew for preserving his identity.

What would the Jews have been if they had compromised with Titus? Where would the Jews be if they had compromised with Babylon? How many times in their history might not the Jews have disappeared from the scene as Jews, had they not known who they were and what they expected of themselves? So I say that binationalism or even federation may not be the answer. Instead, the answer may be good-neighborliness.

Every faith has its own strength. Islam conquered many countries by the sword, but many other countries it won solely by its spiritual power. I have lived in the Far East where no Moslem army ever set foot. Yet millions and hundreds of millions of people there have been converted to Islam—through the moral strength of Islam, its humane concepts, its sense of justice, its righteousness which is greater than any those people had ever known before.

Now I believe that the Jewish people are entitled to self-realization, and I have no quarrel with them. All I ask of them is to be good neighbors, respecting other folk and putting limits on themselves as we all have to do in the course of our lives. Many people strive for riches, others for power; but every one of us has to acknowledge some time or other that there are limits to everything he does, to everything he has set his heart on. I believe the time has come for Zionism to draw in its reins. Zionism must come to terms with itself as David did when he said: I am a man of war, I can't build a temple, I can't build a house for the Lord, because I'm a man with bloody hands. Israel should take an inward look at itself in the same way. Israel should set limits upon its ambitions after having achieved self-realization, not only by the force of its own arms, but also by virtue of universal support. And no matter how this came about, I must respect the majority opinion of the world. But we cannot leave this question of limits unresolved. Perhaps what Mr. Nusseiba has thrown into the ring is a beginning—and a very good beginning—that will lead to peace talks.

9. The Future is the Son of the Past

BY ATALLAH MANSOUR

Jerusalem October 20, 1968

The atmosphere is saturated with talk on war, political solutions and peace. By "atmosphere," I mean mass communications, radio and television, and lobbies of politicians, of whom, alas we have many in our country. Everybody talks about politics and the news, the student revolt in Europe, the war in Vietnam, and the occupation of Czechoslovakia. But all discussions end with Palestine and what happened or is still happening in it. This seems natural; completely so.

The Palestine case, according to people here, is the story of divided families whose members were deprived of seeing each other. It is the story of people who knew mental tranquility and quiet life, but not a pleasant one. Yet all of a sudden the warning bell rang, and people awoke to find themselves refugees living in tents. To them, the case is that of a nation which lived for centuries under serfdom and slavery. When it got up, its people saw ghosts approaching together with the coming light, involved in strange panic while on their run seeking new accommodation in their "national home." Our people wished the lasting of night and darkness, as well as the keeping away of those ghosts, but the coming light from the west (and I do not say the "ray") dazzled the eyes. However, before my people could rub their eyes and put sleep aside, they discovered themselves thrown out of their homes, which were grasped by the outside ghosts. My people tried to resist, but self-confidence and full assurance in their rights blocked their ears from hearing others' talk. They did not hear some of their own people who were

Printed here for the first time by permission of the author.

lucky enough to know their situation before others, and thus they embarked on an incorrect estimation of matters.

The result was, as the world knows, that 350,000 remained in their homes, accepting what rights the Israeli government would bestow upon them. They felt, in breathing the air of their land, an atonement and a complement to the mental ease of which they were short. About a million lived in the Gaza Strip and the West Bank, the occupied areas administered by the Israeli army authorities; and a further million refugees were dispersed in Syria, Lebanon, Jordan and the United Arab Republic; all of them—2,350,000 brothers, cousins and relatives—are waiting for a solution to the problem which is personal for every one of them. . . .

MENTAL TRANQUILITY AT DARKNESS

The country which was later known as Palestine was an Ottoman principality before it was occupied by General Allenby during World War I. This principality was not different from other principalities of the aged Ottoman Empire, which was suffering from arteriosclerosis; a situation which did not prevent it from remaining important to the three monotheistic religions, or from occupying a strategic position bordering the Suez Canal and on the crossroads to Africa and Asia, or from being of economic importance to the British Empire. The industrial revolution in Europe and the advent of the masses into history following the French Revolution, constituted information still missing from the school textbooks taught at the few schools which this country had at the time. But the nationalist awakening had by then reached a number of limited circles, particularly among students of missionary schools and colleges which were influenced by European institutions involved in religious, political or scientific activities. These circles were thin and limited in numbers and in the effect they had. On the whole, they were composed of children of wealthy and luxurious people who considered education something like a face powder, used only to varnish and beautify the face for proper appearance in society. Or perhaps to them it was like spices intended to intensify the appetite when eating to fatten the bellies. As to the needs and welfare of their people, this class was somewhat like the foreigners, not in a position to worry for the sake of others. They used to fear them, in the same way as they hated the filth of mud rubbing into their white dresses.

Palestinians were in complete darkness and far from the light of enlightenment and modern awakening. And all that was written or said on the influence and effect of the European Renaissance on the Arab East, at that period, was nothing but a Byzantine discussion similar to that of theologians when they wanted to determine the number of angels the pin's head could hold.

My people were, when my father was my age, living in an era of blind confidence in the One God able to solve problems and capable of revenge from all evils. My people used to live happily in mental tranquility, fully trusting, beyond any doubt, the will and the ability of God.

My people, then, were a mixture of Moslems, Christians and Jews; all working hard, praying fervently, paying taxes to the Sultan, even if it was at the expense of their hungry children. But despite all of this, they knew that God would bestow upon them the good, if He willed it, and would prevent the good, when He desired it.

And as my people were farmers dependent on rain, since irrigation water was not available, the Heaven-sent rain was enough proof to convince my people of their true faith in God. My people, the Palestinians, were at the beginning of the twentieth century very satisfied with their faith, happy with it despite poverty, dire need and rulers' oppression. He who used to deviate from this rule and felt like overthrowing it, used to walk on foot to Mediterranean ports, such as Jaffa, Acre, Tyre, and would leave for the "new world" seeking a new home in the USA, Brazil or Cuba.

MISERABLE MEN IN THE LIGHT

Further behind the Mediterranean Sea, the rays of light (and I do not say light) in Europe defeated the solidity of darkness. The masses struggled everywhere, and the demand for their rights took shape. The ruling classes tried to divert the anger of the people against an obscure phenomenon in society and to put the blame on those "foreigners, the Jews," and whoever was among the minorities. They were accused of stealing the peoples' shares of land, their resources, and of betraying the general welfare. These ruling classes succeeded in misleading quite a large ratio of the people who rid themselves of their drowsiness in order to divert their anger toward the Jews.

Some Jews, at least, awakened and dreamt of their National Home, advocating it, and offering their services for the cause of any who could help in its realization. The Ottoman Sultan, the German Kaiser and the Roman Pope refused the offer, but the young British Lion, allied to the Jewish people, accepted and fought against aged Turkey. The Balfour Declaration was released, carrying on its young shoulders the bridge to the East in order to facilitate the establishment of a National Home for those who bore the brunt of prejudice in enlightened Europe, while the population of Palestine was still happy with its darkness and dreams.

A HEAVY LEADERSHIP

In this fashion occurred the meeting between victims and those who were still full of faith. Arab leadership had told the masses that the foreigners intended to conquer their land and eject them from it. The Zionists, who came to the East guarded by European bayonets to be freed from European oppression, behaved in a manner that confirmed earlier statements of the Arab leaders to their people. They started buying land from owners, mostly feudal, and expelled the farm laborers. And despite their talk of socialism and labor cooperation, these Zionist pioneers were not able to win the confidence of Arab laborers and farmers. These pioneers were unwilling to accept the Arab laborer within their community on an equal footing. Actually world Zionism and the Jewish settlement movements were always ready to speak of better understanding with the Palestine Arab laborers, but they were, and to an extent still are, adopting a "Jewish Labor" program and policy. In other words, the trend was and still is to secure employment for Jewish laborers living in Israel, or those immigrants who were to be brought from abroad. As to Arab laborers, the policy of the Zionist leadership was always to buy lands in which Arab laborers lived and worked, and then to expel them. Such action led the poor Arab laborers in their struggle against Zionism, to attach themselves to the Arab leadership which was largely feudal.

On the other hand, the British Mandate, which shouldered the responsibility for pioneer Jewish settlement in response to the Balfour Declaration, knew how to keep the Arab Palestinian community behind the black banners waved by its traditional leadership. The Mandate also knew how to increase the influence of its leadership and how to ensure its domination over the people, just as the farmer was preoccupied with internal problems and blood feuds.

In the spring of 1920, demonstrations broke out in Jerusalem against Zionism and the Balfour Declaration. As a result, some Jews were either killed or injured; and the British military authority were on the lookout for those who arranged these demonstrations. This made Haj Amin Husseini, the religious leader, and his colleague, Aref al-Aref, the journalist, flee to Transjordan. Relations between the Arabs and the military authorities worsened as a result of this, and the authorities resorted to the dismissal of the Jerusalem mayor, Mr. Mousa Kazem al-Husseini, replacing him by a son of a feudal family, Mr. Ragheb Nashashibi. This act established the basis for the feud which prevailed between the two big families of Jerusalem. In order to ensure better relations with the Husseini family, the military authority then decided to return Haj Amin Husseini. Sir Herbert Samuel, the first British High Commissioner in Palestine at the time, decreed that order under an amnesty act. He later appointed Haj Amin to fill the leading religious position of a grand mufti, and assigned him to the chairmanship of the Islamic Waqf Council, a department which used to have an annual income of seventy-five thousand Palestinian pounds. By such action, the Mufti became responsible for some one thousand Arab employees working for the Awqaf department. It is worthwhile mentioning also, that Mr. Aref al Aref, a colleague of Haj Amin Husseini, was also appointed by Sir Herbert Samuel to serve the Palestine administration.

One of the most important events which affected the Palestine case, second to the Balfour Declaration, was the appointment of Haj Amin Husseini as Grand Mufti. It was later revealed that Haj Amin was one of the very few Palestinian leaders who was not accused of secret cooperation with the Jews, yet he showed the least flexibility and readiness to distinguish friend from foe. He was also the most prepared to make sacrifices in order to keep his leadership. In any case, as soon as he assumed his official position, he started using department funds, for which he was held responsible, to establish his leadership, even if this was to be accomplished over other peoples' accounts. He criticized and prejudiced his rivals, he dumped his critics, and eventually he led his Palestinian people blindfolded to their destruction.

These unlucky people were to tolerate the leadership which

sat on its chest, and the blazing fire that poured forth from the masses that suffered European hate, a fire which swallowed up piece after piece of this land. What were the Palestinian Arabs to do facing such a situation, when they were in the initial stages of their own awakening in the aftermath of hundreds of black years during which they were subdued by a regime concerned only with collecting taxes and suppressing personal freedom, such as happened under Ottoman rule?

LEADERS AND AGENTS

Truth forces me to say that British policy in Palestine did not adopt a straightforward line in serving Zionism and its objectives. It so happened, more than once, that the Mandatory government suggested to the imposed Palestinian leaders the establishment of a government (or parliament) for the country, the majority of which was to be Arab. These leaders, however, decided and insisted on sticking to their policy which could be summarized in one word: *No.* They refused every form of cooperation with the Mandatory government and declared more than one revolt against the Mandate. During these revolts, many more Arabs fell by Arab hands than did the British or the Jews, simply because Arab leadership refused to hear a word of objection or any criticism. The leadership requested from the poor people that they swallow only nationalist words, which was insufficient to feed them, while the leadership was simply oversaturated with meat.

Numerous are the stories told about the big nationalists who led the boycotting campaigns during the period 1936–39, and who set themselves up as intermediaries for the transactions in the market. It so happened that this intermediary action reached its peak when the leaders decided to hand over the Palestine case against British imperialism and Zionist settlement to the British agents in the kingdoms and republics of the adjacent Arab states. Palestine leaders requested Arab rulers to mediate with the British government, which "as a friend to the Arabs," promised the kings enthroned in Iraq, Jordan, Saudi Arabia, Yemen and Egypt to do good. It was natural that it aimed at nothing but to calm things down in Palestine while World War II was in flames.

NO: BY ALL MEANS

As a result of World War II, concentration camps were established in Germany and all Nazi-occupied countries. The spirit of ghettoed European Jews, who blasphemed for the European human values, were inflamed. They started to flee in panic from the hell of Europe to seek safer places. Many flocked, during the war and after, to Palestine. The British government did not know, then, how to act. It blocked the way of some, and it gave way for others under the heavy pressure of world opinion, despite the high wave of criticism from those forces which did not lose their values. Neither Palestine Arab leadership nor the regents sovereign in the Arab countries knew how to behave. The struggle between Arabs and Jews continued; it even deepened so that the British Mandatory government was finally compelled to decide to refer the case to the UN. Under the influence of the catastrophe which befell the Jews in Nazi Europe, the UN decided on Palestine's partition. Things were thus shaped, while Arab leadership in Palestine and Arab countries hurried to prove themselves nothing but parrots, solely dedicated to one word: *No*. While in the meantime, the USA and USSR supported the partition scheme, which if enforced then, would have given the Jews a small state, half the residents of which would have been Arabs.

Prior to the entry of Arab armies on May 15, 1948, the Arabs, lacking the knowledge of the military and economic possibilities of the Jews, as well as the inability of Palestinian Arabs (and the Arab League as well) to resist armed Jewish forces, some important coastal Palestinian cities (Haifa, Jaffa), as had earlier happened to Tiberias, Safad, Beisan and Acre, the principal Galilee townships, fell into Jewish hands. Arab armies entered following the British evacuation, but were in no position to win the battle against Israeli forces. Moreover, these armies, joining forces in accordance with their respective governments' instruction to prevent the establishment of the state of Israel, operated neither in harmony nor single-handedly. In most instances, they themselves harmed Arab military efforts.

DEPORTATION OF PALESTINIANS

To clarify the general Arab position, militarily and politically, it is enough to mention the fact that Egypt, the largest and most important of all Arab countries, did not decide to participate in the war, except at the last moment. Even then, the Zionist organizations were allowed to operate openly among Egyptian

Jews. Some Egyptian newspapers used to write about the Zionist settlement movement in Palestine as if they were writing
about adventures of the new settlers in the USA, not mentioning
the Palestinian Arabs or even aligning themselves with them.
Why, then, did the Egyptians participate in the war? Most probably, because they feared the influence of the Hashemites in
Iraq and Jordan, and their threat of encroaching on Egyptian
borders. They also feared any future accusation by Arab nationalist
and Islamic circles of defeatism and retardation, if they did not
join forces. It was apparent enough, however, that the Egyptian
forces that entered Gaza and Hebron in southern Palestine
under the banner of welcome and the national anthem, wanted
to occupy Palestine rather than assist or liberate it. In his book,
Al Nakba (The Catastrophe), Aref al Aref said that the Egyptian
army, when entering Gaza, used to insult Palestinians and
confiscate arms, particularly those of the Holy Jihad Force
which was then the elite of the Palestine Army groups. He also
noted that in Hebron, the Egyptian army confiscated arms from
the populace when the town leaders were banqueting with
Egyptian army commanders. It was even more ironic that the
Egyptian army commander, upon entering into Arab Hebron,
reported to his superiors that his forces "occupied Hebron following very minor resistance."

The Jordanian army was not different from the Egyptian one,
except in that its men used to maltreat the unarmed Palestinians. Arab Jerusalemites are still talking about the Arab Legion
and the lootings they committed in their towns. Colonel Abdullah Tell, Commander of Jerusalem at that time, wrote about
King Abdullah's instructions to his army, to arrest "Holy Jihad"
leaders and confiscate their arms. Like others, he submitted
proof that King Abdullah was negotiating with the Jews during
the war to share the ruling of the country with them.

This is how Palestine's fate was decided, and how Palestinians
were sentenced to be paralyzed while their official leadership,
the Arab Higher Committee, was summer vacationing in the
Lebanon, the Damascus' cafés, and the bars of Cairo. They were
sharing the funds collected from Arab and Muslim nations for
the rescue of Palestinians, and they were apportioning positions
in the so-called "Palestine general government." All but one,
Mr. Ahmad Hilmi Pasha, were outside Palestine. Strangely
enough, this one leader was not Palestinian but a Lebanese by
birth who came originally from Sidon.

A FRAGMENTED PALESTINE

As a sequence to war, Palestine was divided. Israel occupied the largest part, Jordan finally annexed Jerusalem and the mountainous region occupied by Iraqi and Jordanian troops, and Egypt retained the Gaza Strip according to the armistice agreement. The armistice agreements between Israel and some of the Arab countries were thought to be a step toward peace. Unfortunately this did not prevail. The UN by then had decided on the return of the Arab refugees, who despite these decisions remained living in tents and on UNRWA's relief assistance. The Arabs, brothers to the Palestinians, swallowed parts of their homeland. Jordanians decided on the annexation of the West Bank; the Egyptians decided to establish the "Palestine general government" at the end of 1948, in Gaza. A meeting for leading Gaza dignitaries was convened, after which the new government was proclaimed, which was acknowledged by all Arab states except Jordan, and which had no annual support except talk. This government did not exercise any authority, not even in Gaza, and was never allowed to levy taxes or form an army. Though established in Gaza, the members of this government were confined to Cairo, and in 1952 when its head, Mr. Ahmad Hilmi Pasha, died, the idea passed away with him.

As to the territory occupied by the Arab Legion, it was annexed in April 1950 to Jordan to form the Hashemite Kingdom of Jordan, and Palestine was erased from the political map and converted into an image and a symbol for Palestinians, residents and refugees alike.

PALESTINIAN RESURRECTION

The story followed a long course and the refugee tents became worn. UNRWA built shelter units for them, but the refugees were unable to find a basis for decent living conditions. Doors to their return, and the possibilities of securing citizenship in host countries were not available except in Jordan, where the Palestinians felt that bedouins mastered their own fate in a state which practices neither freedom nor democracy. The days passed, while the wound was still bleeding and incurable. On the other hand, Arab armies, which were made to fight the Palestine war without prior preparation, were still licking their wounds while pouring blame on the political leadership which betrayed them and provided their spoiled arms (in

Egypt), or imposed British officers on them (in Jordan), or did not pay them much care (in Syria).

The *coup d'états* began. King Abdullah was assassinated in Jordan and several abortive efforts to depose the Hashemite regime took place. Syrian officers attained power through coups aimed at imposing internal reforms and at supporting the military front. King Farouk was at last deposed. The new, powerful rulers of Egypt tried in vain for three years to procure arms from the West, and when they directed their attention to the Communist bloc, a confrontation in the Middle East between East and West became obvious. As a result, Egypt, Syria, Iraq, Algiers, Yemen and the Sudan resorted to buying Russian arms. Egypt was destined to become the leading leftist power in the Arab world. ⅃t followed also that the Egyptian government decided to reactivate the Palestine case, but it did not take any action to establish a Palestinian government in the Gaza Strip. Instead, it decided to establish a Palestine entity movement among Palestinian communities. This was temporarily doomed to failure until 1964, when the Palestine Liberation Organization was established, although it was in practice unable to organize Palestinians outside the Gaza Strip. Lebanon objected to it, fearing its operation on Lebanese soil, Syria was unhappy out of fear that Cairo would control its right to Syrian land, and Jordan feared a challenge to its unity. Other Arab countries refrained also, sensing a threat in it, if the Palestinians were used by Cairo. Thus, the PLO was born paralyzed, especially after the organization and other Arab circles decided to keep the party-liners away from its executive and administration. It only accepted nonpartisans and traditional leaders from known families.

During the June 1967 war, the role of Palestinians was nothing more than silly rhetoric emanating from a lawyer who professed politics by serving Syria and Saudi Arabia before he served Palestine, and a tough battle was fought gallantly by the Palestine Liberation Army, as testified by Israeli military commanders. This army, due to its small size and poor equipment, was unable to do more than what had been done. And as a result of this war, the rest of Palestine was occupied by Israeli forces, while parts of Syria and Egypt were overrun.

THE OCCUPATION

Palestinians residing in occupied parts and refugees abroad

awoke one week after the war to find themselves face to face
with Jews and Zionists for the second time. For many the
surprise was astonishing. A flow of Arab deserters started east-
ward passing through bridges destroyed by war, escaping a new
unbearable fate. A few weeks passed before Palestinians started
facing Israeli soldiers with their wives and families, exchanging
greetings with them while buying transactions from Arab shops.
Soldiers sometimes paid double or more prices, yet smiles in the
faces of the occupiers, previously expected to be murderers and
usurpers, were also apparent on the faces of the occupied.
During the exchange of smiles, the sounds of explosives hit the
ears. The sound of the "Thunderstorm" (Assifah) followed, calling for "Liberation" (Tahreer) by force. Cemeteries started receiving victims' corpses; those of the young who were hoping
for a respectable life. The painful shouts of the wounded rose
higher and higher, and hawks shouted anew to fight again a war
which did not, and will not, end. In this manner, the Middle
East fell again a victim to a dark pessimism. The light of these
explosions became, for the masses, the only hope.

IS THERE A WAY OUT?

Is there a way out of this damned cave? My answer is *Yes;* I
repeat *Yes;* absolutely *Yes.* But how? Here I would say that
Palestinian history offers a good lesson for those looking for a
solution. The Palestinians, throughout their struggle and the
hard experience of the past fifty years, were subjected to the
general feeling that every solution which does not ensure right
and just national integrity and respect is unacceptable. But does
this mean the eradication of Israel? No, of course not. The land
of Palestine coupled with Israeli Jewish genius and that of the
Palestinian Arabs, as well as the technology of the industrial
revolution, are enough guarantees to enable the land of Palestine to provide for its people. There is no doubt that if current
relations among Palestinians and Jews had existed prior to the
industrial revolution, there would have been no possibility for
compromise, but as we are destined to face the problem today,
there cannot be much doubt about economic coexistence, or an
inferiority complex, or the loss of faith and confidence in either
one of the two conflicting nations, or in both of them. Why
cannot Palestine do what Switzerland, Holland or Belgium have
done? The area of each is similar. The Palestinian population

(Arabs, Jews, plus refugees) does not measure up to the population of Switzerland (4.8 million), nor does it reach half that of Belgium (9.2 million), nor that of Holland (11.8 million).

It is true that Palestine does not possess the experience to invade the world industrially; neither does it have enough rain or unlimited water resources. But a calm and stable Palestine does possess a moderate climate and a treasure of holy and historic places, which attract millions of tourists from the Christian, Islamic and Jewish worlds. I do not doubt that a free, stable, quiet and flourishing Palestine can be a world center for all who seek prayer and ease of mind. It would be an attraction to those looking for a happy and joyous holiday, in which there is enough income for the country and the people. At that time, it would be less than Switzerland, Holland or Belgium. There is also, in the Israeli industrial experience, enough experience to develop local production depending on human trials and cultural capabilities. This will provide support for the country's economy in a developing and industrial world. But war and struggle do not render the evolution of an economy easy. Why, therefore, do we not try a solution? My answer is that the USA, although it tries to bring about peace between Jordan and Israel, is actually blocking the way for peace between Israel and the Palestinians. Neither Jordan nor King Hussein can act freely to negotiate peace, because Palestinians in Jordan and abroad threaten the King against negotiations. The situation in Israel, particularly that of the right wing in the government, which has decided on the nonnegotiability of Jerusalem (second Islamic world capital), does not leave much for Hussein to say to East Bankers. Why then should he negotiate? Why should he deviate from Arab unity? And this Arab unity, does it mean more than one country waiting to list the faults of the other, or to compete with it in speeches?

The USSR is also taking a stand which does not ensure peace. It backs Arab governments which, in turn, do not take an official position on the Palestinian case, since this means the splitting of Jordanian territory. In 1947, the USSR stood for the partition of Palestine, like the US; today both agree to keep away the only reasonable solution, which entails the reciprocal acknowledgement of the legal rights of Israelis and Palestinians. America is doing it to keep Hussein on his throne and to keep all its protégés in the Arab World, while Russia is safeguarding its position in the Middle East and its friendly relations with the Arab states, Jordan being one of them. Leftist Arab states, on the other hand, are not yet united. Everyone is trying to be the first in a race, yet everyone is somehow bound to the other. These states, which are dependent since the last war on the financial backing of the so-called "conservative" Arab states, will not be able to adopt a policy which entails the split of Palestine from Jordan or acknowledges the right of Palestinians to establish their own state. Two possibilities remain open to us:

(1) The USA should press Israel to give Hussein concessions which might enable him to deal alone, or with some other Arab states, such as the United Arab Republic or Lebanon. This, as I see it, will not be a final solution, as I am sure Palestinians will revolt against Hussein as soon as he concludes peace, or even before, until they hoist the Palestine flag.

Or that:

(2) The Israeli government should act and deal with the Palestinians under its military rule as though they were partners in the national and economic rights of the country. Palestinians should be allowed to bring back their refugee relatives who wish to return. They should be given the chance of establishing national institutions which they were prevented from doing previously.

Such deeds will lead to:

(a) establishment of a binational state in Palestine;
(b) establishment of two separate and independent states, having economic, military and cultural agreements;
(c) establishment of a federal state in Palestine for both Arabs and Jews.

It is possible that if the Israeli government acted in good faith, this would have positive effects on nearby Arab states, and eventually the contagious effect would spread to all of the Middle Eastern countries, which in turn might lead, through mutual confidence, to a lasting, peaceful coexistence.

This is my hope, and for it I live; for my children's future as well as for the future of all other children.

Notes on Authors

1. ABDEL-MALEK, ANOUAR. Egyptian journalist, former professor of philosophy, writer and analyst of political and social developments in Egypt. Since 1959, he has been a resident of France.

2. ABU-ZULUF, MAHMUD. Journalist, currently editor of Arabic newspaper published in Jerusalem, *al-Quds*. Formerly edited and published Arabic daily in Jerusalem, Jordan.

3. ALAMI, MUSA. Palestinian Arab, student of law in England, member of government of Palestine and Arab Secretary to the High Commissioner during Mandatory period. Associated with project for economic and social rehabilitation of Palestinian peasantry.

4. ARAB HIGHER COMMITTEE. Along with the Jewish Agency, it was allowed to present evidence before the Political and Security Committee of the United Nations in 1948. An unofficial—that is to say, a nongovernmental—organization, the Arab Higher Committee was formed in 1936 by the loose coalition of the existing parties in Palestine; headed by the Mufti of Jerusalem, Haj Amin al-Husseini.

5. AVNI-SEGRE, DAN. Wolfson Fellow in St. Antony's College, Oxford. He was Senior Lecturer in Political Science at Bar Ilan University and Ford (Visiting) Professor of Comparative History at MIT. His study of Israel's political society will be published in the spring of 1969 by Oxford University Press.

6. BEN GURION, DAVID. Israeli Prime Minister and Minister of Defense, 1949–53, 1955–63; co-organizer of Mapai (Jewish Labor Party) and Histadrut (General Federation of Jewish Labor), its Secretary 1921–35; Chairman, Jewish Agency for Palestine 1935–48; following UN Partition Resolution (1947), elected Chairman, National Council in Charge of Security and Defense; proclaimed the independence of the state of Israel, May 14, 1948.

7. COHEN, AMNON. Israeli-born assistant at the Hebrew University Institute of Asian and African Studies, specializing in Middle East affairs.

8. DAYAN, MOSHE. General and Israeli Minister of Defense. Palestinian by birth, he participated in the critical years of the nation's life and defense before and after 1948. Closely associated with the chief architect of the nation, David Ben Gurion.

9. FLAPAN, SIMHA. Member of Mapam, one of the editors and frequent contributors to the Israeli periodical, *New Outlook*, and for a number of years, its representative in France. Associated with a variety of endeavors to encourage Arab-Jewish *rapprochement*.

10. HOURANI, CECIL A. Formerly adviser to President Bourguiba of Tunisia, frequent writer and speaker on contemporary Arab affairs and, more recently, on the Palestine question.

11. AL-HUSRI, KHALDUN. Free-lance writer of Iraqi origin. Formerly columnist, news analyst, director of the Beirut Bureau of Iraqi News Agency, and editor of Arab Political Documents with other political scientists of the American University of Beirut.

12. JAMALI, M. FADHEL. Former Foreign Minister and Prime Minister, on numerous occasions, in Iraqi governments prior to 1958. Sentenced in 1958 by the Revolutionary Military Tribunal, he was released in 1961; has lived since that time in Tunisia and Switzerland. At the present time, Dr. Jamali is a professor at the University of Tunis.

13. KERR, MALCOLM. Professor of Political Science and Chairman of the department at the University of California, Los Angeles. Author of numerous studies on modern trends in Islamic thought, current ideological developments in the Arab world, and the relationship between the two.

14. KHALDI, HAZEM. Palestinian who has worked in Syria, Europe, and Far East; for some time with the United Nations Relief and Works Agency; active in Kuwait Shell Petroleum Development Company and Shell Company in the Persian Gulf. In 1965, he was appointed General Director of Tourism in Jerusalem and the West Bank.

15. LAQUEUR, WALTER. Director of the Institute of Contemporary History and the Wiener Library in London; Professor at the University of Reading and Professor in the History of Ideas and Politics at Brandeis University; specialist in contemporary Middle Eastern political history, particularly in Soviet interest in that region.

16. MAGNES, JUDAH L. (1877–1948). Prominent American Zionist,

pacifist during World War I; Chancellor and then President of the Hebrew University in Jerusalem. Advocated binationalism along with Professor Martin Buber and others, and in 1942 founded the Ihud association, which attempted to increase support within Palestine and in the world at large for the creation of a binational state in Palestine.

17. MANSOUR, ATALLAH. Israeli Arab journalist and novelist. Formerly wrote in *Haolam Hazé*, newspaper published by Uri Avnery; currently correspondent for the daily, *Ha'aretz*. Author of two novels set in Israel since 1948, and contributor in 1967 to the special issue on *Le Conflit Israélo-Arabe*, published by *Temps Modernes*.

18. MAQSUD, CLOVIS. Lebanese socialist and writer on political affairs. Increasingly concerned with ideological questions, in theory and practice, in the Arab world. In 1958–59 he was Director of West Asian Studies at the Indian School of International Studies, New Delhi.

19. MERHAV, PEREZ. Israeli author, editor, member of kibbutz. Active in Mapam-sponsored work, currently head of its international department; one of the editors of *New Outlook*, and author of various studies on the labor movement in Israel.

20. NAHUMI, MORDEHAI. Member of Editorial Council of *New Outlook;* frequent writer on foreign affairs and international relations of Israel.

21. NUSSEIBA, ANWAR. Lawyer, active Palestinian politician; formerly Secretary of the Arab National League in Jerusalem; Secretary General of the "All-Palestine Government," in Cairo; in 1950 became member of the first Jordanian Parliament; subsequently frequently held Cabinet positions in Jordanian government. From 1962 until his resignation in 1967, Jordanian Ambassador in London.

22. PERETZ, DON. Director of the Southwest Asian and North African program at the State University of New York at Binghamton; author of numerous studies on the contemporary Middle East, the situation of the Arab refugees, and the significance of binationalism in the Israeli-Arab experience.

23. RABBATH, EDMOND. Lawyer and writer on Syrian political history during the Mandate period; one of the early exponents of Arab unity and member of the committee that produced the Draft Constitution for a Federal Union of Arab states.

24. REJWAN, NISSIM. Iraqi-born Israeli, active as journalist and writer on cultural and political developments in Israel and the Arab world; formerly editor of Arabic daily, *al-Yaum;* more recently,

free-lance journalist concerned with contemporary trends in the Arab world and communal relations between eastern and western populations of Israel.

25. ROULEAU, ERIC. Correspondent in the Middle East for *Le Monde* and frequent contributor to journals on international relations and internal developments in the Arab world; author, with J. and S. Lacouture and J.-F. Héld, of *Israel et les Arabes* (Paris, 1967).

26. SEALE, PATRICK. Middle East correspondent for *The Observer* and contributor to *The Economist, The Financial Times,* and other periodicals on matters pertinent to the Arab world.

27. SHAMIR, MOSHE. Israeli novelist, playwright, publicist; former captain of Palmach, now editor of Hebrew publishing house, Maariv Library.

28. SHARABI, HISHAM. Lebanese, now an American citizen and Professor of History at Georgetown University; author of articles and books on nationalism and revolution in Middle East.

29. SHEHADEH, AZIZ. Palestinian lawyer and politically committed Palestinian; member of the Arab Youth Congress and the Arab Youth Party in 1948; subsequently Secretary of the Arab Refugees' Congress and member of the Palestinian delegation to the 1949 Lausanne Conference of the UN Conciliation Commission.

30. SHLOMI, DAVID. Author of numerous studies on political and social problems; editor of the *Haoved Hazioni* since 1945; one of the leaders of the Progressive Party and a member of its National Executive. He is also editor of publications for the Culture and Education Center of the Histadrut.

31. SNEH, MOSHE. Head of the anti-neo-Stalinist faction of the Communist Party in Israel; editor of the Hebrew daily, *Kol Haam;* prominent in the Hagana, the Jewish underground army, of which he was Commander in Chief from 1940–60; member of the Jewish Agency Executive from 1945–47; joined Mapam in 1948 and headed its left wing, which joined with the Israeli Communist Party in 1954.

32. SYRKIN, NACHMAN (1867–1925). Russian-born author, founder and theoretician of the Socialist-Zionist movement; participated in the First Zionist Congress; in 1907 settled in the US; during World War I, helped to found the American Jewish Congress. In his commitment to socialist Zionism, he sought to combine the ethical concepts and the social values of socialism with an historic conception of nationalism as it existed for the Jewish people in the form of Zionism.

33. TAMIR, SHMUEL. Member of the Israeli Knesset; formerly Acting Commander of Irgun Zvai Leumi, clandestine Jewish resistance organization, 1946–47; member and General Secretary of the Israel Bar; co-founder of right-wing Heirut Party in 1948; subsequently formed the Free Center Party.

34. WEIZMANN, CHAIM. First President of Israel from 1949–52; one of the founders of the state; a dedicated Zionist since the turn of the century, a laborer on behalf of diplomatic recognition for Zionist aims, and President of the World Zionist Organization from 1920–46, with the exception of the period 1931–35.

35. YOST, CHARLES W. US Ambassador to the United Nations; formerly Deputy US Representative to the United Nations, 1961–66; former Ambassador to Laos, Syria and Morocco; writer on international affairs and diplomacy.

Notes

PART I: REFLECTIONS ON RADICAL CHANGE IN THE ARAB EAST AND ISRAEL

1. Malcolm Kerr. Arab Radical Notions of Democracy.

Note: Where the essays reproduced have been cut, in order to assure clarity in subsequent referrals to the original, note numbers have not been changed. In the following article, therefore, the first note is numbered 22.

22. Jamal Mohammed Ahmed, *The Intellectual Origins of Egyptian Nationalism* (London, 1960), p. 123.
23. Hasan al-Banna, *Al-Rasa'il al-thalath* ("The Three Articles") [Cairo, n.d.], pp. 113–20; French translation by J. Marel, *Orient*, No. 4 (1957), pp. 59–62.
24. Cairo, 1953; Beirut, 1960.
25. Razzaz, pp. 175–76.
26. *Ibid.*, p. 112.
27. *Ibid.*, pp. 200–02.
28. *Ibid.*, p. 193.
29. *Ibid.*, pp. 198–99.
30. *Ibid.*, pp. 201–02.
31. *Ibid.*, p. 243.
32. *Ibid.*, p. 120.
33. *Ibid.*, p. 190.
34. *Ibid.*, pp. 205–06.
35. *Ibid.*, p. 199.
36. Abdullah Abd al-Da'im, *Al-Jil al-'arabi al-jadid* ("The New Arab Generation") [Beirut, 1961], p. 167.
37. *Ibid.*, p. 175.
38. *Ibid.*, pp. 137–39.
39. *Ibid.*, pp. 182–83.
40. Article entitled "Our View of Capitalism and the Class Struggle" in *Dirasat fi al-ishtirakiya* ("Studies in Socialism"), by various contributors (Beirut, 1960). p. 27.
41. *Ibid.*, p. 29.
42. Michel Aflaq, *Ma'rakat al-masir al-wahid* ("The Battle for a Common Future") [Beirut, 1958], pp. 18–21.
43. *Ibid.*, pp. 37–39.
44. Abdullah al-Rimawi, *Al-Mantiq al-thawri* ("Revolutionary Logic") [Cairo, 1961], pp. 166–67.
45. Fayez Sayegh, *Risalat al-mufakkir al-'arabi* ("The Mission of the Arab Thinker") [Beirut, 1955], p. 97.
46. Clovis Maqsud, *Azmat al-yasar al-'arabi* ("The Crisis of the Arab Left") [Beirut, 1960], pp. 57–58.
47. *Al-Ulum* magazine (Beirut), July and September 1959.

48. *Ibid.*, pp. 167–68.
49. *Ibid.*, pp. 170–71.
50. Speech of November 25, 1961.
51. Muhammad Hasanain Haikal in *al-Ahram*, June 2, 16 and 30, 1961.
52. Lutfi al-Khawli in a panel discussion on "The Crisis of the Intellectuals," *al-Ahram*, June 14, 1961.
53. Ihsan Abd al-Quddus in *Rose al-Yusuf*, Dec. 4 and 11, 1961.
54. Muhammad Hamid al-Gamal, *Adwa' 'ala al-dimuqratiya al-'arabiya* ("Light on Arab Democracy") [Cairo, 1960], p. 83.
55. *Ibid.*, pp. 95–96.
56. *Ibid.*, p. 159.
57. Auguste Comte, quoted by Isaiah Berlin in *Two Concepts of Liberty* (Oxford, 1958), p. 36.
58. Article 53 of the UAR Provisional Constitution provides that "while the National Assembly is not in session, the President of the Republic may issue any legislation or decisions originally within the competence of the Assembly, should the necessity arise. Such legislation and decisions must be submitted to the Assembly at its following meeting." But before the Assembly could meet to consider the July decrees, it was dissolved by the President.
59. Haikal in *al-Ahram*, Nov. 6, 1961.
60. Salah Abd al-Sabur in *Rose al-Yusuf*, Oct. 16, 1961.
61. Muhammad Khafif in *al-Ahram*, Nov. 27, 1961.
62. Haikal in *al-Ahram*, Nov. 7, 1961.
63. Khahled Muhammad Khaled, *Al-Dimuqratiya abadan* ("Democracy Forever") [Cairo, 1953; third printing, 1958], p. 24.
64. *Considerations on Representative Government* (Forum Books, New York, 1958), p. 60 (Chapter 4: "Under What Social Conditions Representative Government is Inapplicable"). Cf. the application of Mill's ideas to Arab problems by Manfred Halpern in Chapter 11 of *The Politics of Social Change in the Middle East and North Africa* (Princeton University Press, 1963), to which I am indebted.

2. Hisham Sharabi. The Transformation of Ideology in the Arab World.

1. See Albert Hourani, *Arabic Thought in the Liberal Age, 1789–1939* (London, 1962), pp. 67–102.
2. See, for example, the editorial comments of *Al-Jinan* (Beirut, Jan. 15, 1878).
3. See *Ibid.*, July 23 and Aug. 3, 1880.
4. "Our period is the period of imperialism," Jamal al-din al-Afghani (d. 1897), in *Khatirat*, ed. Muhammad Makhzumi (Beirut, 1931), p. 373.
5. Rifa'ah Bey Rafi (al-Tahtawi), *Manahij al-albab al-misriyya fi mabahij al adab al-asriyah* ("Courses for Egyptian Minds in the Delights of Modern Literature") [2nd ed., Cairo, 1912], p. 373.

6. Tahtawi states that the student missions were sent to Europe "in order to relearn the scientific knowledge," that Europe had borrowed from the Arabs. *Takhlis al-ibriz fi talkhis bariz* ("The Extraction of Gold in the Summary of Paris"), 1st ed. 1834 [4th ed., Cairo, 1958], p. 79. "The scientific knowledge which appears to us to be European is in fact Islamic translated from the Arabic . . ." *Manahij*, p. 373. Even Jurji Zaydan (d. 1914) states practically the same point, *Tarikh adab al-lugha al-arabiyyah* ("The History of Arabic Literature"), Vol. IV [2nd. ed., Cairo, 1937], p. 165.

7. "Anyone who has mixed with Europeans and has come to know them well knows that they are not better than we in rational power, in understanding, in intelligence. . . . or in any other attribute. Indeed that we are better than they in all these qualities is as evident as the sun itself. No matter how great their (current) progress in the sciences and the arts happens to be they still lag behind us in intelligence and intellectual stamina; as for refinement of taste, they are immeasurably behind us . . . ." Faris Ahmad al-Shidyaq in an editorial in his Constantinople newspaper, *al-Jawa'ib*, April 28, 1869.

8. For example, al-Afghani: "The decline of Muslim society cannot be attributed to true Islam but rather to the Muslims' ignorance of what true Islam is." *Khatirat*, p. 218.

9. By the term "liberalism" is here intended neither classical economic liberalism nor the complex and often vague creed of contemporary political life, but rather the broad view based on the nineteenth century optimistic view of man and society with its belief in constitutional government, human progress, the perfectability of human nature, etc.

10. Cf. Farah Antun, *Muqtatafat* ("Selections") [Beirut, 1951], which includes selections from his writings between ca. 1900–14; Shibli al-Shumayyil, *Majmu'ah* ("Collections") [Cairo, 1909–10], consists of most of his writings in two volumes; Ahmad Lutfi al-Sayyid, *Al-Muntakhabat* ("Selections") [Cairo, 1945?], includes most of his articles in *Al-Jaridah* for 1908–13. On Antun and al-Shumayyil see Shukri Ghali, *Salamah Musa wa azmat al-fikr al-arabi* ("Salamah Musa and the Crisis of Arab Thought") [Cairo, 1962], p. 9 ff.; on al-Sayyid, see Jamal Ahmed, *The Intellectual Origins of Egyptian Nationalism* (Oxford, 1960), pp. 85–112. For a general analytical survey of the works and thought of these and other writers of the nineteenth and first quarter of the twentieth centuries, see Albert Hourani, *op. cit.*

11. Neither the classical economists nor Marx and the "scientific" socialists seem to have made any imprint on the pre-World War I intellectuals. They were fairly familiar with Montesquieu, Voltaire, Rousseau, Comte, Mill, Spencer, Darwin, Renan and Le Bon, but hardly at all with Hegel, Marx, Proudhon, Mosca, Sorel or German historicism.

12. Sami al-Dahhan, *Qudama wa mu'asiruh* ("The Ancient and the Contemporary") [Cairo, 1961] pp. 173–179.

13. For an authoritative assessment, see Majid Fakhry, "Ba'd wujah fikruna al-mu'asir fi al-din wa al-falsafah," ("Some aspects of contemporary thought in religion and philosophy") *Hiwar*, Beirut, Vol. III, No. 15, pp. 6–16.

14. *The Future of Culture in Egypt,* trans. Sidney Glazer (Washington, 1954).

15. See his *Al-Islam fi risalatayhi al-muhammadiyyah wa al-masihiyyah* ("Islam in its Muhammadan and Christian Versions") (Damascus, 1952).

16. *Al-nizam al-jadid* ("The New Order") (Damascus, 1951), p. 6.

17. *Risalat al-mu'tamar al-khamis* ("Message of the Fifth Conference") [Cairo, n.d.], pp. 10–11.

18. *Al-mithaq, qaddamahu al-ra'is Jamal Abd al-Nasir lil-mu'tamar al-watani lil qiwa al-sha'biyyah* ("The Pact: Presented to the National Congress of Popular Forces by President Jamal Abd al Nasser") [Cairo, May 21, 1962]; *Al-Muqarrarat al-ammah lil-mu'tamar al-sadis li hizb al-ba'th al-arabi* ("General Resolutions of the Sixth National Congress of the Arab Ba'th Party"), text in *al-Nahar* (Beirut, Oct. 29, 1963); *Barnamaj jabhat al-tahrir al-jaza'iriyyah* ("Program of the FLN") [May 27, 1962]; *Watha'iq wa dirasat* ("Documents and Studies"), Vol. III (Nov. 1962).

19. *Mithaq,* pp. 62–63.

20. *Ibid.,* p. 74.

21. *Ibid.,* pp. 110–11.

22. *Muqarrarat,* sixth resolution.

23. *Ibid.,* seventh resolution.

24. *Barnamaj,* p. 114.

25. *Ibid.,* p. 117.

26. *Ibid.,* p. 116

27. *Ibid.,* p. 117

28. Charles Malik, "The Near East: The Search for Truth," *Foreign Affairs,* Vol. 1, No. 2 (Jan. 1952), p. 263.

29. *Ibid.*

30. *Les Damnés de la terre* (Paris, 1961), pp. 37, 38–39.

PART 2: THE TRANSFORMATION OF SOCIETY

2. Anouar Abdel-Malek. The Crisis in Nasser's Egypt.

1. See the various texts scattered in the national archives of Egypt, Britain, France, Turkey and Italy; the rare serious studies by members of the Free Officers, such as those by Colonel Sarwat Okasha, Major Salah Salem, the autobiographical essay written by Jamal Abd al-Nasser for the *Sunday Times, Egypt's Destiny* by Mohammad Neguib (1955), the two volumes by Colonel Anouar el-Sadat; also the monograph by P. J. Vatikiotis, *The Egyptian Army in Politics,* Indiana University Press (1961). I have sketched a critical synthesis of this literature in *Egypte, Société Militaire,* pp. 204–18.

2. Text of the first edition, *The Charter,* Department of Information (Cairo, 1962), p. 7.

3. See, in European languages, J. &
   S. Lacouture, *L'Egypte en Mouvement*, Le Seuil (Paris 1956; 2nd
   edition, 1962), pp. 435–72; John
   Marlowe, *Anglo-Egyptian Relations 1800–1956*, F. Cass (1965),
   pp. 381–432; Mahmud I. Zayid,
   Egypt's Struggle for Independence
   (Khayat Beirut, 1965).
4. A. Abdel-Malek, "La Question
   Agraire en Egypte et la Réforme
   de 1952," *Tiers Monde*, III No.
   9–10 (1962), pp. 181–216.
5. Detailed account in *Egypte, Société Militaire*, pp. 55–297. For the
   economic sector, see the critical
   analysis of Hassan Riad, *L'Egypte
   Nassérienne*, Ed. de Minuit, Paris
   (1964), and the more detailed and
   favorable account by Patrick
   O'Brien, *The Revolution In Egypt's
   Economic System*, Oxford University Press (1966). Occupying an
   intermediate position is Charles
   Issawi, *Egypt in Revolution*, Oxford University Press (1963), pp.
   46–285.
6. Cf. *Egypte, Société Militaire*, pp.
   189–297, and the texts cited in
   note I. Cf. the detailed analysis of
   "socialism" in Fayez Sayegh, "The
   Theoretical Structure of Nasser's
   Socialism," St. Antony's Papers,
   No. 17, *Middle Eastern Affairs*, No.
   4, Albert Hourani, ed. (Oxford
   University Press, (1965), pp. 9–55.
7. *The Charter*, pp. 63–66.
8. *al-Ahram*, July 23–27, 1962.
9. This was the principal justification
   given for the self-dissolution of the
   Central Conference of the Egyptian Communist Party in April
   1965.
10. Niyazi Berkes, *The Development
    of Secularism in Turkey*, McGill
    University Press (1963).

11. Cf. my paper on "The Emergence
    of New Social and Political Forces
    in Egypt: 1939–52," delivered at
    St. Antony's College, Oxford, Oc-
    tober 22, 1965.
12. On the application of Marx's
    "principle of historical specificity"
    to Egypt, cf., in addition to
    previous publications, A. Ab-
    del-Malek, "Sociology and Eco-
    nomic History, an Essay on Media-
    tion," paper presented at the
    Conference on the Economic His-
    tory of the Middle East, SOAS,
    University of London (July 4–6,
    1967), p. 16; and for a compara-
    tive sociological analysis: "Es-
    quisse d'une typologie des forma-
    tions nationales dans les 'Trois
    Continents'," *Cahiers Interna-
    tionaux de Sociologie*, Vol. 42
    (1967), pp. 49–57.
13. Cf. *The Holy War, The Sunday
    Times* (London, 1967); M. H. Hai-
    kal: "Al-wathâ'eq toudin Amrika,"
    al-Ahram, June 23, 1967, and the
    speech of Jamal Abd al-Nasser on
    July 23, 1967.
14. Eric Rouleau: "the Egyptians view
    the conflict as the logical result of
    the deterioration of their relations
    with the United States," *Le
    Monde*, June 6, 1967.
15. Cf. Eric Rouleau's description and
    analysis in his forthcoming book,
    with J.-F. Held: *Le Troisième
    Combat Israélo-Arabe*, J. and S.
    Lacouture, ed., Le Seuil (1967);
    also Jacques Coubard: "Egypte,
    sur les lignes du front intérieur,"
    L'Humanité, July 28, 29, 31, and
    Aug. 1, 1967.
16. In the series of interviews, "Hiwâr
    maftouh ma'a Ali Sabri,"
    al-Ahram, April 22–26, 1967.

3. Walter Laqueur. Syria on the Move: Ascendancy of the Left Wing.

1. *Kul Shai'*, December 13, 1955.
2. See below.

3. It has denied however, that it gives
   or transmits instructions to the

other Arab communist parties, stressing that "all parties are equal" *(Al-Tali'a,* November 13, 1955).

4. See "Perspective of the Arab World," in *The Atlantic Monthly,* October 1956.

4. Eric Rouleau. The Syrian Enigma: What is the Ba'th?

1. "Un neutralisme à sens unique," *Le Monde,* October 19, 1966.
2. Kamel S. Abu Jaber, *The Arab Ba'th Socialist Party—History, Ideology and Organization.* Syracuse University Press.
3. *Le Monde,* March 21, 1963.
4. Abu Jaber, p. 14.
5. *Al siyassa al arabiya bayn al mabda wal tatbiq* ("Arab Politics Between Principles and Practice"), cited by Abu Jaber, p. 15.
6. According to one of their companions at the time, now a professor

at the University of Damascus, who wishes to be anonymous.
7. "L'Idéologie du Parti de la Résurrection Arabe," reproduced in *Fi Sabil al Baas,* Dar al Talia Publishing House (Beirut, 1963), pp. 193–97; translation published by the review *Orient,* No. 29 (1964).
8. Abu Jaber, p. 29.
9. For the Ba'th, Arab countries are "regions" of the "national" Arab territory, which extends from the Atlantic to the Arab (Persian) Gulf.

6. Khaldun al-Husri. The Iraqi Revolution of July 14, 1958. Part I

1. Amin al-Mumeiz, *The Kingdom of Saudi Arabia As I Knew It,* in Arabic (Beirut, 1963), pp. 399–400.
2. Marouf al-Rissafi, *Diwan al-Rissafi* (Cairo, 1949), p. 458.
3. *Ahl al-Naft,* No. 18, 1956; *The Sphere,* July 28, 1956.
4. Desmond Stewart and John Haylock, *New Babylon, A portrait of Iraq* (London, 1956), p. 77.
5. al-Rissafi, (4th ed.; Cairo, 1953) p. 283.
6. *Baghdad,* in Arabic, July-August 1964.
7. Philip Willard Ireland, *Iraq, A Study in Political Development*

(London, 1937), Chapters XVII
8. Majid Khadduri, *Independent Iraq, A Study in Iraqi Politics from 1932 to 1958,* (London, 1960), p. 235.
9. Abdul Razzak al-Hassani, *The History of Iraqi Cabinets,* in Arabic (Saidon, 1953), Vol. 2, pp. 140–41.
10. Khadduri, op. cit.
11. al-Hassani, Vol. 6, pp. 169–172.
12. Stephen Longrigg, and Frank Stoaks, *Iraq,* (London, 1958), p. 102.
13. *Ibid,* p. 223.
14. al-Hassani, Vol. 4, p. 268.

1. Waldeman J. Gallman, *Iraq Under General Nuri, My Recollection of Nuri al-Said, 1954–1958,* (Baltimore, 1964), pp. 85, 86.
2. *Ibid.,* pp. 32, 56.
3. Anthony Nutting, *I Saw for Myself* (London, 1958) p. 39.
4. "The Last Testament of the Iraqi Premier," in *Life International,* Aug. 18, 1958. On this article, see also Gallman, pp. 168–169, and Lord Birdwood, *Nuri As-Said, A Study in Arab Leadership* (London, 1959), pp. 251–252. (Although missing in the original, footnote 4 refers to the statements immediately preceding number 4, which I have taken the liberty of adding to the text. ILG, *ed.*)
5. Speech delivered in January 1956; Fadhel Jamali, *From the Reality of Iraqi Politics,* in Arabic (Beirut, 1965), p. 64.
6. Stephen Hemsley Longrigg, *Iraq, 1900 to 1950* (London, 1933), p. 345; Gerald de Gaury, *Three Kings in Baghdad, 1921–1958,* (London, 1961), p. 152. (Footnote number added to the text by the editor.)
7. Sir Anthony Eden, *Full Circle* (London, 1960), p. 220.
8. *Parliamentary Debates (Hansard),* House of Commons, Vol. 539, No. 67, Col. 897.
9. *Ibid.,* Col. 838. Italics mine. (Footnote number added to the text by the editor.)
10. Nutting, p. 46.
11. Eden, p. 421.
12. *Department of State Bulletin,* Vol. 36, April 22, 1957, p. 642.
13. Eden, p. 424.
14. Birdwood, p. 240.
15. De Gaury p. 177.
16. *al-Ahram,* Dec. 23 and 24, 1957.

17. Fadhel Jamali, *Memories and Lessons,* in Arabic (Beirut, 1964), pp. 77–78.
18. Birdwood, pp. 240–41.
19. Eden, p. 345. The parentheses in this quotation are Eden's.
20. Speech of Nuri to Parliament, *al-Shaab,* Baghdad daily Nov. 3, 1957.
21. *Times,* Dec. 29, 1956, Jan. 1, 1957.
22. De Gaury, p. 175.
23. Gallman, p. 223.
24. Ministry of Defense, *Official Minutes of the Higher Military Tribunal,* in Arabic (Baghdad, 1956, Vol. 3, p. 1164; see also pp. 1137, 1146, and Vol. 6, p. 2332.
25. *Ibid.,* Vol. 3, p. 1175. Footnote number added to the text by the editor.
26. *Ibid.,* p. 1176.
27. *Ibid.,* p. 1013.
28. *Proceedings of the Chamber of Deputies* (Ordinary Session, 1943), p. 21.
29. Ministry of Defense, *op. cit.,* Vol. 3, p. 1163.
30. *Ibid.,* p. 1022.
31. *Parliamentary Debates (Hansard),* House of Commons, Vol. 539, No. 67, Col. 866.
32. Doreen Warriner, *Land Reform and Development in the Middle East* (London, 1957), p. 126.
33. Lord Salter, *The Development of Iraq, A Plan of Action* (London, 1955) pp. 54–55.
34. Gallman, p. 221.
35. De Gaury, p. 175.
36. *Ibid.,* p. 181.
37. Caractacus, *Revolution in Iraq* (London, 1959), p. 53.
38. Nutting, p. 41.
39. Speech of Dec. 17, 1956.
40. *Al-Amal,* Baghdad daily, Mar. 17, 1958.
41. Gallman, p. 139.
42. *Times,* June 27, 1958.
43. Ministry of Defense, *op. cit.* (Baghdad, 1959), Vol. 6, p. 2482.

8. Dan Avni-Segre. Israel: Society in Transition.

1. The very special conceptions of Zionist sovereignty have been forcefully analyzed by Ben Halpern in *The Idea of the Jewish State* (Cambridge, Mass., 1961) pp. 20–43.
2. The most important Zionist reaction at the time was L. S. Pinsker's pamphlet, *Autoemancipation*, published in Odessa in September 1882 under the *nom de plume* "A Russian Jew"; reprinted in Arthur Hertzberg, *The Zionist Idea: A Historical Analysis and Reader* (New York, 1959), p. 182.
3. Theodor Herzl, the founder of political Zionism, was born in Budapest in 1860 and died in Austria in 1904. For a detailed biography, see Alex Bein's definitive *Theodor Herzl: A Biography*, M. Samuel, trans. (London, 1956). For a concise and penetrating assessment of his ideas, see Hertzberg, pp. 45–51.
4. The "Lovers of Zion" movement originated in Rumania as a reaction to the anti-Semitic policy followed by the Rumanian government especially after 1867. The movement quickly spread to the Jewish communities of Russia. For a critical discussion of the movement's aim and methods, see Ahad Ha-Am (A. Ginsberg), *Al Parashat Derakim* [*At the Parting of the Ways*], (4 vols., Berlin, 1921), 11, pp. 247 and 267. Ahad Ha-Am was the leader of "spiritual Zionism," a movement that, contrary to Herzl's "political Zionism," held that Palestine could and should become a center not only of Jewish political revival but also of a Jewish spiritual revival. For a concise critical assessment of the views of Herzl and Ahad Ha-Am, see Hertzberg, pp. 45–80, and also Leo Simon, *Ahad Ha-Am: A Biography* (London, 1960).

5. See Israël Margalith, *Le Baron Edmond de Rothschild et la colonisation Juive en Palestine,* 1882–1899 (Paris, 1957).
6. The implications of the application by Herzl of an old solution of the Jewish problem to its modern situation have been discussed by Joseph Agassi in "The Novelty of Popper's Philosophy of Science," *International Philosophical Quarterly,* VII (September 1968), pp. 446–49; see also Hertzberg, pp. 202–03.
7. Martin Buber, *Paths in Utopia* (London, 1949) especially pp. 143–49, and Ben Halpern, pp. 58–94; for the relations between Zionist socialism and other Jewish socialist parties, especially the Bund, see Bernard K. Johnpoll, *The Politics of Futility: The General Jewish Workers' Bund of Poland, 1917–1943* (New York, 1967), p. 18.
8. The views of Ber Borochov (1881–1917) are discussed in Hertzberg, pp. 365–66. For more detail, see Alex Bein, *The Return to the Soil* (Jerusalem, 1952), and W. Preuss, *Die Jüdische Arbeiterbewegung in Palästina* (2 vols.; Berlin, 1932–33). However, most of the statements and opinions of the Jewish socialist leaders are scattered in periodical literature such as *Hapoel Ha Zair,* Hebrew weekly labor organ which appeared from 1908 to 1914 in Jerusalem; *Davar,* Tel Aviv, since 1937, Hebrew daily organ of the General Federation of Jewish Labor; and *Kuntress,* Hebrew weekly labor organ, which appeared in Tel Aviv from 1919 to 1929. See also Samuel Halperin, *The Political World of American Zionism* (Detroit, 1961), pp. 157–75 for a concise description of Zionist socialism and American labor.

9. There is a large literature on the Zionist collective and cooperative movement, the most exhaustive work being Harry Viteles, *History of the Cooperative Movement in Israel: A Source Book in 7 Volumes*. The first 4 volumes are published thus far in London. They are *The Evolution of the Cooperative Movement in Israel* (1966), *The Evolution of the Kibbutz in Israel* (1967), *An Analysis of the Sectors of the Kibbutz Movement* (1968), and *Cooperative Smallholders Settlements (The Moshav Movement)* (1968). See also S. N. Eisenstadt, *Israeli Society* (London, 1967).

10. Emil Marmorstein, an orthodox Jewish scholar, has prepared an interesting study of the conflict between Zionism and Jewish orthodox nationalism, mainly from religious sources, to be published shortly in London. A typical and interesting anti-Zionist statement by the Rabbi of Zichover, in 1900, is to be found in E. Kedourie, *Nationalism* (London, 1962), pp. 75–76. See also B. Halpern, pp. 16–18, 81–88, who also gives the text of press release issued by the "Protest Rabbis"—all of them from Germany—against the first Zionist congress in July 1892, p. 144.

11. W.H.G. Armytage, *The Rise of the Technocrats* (London, 1965). See also David Patterson's penetrating analysis of the sociological and psychological evolution of the kibbutz in "The First Fifty Years of Collective Settlement in Israel," *Jewish Journal of Sociology*, II (1960), pp. 42–55, where the social image of the *kibbutz* in Israel is discussed with rare insight.

12. The best known prophet of the "religion of the land and work" was A. D. Gordon (1856–1912), a Russian-born Jew strongly influenced by Tolstoian ideas, who emigrated to Palestine in 1903. His philosophy is reflected in a short essay, "People and Labor," 1911, reprinted in Hertzberg, pp. 372–74.

13. At the turn of the century, in the twelve villages established with the help of Baron de Rothschild, the number of Jewish laborers was only 673. See David Ben Gurion. *First Ones: Israel Year Book 1962–1963* (Jerusalem, 1963).

14. See Haim Darin, *The Other Society* (New York, 1962), pp. 78–82, for the early industrialization of the kibbutz, and p. 115 ff. for the impact of the 1935–39 German immigration on the mechanization of collective agriculture. According to a recent report, *Haaretz*, October 25, 1968, on the occasion of the 35th anniversary of the beginning of the German Jewish immigration in Palestine, more than £13,000,000 were transferred from Germany into Palestine from 1933 to 1939, and £5,000,000 invested in industry.

15. In 1948 the ratio, in market value, between agricultural and industrial production in Israel was 1:3. It was reduced to 1:2 in 1959 because of the big agriculture expansion due to Israel's acquisition of Palestine government land and Arab-abandoned properties after the war of independence. It jumped to 1:4 in 1965 and has continued to increase. See Central Bureau of Statistics, *Statistical Abstract of Israel: 1966*, pp. 373–423.

16. Masao Maruyama, *Thoughts on Behavior in Modern Japanese Politics* (London, 1963), pp. 11–13 and 134–53.

17. Cecil Hourani, "The Moment of Truth: Towards a Middle East Dialogue," *Encounter*, XXIX (November 1967), pp. 3–14.

470

The Middle East Reader

18. The idea of an Arab-Jewish community in Palestine is as old as the idea of the Jewish state. Jewish-Arab coexistence and cooperation was one of the topics in Herzl's futurist Zionist novel, *Altneuland*. For more recent Israeli opinions on the subject, see Aaron Amir, "Levant des Patries: Le Dépassement du Sionisme et du Pan-Arabisme" (mimeographed 1967), and Uri Avnery, *Israel Without Zionism, a Plea for Peace in the Middle East* (London, 1968), as well as Uri Avnery, "Une Guerre Fratricide entre Semites," *Le conflit Israélo-Arabe*, special issue of *Les Temps Modernes*, XXII, rev. 253 bis (July 1967), pp. 702–3.

19. According to *The Statistical Abstract of Israel, 1963*, published by the Central Bureau of Statistics (Jerusalem), pp. 15–18, the Jewish population of Israel was composed in 1948 of 54.5 per cent European-born Jews, 8.8 per cent Middle-East-born Jews, and 35.4 per cent locally born Jews. In 1962 the percentages were respectively 33.5; 28; and 38.5. The last figure includes a vast majority of locally born Israelis of Oriental parentage, the birth rate of the Middle Eastern Jews outnumbering that of the Western Jews by three to one. According to Ministry for Foreign Affairs, Information Division, *Facts about Israel 1967* (Jerusalem), out of a total of 168,126 immigrants who entered Israel between 1961 and 1963, only 56,386 were of Western origin. However, out of a total of 1,336,678 immigrants who entered the state between 1948 and 1965, 498,677 were of European origin and 618,763 of Asian and African (Arabized) origin.

20. Some of these typical views are aired by Arab authors writing for *Le conflit Israélo-Arabe*, such as: Sami Hadawi, "Les revendications 'bibliques' et 'historiques' des sionistes sur la Palestine," pp. 91–105; Mounthir Anabtawi, "Le sionisme: un mouvement colonialiste, chauvin et militariste," pp. 106–26; Lotfallah Soliman, "Un transfer de culpabilité," pp. 266–80; and Tahar Benziane, "Le Problème palestinien et la question juive," pp. 317–44.

21. See in particular Georges Friedmann, *Fin du Peuple Juif?* (Paris, 1966), Ch. 8; Judith T. Shuval, *Immigrants on the Threshold* (New York, 1943), and "Emerging Patterns of Ethnic Strain in Israel," *Social Forces*, XL (May 1962), pp. 323–30; Alex Weingrod, "The Two Israels," *Commentary*, XXXIII (April 1962), pp. 313–19; Raphael Patai, *Israel Between East and West: A Study in Human Relations* (Philadelphia, 1953); S. N. Eisenstadt, *The Absorption of Immigrants* (London, 1954) and *Israeli Society* (New York, 1967), especially Ch. 7.

22. Such as the one of Michael Selzer, *The Organization of the Jewish State: A Polemic* (New York, 1967).

23. An interesting summary of Arab broadcasts against Israel during the June crisis can be found in "The Arab Call to War," *Wiener Library Bulletin*, XXI (Summer 1967), pp. 2–19.

24. The treaty for German reparations to Israel was signed by Chancelor Konrad Adenauer and the Israeli Foreign Minister Moshe Sharet in September, 1952.

25. According to Walter Laqueur, "Bonn, Cairo, Jerusalem: The Triple Crisis," *Commentary*, XXXIX (May 1965), pp. 29–38, the total amount of restitution money paid to individual Jews all over the world is $4.5 billions. The real

amount paid to Israeli Jews is not available because the statistics concerning restitution funds transferred to Israel cover only a part of the amount, the rest being spent or kept in Europe. It was certainly not less than $1.3 billion by 1969.

26. According to a detailed document published by Georges Friedmann and Marie-Therèse Basse, "Problèmes d'Israèl en statistiques," *Revue Française de Sociologie*, VI (July-Sept. 1965), pp. 349–77, the majority of the 225,000 Jews who entered Israel in 1961–64 were East European. See Tableau VIII, "Les differentes vagues d'immigration juive en Palestine (1882–1948) et en Israèl (1948–1964)," p. 358.

27. See *Israel's Oriental Problem, A Monthly Bulletin of News and Comments Distributed to Opinion Leaders by the Council of the Sephardi Community* (Jerusalem), Nov. 1966 and March-April 1966.

28. For the "Lavon affair," see Michel Bar Zohar, *Ben Gurion, Le prophete armé* (Paris, 1966) pp. 249–58, 365–68, and 373 ff; Uri Avnery, *Israel Without Zionism* (New York, 1968), Chap. 7, "1954: A Spy Story"; S. N. Eisenstadt, *Israeli Society*, pp. 329–32.

29. An analysis of the hostile atmosphere that surrounded Ben-Gurion at the time of his resignation and of the psychological change brought about by his successor, Levi Eshkol, can be found in Ze'ev Katz, "Eshkol's Winds of Change," *New Outlook*, VII (July-August 1964), pp. 16–19.

30. The initials for the Hebrew words meaning "List of Israeli Workers."

31. Like the "Ben-Gurionist" party RAFI—which seceded in 1965 from Mapai (the majority workers' party of Israel)—its bitter opponent Achdut Avodah had also seceded from Mapai twenty-five

years earlier. Both splinter parties returned to their "parent" organization in January 1968, when the new Israel Labor Party was officially launched after more than a year of bitter negotiations for unity. By the end of 1968 also, Mapam, the leftist section of the labor movement in Israel, rejoined Mapai, from which it originally split in 1944.

32. See Pinhas Lavon, "A Chosen People and a Normal Society," *New Outlook*, V (Tel Aviv,) February 1962, pp. 3–8 (italics added). It is interesting to compare Lavon's view of the Israeli "chosen" labor society with some of those currently expressed by Maoist partisans in favor of a perfect society in which people should be "encouraged not to consider work as a way of earning one's life, but as the prime necessity of life"; see W. U. Jiang. "Un partisan de la théorie de la révolution permanente doit nécessairement être un materialiste dialectique conséquent," in *Zhexue Yanjiu*, No. 8, 1958, pp. 23–29, quoted by R. S. Schram, *La révolution permanente en Chine* (Paris, 1963), pp. 19–31.

33. Shimon Peres is considered the creator of the Israeli Defense Establishment and the architect of the military alliance between Israel and France in 1956. He was director general of the Ministry of Defense when the Lavon Affair first broke out in 1954. He is known to have clashed often later with Lavon, then secretary general of the Histadrut, over the role and organization of the military industry, and especially over the establishment of Bedek, the Israeli center for the repair and maintenance of the military and civil aircraft that became one of the important technological factors of the Israeli air superiority over the Arabs.

34. See "Making a Modern Israel: A 'Young Mapai' View of Planning," *The Jerusalem Post* (February 12, 1965), and "What Ben-Gurion Group Stands For," *The Jerusalem Post* (July 14, 1965). Significantly, in 1967 Shimon Peres originated the idea of a detailed study of Israeli society by the end of the century, and wanted to include among the tasks of the RAFI Party the preparation of plans for Israeli "postindustrial" society.

35. No detailed study has so far been made of the effect on the civilian economic sector of the transfer of young, early-pensioned Israeli military leaders. The Israeli economy is already run today, both in the Socialist-controlled sector and in the private one—to say nothing of the government agencies—by an increasing number of administrators recruited from among retired army officers. For example, the Dead Sea mineral complex has been run for the last thirteen years by a former chief of staff, and another heads the Israeli port authority. A former chief of intelligence runs one of the largest mechanical concerns of the Histadrut, while the tourist-amenities center of Eilat is run by a former navy commodore. See Amos Perlmutter, "The Israeli Army in Politics: The Persistence of the Civilian Over the Military," *World Politics,* XX (July 1968).

36. The shock of the Nazareth riots was great, especially among the Jewish labor organizations. It was best expressed by a poem by Nathan Alterman, a leading poet and political figure, published by the Histadrut paper *Davar,* translated into English by *New Outlook,* I (July–August 1958), pp. 48–49, under the title "After the Riots in Nazareth."

37. The Wadi Salib (a very poor quarter of Haifa) where riots broke out

in July 1959, shortly before general election; they spread to Beersheba in the south and to Migdal Emek in the east.

38. One of the most outspoken supporters of the economic and social integration of the Arab minority into the Jewish majority is Rustum Bastuni, an Arab engineer and former member of the Israeli Parliament. See [his] "Arab Society in Israel," *Hamizrach He'Hadash* (Jerusalem), XV (1965), pp. 1–2. It is interesting to note that the riots in Ramleh in August 1965, and in Nathania in March 1966, between Arabs and Jews were caused not by political tension, but by rivalry between young workers of the two communities over the favors of the same Jewish girls. See also "Integrating Israel's Arabs," *The Jerusalem Post,* September 25, 1964.

39. See Amos Eilon, "Letter from Jerusalem," *Encounter,* XXIX (February 1967).

40. See Jamal Abd al-Nasser, *The Philosophy of the Revolution* (Cairo, 1952).

41. For the struggle of the Palestinians to maintain their own autonomous institutions against Jordanian and Egyptian control, see Marcel Colombe, "Le problème de l'Entité Palestinienne dans les relations arabes," *Orient,* XXIX (1964), pp. 57–87; and Joseph B. Schecterman, *The Mufti and the Fuehrer: The Rise and Fall of Haj Amin al Hussein* (London, 1965), pp. 200–80. Also Rony E. Gabay, *A Political Study of the Arab-Jewish Conflict: The Arab Refugee Problem* (Geneva, 1959), pp. 202–71; and Musa Alami, *Ibrat Palestin* [*The Lesson of Palestine*] (Beirut, 1949), condensed in "The Lesson of Palestine," *Middle East Journal,* III (October 1949), pp. 373–405.

PART 3: ISRAELI PERSPECTIVES AND ARAB UNITY

5. Cecil A. Hourani. The Arab League in Perspective.

1. The Arabic text of the Alexandria Protocol was published in *al-Ahram* (Cairo, Oct. 8, 1944), p. 3.
2. The Pact of the Arab League has been published in English by the Arab Office, Washington, D.C. For an unofficial translation, see also the *American Journal of International Law*, Vol. 39, No. 4 (October 1945), Supplement, pp. 266–72.
3. H. A. R. Gibb, "The Future for Arab Unity," *The Near East: Problems and Prospects*, Philip W. Ireland, ed. (Chicago, 1942), p. 93.
4. Robert Montagne, "L'Union Arabe," *Politique Étrangère*, IIe année, nr. 2 (April-May 1946), p. 181.

8. Patrick Seale. The Breakup of the United Arab Republic.

1. BBC Monitoring Report, ME/765/A/2, October 11, 1961.
2. *Ibid.*, ME/759/A/8, October 4, 1961.
3. *Ibid.*, ME/765/A/5, October 11, 1961.
4. *Ibid.*, ME/757/A/4, October 2, 1961.
5. *Ibid*, ME/755/A/7, September 29, 1961.
6. *Al-Ahram* (weekly supplement), March 21, 1961, translated in *Orient*, No. 17 (Paris, 1961), pp. 181-7.
7. BBC Monitoring Report, ME/762/A/4, October 7, 1961.

PART 4: SQUARING THE CIRCLE: ISRAEL AND THE ARABS

1. Chaim Weizmann. Palestine's Role in the Solution of the Jewish Problem.

1. Address delivered at the Overseas League, London, April 8, 1941.
2. See the "Palestine Report: Alternatives to Partition," by Viscount Samuel, and "The Arabs and the Future of Palestine," by H. St. J. Philby, both in *Foreign Affairs*, Oct. 1937. (Note by ed. of *Foreign Affairs*, 1942.)

2. Judah L. Magnes. A Solution Through Force?

1. See the article by Professor Koebner, *Ireland—the False Analogy*, in this booklet.
2. "Palestine—A Bi-National State." Publ. by IHUD (Union) Association of Palestine, New-York, August 1946.
3. See the article by G. Baer, *Jewish and Arab Workers—Divided or United?*

4. That was the name of the first article by Ahad-Haam, the leader of spiritual Zionism, criticising some ways of the Zionist Movement.

The title of that article has become a slogan of earnest criticism.—Ed.

3. Why the Arab States Entered Palestine.

1. The American Journal of International Law, Vol. 42, p. 397.
2. Letter to New York *Times* May 20th, 1948.
3. Hackworth, *Digest of International Law.* Vol. I p. 175.
4. *Moore International Law Digest,* Vol. I, pp. 138–9.

Bibliography

The following are offered as supplements to the material in the text. In numerous cases books listed under one particular section are relevant to others. In all cases the suggested readings constitute a small portion of what is available in each field. Titles are listed in accordance with the subjects they concern, as these appear in the text. The first part of the material listed for Part 1 consists of titles of anthologies and general readers of particular use to beginning students.

PART 1: REFLECTIONS ON RADICAL CHANGE IN THE ARAB EAST AND ISRAEL

Karpat, Kemal H., *Political and Social Thought in the Contemporary Middle East*, ed. New York, Praeger, 1968; Laqueur, W. and Mosse, G. L., *The Middle East, The Journal of Contemporary History*, eds. London, Weidenfeld and Nicolson, Vol. 3, No. 3, 1968; Rivlin, B. and Szyliowicz, J. S., *The Contemporary Middle East*, eds. New York, Random House, 1965; Thompson, J. H. and Reischauer, R. D., *Modernization of the Arab World*, eds. Princeton, D. Van Nostrand Company, Inc., 1966; Sharabi, Hisham B., *Nationalism and Revolution in the Arab World*, ed. Princeton, D. Van Nostrand Company, Inc., 1966.

Binder, Leonard. *The Ideological Revolution in the Middle East*, New York, John Wiley and Sons, 1964; Halpern, Manfred, *The Politics of Social Change in the Middle East and North Africa*, Princeton University Press, 1963; Laroui, Abdallah, *L'Idéologie arabe contemporaine*, Paris, Seuil, 1967; *Beginnings of Modernization in the Middle East*, W. R. Polk and R. L. Chambers, eds. Chicago, Chicago University Press, 1968; Shamir, Shimon. "The Question of a 'National Philosophy' in Contemporary Arab Thought," *Asian and African Studies*, Vol. 1, 1965, pp. 1–48; Hurewitz, Jacob C. *Middle East Politics: The*

Military Dimension, New York, Praeger, 1969; Lissak, Moshe "Patterns of Change in Ideology and Class Structure in Israel," *Jewish Journal of Sociology,* Vol. VII, No. 1, June 1965, pp. 46–62; Perlmutter, Amos "The Israeli Army in Politics: The Persistence of the Civilian Over the Military," *World Politics,* Vol. XX, No. 4, July 1968, pp. 606–643; Tartakower, Aryeh. "The Sociology of Political Life in Israel," *Jewish Social Studies,* Vol. XXII, No. 2, pp. 83–96.

PART 2: THE TRANSFORMATION OF SOCIETY

Abdel-Malek, Anouar. *Egypt: Military Society,* New York, Vintage Books, 1968; O'Brien, Patrick. *The Revolution in Egypt's Economic System,* London, Oxford University Press, 1965; Vatikiotis, P. J. *The Modern History of Egypt,* London, Weidenfeld and Nicolson, 1969; Abu Jaber, Kamel S. *The Arab Ba'th Socialist Party. History, Ideology and Organization.* Syracuse, Syracuse University Press, 1966; Colombe, Marcel. "Remarques sur le Ba'th et les institutions politiques de la Syrie d'aujourd'hui," *Orient,* No. 37, pp. 57–67; Seale, Patrick. *The Struggle for Syria,* London, Oxford University Press, 1965; Khadduri, Majid. *Independent Iraq, 1932–1958,* Oxford University Press, 1960; Penrose, Edith F. "Une tentative de gouvernement civil en Irak," *Orient,* No. 39, pp. 2–34; Gaspard, J. "Penetrating the Ba'th—an Ideology in Search of Leadership," *The New Middle East,* No. 8, pp. 30–34; Fein, Leonard. *Politics in Israel,* Boston, Little Brown and Company, 1967; Halpern, Ben. *The Idea of the Jewish State,* Cambridge, Mass., Harvard University Press, 1960; Perlmutter, Amos. "The Institutionalization of Civil-Military Relations in Israel: the Ben Gurion Legacy and its Challengers (1953–1967)," *The Middle East Journal,* Vol. 22, No. 4, pp. 415–432; Safran, Nadav. *The United States and Israel,* Cambridge, Mass., Harvard University Press, 1963.

PART 3: ISRAELI PERSPECTIVES AND ARAB UNITY

Calvocoressi, Peter. *Suez Ten Years After,* New York, Pantheon Books, 1966; Patai, Raphael. *Israel Between East and West,* Philadelphia, Jewish Publication Society of America, 1953; Rejwan, Nissim, "The Two Israels: A Study in Europeocentrism," *Judaism,* Vol. 16, No. 1, pp. 97–108; Weingrod, Alex. *Israel: Group Relations in a New Society,* New York, Praeger, 1966; Badeau, John S. *The American Approach to the Arab World,* New York, Harper and Row, 1968; Cremeans, Charles D. *The Arabs and the World,* New York, Praeger, 1963; Kerr, Malcolm, *The Arab Cold War, 1958–1967,* London, Chatham House, 1967; Macdonald, Robert W. *The League of Arab States,* Princeton, Princeton University Press, 1965; "Minutes of the Tripartite Union Talks Held in Cairo Between the U.A.R. and the Syrian and Iraqi Republics," *Arab Political Documents,* 1963, W. Khalidi and Y. Ibish, eds. Beirut, Published by the Political Studies and Public Administration Department of the American University of Beirut, 1963.

PART 4: SQUARING THE CIRCLE: ISRAEL AND THE ARABS

Avnery, Uri. *Israel Without Zionists*, New York, The Macmillan Company, 1968; Sartre, J.-P., ed. *Le conflit israélo-arabe, Les Temps Modernes* XXII, rev. 253 bis (July 1967); Hurewitz, Jacob, C. *The Struggle for Palestine*, New York, W. W. Norton and Company, Inc., 1950; Laqueur, Walter. *The Israel-Arab Reader*, New York, Bantam Books, 1969; Peretz, Don. *Israel and the Palestine Arabs*, Washington, D.C., The Middle East Institute, 1958; Rodinson, Maxime, *Israel and the Arabs*, New York, Pantheon, 1969; Rouleau, E., Held, J.-R., Lacouture, J. and S. *Israel et les Arabes*, Paris, Seuil, 1967; Safran, Nadav. *From War to War*, New York, Pegasus, 1969; Sykes, Christopher, *Crossroads to Israel. Palestine from Balfour to Bevin*, London, Collins, 1965.